MW01044632

HATCHES II

Also by the Authors:

Comparahatch

Flytiers Color Guide

Instant Mayfly Identification Guide

HATCHES II

A Complete Guide to Fishing the Hatches of North American Trout Streams

Al Caucci *and* **Bob Nastasi**

Illustration and Photography by the Authors

Introductions by
Art Flick *and* **Al Caucci**

With a Preface by
Nick Lyons

Postscript by
Gary LaFontaine

THE LYONS PRESS
Guilford, Connecticut
An imprint of The Globe Pequot Press

Copyright © 2004, 1986, 1975 by Al Caucci and Bob Nastasi
All rights reserved. No part of this book may be reproduced or transmitted in any form by any means, electronic or mechanical, including photocopying and recording, or by any information storage and retrieval system, except as may be expressly permitted in writing from the publisher. Requests for permission should be addressed to The Lyons Press, Attn: Rights and Permissions Department, P.O. Box 480, Guilford, CT 06437.

The Lyons Press is an imprint of The Globe Pequot Press.

10 9 8 7 6 5 4 3 2 1

Printed in the United States of America

Library of Congress Cataloging-in-Publication Data

Caucci, Al.
Hatches II : a complete guide to fishing the hatches of North American trout streams / Al
Caucci, Bob Nastasi ; illustration and photography by the authors ; with introduction by Art Flick and Gary LaFontaine.—New ed.
p. cm.
Includes bibliographical references (p.).
ISBN 1-59228-322-5 (trade paper)—ISBN 5-55821-060-1 (trade cloth)
1. Trout fishing—North America. 2. Mayflies—North America—Identification. 3 . Fly fishing—North America. I. Title: Hatches 2. II. Title: Hatches two. III. Nastasi, Bob. IV. Title

AH688.N7c38 2004
799.17'57—dc22 2004044231

IN MEMORY OF BOB NASTASI

A week after I wrote the introduction to the sixth edition of *Hatches,* I received a call in the Keys from my son, Blair. "I hate to tell you this, Dad," he hesitated. "Bob Nastasi died this morning." Although I knew it didn't look good for Bob from my frequent phone calls with him over the past few months, it still didn't prepare me for those terrible last words.

Bob Nastasi, one of the most respected fly fishermen of our time, died at 1:30 A.M. on February 8, 2004. His death followed a six-year battle with kidney failure, a kidney transplant, and finally, lung cancer. As incredible as it may seem, Bob told me many times that these were the best days of his life. Bob shared these years with his wife, Roseanne, his sons, Robert, Christopher, and Matthew and his grandchildren at his home on Barnegat Bay. Most of his spring, summer, and fall days were spent at his fishing trailer on the West Branch of the Delaware, where he was an idol to a band of hard-core regulars at our Delaware River Club campground. Bob was and still is my hero—we were like brothers.

Bob's trailer sits on a high bank overlooking the river only a half a mile upstream from my office. Whenever possible, I'd drive over to his camp to get away from the action at the "Club." We'd sip a beer and chat about the "good old days," about new books we should write, and if he was feeling good, we'd take a float down the river and stick a few wild trout.

These really were "the best" days. I will miss Bob dearly, but more importantly, I will always remember the great adventures we shared on countless rivers across the country, and on our home rivers of the Upper Delaware.

Al Caucci
February 21, 2004

HATCHES II

CONTENTS

NOTE: Color insert appears after page 252

INTRODUCTION
Al Caucci

I grew up in a tough Italian neighborhood outside of Philadelphia in the forties and fifties. The blue-collar town of Bristol, Pennsylvania, was a million miles away from the heart of America's fly-fishing culture. I was the oldest of five children, and the only fishing I did was for catfish and carp in the tidal waters of the Delaware River, a block away from my house. The lower Delaware near Philly was severely polluted back then, but that didn't stop us from swimming and fishing. We used chicken guts scrounged from the neighborhood grocer and cornmeal balls as bait.

After high school, I went to work in a factory to help support my family. I'd give my mom my check, and she would give me an allowance. My three kids (now ages thirty-eight to forty-two) still have a hard time believing that! In the late 1950s, I worked as a mechanical draftsman while studying mechanical engineering at night, but managed to find the time for spinning and baitcasting for bass and pickerel in the gravel pits evacuated for the building of Levittown, Pennsylvania. When I could, I also loved fishing for stripers and bluefish along the Jersey shore with plugs, spoons, and bait.

My obsession with fly-fishing began in 1962, just after my marriage to Betti LeCompte. Betti supported my fishing habit, and encouraged me to pursue my dreams. There were no fly-fishing magazines or schools in those days, and the few fly-fishing books available were hard to come by in my neighborhood. My interest in fly fishing was fueled by the occasional fly-fishing articles in *Field & Stream, Outdoor Life* and *Sports Afield.* One day I saw an ad in the back of *Field & Stream* about a camp in Maine that specialized in fly fishing for wild brook trout. I called the camp and the owner, George, told me to buy a Shakespeare Wonder Rod and a Pfleuger Medalist reel with an HCH tapered flyline. Then he gave me directions to the camp.

It wasn't long before Betti, who was pregnant, and I were driving to Maine, to the northern end of Baxter State Park. It took us two days, and then four hours on a dirt road, to get there. After we settled in to our quaint little lakeside cabin, George took me out on the lawn, held out my new fly rod, and began waving it back and forth. "Just go like this and go like that," he said. He cast a few times, and then he said, "It takes a long time to learn. Just keep practicing. See ya later."

"Wait a minute," I protested. "What flies should I use?" "We only use two flies here: big Paramachene Belles and Hornberg Specials," he said. He gave me a couple and sent us on our way. Betti and I took the motorboat out on this beautiful lake at sunset. There were fish rising all over the place, and I cast right up until dark without hooking one. Something was wrong, and I couldn't figure it out. It was either my casting, or George had given me the wrong flies. That night I asked him, and he told me I was being impatient. "And you've got to keep practicing," he told me. "It takes a long time to become a flyfisherman."

I couldn't sleep that night. At 6 A.M. I got out of bed and told Betti, "We've got to go fishing now." She complained, but she knew what the answer was going to be, so off we went.

After boating through the mist for half an hour, we pulled into a cove that was just loaded with rising fish. We quickly tied on our flies, started casting, and, nothing. "Something's wrong here Betti," I said. "Give me that flybox." Taking the box, I took all of the flies out, then used the box to scoop up some of the insects that were on the surface of the lake. Then I hit the motor and went racing back to the camp.

When we got there, I raced into the office. "George, these flies aren't working," I said. "I need flies that look like these insects" (the ones I had scooped off the lake). George went into the back and, after rummaging around a bit, came out with a cigar box full of gnarly old flies. I picked out a dozen that looked like the naturals and off we went. When we got back to the cove, I tied one of George's flies and, bingo, I started catching fish right away. In fact, I limited out in about half an hour (nobody had heard of catch and release in those days).

I learned a big lesson that day, or, better, I taught it to myself. If you don't look at what is on the surface, and figure out what the fish are feeding on, you can go for days without catching anything. That approach became my credo and led directly to my lifelong study of entomology and, eventually, to my books with Bob Nastasi.

Bob Nastasi grew up in the Bedford Stuyvesant section of Brooklyn back in the forties and fifties. He lived in a tenement building with two older brothers and two younger sisters. His mother was Lithuanian and his dad was Italian. Bob spent his childhood summers in upstate New York, where he developed a love of the outdoors through his aunt and cousins. When Bob was a teenager, he spent weekends fishing with Uncle Pete on board the *Two Brothers* out of Howard Beach. Using live and cut baits they fished the wrecks of Manhattan and Long Island.

Bob began his career as a graphic artist in the advertising business in New York City, specializing in the movie industry. He married Roseanne in the mid-sixties and moved to Wayne, New Jersey, where they raised a family of three boys.

I met Bob in 1970 through a mutual friend at my vacation home in the Poconos. He came to check out my house, but when Bob saw my fly-tying and "bug" aquarium setup, he started asking questions, and never stopped. We talked all day and into the night about insect's, and flies, and trout, and a lifelong friendship was born — one that lasts to this day.

We eventually formed "Comparahatch Limited," a corporation for our published works, fly-tying materials, and trout flies. It was also the namesake of our first book, *Comparahatch*, and our line of trout flies, which included Comparadun, Compara nymph, Compara spinner, and so on.

Through necessity, Bob and I learned the intricacies of fly fishing through trial and error over many years. In contrast, today's anglers have an incredible amount of resources at their disposal. There are any number of excellent fly-fishing schools, instructors, and guides; dozens of fly-fishing magazines; and thousands of books and videos to get you started in the right direction. My fly-fishing school advertises, "We can save you five years of trial and error." And it's true; we really can. So can a number of good schools around the country. Stick to those that have good reputations or get a recommendation from a friend who already fly fishes. As in golf, tennis, or skiing, progress will depend on the quality of training that you receive early on. Ask questions before you plunk down your money and you can avoid problems later on. Ask for detailed written itineraries before you select a school.

Schools are not only for beginning fly fishers, either. I recommend them for fly fishermen at every stage and level: intermediate, advanced, and expert. Technology, tactics, and tackle are constantly changing, and the best way to stay informed is to spend time with a real pro. A good fly-fishing school will provide instructors with exceptional teaching knowledge in casting, presentation, entomology, fly patterns, knots, equipment, and accessories. On-the-river instruction is mandatory if you want a jumpstart into fly fishing. Techniques for fishing nymphs, streamers, dry flies, and emerger patterns are best taught in a trout river, over feeding fish, with an instructor at your side.

A school should teach proper wading, sighting fish, analyzing the rise forms, match-the-hatch fly selection, nymph and streamer tactics, sink-line techniques, and correct presentation. Fly fishing for trout is largely an intellectual sport, where you have to think things through, but when all is said and done, you still must be able to accurately cast the fly to the fish to be successful. Because of this, the ability to double haul a tight loop into the wind is a necessity. So is the ability to throw seventy feet of line with an effortless cast, utilizing the power in the rod (not your arm). This is not difficult when you combine proper technique with today's excellent rods.

Nowadays you don't have to struggle with a whippy Shakespeare Wonder Rod, as I did. High-tech rods, precision-machined reels, and slick-surfaced lines that cast like laser beams have replaced the primitive equipment of the early sixties. Unless you're fishing on small or tiny streams, anglers should consider light, stiff rods with fast taper actions. They produce higher line speed, tight loops, more distance, and control in the wind. Soft rods generate slow line speed, less distance, and contribute to tailing loops. Tight loops and long distance casting are necessary on my home rivers of the Upper Delaware system. A sixty-foot reach cast will give you an advantage over big, wild, sipping fish in flat water, which is so typical on these waters. If you get close, they will spook.

American manufacturers produce terrific fly reels today. Starting at less than $100.00, you can buy a reel machined from aluminum bar stock with perfectly fitted parts, held to tolerances of one ten-thousandth of an inch, and with a drag system that is both smooth and powerful. With technology developed from such areas as the space program and the military, we now have so much top-quality gear it's unbelievable. For example, we now have all kinds of light, effective materials for equipment and clothing. Breathable, lightweight waders that keep you as dry as a bone fall into this category, for instance. Then there's eyewear, tying materials, lines, leaders, clothing, and gadgets. I could go on and on.

But to conclude this introduction for the sixth edition of HATCHES II, let me state, simply, that fly fishing has come a long way. Streams are less polluted and, thanks to catch-and-release policies and a more conservation-oriented frame of mind among anglers, the trout are bigger and generally more selective. The hatches are still prolific, and today's imitations are more effective. It's a wonderful time to be a fly fisherman!

INTRODUCTION
Art Flick

Back in the 1930's, when I was collecting mayflies, I spent many hours on our streams; day after day, through most of the fishing season when the flies were emerging. The data I was able to gather later went into my book *Streamside Guide To Naturals and Their Artificials.*

I mention this only because I know how many hours went into collecting the comparatively few species I reported; to say nothing of the effort required in obtaining photographs of them.

In recent years, very important books were published about the hatches, the photography of them, the artificial flies, etc. Authored by Vincent Marinaro, Ernest Schwiebert, Swisher/Richards, they are of great importance to the fly-fisher.

Now comes Hatches: *A Complete Guide to Fishing the Hatches of North American Trout Streams* by Al Caucci and Bob Nastasi, which in my judgment has so much more than all the others that it should be the last word on the subject.

Although I cannot be sure, I doubt if there has ever been a book published for fly-fishers that is nearly so complete as this one on the subject of mayflies and their identification. I'm certain there have never been photographs of so many species, including nymphs, subimagoes and spinners. It is truly amazing that the data could be accumulated to the extent that it was in the comparatively short span of time required.

Collecting and identifying the 21 genera and more than 100 species treated in this book was in itself a terrific task, to say nothing of obtaining the nymphs and correlating them with the flies. Gathering them was only a small part of it—keeping them alive through their numerous moults was one helluva chore. Many are extremely difficult to raise, for different species require different water temperatures and conditions.

The photographs are truly outstanding. Nymphs and flies are notoriously poor models and although the former will stand some handling, the flies are extremely fragile, particularly the spinners. To get them into the proper position for a good picture can be frustrating to say the least.

The pictures and illustrations in this book are probably as fine as one will ever see. A person should have no trouble identifying the natural flies from them as their detail makes identification quite easy. This help will be invaluable to the fly-fishers, enabling them to offer the proper imitation to the trout.

Actually, Al and Bob's book does the trout dirt, by giving the angler so much valuable information. Just one example

are the chapters on the little-known Tricorythodes genus. This tiny but terribly important mayfly is finally coming into its own.

Never before have I seen it covered so thoroughly as here and although it is a fly that truly "separates the men from the boys", it is one that pays off for those who know it. Not too many anglers are familiar with this genus, but if it occurs in the waters in which you fish, it can add many pleasurable hours and days to your season. Although mighty tough fishing, this little rascal can make your season, coming as it does when there are few, if any, other mayflies.

You won't know what a real thrill trout fishing can be until you take a 17 inch or better fish on one of the tiny imitations of "Trico". I sincerely wish that they were present in quantity in the turhulent mountain streams that I normally fish.

If you think this book is only for the neophytes, forget it; any angler who thinks he has all the answers will find he is wrong. My fishing covers over fifty years and I thought I knew something about fly life. However, one of the important flies that has "bugged me" over the years is Ephemerella *attenuata*, the so-called Blue-Winged Olive, an important mayfly that appears on most Catskill Mountain streams.

On some days I've had wonderful dry-fly fishing when fish were surface feeding—on others I couldn't even get a "salute", despite the fact that I knew from careful observation that the fish were taking the subimagoes and not the nymphs as they reached the surface.

Thanks to *Hatches*, I learned that there are two different flies that are "look-alikes," E. *attenuata* and E. *cornuta*. This was one of those cases where a person takes too much for granted, but a study of the photographs of the two insects and the text, shows that there *is* a difference. It may not appear like much to us, but, to a trout that can see an insect no larger than a period, he can certainly differentiate; their very lives depend to a great extent on their vision.

Another case of "look-alikes" mentioned in the book is E. *invaria* and E. *dorothea*, both important flies on most streams. This pair I *was* familiar with, but the chances are at least 50 to 1 that the average angler isn't. Compare the photographs and read the text covering these two insects.

It seems to me that Caucci and Nastasi are bad news for our trout, as far as mayflies are concerned. I fear that because of them, or, rather, due to the heretofore not known facts divulged in their book, many more trout will be creeled. One can only hope that most of them will be taken by folks who "Limit Their Kill and don't Kill Their Limit".

If it seems from what I have said that I think the book is good, YOU ARE CORRECT!

Acknowledgments

A very special thanks to A.J. McClane, Nick Lyons, Dick Surette, John Randolph, Jack Russell, Bing Lempke, Bill Cairns, Chris Tafuri, Dave Popa, Ron Cordes and Paul Romaniello for their support and friendly advice. And to Charles Walther of Winchester Press for his enthusiasm and suggestions for this new edition of HATCHES.

Heartfelt thanks to Gary LaFontaine and Leon Chandler for their friendship, companionship and expert advice. And to our good friends: Ken Begies, Mike Chain, Jim Charron, Paul P. Dickes, David V. Grow, William Hurt, Dick Stewart and Pres Tolman for their companionship on our home rivers.

We also wish to express our sincerest appreciation and gratitude to the following individuals who have helped make this book possible: Dr. Alvin R. Grove, Eric Peper and Art Flick for their friendly advice and encouragement; Dr. George Harvey for his warm friendship and assistance on Western Pennsylvania streams; Harry Darbee for his help through the years on Catskill waters, especially the Beaverkill; Gary Schnicke for his expert advice on Michigan hatches, including his assistance with the Limbata emergence sequence on the Au Sable River; Professor Dwight Webster of Cornell University for his help with the phonetics; Jack Davis for his friendship and knowledgeable advice on the gentle Lehigh Valley streams; John Hicks for his invaluable help and companionship during our Western and Midwestern research; Shelly Young for friendship and hospitality extended in the typical tradition of the Midwest; Del Mazza for his assistance with Ephoron specimens on Southern Adirondack waters; Stan and Carol Molinski of Anglers Cove in Cadosia, N.Y., Cathy and Barry Beck of Beckies in Berwick, P.A. and Paul Filippone of Donegal, Fort Montgomery, N.Y. for their friendship and expertise in hooks, fur and feathers.

We also want to express our admiration for a job well done to the energetic membership of the TGF and to the various chapters of TU and FFF across the country that we have come to know personally.

An Update from the Authors

The 1985 edition of HATCHES is a 10 year update of our original 1975 edition. From the moment President Charles Walther of Winchester Press mentioned that they were interested in co-publishing a revised version of HATCHES with Compara-hatch, Ltd., we must say that we were thrilled about the prospects of updating the entomology as well as other aspects of the book.

In many respects the changes were prompted by Dr. George F. Edmunds, one of the world's most renowned mayfly experts, who wrote a meticulous book review on HATCHES in the entomological vehicle, Etonia, shortly after HATCHES was released. In his review, Dr. Edmunds both praised and critiqued the book, mostly for minor or nuisance mistakes. We are flattered and thankful that Dr. Edmunds took the time and effort to scrutinize HATCHES in such detail, and we have heeded his advice in correcting the entomology in this new edition for future researchers in the field.

Entomology is an ever expanding field of knowledge. As new facts are discovered, the families, genera and species may be revised. When a mayfly is moved from one genus to another, the name may change. This new edition of HATCHES follows the nomenclature of *Mayflies of North and Central America*, 1976, 2nd printing 1979, by Edmunds, Jensen and Berner. The 1975 edition followed that of the *Biology of Mayflies*, 1935, by Needham, Traver and Hsu and Burks.

In addition to updating the entomology, this revised edition also gives us the chance to reveal more of our latter day research on certain mayfly hatches as related to mayfly biology, tactics, presentation and imitation; although the structure of the book stays mainly intact.

One of the most important changes in the book, which the original *HATCHES* lacked, is the addition of the Quick Reference Charts. There are charts for the East/Midwest and the Western United States. All the important species from every part of the country are listed in these charts, along with the emergence dates, hook sizes, body sizes, page references and common names.

Other additions are more elaborate tying instructions for the Compara-dun, plus tying instructions for our effective Deerhair Compara-emerger. This fly pattern section has been revised and expanded along with some of the dressings. Some of the major revisions will be found in the following chapters: Family Tree; Genus Ephemerella; Ephemerella subvaria; Ephemerella cornuta; Family Heptageniidae; Leptophlebia species and Ephemera simulans.

Most of these chapters contain new information. Practically all the Genus chapters have been affected and revised to reflect new information and entomological changes.

In addition to the above, the phonetics and glossary chapters have been revised and expanded. We have also added new chapters on three genera. These are Genus Baetisca, Genus Cinygmula and Genus Ameletus, which are popular in the west.

In defense of the flyfishing amateur entomologist, we'd like to make a plea to the scientific entomological community to do more original work at the species level. It appears that much shuffling is done at the family and genus levels with laboratory specimens, while very little is attempted on the streams to solve current identification problems at the species level. We have come across dozens of prolific mayfly species that can't be identified for lack of entomological keys.

An updated comprehensive study at the species level similar to the 1935 *Biology of Mayflies* by Needham, Traver and Hsu; *Mayflies of Michigan Trout Streams* by Justin and Fannie Leonard; *The Mayflies, or Ephemeroptera, of Illinois* by Burks, would surely be welcomed by these two authors.

Al Caucci
Bob Nastasi

Notes About the Text

The rationale concerning the mayfly-trout relationship; stream and lab research; photomacrography; imitations (selection, design and usage); hook size and other major issues that affect the fly-fisherman or the student of entomology are highlighted and explained throughout the respective sections and chapters of this book. More subtle points in our approaches which are not highly emphasized are explained as follows:

The information given in the text about the mayfly is a result of our actual stream and lab experiences with the live insects which was recorded over the years in notes, tape casettes and photography. Wherever information is given in the text that did not derive from our actual experience, it is noted as such. Final identification of the individual mayfly species evolved from cross-checking and comparing our specimens and photographs with the identification descriptions in many entomological texts (mainly the definitive works of Needham, Travers and Hsu; Justin and Fannie Leonard; Edmunds, Berner and Jensen; and Burkes—see Selected Bibliography on page 23. Many additional works and materials were drawn on freely as reference for which we are greatly appreciative and credit has been given for much of this information wherever possible throughout the text. The coloration and physical characteristics of each major species and even the lesser ones are displayed in both color and black-and-white photography to eliminate any possible error through language interpretation.

Included at the end of each genus chapter are identification charts of the nymphs and the adults that facilitate efficient comparisons of the important species as well as the lesser species within the genus. Although there are many identification characteristics, we chose only those that will help the angler make the quickest identification. The important species are in Bold typeface.

The emergence periods of all the specific major mayfly species are graphically illustrated with emergence calendars both in the Quick Reference Charts as well as the more detailed calendars within the species chapters. The calendars were developed and data collected over many seasons and are surprisingly accurate, although not infallible. The general emergence span for each area is depicted by a bar, the darkened area indicates when the best hatches normally occur, while the dotted extension of the bar indicates sporadic hatching activity over a longer period. Emergence calendars are not given in the Western species chapters because chapters seasonal emergence varies tremendously on streams from one mountain range to another and even on neighboring streams due to contrasting geological influences of thermal activity, glacial influence, altitude, subterranean springheads, etc. Instead, general emergence dates are given for freestone streams that experience runoff as well as those of spring origin which are unaffected by snow melt. General emergence dates are also given for multi-species treated on a genus level as species within the genus may emerge months apart rendering the calendar method impractical for illustration.

The reader will also notice that each species chapter has abbreviated marginalia data which includes: 1) sketches of the adult mayfly in actual average size, 2) the body size range of the natural nymph and dun, 3) common names, 4) recommended fly patterns, (traditional and the Comparaseries) and 5) recommended hook sizes. The angler should note that some of our hook size recommendations may vary with those given in the first edition of *Hatches*, especially those for the larger insects. Over the years we've concluded that it is easier to fool a trout with a smaller imitation (the trout has less to scrutinize). For instance, if a mayfly species ranges from 12mm to 20mm (#10 std. #94840 to #8, 4 × long #79580) our recommendation is to lean toward the smaller #10 or #8 std. (#94840) hook.

Unless otherwise specified in the text, all daily hatching periods are expressed in Daylight Savings Time.

A phonetic table is given to aid the angler with the Latin. It should be noted that, just as there are acceptable differences in the pronunciation of English, so are there acceptable differences in Latin. Such differences are exhibited in English by the words data or tomato. Where common usage of a Latin word is different from the more rigid pronunciation, we show them both.

Traditional biological typesetting dictates that the genus and species should be both set in italic. However, since we commonly refer to a species without relating it to its genus, we have placed only the species in italic. In this manner, when written separately, one can always determine whether a genus or a species is under discussion.

PREFACE TO THE 1995 EDITION

Nick Lyons

This season marks the twentieth anniversary of *Hatches*—a book privately published by its authors in 1975—and it thus remains one of a handful of modern fly-fishing books (of the many hundreds published) that endures for the simplest of reasons: serious fly fishermen keep wanting to read it.

We recommend our favorite fly patterns and go back to them when we fish because they catch fish. One reason that we recommend books, and that these books remain in print, is because what they say helps the reader catch more fish. *Hatches* is this kind of book. It offers a fly-fishing "system" that matches the probing entomological research by Al Caucci and Bob Nastasi with the development of practical fly patterns and stream tactics. The basic fly pattern presented is the durable Comparadun that uses deer hair for its winging and eliminates hackle. Patterns that fall from favor after their fifteen minutes in the sun do so for one or more of a number of reasons: the first, always, is that they simply do not gull fish as billed. Some require the genius of Leonardo to tie, others are difficult to cast or fail to float properly. In the end, though, all flies vanish if they are not durable.

The Comparaduns, with their strong deer-hair winging, are easy to tie, they gull the most recalcitrant trout, and they will, literally, take dozens of fish before they come apart. That new versions of the fly, and of the Compara-spinner, have been developed by others in recent years, is only testimony to the fly's basic effectiveness—and to credit the early version to Bob and Al in no way diminishes the value of the various refinements and improvements made by such great innovators as Craig Mathews (Sparkle Dun), René Harrop (Hairwing Dun), John Betts, Al Troth, and a small group of others. Synthetic materials have become more and more important, of course, for the body and tail in particular; but the basic concept of the fly, and the use of deer hair, remains the same.

So it is with much pleasure that we honor the book with still another printing, above 50,000 copies that have already been sold. The entomology—won through years of original research—has proven sound; the fading color plates from the earlier editions have been re-made; and the concepts of fly design and stream tactics await the tests of still another generation—confidently, since they have passed all tests to date.

Restless and inquiring as they are, Al and Bob are already looking beyond this book to another. But this one remains, and should always remain in print. It is one of the foundations on which modern fly-tying is built; it is one of the half dozen seminal books that every fly fisherman should own and study, and then study again.

An Introduction to the Mayfly

The Mayfly-Trout Relationship

The mayfly has been associated with fly casting for trout for almost five centuries. The earliest literary reference was permanently recorded by Dame Julianna Burners in 1496 in *Treatys of Fyshing with an Angle*, where she lists the dressings of 12 flies, most of which represent various species of mayflies. Great works by Issac Walton and Charles Cotton followed on the subject in the 1600's, which later touched off one of the most prolific literary splurges ever devoted to a singular sport. Thus, the incomparable mayfly became the symbol associated with fly-fishing for trout.

Through the centuries, the mayfly has retained its lofty status, and rightly so, as it still today makes up the bulk of the trout's diet. Although the population sprawl has taken its toll on their populations, the resilient mayfly endures and remains synonymous with our North American trout streams because the specialized families within the order have the ability to adapt to every conceivable stream habitat.

In addition to the upwinged mayflies, the tent-winged caddisflies of the Tricoptera order are also extremely important aquatic insects on our trout streams. Their importance parallels the mayfly on many streams, due to their seemingly greater tolerance for pollution. Our initial studies on the various caddis genera have made us well aware of their angling importance. Although our primary research thus far has been on the mayfly, with which this book deals specifically, we are looking forward to our continuing research on the caddis and other lesser, yet important, orders. High on this list are the stonefly, (Plecoptera) and the down winged midges of the Diptera order.

A brownie caught during a mayfly hatch being released to feed again.

The Evolution of the Mayfly

The mayfly is an upwinged insect belonging to the scientific order of Ephemeroptera. There are about five hundred species of this prominent insect in North America; their genesis dating back over 300 million years. Evidence of their populations indicate that they were abundant toward the end of the reptile age or Paleozoic Era, where their story is permanently recorded on fossils of Permian shale which is between 220 and 270 million years old. The story of their evolution is subsequently recorded on fossils of the Jurassic Age (135 to 180 million years ago—a period of the Mesozoic Era) and during the more recent Tertiary Period (1 to 70 million years ago), where fossils of winged mayfly adults were found in fossilized coniferous tree trunks.

The prehistoric Permian fossils of the famous Elmo, Kansas shale beds are amazingly preserved; even the wing veinations are reported to show as clearly as recent specimens. It should also be noted that the nymph fossils from this period bear gills which show that the mayflies were aquatic. Dr. F. M. Carpenter (1933) studied and constructed a restoration drawing of a primitive adult mayfly from the fossils of this period. His drawing shows a long-winged, slender-legged, three-tailed insect with a long, slender body. The three pairs of legs are nearly equal in length as are the three tails, but the most noticeable difference from the modern day mayfly is that this primitive insect has four oblong wings which are nearly equal in length.

Dr. R. J. Tillyard, who conducted studies of the Permian mayflies prior to Dr. Carpenter, said of the primitive mayfly, "there is not a single character which fails to agree with our conception of the arche-type for modern mayflies, before the reduction of the hind wing began. All the characteristics of the head, thorax, abdomen, legs and tail filaments so far as revealed in the fossil Permoplectoptera agree admirably with what is required in such an ancestor."

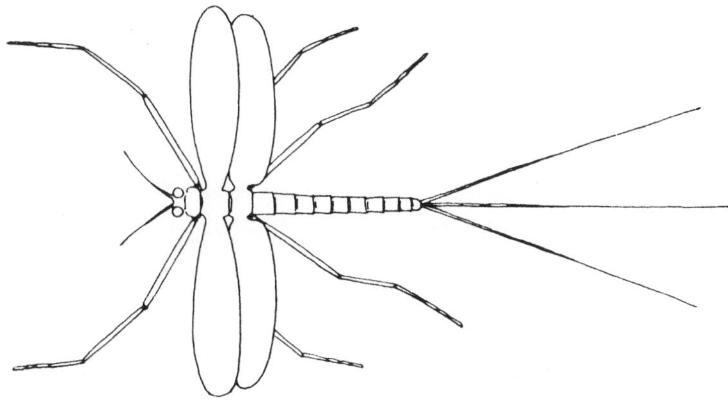

Dr. F. M. Carpenter's restoration of the prehistoric mayfly, Protereisma *permianum*.

The Jurassic mayfly of the Mesozoic Era (the age of dinosaurs) shows obvious signs of evolution; principly the hind wings are much thinner and noticeably shorter (2/3 to 3/4) of the length of the forewing). Mayflies of the subsequent Tertiary period are similar to the present species, having large eyes that meet at the top of the head of the male specimen and further reduced hind wings.

The fossil records from each age clearly show the progressive steps to the modern mayfly and the trends and specializations that have been carried forth to recent days. The main trends are the enlargement of the eyes in the male, the reduction in size, or the loss entirely of the hind wings and the consolidation of the thorax.

In conclusion of the evolutionary aspects of the mayfly, it seems appropriate to quote from *The Biology of Mayflies* by Needham, Traver and Hsu about the fragility but surprising resilience of these prehistoric insects, "Adult mayflies are specialized in their own ways far beyond any other group of insects. They have departed so far from the insect norm that they may be characterized in good part by the losses they have sustained; loss of mouth parts and of all capacity for feeding; loss of legs and of the walking habit*; loss of all defensive equipment, and of all instincts to defend themselves. It seems a marvel that after such losses they still survive and flourish, such fragile creatures in so rough a world!"

*loss or degeneration of legs in the adult mayfly only occurs in some species that are unimportant to the trout angler. To our knowledge, the only species of significance to the angler that fall into this category are of the Ephoron genus.

The Life Cycle of the Mayfly

The futility of the mayfly has been an ideal subject for philosophers since ancient Greece due to its very brief existence as an adult. This poetic reference however is misleading in terms of the mayfly's primary underwater existence as a nymph, which constitutes approximately 99% of its entire lifespan. The nymphs are surprisingly resilient and prolific; their elimination in any one geographic area could only come about by natural calamity or man-made tragedy caused by thermal, toxic, organic or silt pollution. Some mayfly species that require exceptionally long moulting periods as adults have been depleted by severe changes in or elimination of their immediate streamside habitat.

The four stages in the cycle of the mayfly are; egg (ovum), nymph (larva), dun (subimago) and spinner (imago). Because it lacks the pupal stage, this cycle is considered an incomplete metamorphosis. The life span ranges from about 4 months for nontypical species in ideal habitats to as long as three years for some of the large burrowing genera, but the average lifespan of most of the principal species is almost exactly one year.

The peculiar-looking eggs are laid in water, where they settle and adhere to the stream's bottom or to underwater vegetation. They are extremely diverse in size, shape and form. Some are rounded, elipsoid or ovoid in shape and the eggs range in size from .07mm (.002 inches) to .30 or .40mm (.012-.016 inches) across the larger axis which is the size range of the Hexagenia mayfly eggs. Some eggs have polar caps, while still others have ganglion type strings attached. The normal incubation period of the eggs is between one and three weeks according to water temperature, with two weeks being about average. This embryonic development is the first period of the mayfly's life cycle. During this period, the antennae, mouth parts, legs, tails and all of the necessary internal organs are developed and made ready to function at eclosion.

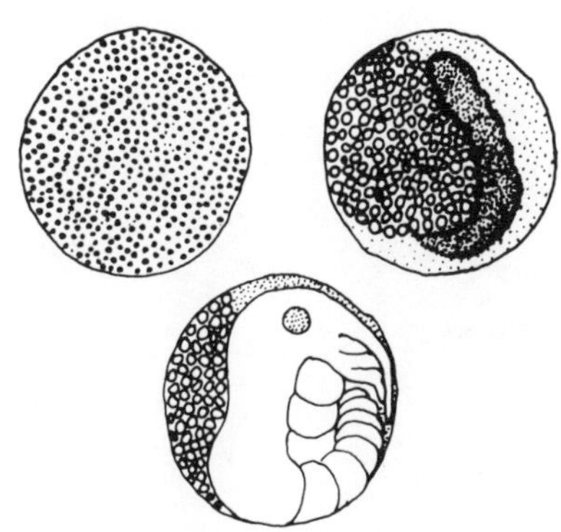

Stages of egg development.

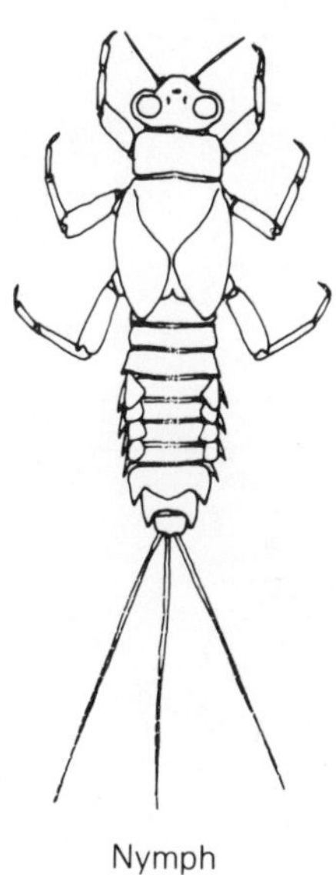

Nymph

Left: Dun (subimago). *Right:* Spinner (imago).

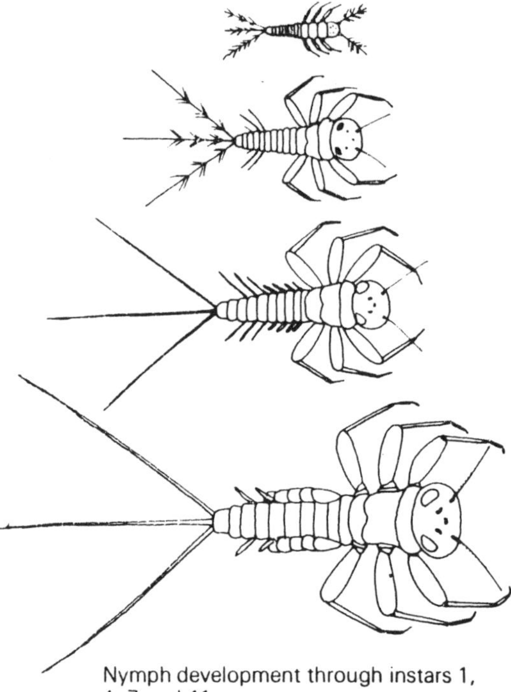

Nymph development through instars 1, 4, 7 and 11.

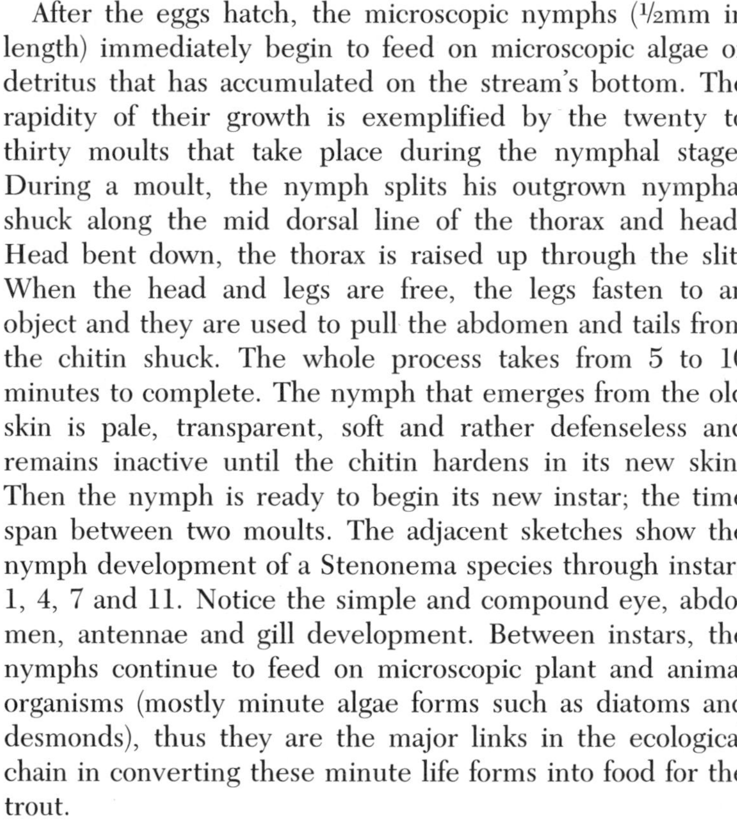

After the eggs hatch, the microscopic nymphs (½mm in length) immediately begin to feed on microscopic algae or detritus that has accumulated on the stream's bottom. The rapidity of their growth is exemplified by the twenty to thirty moults that take place during the nymphal stage. During a moult, the nymph splits his outgrown nymphal shuck along the mid dorsal line of the thorax and head. Head bent down, the thorax is raised up through the slit. When the head and legs are free, the legs fasten to an object and they are used to pull the abdomen and tails from the chitin shuck. The whole process takes from 5 to 10 minutes to complete. The nymph that emerges from the old skin is pale, transparent, soft and rather defenseless and remains inactive until the chitin hardens in its new skin. Then the nymph is ready to begin its new instar; the time span between two moults. The adjacent sketches show the nymph development of a Stenonema species through instars 1, 4, 7 and 11. Notice the simple and compound eye, abdomen, antennae and gill development. Between instars, the nymphs continue to feed on microscopic plant and animal organisms (mostly minute algae forms such as diatoms and desmonds), thus they are the major links in the ecological chain in converting these minute life forms into food for the trout.

Before proceeding further with the life cycle, let us pause to touch on the basic nymph types. There are six mayfly families that are extremely important to the angler and we believe that the nymphs should be classified into four basic types; crawlers, clingers, swimmers and burrowers. Each type is equipped with specific body characteristics and appendages, enabling it to survive in its required habitat. The *crawlers* are variable in size and generally inhabit stretches of medium current, although they may also be found in fast and slow water types; they consist of the prolific Ephemerellidae family, the feeble-legged Leptophlebiidae family and the tiny mayflies of the Tricorythidae and Caenidae family. The *clingers* are of the swift-water Heptageniidae family and the enormous Baetidae family is made up of quick *swimmers*, while the *burrowing* types are of the families Ephemeridae, Potamanthidae and Polymitarcyidae. The mayflies that fall within these basic nymph types, including all of the related genera and species, are treated comprehensively in the subsequent chapters of this book.

Prior to emergence, the nymphs become increasingly available to the trout, as they congregate in advantageous emergence positions behind underwater obstructions or on sticks and other submerged objects; most fast water nymphs normally migrate to side eddies and quiet pockets within the swift water to prepare for emergence.

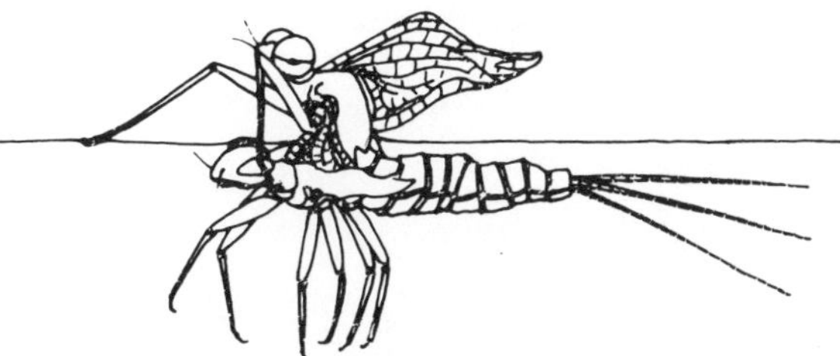
Dun emerging from nymphal shuck.

As the emergence approaches, the nymphs undergo many internal physical changes which are less obvious than the magic-like transformation it will undergo when changing from a rugged nymph to a delicately winged dun. During these last days, the nymphs cease feeding and their sexual products (eggs and sperm) mature quickly. The eyes, wings, genitalia, tails and legs which are needed during the mating and egg-laying processes mature rapidly, while those parts which are not functional during adulthood degenerate or are lost. Some of the more significant changes that take place are the atrophication of the mouth parts and the degeneration of the digestive system. The stomach is then used as ballast to assist in emergence from the stream's bottom. The nymph gulps and fills its stomach with water which is later replaced by air.

Fly-fishermen commonly refer to the emergence of the subimago as "the hatch". Each species has its own emergence characteristics and time period. For example, some crawl out of the water onto stones and twigs like the Isonychia and Siphlonurus mayflies, while others shed their skin on the stream's bottom and rise to the surface as a subimago like those of the Epeorus genus. Most species, however, swim or struggle to the surface as a nymph and hatch within or on the film where the surface tension assists them in the evacuation process. The "hatch" or evacuation process is almost identical to the nymph's moulting process previously described, except that this final moult produces a graceful winged subimago.

During its preoccupation with emergence, the nymph or dun reaches its peak of vulnerability. In the water, they are subjected to relentless attack by the trout. Anglers should note that, during this time, the trout become extremely selective to the physical size, color and shape of the particular species emerging and their emergence characteristics and that one must duplicate this activity if successful angling is to be experienced. As the nymphs pass through this medium and into the atmosphere as a dun, the danger is intensified as swooping birds and other predators join the trout in the frenzied onslaught. Principal animal and insect predators are: dragonflies (both nymph and adult), diving beetles, back swimmers, frogs, salamanders, swifts, swallows and phoebes to name a few. Just when it seems these subimagoes will never survive to perpetuate the species, the duns are off in a wink. Once airborne, they rise slowly and steadily, helicopter-like, toward their tree top destinies, their bodies arched in a semicircle toward the heavens, the survival of some species being proportionally related to the distance they must travel to obtain protective cover.

When the relative safety of the foilage is reached, the duns seek the protective undersides of leaves to serve as protection from the elements and as camouflage from tree-dwelling predators.

Once the duns are settled, they become inactive as further development of the vital reproductive equipment continues to take place within the thin sub-imago skin. The genitalia mature, the eyes of the males enlarge and the legs and tails extend, causing pressure on the thin outer skin. Also, their energy must be reserved for the mating flights and the completion of the life cycle as the mouth parts are atrophied and they cannot eat.

The appearance of the subimago (dun) differs from that of the imago (spinner) in that it is of softer color due to its veil-like chitinous shuck which tones down the vibrant colors of the spinner within. This cloudy or dull appearance is also very evident in the wings, which gives them an opaque appearance as opposed to the sparkling clear or hyaline wings of the spinner.

Mayflies are the only insects that moult their skins after developing functional wings. The final moult may take place in flight within a few hours after emergence, as in the Tricorythodes and Ephoron genera, or it may take several days to complete, such as in the burrowing Ephemera and Hexagenia genera, but the average span of time before the moult is about 24 to 48 hours. The moulting process from dun to spinner is much like the instar moults of the nymph and the transformation from nymph to dun. However, in this case the difficulty is increased as the large delicate wings must also be pulled from the subimago tissue in which they are encased. Any damage, no matter how slight will usually result in disaster! When rearing these mayflies in our lab, the casualties during the final moult were considerable due to unnatural conditions, but we have also observed considerable casualties under natural conditions.

Shortly after the final moult, the lively males mass in swarms over the riffles. The timing and characteristics of the nuptial flight or mating swarm varies from species to species and each is comprehensively covered in the individual chapter. The females flit into the undulating swarms intermittently, each securing a mate. Once paired, they leave the swarm to copulate. Mating occurs in flight; the required positions can only be obtained in the air. The male flies beneath the female and reaches up with his extremely long forelegs and reversed forefeet, holding her in front while he arcs the rear end of his abdomen and clasps her with his forceps at about the ninth abdominal segment. In this manner, the male genitalia contact the duct openings of the female and copulation is accomplished. Eggs fertilized, the female deposits her precious cargo into the stream.

According to the species, the eggs are deposited in various methods. Some species of Ephemerella jettison them, en masse, a safe distance above the stream. The large quivering Ephemera lies prone on the surface and extrudes its eggs while species of Baetis crawl beneath the surface to deposit them.

Their mission accomplished, both males and females soon fall to the surface spent, completing their cycle in a final sacrifice to the dependent trout, who gobble them up greedily.

Cast shuck of dun.

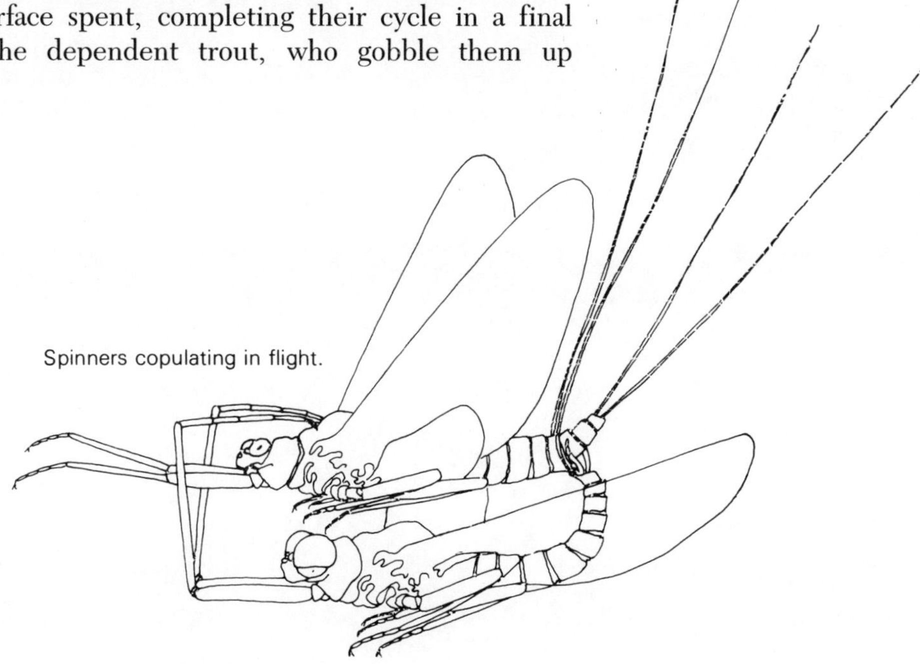

Spinners copulating in flight.

The Anatomy of the Mayfly

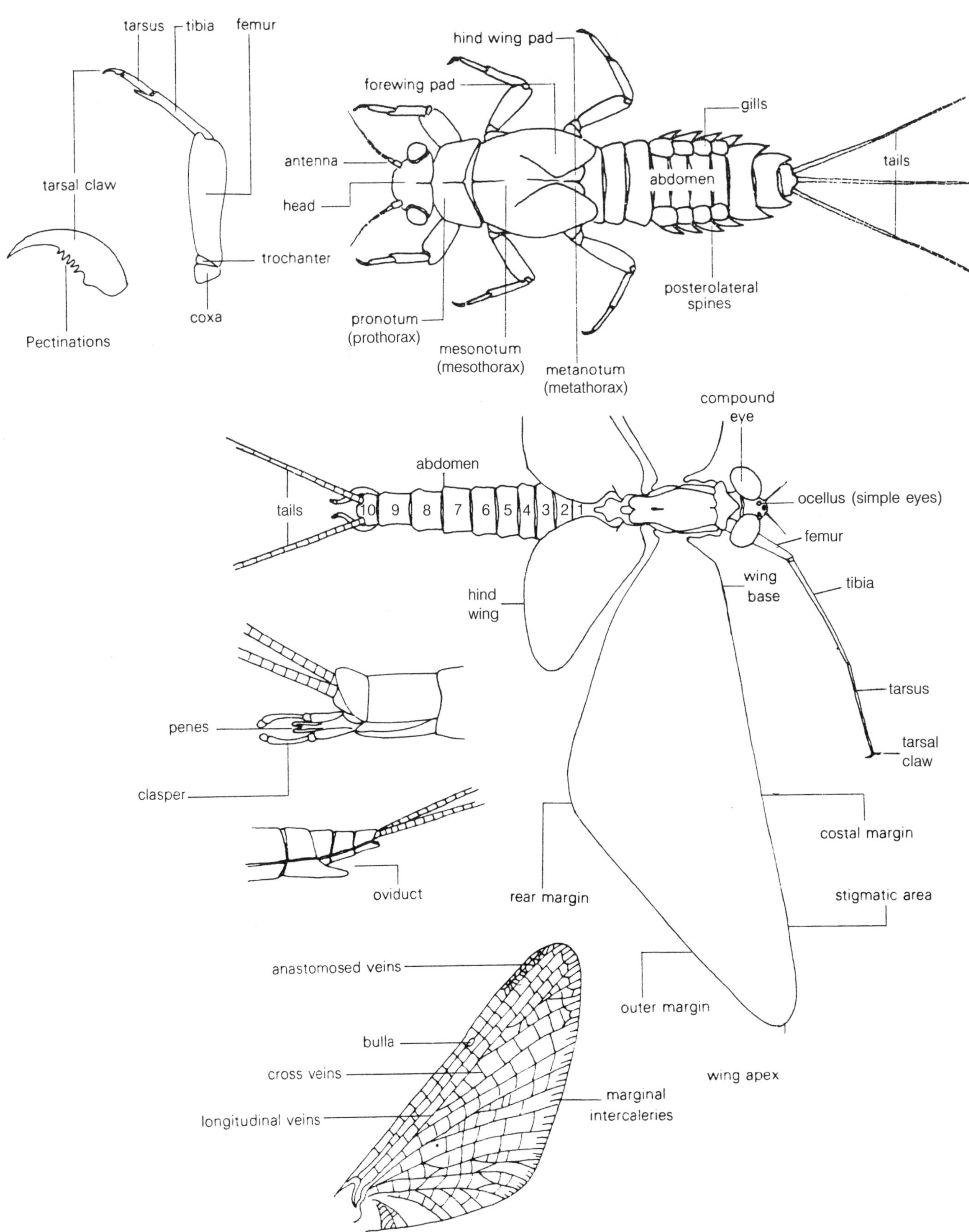

Phonetics

adoptiva . . . . . . adopt tee vuh
albertae . . . . . . al ber tay
album . . . . . . album
allectus . . . . . . ah leck tus
alternatus . . . . . . alter nate us
ameletus . . . . . . am a lay tus
amica . . . . . . am ick uh
anoka . . . . . . an oh cuh
atratus . . . . . . ah trait us
atracaudata . . . . . . atra caw date uh
attenella . . . . . . ah ten ella
attenuata . . . . . . ah ten you ah tuh
baetidae . . . . . . bait ah day
baetis . . . . . . bait iss
baetisca . . . . . . bay tisk ah
baetiscidae . . . . . . bay tisk ah day
basale . . . . . . bah sally
bicaudatus . . . . . . bye caw date us
bicolor . . . . . . bye color
bicornuta . . . . . . bye cor new tuh
blanda . . . . . . bland uh
brachycercus . . . . . . bra key circus
bruneicolor . . . . . . brun eye color
caenidae . . . . . . cane uh day
caenis . . . . . . cane iss
callibaetis . . . . . . caley bait iss
campestris . . . . . . cam pess triss
canadense . . . . . . can uh den see
carolina . . . . . . carolina
caudatella . . . . . . caud a tella
centroptilum . . . . . . sen trop till um
cingulatus . . . . . . sing you late us
cinygmula . . . . . . sin ig mule uh
cloeon . . . . . . clo ee on
coloradensis . . . . . . cholera den sis
columbianus . . . . . . co lum bee ann iss
compar . . . . . . com par
convexum . . . . . . con vex um
cornuta . . . . . . cor new tuh
cornutella . . . . . . corn new tell uh
costalense . . . . . . cah stuh len see
criddlei . . . . . . crid el eye
cupida . . . . . . cupid uh
dannella . . . . . . dan ella
debilis . . . . . . de bill us
deceptivus . . . . . . de cept ee vus
deficiens . . . . . . dee fiss ee ens
depressa . . . . . . depress uh
devinctus . . . . . . dee vinkt us
diaphanus . . . . . . dye ah fane us
distinctus . . . . . . distinct us
doddsi . . . . . . dodds eye
doris . . . . . . door iss
dorothea . . . . . . door uth ee uh
epeorus . . . . . . ee pee or us
eurylophella . . . . . . your ee lop fella
excrucians . . . . . . ex crew see anns
fallax . . . . . . fall ax
ferrugineus . . . . . . fare oo genius
flavilinea . . . . . . flah vil lynn ee uh
fluctuans . . . . . . fluck chew anns
forcipata . . . . . . for sip ah tuh
fuscum . . . . . . fuss come
futile . . . . . . few tilly
glacialis . . . . . . glay see alice
grandis . . . . . . grand iss
gravastella . . . . . . grav uh stella
guttulata . . . . . . gut you lot uh
hageni . . . . . . hog en eye
harperi . . . . . . harper eye
hebe . . . . . . hee bee
hecuba . . . . . . heck cu ba
heptagenia . . . . . . hep tuh gene ee uh
heptageniidae . . . . . . hep tuh gene uh day
heteronea . . . . . . het er roon ee ah
heterotarsale . . . . . . het er o tar sally
hexagenia . . . . . . hex uh gene ee uh
hiemalis . . . . . . he mal iss
hilaris . . . . . . hill air iss
inqualis . . . . . . in ee equal is
inermis . . . . . . in er miss
infrequens . . . . . . in freak whens
ingens . . . . . . in gens
insignificans . . . . . . insignific anns
integrum . . . . . . in tuh grum
intercalarus . . . . . . inter cal ar us
interlineatum . . . . . . inter lynn ee ate um
interpunctatum . . . . . . inter punk tate um
invaria . . . . . . in vair ee uh
isonychia . . . . . . eye son ick ee uh
ithaca . . . . . . ith uh cuh
jocosa . . . . . . jock os suh
johnsoni . . . . . . johnson eye
lacustris . . . . . . lah cuss triss
lata . . . . . . lah tuh
latipennis . . . . . . lay tee pean us

leptophebia .... lept oh flee bee uh
leptophelbiidae .... lept oh flee bee ah day
leukon .... loo con
limbata .... lamb bait uh
levitans .... lev ee tans
lineatus .... line ee a tus
litobracha .... lit o branch uh
longimanus .... lon gee man us
ludens .... lou dens
margarita .... mar guh reet uh
mendax .... mend ax
metretopodidae .... mee tree top uh day
minutus .... my new tuss
mollis .... mahl us
mollita .... mahl ih tee uh
morrisoni .... morris own eye
nebulosa .... neb you low suh
needhami .... need ham i
neglectus .... neglect us
neoclroeon .... knee oh clo ee on
nepotellum .... nep oh tell um
nigritus .... knee greet us
nitidus .... knee tide us
occidentalis .... ox id den tale us
pacifica .... pacific uh
packi .... pack eye
paraleptophlebia ...... para lept oh flee bee uh
parvus .... par vus
pleuralis .... ploor alice
polymitarcyidae .... polly mih tar sid day
potamanthus .... pot uh manth us
potamanthidae .... pot uh manth uh day
prudens .... prude ens
pseudocloeon .... soo doe clo ee on
pulchellum .... pull chell um
pulla .... pull uh
quebecensis .... quebec en sis
remaleyi .... ray moll ee eye
rapidus .... rah pee duss
recurvata .... ree curve ah tuh
reticulata .... rah tick u lata
rhithrogena .... rye throw gene uh
rigida .... rige eye dah
rotunda .... row ton duh
rubrum .... rub rum
rufostrigatum .... roof oh stry gay tum
rufous .... roof us
sadleri .... sadler eye
serrata .... sir ah tuh
serratella .... sir ah tell uh
sicca .... sick uh
signatum .... sig nate um
simplex .... sim plex
simplicioides .... sim plick ee oh dees
simulans .... sim yule anns
siphlonuridae .... sif lun or uh day
siphlonurus .... sif lun or uss
siphloptecton .... sif low pleck ton
sparsatus .... spar sate us
speciosum .... spee see oh sum
stenacron .... sten oh cron
stenonema .... sten oh knee muh
stygiatus .... sty ghee ate us
subvaria .... sub vary uh
tardata .... tar date uh
temporalis .... temper alice
timpanoga .... tim pan oh ga
tricaudatus .... try caw date us
varia .... vair ee uh
velma .... vel muh
verticis .... vert tee sis
vicarium .... vie care ee um
vitreus .... vit ree us
walshi .... wall shy

NOTE: Over the years we have tried to discourage the use of common names because we sincerely believe that it leads to confusion in identification and communication. One has only to count the use of the name Blue Winged Olive to realize the futility of this practice.

Glossary

Appendage: Any part joined to or diverging from the axial trunk (body) or from any adjunct of it, such as legs, tails, gills, antennae, etc.

Adult: Imago or spinner stage of mayfly.

Anastomosed: Branching and rejoining of veins in wing creating crisscross-like network of veins, usually in stigmatic area of wing.

Antenna: (pl. antennae) Paired appendages of head, usually located between eyes.

Anterior: At or toward head or forward part of body.

Apex: (adj. apical) The tip, end, or highest point of structure.

Atrophy: (v. atrophied) Withered structure, no longer fully formed or functional.

Basal: (adv. basally) Base of structure or part, generally at or near point of attachment.

Brood: One of the generations of species having more than one generation per year.

Bulla: Bubble-like node in subcostal vein found approximately midway between base and apex; sometimes found in other longitudinal veins.

Carapace: Hardened shield covering part of body dorsally.

Caudal: Pertains to posterior end of body.

Caudal filament: synonymous to tail.

Cercus: (pl. cerci) Pair or outer tails as compared to middle.

Cervical: Area immediately behind head and before thorax.

Chitin: Outer, hardened skin of insect.

Clasper: Paired, jointed structure of male adult used to clasp female abdomen during mating.

Compound eye: Large, multifaceted eyes as compared to smaller ocellus.

Conical: Cone-shaped; usually in reference to front portion of head.

Contiguous: Touching or joining at edge or boundary.

Costa: (adj. costal) Front or fore margin of wing.

Costal angulation: Point or angulation of fore margin of wing; usually in reference to hind wing.

Costal vein: Longitudinal vein forming anterior margin of wing.

Coxa: (pl. coxae) Basal segment of leg connecting distally to trochanter and basally to thorax.

Crossveins: Short horizontal-like veins extending between and often connecting longitudinal veins.

Cubital veins: Network of veins stemming from cubitus.

Cubitus: (adj. cubital) Fifth longitudinal vein that connects to base of wing, located in rear or hind margin of wing.

Denticles: Tooth-like projections.

Distal: At or toward outermost area or end of structure, as opposed to basal.

Dorsal: Top or upper surface.

Dun: Subimago stage of mayfly in fully winged form prior to shedding its thin outer skin.

Eclosion: Hatching of the egg.

Emergence: "Hatching" or transformation from nymph to adult stage.

Entomology: The study of insects.

Exoskeleton: External body wall of insect as in chitin shuck.

Facet: Lenslike divisions of compound (multifaceted) eye.

Facial: Referring to forepart of head.

Femur: (pl. femora) "Thigh" portion of leg, distal to trochanter and preceding tibia.

Filamentous: Threadlike, usually in reference to antennae or gills.

Ganglion: (pl. ganglia) Collection of nerve cells acting as a center of nervous influence.

Genitalia: External sexual organs or structure.

Gills: Respiratory appendages of nymph located on abdomen either laterally or dorsally.

Hatch: Birth of larva from egg. Emergence from aquatic to winged state.

Hyaline: Glassy, transparent, usually in reference to wing of Spinner or Imago.

Imago: (pl. imagoes) Sexually mature adult or spinner stage of mayfly.

Incomplete metamorphosis: Life cycle in which no pupal stage preceeds the adult, as in mayfly.

Incubation: Period of egg stage necessary for development and eclosion.

Instar: Insect between two molting events.

Intercalary: Short veins not connecting to main longitudinal veins, usually extending from rear margin of wing.

Labium: Area covering undersides of mouth parts.

Labrum: Area overhanging mouthparts from top.

Larva: (pl. larvae) First major mobile life stage, usually referred to as nymph.

Lateral: At, or toward sides.

Longitudinal veins: Long, major veins, or long veins attaching to major veins that connect to base of wing.

Mandible: (pl. mandibles) Paired mouthparts directly behind labrum.

Marginal intercaleries: Single veins located at outer and rear margins of forewing, not being connected to any other veins.

Maxilla: (pl. maxillae) Paired mouthparts between mandibles and labium.

Medial: At or toward midline of body.

Metapleuron: Side area of metathorax, from which base of hind wings are attached.
Metasternum: Bottom area of metathorax, from which hind pair of legs are attached.
Metathorax: Rear and smallest part of thorax.
Mid-dorsal: Longitudinally along the center of body.
Molting: To shed exoskeleton or thin outer skin.
Morphology: Study of structure and form of organisms.
Naid: Nymph
Node: A bulla-like nodule.
Notum: Dorsal surface of a body segment.
Nymph: Larval stage of insect, in reference to mayfly.
Occiput: Rear of head.
Ocellus: (pl. ocelli) Simple eye, in sets of three located on head between the larger, compound eyes.
Operculate: Lid or cover-like, usually in reference to gill covers.
Oviposition: (v. ovipositing) The act of laying eggs.
Ovipositor: Specialized structure of female adults used to deposit eggs.
Ovum: (pl. ova) Egg (eggs) of female adult.
Pectinate: (pl. pectinations) Usually in reference to toothed, comb-like spines in tarsal claw.
Penes: Paired structures of male located between base of claspers, from which sperm is transferred to female eggs.
Pluera: Generally in reference to sides of thorax in adult.
Posterior: At or toward the hind, or tail end of body.
Postero-lateral spines: Structures eminating from rear and sides of abdominal segments.
Pronotum: Dorsal area of prothorax.
Propleuron: Side area of prothorax.
Prosternum: Bottom surface of prothorax, from which forelegs are attached.
Prothorax: The front or first portion of thorax.
Median veins: Longitudinal veins located between radial and cubital veins, in reference to forewing.
Mesonotum: Top or dorsal area of mesothorax.
Mesopleuron: Side area of mesthorax from which base of forewings are attached.
Mesosternum: Bottom area of mesothorax from which middle pair of legs are attached.
Mesothorax: Middle and largest part of thorax.
Metamorphosis: Transformation from egg to larva to pupa to adult; in reference to mayfly, from egg to larva (nymph) to dun (subimago) to adult (imago or spinner).
Metanotum: Top or dorsal area of metathorax.
Pupa: Quiescent stage of insect that undergoes complete metamorphosis, following larval, and preceeding adult stage.
Quiescent: Generally inactive.
Radial veins: Longitudinal veins located between subcostal and median veins, in reference to forewing.
Spinner: The sexually mature adult or imago stage of mayfly after it has shed the thin outer skin of subimago.
Subcostal: In reference to the first longitudinal vein after the costal vein and before the first radial vein of the forewing.
Subimago: The sexually immature "Dun" stage of mayfly in fully winged form after emergence from nymph, and prior to shedding its thin outer skin to become a spinner or imago.
Tarsal claw: Located at tip of tarsus (paired in adults and usually single in nymphs).
Tarsus: (pl. tarsal) Most distal major leg segment, immediately beyond tibia, often subdivided into two to five tarsal segments.
Tergite: Upper or dorsal surface of an individual abdominal segment.
Thorax: (adj. thoracic) Portion of insect body located between head and abdomen consisting three sections; prothorax, mesothorax and metathorax (from which legs and wings are born).
Tibia: Major leg segment located between femur and tarsus.
Trachea: As referred to in this text, branching vein-like tubes in gills of nymph.
Trochanter: Small joint located between femur and coxa.
Truncate: Squared off or blunt at end.
Tubercles: A rounded eminence or nodule.
Tusks: Paired, horn-like prominance extending from front of head, usually located between or just outside of antennae.
Veinlet: Short vein in wing that leads from a major longitudinal vein to wing margin, particularly to hind region.
Venation: Structural network of veins in wing.
Ventral: Bottom or underside.
Vestigial: A appendage surviving in a dwarfed or degenerate form.
Wing pad: Sheath of a developing wing, referring to a nymph.

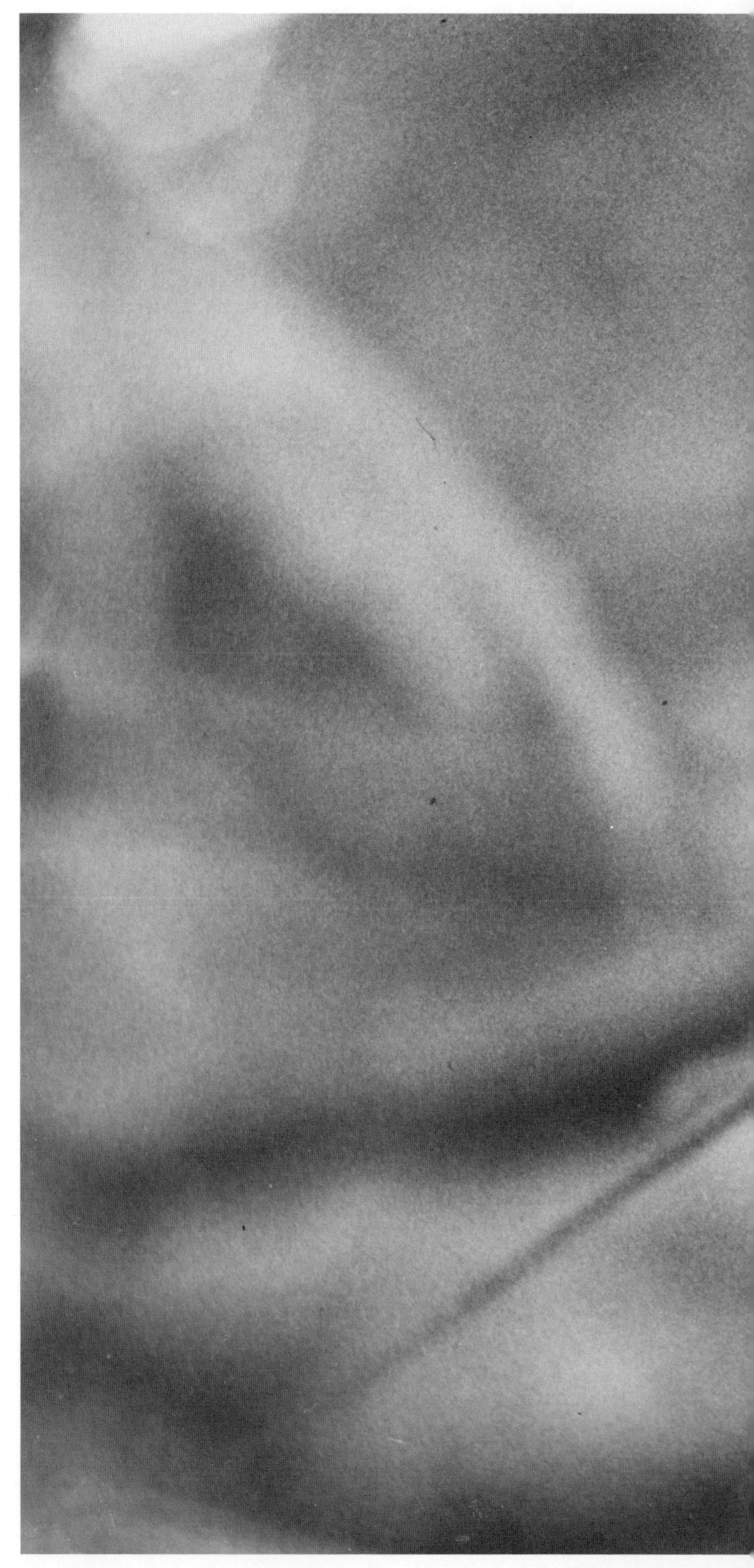

The Hatches

QUICK REFERENCE EMERGENCE CHARTS—EASTERN & MIDWESTERN NORTH AMERICA

GENUS	SPECIES	GENERAL EMERGENCE								BODY SIZE MM	HOOK SIZES-MUSTAD Dry-Std. 94840 94833	HOOK SIZES-MUSTAD Wet-Std. 7948A	SPECIES INFO	MOST ACCEPTED COMMON NAMES
		MAR	APR	MAY	JUNE	JULY	AUG	SEPT	OCT					
Baetis	*vagans (E,M)*	20		15						6½-8mm	#16	#16	Pg. 252, 253 Color Pit XIX & XX	Blue Winged Olive
Baetis	*tricaudatus (M)*		1	15				6	15	8-9mm	#14	#14	Pg. 252, 253	Blue Winged Olive
Emphemerella	*subvaria (E,M)*		7		7					10-12mm	#10, #12	#10, #12	Pg. 65, 68 Color Plt I	Hendrickson (f) Red Quill (m)
Baetis	*cingulatus (now quebe censis) (E, M)*		10		30					5-6mm	#18	#18	Pg. 252, 253 Color Pit XIX	Blue Winged Olive
Epeorus	*pleuralis (E, M)*		10		30					9-12mm	#10, #12, #14	#10, #12	Pg. 178, 179 Color Plt XII	Quill Gordon
Paraleptophlebia	*adoptiva (E,M)*		14		12					6-8mm	#16, #18	#16, #14	Pg. 121, 122 Color Pit VI	Blue Quill, Blue Dun, Slate Winged Mahogany
Leptophlebia	*species (E,M)*		15		20					10-13mm	#14, #12, #10	#10, #12	Pg. 128, 129 Color Plt VI	Black Quill, Whirling Dun
Ephemerella	*rotunda (E,M)*		30		14					9-10½mm	#12, #14	#12, #14	Pg. 65, 75 Color Plt II	Dk Hendrickson Red Quill (f)
Ephemerella	*invaria (E,M)*			7	13					7½-9½mm	#14	#14	Pg. 65, 75 Color Plt III	Sulphur Pale Evening Dun
Ephemerella	*cornuta (E,M)*			14		14				9-10mm	#16, #14	#14, #12	Pg. 66, 94 Color Pit I	Blue Winged Olive
Hexagenia (now Litobrancha)	*recurvata (E,M)*			14		3				16-38mm	#8, #6 & #8 4×lg**	#6, #4 & #6 3×lg***	Pg. 221, 232 Color Pit XV & XVIII	Dk Green Drake

QUICK REFERENCE EMERGENCE CHARTS—EASTERN & MIDWESTERN NORTH AMERICA (*Continued*)

		GENERAL EMERGENCE									HOOK SIZES-MUSTAD			
GENUS	SPECIES	MAR	APR	MAY	JUNE	JULY	AUG	SEPT	OCT	BODY SIZE MM	*Dry-Std.* 94840 94833	*Wet-Std.* 7948A	SPECIES INFO	MOST ACCEPTED COMMON NAMES
Stenonema	*vicarium (E,M)*			14		9				14-16mm	#10, #8* #12 4×lg***	#10 3×lg*** #10*	Pg. 159, 160 Color Pit IX & X	March Brown Amer. March Brn Ginger Quill
Ephemera	*guttulata (E)*			15	28					18-30mm	#8, #6*, #8 4×lg**	#10, #10 3×lg***	Pg. 200, 201 Color Plt XV & XVI	Green Drake, Coffin Fly
Pseudocloeon	*carolina (E)*			16			20			4-5mm	#20, #22*	#18, #20	Pg. 260 Color Plt XXII	Blue Winged Olive
Stenonema	*fuscum (E,M)*			17		9				12-14mm	#8, #10	#10, #10 3×lg***	Pg. 159, 165 Color Pit IX & X	Grey Fox, Ginger Quill
Ephemera	*simulans (E,M)*			21		21				11-14mm	#8, #10	#10, #10 3×lg***	Pg. 200, 217	Brown Drake
Ephemerella	*dorothea (E,M)*			21		7				6½-7½mm	#16, #18	#16	Pg. 65, 82 Color Plt II	Sulphur, Pale Evening Dun
Isonychia	*bicolor (E,M)*			25				6		13-16mm	#10, #8	#10, #10 3×lg***	Pg. 270, 271 Color Plt XXIII & XXIV	Leadwing Coachman, Dun Variant
Siphlonurus	*alternatus (E,M)*			30		15				13-16mm	#12, #10, #8	#10, #10, 3×lg***	Pg. 281, 283 Color Pit XXII & XXIII	Grey Drake
Siphlonurus	*quebecensis (E,M)*			30	15					12-15mm	#10, #8, #12 4×lg**	#10, #10 3×lg**	Pg. 283 Color Pit XXII	Grey Drake
Epeorus	*vitreus (E,M)*				1		18			9-12mm	#12, #14	#14, #12	Pg. 178, 183 Color Pit XII, XIII & XIV	Sulphur, Pale Evening Dun

QUICK REFERENCE EMERGENCE CHARTS—EASTERN & MIDWESTERN NORTH AMERICA *(Continued)*

GENUS	SPECIES	*GENERAL EMERGENCE* MAR	APR	MAY	JUNE	JULY	AUG	SEPT	OCT	BODY SIZE MM	*HOOK SIZES-MUSTAD* *Dry-Std.* 94840 94833	*Wet-Std.* 7948A	SPECIES INFO	MOST ACCEPTED COMMON NAMES
Isonychia	*sadleri (E,M)*				1			2		13-16mm	#8, #10	#10, #10 3×lg***	Pg. 270, 276 Color Plt XXIII & XXIV	Leadwing Coachman, Dun Variant
Baetis	*brunneicolor (E,M)*				3	28				6-7mm	#16, #18	#16, #18	Pg. 252, 253	Blue Winged Olive
Brachycercus	*species (E,M)*				3			7		3-6mm	#18, #24*	#18, #18-24	Pg. 150	
Ephemerella	*attenuata (E)*				3	14				6-8mm	#16, #18	#16	Pg. 67, 113 Color Plt II	Blue Winged Olive
Paraleptophlebia	*mollis (E,M)*				6	15				6-8mm	#16, #18	#14, #16	Pg. 121 Color Plt VII	
Centroptilium	*species*				6				15	5-6mm	#18	#18	Pg. 268	
Stenonema	*canadense (E,M)*				9		28			9-11mm	#14, #10	#14, #12	Pg. 159, 170 Color Plt IX	Light Cahill
Stenonema	*ithaca (E)*				8		30			10-12mm	#10, #12	#10, #12	Pg. 159, 170 Color Plt IX & XI	Light Cahill
Hexagenia	*limbata (E,M)*				11		10			16-35mm	#6, #8 4×lg**	#4, #6 3×lg***	Pg. 221, 222 Color Plt XV, XVII, XVIII	Michigan Caddis
Potomanthus	*distinctus (E,M)*				14		21			13-16mm	#10, #8	#10, #10 3×lg***	Pg. 237, 238 Color Plt XV & XVII	Golden Drake Yellow Drake Cream Variant
Ephemera	*varia (E,M)*				15		18			13-16mm	#10, #8	#10, #10 3×lg***	Pg. 200, 211 Color Plt XV, XVI & XVII	Yellow Drake, Yellow Dun, Cream Variant

QUICK REFERENCE EMERGENCE CHARTS—EASTERN & MIDWESTERN NORTH AMERICA (*Continued*)

		GENERAL EMERGENCE									HOOK SIZES-MUSTAD			
GENUS	SPECIES	MAR	APR	MAY	JUNE	JULY	AUG	SEPT	OCT	BODY SIZE MM	*Dry-Std.* 94840 94833	*Wet-Std.* 7948A	SPECIES INFO	MOST ACCEPTED COMMON NAMES
Callibaetis	*species (E,M)*				20			25		6-9mm	#18, #16, #14	#18, #16, #14	Pg. 266 Color Plt XX	Gray Quill
Ephemerella	*cornutella (E,M)*				20		15			6-7mm	#18, #16*	#18, #16	Pg. 66	Blue Winged Olive
Psedocloeon	*anoka (M)*				20	21	28	30		4-5mm	#22, #20*	#18, #20*	Pg. 260	Blue Winged Olive
Tricorythodes	*species (E,M)*				20				30	3-3½mm	#24, #26*	#24, #26*	Pg. 134, 135 Color Plt VIII	Trico, Tiny White Winged Black, Caenis
Cloeon	*species (E,M)*				21			30		3-5mm	#26, #24, #22, #20*	#26, #24, #22*	Pg. 260 Color Plt XXIII	Blue Winged Olive
Ephemerella	*deficiens (E,M)*					1		30		4-5½mm	#20, #22*	#18, #20	Pg. 67	
Ephemerella	*depressa (E,M)*					1		30		6-8mm	#18, #16	#16	Pg. 66	Blue Winged Olive
Paraleptophlebia	*debilus (E,M)*					1		5		6-8mm	#18, #16	#16	Pg. 121 Color Plt VII	Blue Quill, Blue Dun, Slate Winged Mahogany
Ephemerella	*lata (M)*					1	15			6-8mm	#18, #16	#16	Pg. 66, 100 Color Plt IV	Blue Winged Olive
Heptagenia	*hebe (E,M)*					15			20	6-8mm	#18, #16	#16	Pg. 190 Color Plt XIII & XIV	

QUICK REFERENCE EMERGENCE CHARTS—EASTERN & MIDWESTERN NORTH AMERICA *(Continued)*

GENUS	SPECIES	*GENERAL EMERGENCE* MAR	APR	MAY	JUNE	JULY	AUG	SEPT	OCT	BODY SIZE MM	*HOOK SIZES-MUSTAD* *Dry-Std.* 94840 94833	*Wet-Std.* 7948A	SPECIES INFO	MOST ACCEPTED COMMON NAMES
Ephoron	*leukon (E,M)*						15	30		13-14mm	#10, #8	#10, #10 3×lg***	Pg. 243	White Fly
	album (E,M)						15	30		11-12mm	#12, #10	#12, #10	Pg. 243	White Fly
Isonychia	*harperi*						20	30		12-14mm	#10	#10	Pg. 270	Lead Winged Coachman, Dun Variant

GENUS	SPECIES	GENERAL EMERGENCE MAR	APR	MAY	JUNE	JULY	AUG	SEPT	OCT	BODY SIZE MM	HOOK SIZES-MUSTAD Dry-Std. 94840 94833	Wet-Std. 7948A	SPECIES INFO	MOST ACCEPTED COMMON NAMES
Baetis	*tricaudatus*		1	15				10	30	8-9mm	#16, #14	#14	Pg. 252, 254	Blue Winged Olive
Rhithrogena	*morrisoni*		7	15						8-9mm	#16, #14	#14	Pg. 192	Black Quill
Baetis	*bicaudatus*		10						30	4-5mm	#18, #16	#18, #16	Pg. 252	Blue Winged Olive
Leptophlebia	*nebulosa*		10			1				10-13mm	#14, #12, #10	#12, #10	Pg. 128, 129	Black Quill, Whirling Dun, Borchers Drake
Leptophlebia	*gravestella*		10			1				10-12mm	#14, #12	#12, #10	Pg. 128	Same as above
Leptophlebia	*pacifica*		10			1				13-14mm	#12, #10, #8	#10	Pg. 128	Same as above
Siphlonurus	*alternatus*			5	15					13-16mm	#12, #10, #8	#10, #10 3×lg***	Pg. 283 Color Pit XXII & XXIII	Grey Drake
Baetis	*brunneicolor*				1	25				6-7mm	#18, #16	#18, #16	Pg. 252, 253	Blue Winged Olive
Hexagenia	*limbata*				1			1		16-35mm	#6, #8 4×lg**	#4, #6 3×lg***	Pg. 221, 222 Color Pit XV, XVII & XVIII	Michigan Caddis
Brachycerus	*species*				5			20		3-4mm	#26, #24	#26, #24	Pg. 150	——
Caenis	*species*				10			25		3-4mm	#26, #24	#26, #24	Pg. 148, 149	Caenis
Rhithrogena	*hageni*				10		7			9-10mm	#14, #12	#12	Pg. 192	Black Quill
Cinygmula	*species*				12				20	7-10mm	#16, #14	#16, #14, #12	Pg. 193	——
Ephemera	*simulans*				15		5			11-14mm	#12, #10	#12, #10	Pg. 200, 217	Brown Drake

QUICK REFERENCE EMERGENCE CHARTS—WEST *(Continued)*

GENUS	SPECIES	*GENERAL EMERGENCE* MAR	APR	MAY	JUNE	JULY	AUG	SEPT	OCT	BODY SIZE MM	*HOOK SIZES-MUSTAD* *Dry-Std.* 94840 94833	*Wet-Std.* 7948A	SPECIES INFO	MOST ACCEPTED COMMON NAMES
Isonychia	*velma*				15	25	1	15		13-16mm	#12, #10, #8	#10, #10 3×lg***	Pg. 270	Leadwing Coachman, Dun Variant
Centroplilium	*species*				20				10	5-7mm	#18, #16	#18, #16	Pg. 268	——
Ephemerella	*doddsi*				20		10			14-16mm	#10, #8	#10 3×lg***	Pg. 66, 104 Color Plt V	Western Green Drake
Ephemerella	*glacialis*				20		10			13-15mm	#12, #10	#10	Pg. 66, 104 Color Plt III	Western Green Drake
Ephemerella	*grandis*				20		10			12-13mm	#12, #10	#10	Pg. 66, 104	Western Green Drake
Heptagenia	*elegantual*				20		1			8-10mm	#16, #14, #12	#14, #12	Pg. 190	Grey Drake
Heptagenia	*simplicioides*				20			15		9-10mm	#14, #12	#12	Pg. 190	Grey Drake
Tricorythodes	*minutus*				22			20		3-3½mm	#26, #24*	#26, #24*	Pg. 134, 135	Trico, Tiny White winged Black, Caenis
Tricorythodes	*fallax*				22			20		5mm	#20	#18	Pg. 134, 135	Same as above
Ephemerella	*inermis*				30				2	5½-6½mm	#18	#16, #18	Pg. 65, 87 Color Plt V	Pale Morning Dun
Ephemerella	*infrequens*				30				2	7-8mm	#16	#16, #14	Pg. 65, 87 Color Plt III	Pale Morning Dun
Cloeon	*ingens*					1	25			8-9mm	#16, #14	#14	Pg. 260, 265	Blue Winged Olive

QUICK REFERENCE EMERGENCE CHARTS—WEST *(Continued)*

GENUS	SPECIES	*GENERAL EMERGENCE* MAR	APR	MAY	JUNE	JULY	AUG	SEPT	OCT	BODY SIZE MM	*HOOK SIZES-MUSTAD* *Dry-Std.* 94840 94833	*Wet-Std.* 7948A	SPECIES INFO	MOST ACCEPTED COMMON NAMES
Paraleptophlebia	*debilus*					1		15		6-8mm	#18, #16	#16	Pg. 121 Color Plt VII	Blue Quill, Blue Dun, Slate-wing Mahogany
Ephemerella	*flavilinea*					2	30			8-10mm	#16, #14, #12	#14, #12	Pg. 66, 111 Color Plt IV	Slate-wing Olive, Western Slate-wing Olive
Pseudocloeon	*dubium*					2		25		3-4mm	#26, #24*	#26, #24*	Pg. 260, 265	Blue Winged Olive
Pseudocloeon	*futile*					2		30		3-3½mm	#26*	#26*	Pg. 260, 265	Blue Winged Olive
Callibaetis	*coloradensis*					3		30		7-9mm	#16, #14	#16, #14	Pg. 266	Grey Quill
Callibaetis	*nigritus*					3		30		8-10mm	#16, #14, #12	#14, #12	Pg. 266	Grey Quill
Rhithrogena	*undulata*					5		30		7-8mm	#16	#16, #14	Pg. 192	Red Quill
Ephoron	*album*						5	30		11-12mm	#12, #10	#12, #10	Pg. 243	White Fly
Paraleptophlebia	*bicornuta*						1	28		9-11mm	#14, #12	#12	Pg. 121	——

The Family Concept of Identification

The "family concept of identification" is based on the angler's ability to recognize the specialized physical characteristics (body shape and appendages) of the four basic nymph types. These characteristics, relative to the environment in which the nymph lives, are the real key to positive identification of the species. Once the angler learns these characteristics, he should have little problem in distinguishing the basic nymph types of families; the flattened clingers, the more rounded feeble-legged crawlers, the tusk-bearing burrowers and the swift swimmers. After some experience he will be able to discriminate the genus of the nymph and, finally, if he does his homework, the species.

The following is a systematic approach to this identification process.

The Basic Nymph Types

The Variable Crawlers

The Flattened Clingers

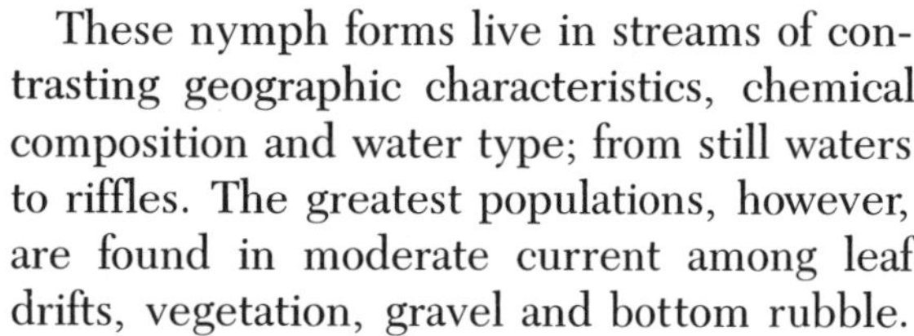

These nymph forms live in streams of contrasting geographic characteristics, chemical composition and water type; from still waters to riffles. The greatest populations, however, are found in moderate current among leaf drifts, vegetation, gravel and bottom rubble.

Although their body characteristics are as extreme as their environment, most species have feeble legs, round or ovoid cross-sectional bodies and are poor swimmers. Their varied and diverse features make them easy to recognize when compared to the specific physical characteristics of the remaining three basic nymph types. The eyes of these nymphs are always located at the sides of the head.

There are three major families in this prolific group that are important to the angler. They are Ephemerellidae, Leptophlebiidae, and Tricorythidae. Caenidae and Baetiscidae make up the minor families in this group.

These oxygen-loving clinging nymphs are extremely flattened. Their heads and bodies are perfectly designed to deflect the swift currents where they live.

They are of the easiest nymphs to recognize due to their saucer-like heads which are normally wider than their thorax. The eyes are located on the top lateral edge of the head. Most species have large plate-like, overlapping gills which act as suction cups even on the smoothest of stones located at the bottoms of white water torrents.

Although they are fast-water dwellers, some species migrate to quiet-water pockets, side eddies or nearby quiet pools prior to hatching. Their presence can be detected by lifting and inspecting the undersides of medium-sized rocks along the shore.

All of the clinging nymph forms belong to the family Heptageniidae.

The Tusked Burrowers

The elusive burrowing nymphs are normally found in the rich silt and marl bottoms of pools, eddies and quiet stretches of our rivers as well as the firm bottom-muck of cold lakes and ponds. They are easily recognized by their outlandish size, long tuskbearing mandibles, three tails, flanged legs and shovel-like heads which are efficiently designed for burrowing into soft bottoms of back waters and the silt that accumulates behind boulders in faster sections.

Their fascinating, serpent-like bodies feature plumage-like gills that are in constant flowing motion, creating current and extracting oxygen from their still-water environment.

These legendary nymph forms are classified under the families Ephemeridae, Potamanthidae and Polymitarcyidae.

The Streamlined Swimmers

The habitat of the swimming nymph is quite extreme in type. The larger swimmers prefer the swift water commonly associated with tumbling freestone streams, while the tiny swimmers prefer medium and, sometimes, quiet water where they range about freely, perching on the lush subaquatic growth in alkaline streams. Unique to these nymph forms is that every genus is transcontinental.

All swimmers are similar in body form and are easy to identify by their slender, sleek bodies, long, fragile legs and plate-like gills on segments 1 through 7. Their tails are normally thickly fringed with hairs that act as paddles enabling the nymph to dart quickly in any direction.

The swimming nymphs are classified under the families Baetidae, Siphlonuridae and Metretopodidae.

The Family Tree

The Crawlers

FAMILY EPHEMERELLIDAE (p. 59)
The Super Crawlers

GENUS EPHEMERELLA
attenuata
cornuta
cornutella
deficiens
depressa (now synonym of *cornuta*)
doddsi
doris
dorothea
excrucians
flavilinea
glacialis (now synonym of *grandis ingens*)
grandis (*grandis ingens*)
inermis
infrequens
invaria
lata
longicornis
lutulenta
margarita
mollitia
needhami
rotunda
serrata
simplex
subvaria
temporalis
walkeri

FAMILY LEPTOPHLEBIIDAE (p. 119)
The Feeble-legged Crawlers

GENUS LEPTOPHLEBIA
cupida
gravastella
johnsoni
nebulosa
pacifica

GENUS PARALEPTOPHLEBIA
adoptiva
bicornuta
debilis
heteronea
mollis
packi

FAMILY TRICORYTHIDAE (p. 133)
The Tiny Crawlers

GENUS TRICORYTHODES
atratus
allectus
minutus
stygiatus
fallix (synonym to *minutus*)

FAMILY CAENIDAE (p. 133)
The Tiny Crawlers

GENUS CAENIS
amica
forcipata
hilaris
jocosa
latipennis
simulans

GENUS BRACHYCERCUS
nitudus *lacustris* *prudens*

FAMILY BAETISCIDAE (p. 151)

GENUS BAETISCA
obesa *laurentina* *rogersi*

The Clingers

FAMILY HEPTAGENIIDAE (p. 155)

GENUS STENONEMA
fuscum
integrum integrum
ithaca
luteum
nepotellum
pulchellum
rubrum
tripunctatum tripunctatum
vicarium

GENUS STENACRON
interpunctatum canadense
interpunctatum heterotarsale
interpunctatum interpunctatum

GENUS EPEORUS
albertae
deceptivus
longimanus
pleuralis
punctatus
rubidus
suffusus
vitreus

GENUS HEPTAGENIA
criddlei
elegantula
hebe
juno
minerva
pulla
rosea

GENUS RHITHROGENA
impersonata
jejuna
hageni
pellucida
sanguinea
undulata
morrisoni

GENUS CINYGMULA
ramaleyi
reticulata

The Burrowers

FAMILY EPHEMERIDAE (p. 197)

GENUS EPHEMERA
blanda
compar
guttulata
simulans
triplex
varia

GENUS HEXAGENIA
atrocaudata
limbata (now *limbata limbata*)
rigida

GENUS LITOBRANCHA
recurvata

FAMILY POTAMANTHIDAE (p. 236)

GENUS POTAMANTHUS
diaphanus
distinctus
inequalis
neglectus
rufus
verticus

FAMILY POLYMITARCYIDAE (p. 243)

GENUS EPHORON
album
leukon

The Swimmers

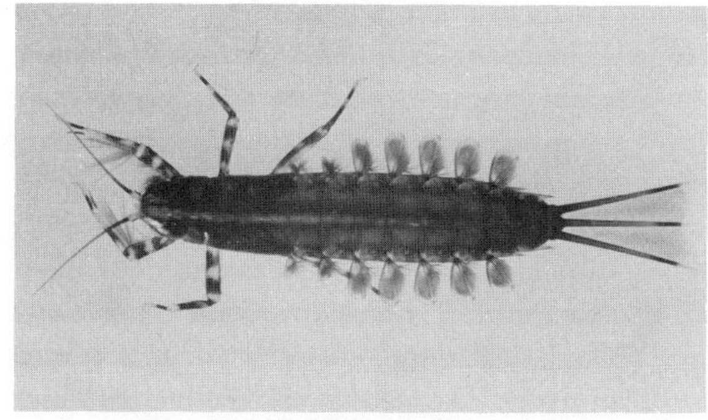

FAMILY BAETIDAE (p. 249)

GENUS BAETIS
bicaudatus
brunneicolor
devinctus
frivolus
hiemalis
intercalaris
levitans
parvus
propinquus
quebecensis (was *cingulatus*)
spinosus
tricaudatus
vagans

GENUS PSEUDOCLOEON
carolina
dubium
edmunsi
futile
anoka

GENUS CLOEON
alamance
ingens
insignificans
mendax
rubropictum
simplex

GENUS CALLIBAETIS
coloradensis
fluctuans
ferrugineus
nigritus

GENUS CENTROPTILUM
album
convexum
elsa
rufostrigatum
walshi

FAMILY SIPHLONURIDAE (p. 269)

GENUS ISONYCHIA
bicolor
campestris (subspecies of *sicca*)
harperi
sadleri
velma

GENUS AMELETUS
ludens
lineatus
sparsatus

GENUS SIPHLONURUS
alternatus
occidentalis
quebecensis

FAMILY METRETOPODIDAE (p. 281)

GENUS SIPHLOPLECTON
basale
costalense
interlineatum
signatum
speciosum

The Crawlers

(Family Ephemerellidae, Leptophlebiidae, Tricorythidae, Caenidae and Baetiscidae

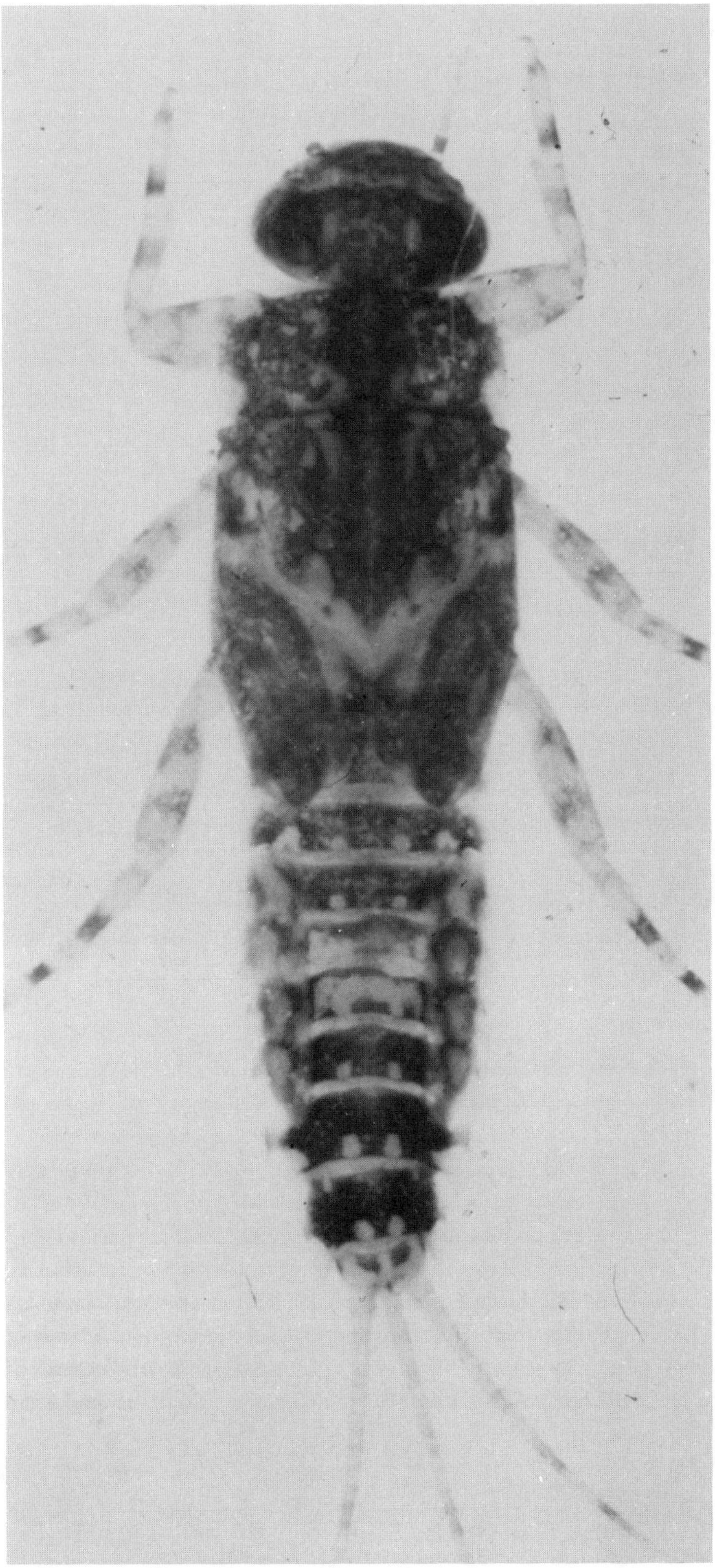

Left: The supercrawlers of Ephemerellidae. *Top:* The feeble-legged crawlers. of Leptophlebiidae. *Bottom:* The tiny crawlers of Tricorythidae

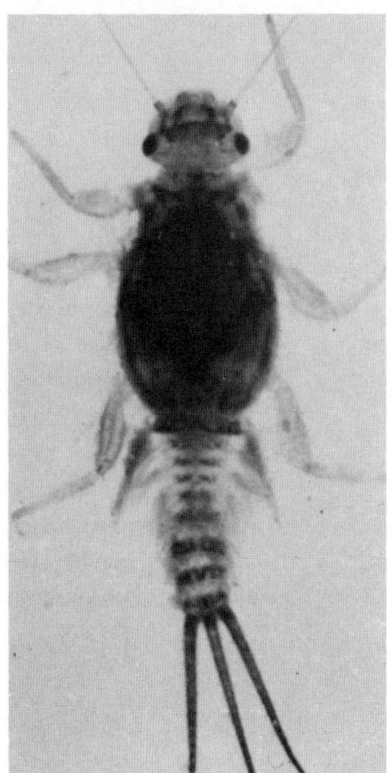

Family Ephemerellidae
(The Super Crawlers)

It is impossible to conceive of a group of aquatic insects that are more important to the trout, the trout stream and the American angler than those of the Ephemerellidae family. Originally this family consisted of the single phenomenal genus Ephemerella which was divided into 7 convenient subgeneric groups by James J. Needham, Jay R. Traver and Yin-Chi Hsu in their entomological milestone *Biology of Mayflies*. These 7 groups have since evolved into 8 subgenera.

It should be noted that since the family Ephemerellidae has but one genus, the description under genus Ephemerella in the following pages are, of course, the same as in the family level. Thus, no family description is needed.

Typical male Ephemerella dun. Note the three tails and large, round compound eyes which are usually reddish-brown to orange.

Genus Ephemerella

This amazing genus consists of no less than 84 species according to the 1978 edition of Edmunds, Jensen and Berners, Mayflies of North and Central America.

The hardy, prolific nymphs of this genus seem to have withstood the onslaught of civilization due to their ability to adjust to various degrees of thermal, silt, organic and toxic pollution. This flexibility is evident in the diverse and highly specialized characteristics of each species which thrive in rivers and streams of contrasting geographic characteristics, chemical composition and water-type; from still back-waters to roaring rapids.

The body-forms and appendages of these nymphs are as extreme as their environment. Yet, surprisingly they are easy to recognize even at a glance once the angler becomes familiar with their basic shape.

Typically stocky Ephemerella nymph.

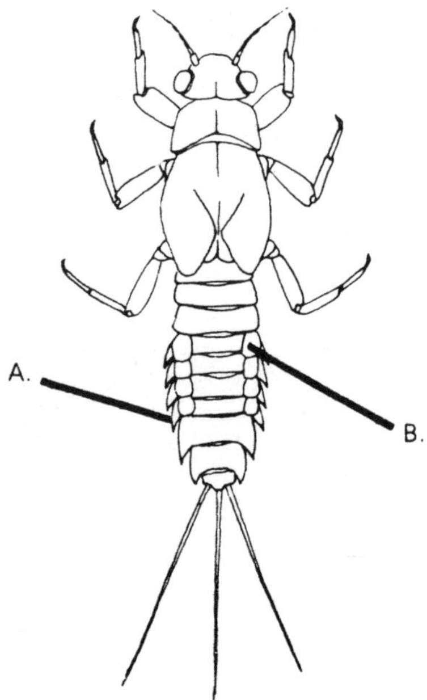

A. Postero-lateral spines; B. Wholly dorsal plate-like gills.

One of the most recognizable features of the genus are the postero-lateral spines which extend from the abdomen. The heads of the nymphs are quite variable, yet they are always wider than they are long. The gills are smallish and platelike, wholly dorsal and are borne on abdominal segments 3 through 7 or 4 through 7, slightly overlapping each other. When observed live, the gills undulate up and down rapidly in a sequential order which is unique and perhaps the best key to immediate recognition.

When the nymphs are ready to hatch, they seek more advantageous emergence sites, exposing themselves in great number to the trout. The fast-water species migrate to quieter eddies within or adjacent to their rapid environment. Slow-to-medium water species seek even more appropriate sites along banks and behind boulders and dead-falls for their emergence. When the "magic hour" arrives, the nymphs swim laboriously toward the surface with a peculiar wiggle. Sometimes their emergence is assisted by gasses released from the nymphal skin, buoying them to the surface. Many species hatch into subimagoes a foot beneath the surface and a few, like the *attenuata* species, actually hatch on the stream's bottom. Where this is the case, the partially emerged duns are buoyed to the surface with their wings still collapsed in folds on their thorax. Once on the surface, many Ephemerella species experience delayed takeoffs, sometimes floating for minutes before they unfold and straighten their collapsed wings.

During this activity, the vulnerable nymphs are a favorite with the trout which feed on them rather exclusively. Anglers should use deep-running, weighted nymphs during the hatchless hours when the nymphs are shuffling on the bottom and switch to emerger and wet-fly patterns when the nymphs are ascending. The nymph and emerger imitations can be murder when fished dead-drift just beneath the surface or manipulated to duplicate the mid-depth struggles of the nymph. A deer-hair emerger pattern (see tying instructions) with pontoon tails can be fished like a dry, right in the surface film throughout the hatch with fantastic results.

Typical Ephemerella, female dun.

The species of Ephemerella are small to moderate in size (6 to 12mm; approximately 1/4″ to 1/2″) but several very important Western species grow to 16mm in length (approximately 3/4″.)

Recognizing the more subtle characteristics of the winged adults is not as easy as distinguishing the more obvious nymph shapes; however, if the angler knows what to look for, the telltale clues to identification are rather simple and as indelible as fingerprints.

The duns and spinners of the Ephemerella genus are one of nine mayfly genera of importance to the angler that have three tails. Four of these are of the burrowing families which are enormous mayflies. The Ephoron genus of the Polymitarcyidae family approaches the size of the larger Ephemerella adults, but they are an unmistakable pure white in color. Of the five remaining genera, three are of the tiny Caenidae and Tricorythidae families—no identification problem here. The final two genera having 3 tails are of the important Paraleptophlebia genus and the less-significant Leptophlebia genus. The angler can discern the Ephemerella mayflies from these two genera quickly by the hind wings. In Ephemerella, the hind wings are well developed in size and the costal angulation near the base is rounded and followed by a shallow depression. In Leptophlebia, and, especially, Paraleptophlebia, the hind wings are rather small as compared to the forewings and are distinctly elliptical in outline.

Hind wing of Ephemerella with rounded costal angulation near base followed by a shallow depression.

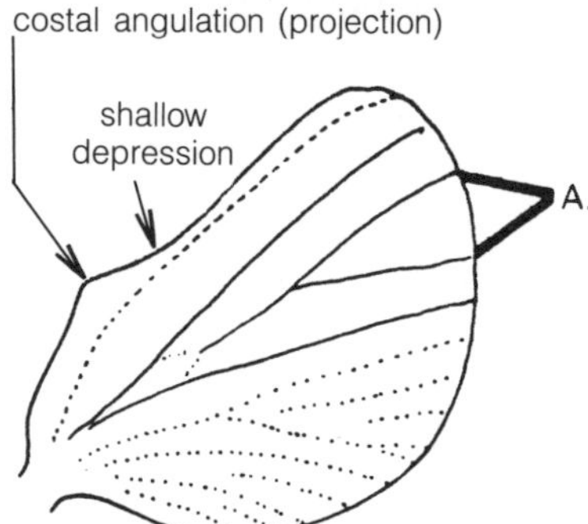

A. The median vein of the Ephemerella hind wing is distinctly forked at slightly less than half way to its base.

Due to their frequent subsurface emergence, the duns normally ride the currents in a placid manner for exceptionally long periods until their wings unfold. When the sailboat-like wings are finally erect and dry, they make several attempts at flight. This whole business is quite ungainly and usually provokes trout into enraged feeding. The Compara-duns are ideal for most of these hatches as their flush-floating characteristics and prominent wing silhouette are very imitative of the naturals. If trout are selective to the more active duns, hackled patterns should be used with timely twitches to imitate the awkward attempts of the naturals.

THE SUBGENERA

Dr. Needham divided the Ephemerella species into seven subgeneric groups. These groups have been modified over the years into 8 subgenera.

SUBGENUS EPHEMERELLA (Was Invaria group)

Ephemerella is the most famous subgenus of the genus and includes the legendary Eastern and Midwestern "Hendrickson" and "Sulphur" hatches: *subvaria* (Hendrickson); *invaria, rotunda, dorothea* (Sulphurs); and the Western hatches, *inermis* and *infrequens* (Pale Morning Dun). All of these mayflies are given extensive treatment in the following chapters. *mollitia* and *excrucians* are important but lesser-known species of the Invaria group and are also mentioned.

E. *rotunda,* (Ephemerella).

SUBGENUS EPHEMERELLA. Gills on segments 3–7. Femora bear rather long spines on posterior margins; on upper surface of fore femur, a transverse band of spines near apical end; short dorsal abdominal spines may be present. No whorls of spines at tail joinings.

SUBGENUS DRUNELLA (Was Fuscata group)

The subgenus Drunella is the most intriguing and underrated group and its growing importance threatens to overtake that of the famous Invaria group.

Needham lists 21 species in the group, but this number has been revised to 17 in recent years. The Drunella nymphs are normally very different from those of the other subgroups, having much flatter body configurations which are accentuated by powerful forelegs resembling the fast-water clingers of the Heptagenidae family; i.e., Epeorus and Stenonema nymphs. Although they may be found in slower waters, their flattened bodies extend their habitat to runs, riffles and eddies of pocket-water.

Characterized by their fat, olive-brown bodies and oversized gray wings, the dun stages of these mayflies are commonly called "Blue-Winged Olives". Among the species tagged with this overused term are the extremely important Eastern *cornuta* species, *lata* of the Midwest and the *flavilinea* mayflies of the West. The unusually large and very important Western hatches of *grandis grandis, grandis ingens* and *doddsi* are also Drunella mayflies and are referred to as the "Western Green Drake". The prolific *cornuta* species is almost unknown; hence, it has no common name. We're hopeful that it will be called by its specific name which is even easier to say than Blue-Winged Olive.

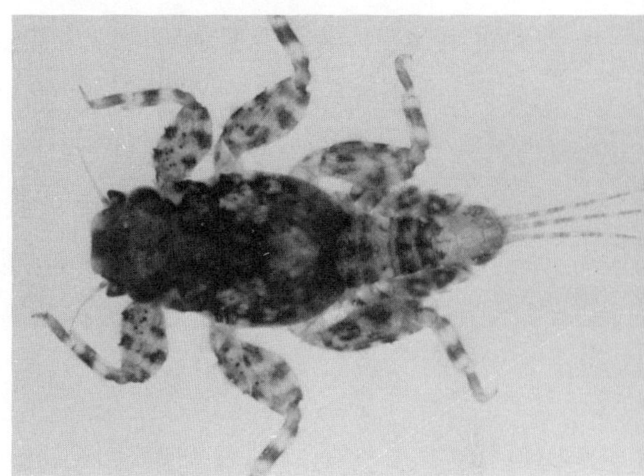

E. *walkeri,* (Drunella).

SUBGENUS DRUNELLA. Often bears spines or tubercles on occiput and dorsum of thorax and abdomen; in many species, the fore femora also bears spines or tubercles on the anterior margin. Gills present on segments 3–7.

SUBGENUS ATTENELLA (Was Simplex group)

attenuata is the most important species of this subgeneric group in the East and Midwest. *margarita* is relatively important in the West. *delantala* and *soquele* round out the lesser species of this group.

These mayflies range from 6-10mm, the gills are located on abdominal segments 3-7 and the tails are covered with minute, black hairs. The body usually has pale dosal stripes.

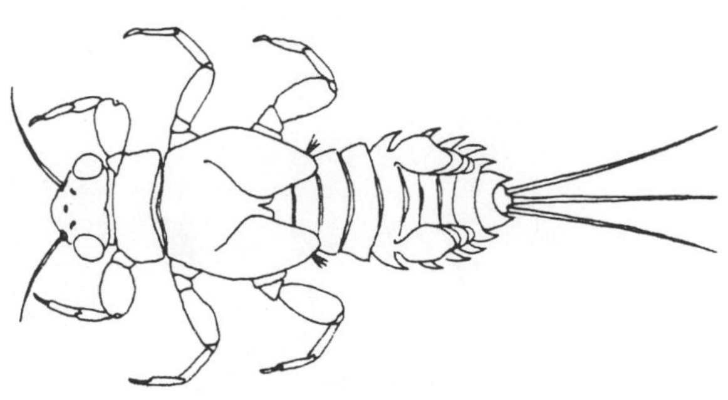

E. *simplex,* (Danella).

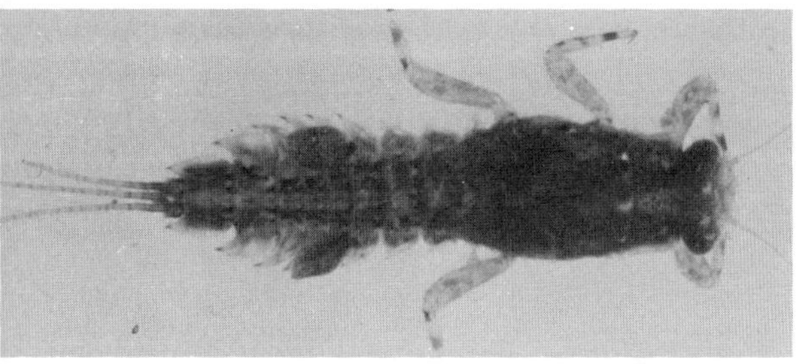

E. *doris*, (Eurylophella).

SUBGENUS EURYLOPHELLA (Was Bicolor group): Nymphs bear a rudimentary gill on segment 1; none on 3; gill on 5 operculate. 9th segment of abdomen longer than the 8th; prominent dorsal abdominal spines; lateral margins of abdominal segments much flattened and expanded, bearing prominent postero-lateral spines.

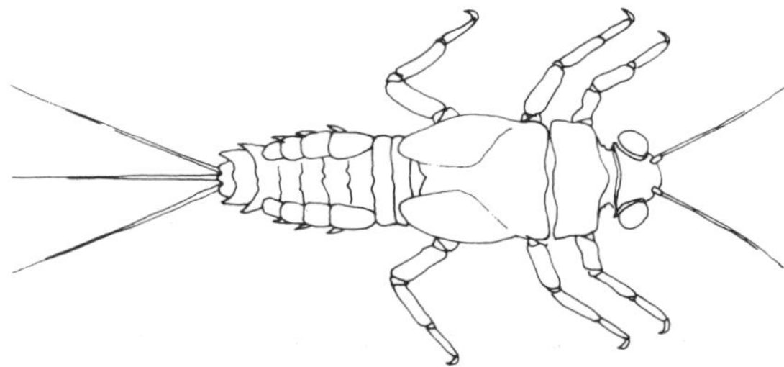

E. *deficiens*, (Serratella).

SUBGENUS SERRATELLA (Was Serrata group): Gills on segments 3–7, none operculate; no spines on anterior margin of fore femur; a whorl of spines at each tail joint.

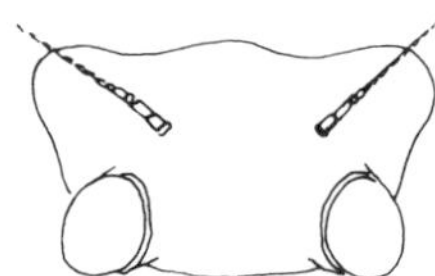

E. *hecuba*, Hecuba group.

SUBGENUS TIMPANOGA (Was Hecuba group): Head very wide on frontal margin; gills on 4–7 only, operculate on 4; dorsal spines on tergites 2–6 only. Lateral margins of segments 2–9 produced into prominent flattened teeth. A sharp spine at apex of each femur.

SUBGENUS DANELLA (Was Simplex group)

Formally of the defunct Simplex group, this subgenus is uncommon and unimportant to the trout fisherman and contains just two species—*simplex* and *lita*.

SUBGENUS EURYLOPHELLA (Was Bicolor group)

We have had little experience with this group and have never found good populations during our stream research. To our knowledge, nothing has been written in angling texts in respect to their angling importance; however, Ernie Schwiebert does mention them in his book, *Nymphs*, along with *lutulenta* and *temporalis*. He states that the *doris* species is distributed from Maryland to Georgia and the others from Quebec to North Carolina.

SUBGENUS SERRATELLA (Was Serrata group)

In recent years we have found the *deficiens* species to be significantly important on rich river sheds like the Delaware River in late summer and fall. *serrata* can be of local importance.

SUBGENUS TIMPANOGA (Was Hecuba group)

In 1959, Allen and Edmunds provided characters to distinguish the nymphs of *hecuba* and *pacifica* which is distributed west of the Cascades and the Sierra Nevada, and *hecuba hecuba* which is distributed east of the same mountain ranges. The *hecuba* species is reportedly a fishable Western hatch, emerging through July and August in accordance with ideal water temperature. They are relatively large (16mm) mayflies, thus they should cause exciting feeding when they appear in good number.

SUBGENUS CAUDATELLA (New Subgenus)

These 5-11mm mayflies are uncommon. Their outer tails are much shorter than the middle tails by 30% to 70%.

NYMPH (Subgenus Ephemerella)

SPECIES	DIST.	SIZE	TEETH ON CLAW	ABDOMINAL DORSAL SPINES	WHITE DOR-SAL SPOTS AT BASE OF SPINE	MISC.
subvaria	E, M	10-12	---	present	present	Abdominal spines blackened.
invaria	E, M	7½-8½	5-6	reduced	variable	Dark "V" on thorax. Yellowish-brown ground color.
rotunda	E, M	9-10½	5-7	short	present	Yellowish-brown ground color.
dorothea	E, M	6½-7½	6-7	absent	variable	Light "V" on thorax. Yellowish-brown ground color.
infrequens	W	7-8	5-6	absent	absent	See color plates.
inermis	W	5½-6½	8	absent	present	Very similar to *mollitia*.
mollitia	W	8-10	8-10	absent	present	See color plate.
excurcians	E, M	5½-6½	---	absent	present	Nearly black ground color.
needhami	E, M	6-8	---	present	absent	Wide pale dorsal stripe. Medium or dark brown, almost black.

MALE SPINNER (Subgenus Ephemerella)

SPECIES	DIST.	SIZE	EYES	VENATION	DUNS
subvaria	E, M	10-12	dark reddish-brown	brown	Body: yellowish or brownish-gray with tinge of pink. Wings: medium gray.
invaria	E, M	7½-9½	deep orange	amber	Body: olive-yellow. Wings: light gray.
rotunda	E, M	9-10½	deep orange	pale amber	Body: olive-yellow. Wings: light to medium gray.
dorothea	E, M	6½-7½	pale orange	amber	Body: pale yellow. Wings: pale gray with tinge of yellow. Legs: pale yellow.
infrequens	W	7-8	light orange	clear	Body: olive-yellow. Wings: pale yellowish-gray.
inermis	W	5½-6½	---	pale	Body: olive-yellow. Wings: pale yellowish-gray.
mollitia	W	8-10	salmon	yellowish	Body: brownish with reddish tinge. Wings: medium gray with touch of brown.
needhami	E, M	6-8	dark brown	smokey	Body: dark brown. Wings: dark gray, almost black. Legs and tails: pale.
excurcians	E, M	5-6	bright orange-yellow	hyaline	Body: reddish-brown. Wings: pale gray. Legs and tails: pale olive.

Penes much as in Needhami group, but with lateral apical processes that are shorter, blunt and directed inward; apical notch between divisions of penes is more shallow.

NYMPH (Subgenus Eurylophella)

SPECIES	DIST.	SIZE	OCCIPUTAL TUBERCLES	ROWS OF ABDOMINAL SPINES (to rear)	WIDTH BETWEEN Spines 5-7*	MISC.
doris	E, M	7-8½	strong	parallel	less	Forefemora 2x as long as wide.
lutulenta	E, M	9-12	reduced	diverge	equal	---
temporalis	E, M	10-11	strong	parallel	less	Forefemora 3x as long as wide. Ground color: medium brown, thickly flecked with tiny pale dots.

MALE SPINNER (Subgenus Eurylophella)

SPECIES	DIST.	SIZE	TERGITES 1-6	TERGITES 8-9	STERNITE BLACK DOTS	EYES	TAILS
doris	E, M	7	yellowish brown	---	indis.	orange	pale, joinings blackish
lutulenta	E, M	9-11	blackish-brown	brown	indis.	---	brown basally, paler toward tips
temporalis	E, M	10-11	deep brown	reddish-brown	present	bright orange	almost white, dark joinings

Penes of male united; swollen at base, but not apex; bear no spines. DUNS: *doris*: similar to *temporalis*. *lutulenta*: brownish insect sprinkled with small dark dots on legs, thorax and abdomen. *temporalis*: Body: tan with tinge of olive. Wings: dark gray.

*Less than or equal to length of their respective tergites.

NYMPH (Subgenus Drunella)

SPECIES	DIST.	SIZE	FRONTAL HORNS	TUBERCLES (BACK OF HEAD)	SPINES PRO-NOTUM	SPINES MESO-NOTUM	MISC.
cornuta	E,M	9-10	yes	no	no	no	Incurved horns with straight median horn-like projection.
cornutella	E, M	6-8	yes	no	no	no	Similar to *cornuta*, but darker.
depressa (now synonym of *cornuta*)	E, M	6-8	yes	no	no	no	Similar to cornuta.
longicornis	E, M	8-10	yes	no	no	no	Frontal horns more than ½ as long as space between them. Tibial "thumb" extends beyond middle of tarsus.
walkeri	E, M	9-11	indic.	no	yes	no	Slight indication of "adhesive disc."
lata	M	6-8	yes	no	no	no	Frontal horns are rudimentary
doddsi	W	12-13	no	no	no	no	"Adhesive disc" present on ventor of abdomen.
flavilinea	W	8 -10	no	yes	no	no	Tibial "thumb" short and blunt. Abdominal spines very short.
glacialis (now synonym of *grandis ingens*)	W	13-15	no	yes	yes	yes	Prominent finger-like dorsal spines. Spines on segments 8-9 relatively longer.
grandis (now *grandis ingens*)	W	14-16	no	yes	yes	yes	Prominent finger-like dorsal spines similar to *glacialis,* but 8-9 not conspicuously longer.

MALE SPINNER (Subgenus Drunella)

SPECIES	DIST.	SIZE	VENATION	TAILS	DUNS
cornuta	E, M	9-10	pale	yellow	Body: medium olive. Wings: medium-dark gray.
cornutella	E, M	6-8	pale	white	Similar to *cornuta* except for smaller size.
depressa	E, M	6-8	pale	white	Similar to *cornuta* except for smaller size.
longicornis	E, M	8-9	pale brown	brown	Very difficult to separate from *cornuta* in both size and color.
walkeri	E, M	8-10	yellowish-brown	yellow-olive fading to gray at tips	Body: dark greenish-black. Legs and tails: olive. Wings: blackish.
lata	M	6-8	pale	white, gray basally	Body: brownish-olive. Wings: dark gray.
doddsi	W	11½-13	dark brown	brown	Similar to *grandis,* but no femoral bands.
flavilinea	W	8-10	pale	black	Body: olive with yellowish-brown. Wings: medium to darkish-grey.
glacialis (now synonym of *grandis ingens*)	W	13-15	dark brown	brown	Similar to *grandis*, body darker.
grandis (now *grandis ingens*)	W	14-16	dark brown	brown	Body: olive. Wings: medium gray with dark venations.

Apical forceps joint is at least twice as long as wide. The long second joint may be distinctly bowed or irregularly swollen.

NYMPH (Subgenus Attenella)

SPECIES	DIST.	SIZE	MISC.
attenuata	E	6-8	Tubercles present on back of head, pronotum and mesonotum.
margarita	W	8-10	No tubercles, but dorsal spines present on abdomen. 8-9 denticles on each claw. Body not conspicuously hairy.

MALE SPINNER (Subgenus Attenella)

SPECIES	DIST.	SIZE	LONGITUDINAL TAILS	VEINS	FORCEPS	DUN
attenuata	E	6-8	white	hyaline	whitish, light brown at base	similar to *cornuta* but smaller.

Penes of male broadened more at apex that at base.

NYMPH (Subgenus Serratella)

SPECIES	DIST.	SIZE	TEETH ON CLAW	DORSAL ABDOMINAL SPINES	MISC.
deficiens	E, M	4½-5½	8-9	absent	Ground color nearly black.
serrata	E, M	5	3-4	present	Thoracic tubercles present.

MALE SPINNER (Subgenus Serratella)

SPECIES	DIST.	SIZE	VENTRAL ABDOMINAL MARKS	MISC.	DUN
deficiens	E	4-5	absent	– – –	Body: blackish. Wings: blackish. Legs and tails: White.
serrata	E	5	present	– – –	Body: dark brown. Wings: dark gray.

Penes broadened at base as much as or more than at apex.

Ephemerella subvaria
(Subgenus Ephemerella)

COMMON NAMES: Hendrickson, Red Quill, Lady Beaverkill

SIZE RANGE: 10 to 12 mm

HOOK SIZES:
SURFACE (dry): #10, #12.
SUBSURFACE (wet): #10, #12; std.

IMITATIONS:
NYMPH: Subvaria Compara-nymph
EMERGER: Subvaria Compara-emerger, Subvaria Deerhair emerger
DUN: Hendrickson, Red Quill, Subvaria Compara-dun
SPINNER: Subvaria Compara-spinner

Ephemerella subvaria, the Hendrickson Hatch, is without a doubt the most exciting mayfly hatch of the early season. For us, this activity is probably the most prolific and reliable hatching of the year, especially on our rich "home" rivers; the West Branch, East Branch and main river; the big Delaware, which separates Pennsylvania and New York. On the Delaware system the subvaria and its related or sibling species can start in mid April and continue until the end of May.

Emergence in southern Pennsylvania and Maryland could take place as early as April 7, but normally occurs around the middle of the month. Hatching in southern Appalachia usually takes place even earlier. The Poconos and northern Pennsylvania are at their best between April 28 and May 8. The Catskill systems peak between May 10 and May 20, while good hatches can linger on the northern rivers of this lush mountain range until the end of the month. The Adirondacks and northern New England usually peak between May 20 and 30.

Midwestern waters are best from late April through May. Michigan's Au Sable and Pere Marquete River systems are excellent during the first week in May.

Some years ago we experienced excellent hatches on the Namekagon River in northern Wisconsin during the first week of May in a blinding snow storm which came out of nowhere just as the *subvaria* duns started to emerge.

A week before this bizzare experience, the *subvaria* hatched on the Prairie and Wolf Rivers, a little further south, were in full swing. Unfortunately this superb activity had gone completely unnoticed as the peak of this hatching occurred a week before "opening day".

Rivers on the extreme northern boundary of Wisconsin like the Bois Brule, Iron R., White R., Brule R. (eastern) as well as the famous rivers of Michigan's Upper Peninsula, generally hatch from the second week in May until early June, in accordance with their water temperatures.

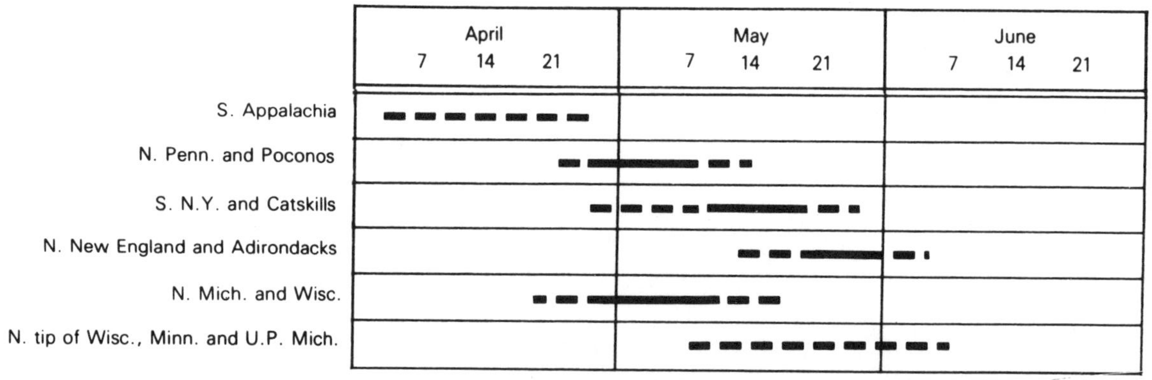

	April 7 14 21	May 7 14 21	June 7 14 21
S. Appalachia			
N. Penn. and Poconos			
S. N.Y. and Catskills			
N. New England and Adirondacks			
N. Mich. and Wisc.			
N. tip of Wisc., Minn. and U.P. Mich.			

The *subvaria* nymphs are robust creatures with relatively feeble legs. They are dark brown in color, being almost blackish, with influences of amber and/or olive. Their 6th and 7th abdominal tergites are wholly pale, while the 5th abdominal segment is only partially pale. There are other distinguishing details which can be observed under magnification (see chart below), but these pale tergite segments, although somewhat variable, are the easiest feature to identify on the stream.

Since the first edition of HATCHES, ten years ago, our continued studies at our base camp on the Delaware, as well as other areas in the East and Midwest, show that there appears to be as many as six (6) subspecies or sibling species that fall within the general description of subvaria, in terms of size, hatching periods, coloration and markings (see chart below). One species which we call Ephemerella "X", for lack of entomological information, starts hatching in late April or early May and continues through May, is a consid-

E. *subvaria*, nymph.

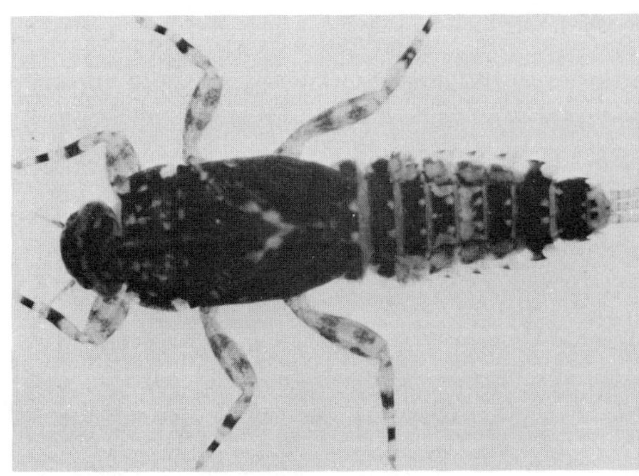

NYMPH

NYMPH SPECIES	SIZE (MM)	ABDOMINAL SEGMENTS 5, 6, 7	ABDOMINAL DORSAL SPINES	SPOTS AROUND DORSAL SPINES	10TH ABDOMINAL SEGMENT	GENERAL COLOR
Subvaria	12	6 and 7 wholly pale; 5 partially pale	well defined almost black on all segments	yes	almost wholly pale	Body: blackish brown; bands on tibia and tarsus
Species I	12	wholly dark	well defined, dark brown on all segments	remote	3 pale dots on distal half	Body: dark brown; bands on tibia and tarsus
Species II	9	5 wholly dark, 6 mostly pale; 7 sparsely pale	well defined, very dark on all segments	visable on segments 7, 3 and 2	pale on distal half	Body: dark brown; bands on tibia and tarsus
Species III	11	6 remotely pale, 5 and 7 wholly dark	well defined, but remote on segments 8 and 9	inconsistant, visible on segments 6, 3 and 2 only	2/3 of distal portion is pale	Body: dark brown; bands on tibia and tarsus
Species IV "Ephemerella X"	9½	partially pale on segment 6 only	moderately defined on all segments	no	wholly dark	Body: blackish brown; bands on tibia and tarsus are remote to absent
Species V	11	5, 6 and 7 a wholly pale reddish brown in coloration	well defined, almost black on segments 8-4 only	no	wholly dark	amber brown washed with reddish brown; no bands on fore tibia
Species VI	9	almost wholly pale on segment 6 only	remote to absent	no	almost wholly pale	Body: medium amber brown; bands are remote to absent

The duns of the above insects range in sizes from 8½ to 12½ mm. Body colorations of the sternum vary from pinkish tan to dark brown with various shades of brownish olive in between. Wings range from medium light to dark gray. Along with the standard subvaria patterns, a deerhair emerger pattern with a darkish brown body and dark wings on #12 and #14 hooks is an imitation that does a good job of bridging the gap between these various species.

Matching your pattern to the natural and close scrutiny of the riseforms is a must in determining whether the trout are taking them just under, in, or on top of the surface film.

Subvaria spinner patterns on #10, #12 and #14 hooks should suffice the imago imitations.

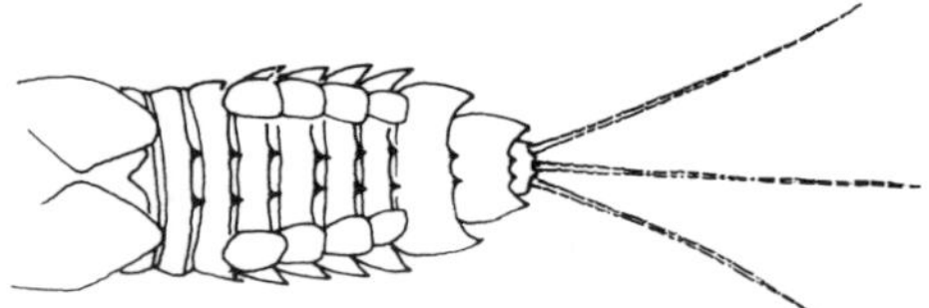

In addition to the pale tergites on segments 5, 6 and7, tiny paired abdominal spines are black.

erably darker insect than the subvaria species in the dun stage. It is also smaller 9-10mm instead of 10-12mm, thus, a size 14 hook is the most effective when these insects are on the water.

Our research on these species continues although we are handicapped by the lack of entomological information at the species level. As more scientific information becomes available, we feel we will eventually unravel the subvaria puzzle.

The subvaria nymphs live in a variety of habitats. Look for them in the gravel and vegetation of our slower meandering streams. On faster rivers, such as freestone mountain streams, look for them in the gravelly riffles, slick runs, or eddies of pocket-water.

Around one in the afternoon, nymph activity is usually well underway in April, by the 2nd week in May this activity may start at two or even three P.M. The nymphs swim to the surface with a peculiar wiggle, where they drift with the current for a time before escaping their shucks which normally takes place just under the surface film. Often, they will swim back to the bottom and repeat this ascent several times before they are finally able to escape their shucks. We have observed the Ephemerella nymphs in our aquariums often, probably more than any other group of mayflies. Their lively underwater antics are normally conducted for a considerable time prior to actual hatching (sometimes for days). There is little doubt that this activity prompts exceptional interest from the trout.

During our aquarium observations, we have noticed several interesting behavior characteristics. Perhaps the angler will glean something from our research that may inspire him to experiment with nymphing tactics and fly pattern creations.

When the aquariums were disturbed by shadows or physical commotion, the Ephemerella nymphs, especially those of *subvaria,* swam excitedly, up and down, in a vertical motion, between the tank's bottom and the surface. They were also the last nymphs to settle down once the disturbances ceased. Although excitable, these nymphs were rarely shy. Instead, they normally perch on convenient vegetation and rocks, in plain view, unlike many species that hide under debris. This trait, we are sure, makes them a favorite with the trout even during hatchless days.

The nymphs swim by executing peculiar movements. They undulate their bodies with exagerated jackknife motions (the thoracic-portion of the body, including the head, moves in the opposite direction of the abdomen and tails) several times per second. The forelegs extend and then fold as in a breast stroke while the middle and rear legs trail motionless. The hackle-shaped hairs, located on the tips of the tails, are paddle-like in outline and they perform important functions in locomotion and steering. When caught in the current-like turbulence of the aquarium filtration and

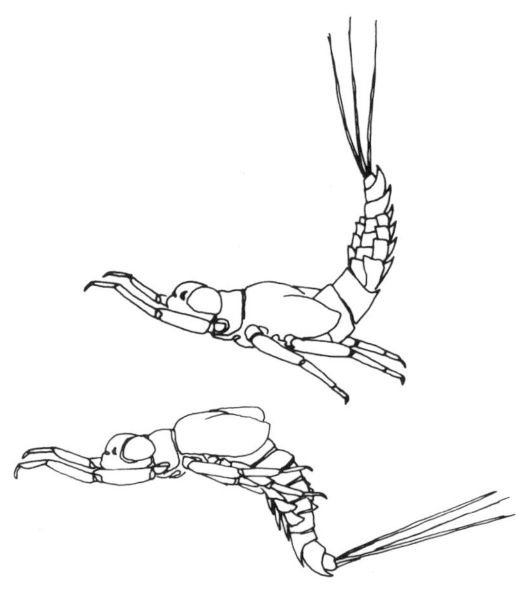

The peculiar wiggle of the *subvaria* nymph is also common to its genus, Ephemerella. Swisher/Richards, in their book, *Selective Trout,* have developed an excellent pattern they call the "Wiggle Nymph." It does a fine job in imitating this movement of the natural.

aeration system, the nymphs would freeze (legs extended), like soaring gliders, until they drifted out of the current's influence, where they would resume their comical swimming motions until a convenient perch was reached, or until they hatched in the surface film area.

In order to duplicate the behavior of these nymphs, the angler should twitch his imitation when fishing the slower water where the nymphs normally wiggle to the surface. On faster stretches, the dead-drift method is more imitative of the "motionless" drifting nymphs.

We designed a "deerhair emerger" pattern for this activity and it can be deadly when fished throughout the hatch. It has pontoon tails, like the Compara-dun, and deerhair in the thorax area. We fish it in the surface film as a partially emerged dun, or pull it under to imitate the struggling behavior of the hatching nymphs.

The ever-popular Hendrickson.

DUN

The "Hendrickson" is truly the exhaulted king of the early season. Few mayflies have been so decorated in the annals of fly-fishing literature. *subvaria* has earned all its credentials and probably deserves even more accolades. The thrilling experience of floating a dry-fly among these delicate and sedate duns can hardly be justified within the confines of these pages. It is our sincere wish that every fly-fishing enthusiast have at least one good fling with the *subvaria* (Hendrickson) hatch.

When the water temperature registers between 50°-55°F, hatching will usually begin. Once emergence starts, daily hatching is normally very reliable. Emergence may take place at any time between noon and 6 P.M., but peak activity is usually between two and four in the afternoon when water temperature is ideal. The exceptions are during unusually hot weather or cold, rainy conditions. Hot weather will ordinarily delay hatching until early evening when the water temperature is more favorable. During cold weather, hatching will normally take place around the warmest part of the afternoon. At this time, the duns float the currents for exceptionally long periods (sometimes several minutes), thus making them extremely available to the trout. The duns are seemingly unperturbed in spite of their inevitable fate of being sucked under by hungry trout or beaked by ravenous birds swooping from above. Throughout the years we have found that this inclement weather offers the best opportunities for fishing the dun immitations.

Trout rise eagerly to these vulnerable duns, and at times they become so preoccupied with feeding, that wading into an advantageous casting position can be accomplished without putting them down. This is a good opportunity to locate a large fish and wade into ideal casting range without spooking him. The most efficient feeding lanes are usually only a few inches wide and under normal conditions, large, streamwise browns will seldom be enticed by offerings outside the

E. *subvaria,* male dun.

Early spring conditions on a good stretch of *subvaria* water.

convenient line of drift. Accurate and drag-free floats are essential and accurate casts will greatly enhance your chances in fooling a dandy.

Smaller trout, or stocked fish, are normally less efficient feeders than are native or holdover trout, and they will often cruise from their stations and slash at floating duns a considerable distance from their normal feeding station. This may also be the case with larger trout if a stream is overpopulated by excessive stocking of trout. The available food supply on these overpopulated streams (especially on the less rich freestone streams where *subvaria* seems to be surprisingly abundant) is generally insufficient to support both natural and holdover trout plus the newly stocked fish which are usually introduced without proper study of the existing natural food supply. Hence, competition for this food supply becomes fierce, forcing even the wisest trout from their normal feeding stations to cruise for their food in desperation. This feeding behavior also leads to inferior trout growth and subsequently, less challenging fly-fishing.

The very "questionable" philosophy of mass trout production by state and federal agencies and the associated problem of overstocking (especially on our prime trout waters) which forces trout to abandon their natural feeding habits is, indeed, a serious one which should be dealt with by all trout fishermen. Anglers should understand that the *subvaria* hatches do occur very early in the season, shortly after the streams are heavily stocked, and that these stockings will affect the fishing of this hatch. Hence, if he is to enjoy the essence of this hatch, he must be able to determine whether trout are being forced to cruise for mayflies or if they are feeding normally, from stations.

If a trout rises several times in the same spot, you can assume he is holding his feeding station. You can now concentrate on selecting the proper imitation and correct presentation. On the other hand, it would be futile to focus your attention where you last saw him rise if the trout is cruising. Chances are by the time you are ready to cast to that trout, he'd be completely out of range. However, there are ways to counteract this problem of unnatural feeding behavior and still enjoy the essence of fishing the hatch. One is to avoid wide, flat stretches where, due to the less tiring current, the trout have even more incentive to cruise. Instead, focus your attention at the head of these stretches or at the tail of the pool where the duns are funneled in a more concentrated formation. Good-sized trout, native or holdover fish, will usually protect these optimum feeding stations and chase out inferior fish. Another good move is to fish the faster pocket-water where trout must hold behind boulders and dead-falls within the white water torrents. These are exciting targets to fish and many fish will be lost once they are hooked.

This is not the case on large, rich river systems like the

Delaware where wild selective browns and rainbows are the rule. The wild trout in rivers of this magnitude will hold station during the hatch and seldom move more than six inches outside of their feeding lanes to take a natural. Thus, dead drift presentation and proper imitation are very critical for success on these rivers. Anglers should object and resist stocking programs by state and federal agencies on rich rivers that support wild trout. Stockings will generally deteriorate the native trout population, causing the large wild fish to move out of the area rather than compete with dumb, pellet fed hatchery fish. Hatchery survivors also have a deleterious effect on the wild strains of fish during reproduction. By the same token, fly-fishermen can't expect a wild fish population to hold its own if it is heavily fished by meat fishermen, so true sporting anglers should push for a reduced limit or "catch and release" program. On rivers like the Delaware system, we believe that the 12 or 13 inch to 20 inch fish should be completely protected.

The Compara-dun is tailor-made for the complacent attitude of the duns, especially in slick feeding lanes. In recent years we have abandoned most patterns for this wonderful fish-getter. If you experience refusals try the deerhair emerger in both the subvaria dressing as well as the Ephemerella "X" dressings.

If you must fish the broader sections where trout are cruising, hackled patterns are probably the best choice. Intermittent skittering and twitching of these imitations will enable you to cover more territory. Plus, this action will entice the trout who, remember, are competing for the limited food supply. Besides the Hackled Compara-dun, two excellent patterns for this application are the well-loved Hendrickson and the Red Quill. Art Flick developed the latter on the Schoharie where he patterned it after the male *subvaria* dun and some of the smaller, darker subspecies. The Hendrickson somewhat resembles the female dun and was originated during the "golden age" of the Beaverkill by Roy Steenrod, a companion of Theodore Gordon.

SPINNER

After mating, the female deposits its eggs en masse. The egg cluster is usually jettisoned from a safe distance above the stream, but at times they will come very close to the surface. It is not unusual for females to break the surface film with their egg sacs. At such times, lemon-colored rabbit fur wound in a ball on size #24 or #28 hooks can be effective.

After egg-laying, highly concentrated spinner-falls take place over runs and riffles. Thousands of spent spinners fall prostrate to the surface to tarry in quiet eddies or to be swept away by the varied currents. These falls take place around 4 or 5 P.M., but as the days pass they will fall progressively later until the last flights fall at dusk. In many areas, the evenings will be too cold to precipitate spinner

subvaria female spinner dropping her egg cluster en masse.

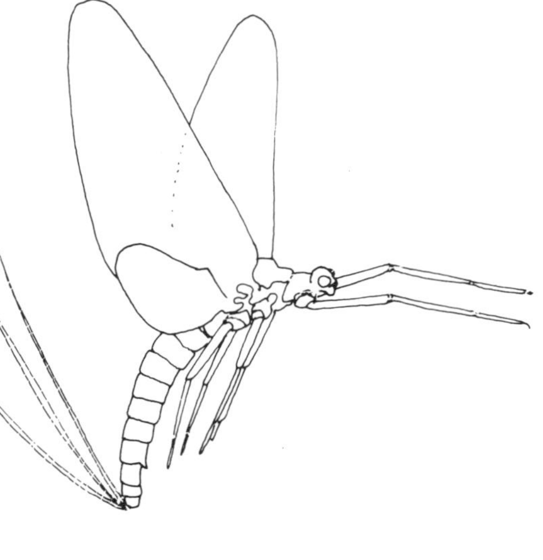

A #12 Subvaria Compara-spinner.

activity. This is common on waters in the Midwest where ideal water temperature exists very early in the season due to the spring-head genesis of the rivers. Yet, the evening air temperatures are relatively low. When this is the case, the spinner activity will normally occur in the morning (between 7 and 9 A.M.) when the air reaches ideal temperature. The spent spinners are difficult to detect on the water and care must be taken to determine whether fish are taking spinners or other emerging insects.

Our experience shows that these spinner-falls are of monumental importance on all types of streams, but especially so on the gentle limestone waters and larger rivers. The spent spinners linger longer in these slower waters, thereby affording the trout a prolonged, leisurely meal. When casting to these lethargic risers, accuracy is imperative as feeding will take place in relatively narrow lanes with the trout seemingly oblivious to anything a few inches outside of its line of drift.

In freestone mountain streams, such as those found in Pennsylvania, New York and New England, fishing to these spinners is surprisingly exciting, but the activity is normally short (about 20-30 minutes) and fly-fishermen must anticipate the spinner-fall by preparing themselves ahead of time.

On these rugged mountain rivers, your signal for preparation should be the sighting of spinner squadrons above the rough pocket-water and riffled sections. Excellent casting spots are within the heavy runs or pockets, so if drag is to be eliminated in these tricky stretches, you must wade as close as you can to your quarry and cast a short line. Casts should be made to side-eddies and at the base of mini-waterfalls. Large boulders create small pools within the white water torrents. Cast your fly at the line where the fast current meets these quiet pockets; chances are you'll get a tackle-smashing rise.

On quieter streams, or on milder sections of faster streams, concentrate your attention at the heads of pools where the spinners are flushed from the rapid white water above. Longer casts are necessary here, but anglers should still wade as close as possible, prior to the spinner-fall, to cut down on some of this distance.

Flush-floating spinner patterns are mandatory for duping trout when they are taking the spent imagoes; the right size and color are also imperative. On blustery days, when the mating imagoes are frequently blown to the surface prematurely, full-hackled spinner patterns may come in handy. They should be twitched to duplicate the struggles of the spinners on the water, however, this seldom works with wild browns.

To sum it up, fishing the *subvaria* spinner activity is extremely exciting business and like most prolific spinner activity it is one of the most reliable aspects of fly-fishing.

Ephemerella invaria and rotunda

(Subgenus Ephemerella)

Throughout the history of American fly-fishing literature, the important activity associated with the Ephemerella *invaria* and *rotunda* species has gone completely unrecognized. Instead, these species have been mistakenly classified with the action of Ephemerella *subvaria*, the early season "Hendrickson Hatch". Our studies indicate that there is absolutely no connection between the *invaria* and *rotunda* action and that of the *subvaria* species—in fact both *invaria* and *rotunda* are contrastingly different mayfly hatches than are those of *subvaria*. Our stream and lab research, as well as our mayfly photography, indicate that the hatches of *invaria* and *rotunda* follow the early season *subvaria* activity by approximately a month and that the size and color of these naturals in the nymph, dun and spinner stages are extremely different.

In 1935, Preston Jennings set the meticulous standard for American fly-fishing entomology, with his surprisingly accurate work, *A Book of Trout Flies*. We say surprising because there were no American angling entomological reference books available for Mr. Jennings to use as reference. Even the Needham-Traver-Hsu classic, *The Biology of Mayflies* wasn't published until 1938. Hence, it's understandable that in his work, Mr. Jennings and Dr. Speith misidentified and grouped the *invaria* and *rotunda* mayflies with those of *subvaria*.

Since these early days, the subsequent flow of angling entomological information has mimicked the Jennings-Speith error. We were also guilty of perpetuating this miscue in *Comparahatch* which we finished in 1972. Before the ink was dry on the initial edition, we became suspicious of the "Subvaria-Invaria-Rotunda" relationship. Our doubts became more acute during the following seasons while we were researching new species and reinvestigating those previously covered by *Comparahatch* for this new work.

During the last two seasons, we have checked hundreds of nymph, dun and spinner specimens captured during the "Hendrickson Hatch" and examined them under high magnification. We also rephotographed scores of naturals during this activity and inspected the transparancies carefully. Our inspections included wing venation checks and pene configuration studies. Color evaluations of each specimen were also conducted. The results of our tests conclude that all naturals captured and studied from these early season "Hendrickson Hatches" were those of the *subvaria* and related subspecies species. We are confident that the *invaria* and *rotunda* mayflies are not a part of this *subvaria* activity.

COMMON NAMES:
rotunda, Dark Hendrickson, Red Quill
invaria, Sulphur Pale Evening Dun

SIZE RANGE: *invaria*, 7½ to 9½ mm; *rotunda*, 9 to 10½ mm

HOOK SIZES:
SURFACE (dry): *invaria & rotunda*, #12, #14;
SUBSURFACE (wet): *invaria & rotunda*, #12, #14; std.

IMITATIONS:
NYMPH: Invaria Compara-nymph
EMERGER: Little Maryatt Wet, Invaria Deerhair emerger
DUN: Little Maryatt, Invaria Compara-dun; Invaria Hackled Compara-dun
SPINNER: Invaria Compara-spinner

Satisfied that there was no connection between *invaria* and *rotunda* species and the *subvaria* hatch (as far as the angler was concerned), we started a program of isolating the Ephemerella nymphs in separate aquariums. Most of the nymphs that took part in the experiment were Emphemerella nymphs; i.e., *dorothea, invaria, subvaria,* and related subspecies, *rotunda, needhami, cornuta,* and *attenuata.*

We recorded these stockings and the resultant hatching activity. The object was to segregate the same specimens in all three stages so there would be no mistake as to which nymphs and adults were related. Special attention was given to the so called "Sulphur" nymphs; *dorothea,* and the slightly larger nymphs that resembled the *dorothea* nymph that we had not yet positively identified. Our suspicions were that these slightly larger nymphs were Ephemerella *invaria* and *rotunda,* but we needed positive proof.

The hatching activity and examinations that followed confirmed our suspicions. The larger nymphs, that had thus far been erroneously linked with the so called *dorothea* or "Sulphur Hatch", were, in fact, those of Ephemerella *invaria* and *rotunda.* What is even more surprising is that as far as we can determine, these nymphs appear to be more common to Pennsylvania and New York trout streams than those of the smaller, familiar *dorothea* species. Our initial seine tests on other waters indicate that this seems to be the case throughout the East and Midwest also. It should be mentioned, however, that the *invaria* and *rotunda* nymphs are more conducive to seine tests because they live in the faster currents; hence, they naturally showed up in greater populations. So, our initial evaluation of the population ratio between these species must be studied further.

Since our discovery of the distinct *invaria-rotunda* activity, we have had the opportunity to experiment with related imitations which has improved our angling success substantially during the "sulphur" activity. As with most new discoveries, interesting new facets crop up every season. Anglers will do well to experiment with this activity on their own streams and record the distinct differences between these hatches and those of the smaller and later-hatching *dorothea.* We believe that even finer breakdowns between the *invaria* and *rotunda* species awaits the ambitious angler who seeks the more sophisticated challenges of his sport.

Our experiences in Pennsylvania and New York indicate that the best *invaria-rotunda* hatching activity takes place during the last two weeks in May and the first week in June. Over the past two years, we've recorded excellent *invaria rotunda* activity between May 13 and 21 on western Pennsylvania streams like Penn's Creek. The best Pocono hatching generally takes place between May 18 and Memorial Day. Hatching occurs on the Lackawaxen River, a little further north, toward the end of the month. The Catskills are generally best during the last week in May and the first week in June. We've caught this hatch in the Adirondacks during the third week in June and have reason to suspect most of the northern New England streams coincide with this hatching activity. The famous trout rivers of Michigan and Wisconsin have an emergence span which is very similar to that of Pennsylvania and southern New York. The uppermost parts of these Midwestern states including Minnesota and Michigan's Upper Peninsula have spans similar to the Adirondacks.

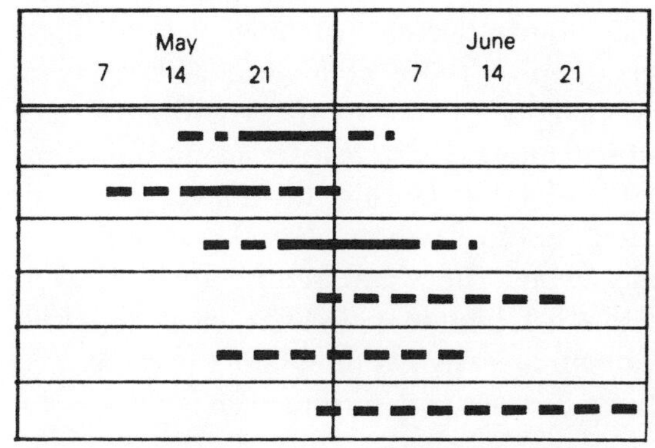

NYMPH

The pale nymphs of Ephemerella *invaria* and *rotunda* closely resemble those of *dorothea*. The main difference is in size. *dorothea* averages 7 mm, while *invaria* and *rotunda* are between 8.5 and 10.5 mm. The *dorothea* nymphs are a buff color, but the larger *invaria* and *rotunda* nymphs vary between yellowish-brown and mahogany. (See plates II & III and verification charts on page 65 for color marking comparisons.)

E. *invaria,* nymph. Notice the dark "V" pattern in the thorax.

Unlike the *dorothea* nymphs (and this is probably the most distinct difference between the habits of these species), *invaria* and *rotunda* prefer much faster currents. Best populations are normally found in medium-to-fast water types. Like most Ephemerella nymphs, they still have a migrating instinct which tends to make them seek out convenient emergence sites adjacent to or within the fast-water currents, but this urge is less than in most of the other species of this genus. The emergence traits of *invaria* and *rotunda* are similar to many Ephemerella species. They wiggle enticingly during their ascent and usually make several attempts to break through the surface tension.

Nymph imitations should be fished in typical Ephemerella fashion; on the bottom prior to hatching and in the film or on the surface during actual hatching.

Unlike *dorothea* nymphs, those of *invaria* and *rotunda* usually hatch between midday and 5 P.M. According to our initial records, best hatching activity takes place in the afternoon between 1 P.M. and 4 P.M. During this time of the year, the normal water temperature is between 50 and 60°F.

During hot spells (when the water temperature is over 60°F), it's possible that hatching may occur in the late morning hours (10 A.M.-noon) or early evening hours (6-8 P.M.). A good tip for catching this activity during heat waves is to pick cloudy or rainy days that mark a break in the weather. We have enjoyed excellent sport in the pouring rain when the *invaria* flies were hatching.

DUN

It is understandable why fly-fishermen have thus far mistaken the duns of *invaria* and *rotunda* for those of *dorothea*. Both are of the pale-winged, sulphur-bodied variety. If the

Left: E. *invaria,* female dun. *Right:* E. *rotunda,* female dun.

angler would capture a natural, however, he would surely be able to discern the difference between these species. When seen side-by-side with a *dorothea* dun, the larger size of the *invaria* or *rotunda* subimago becomes obvious and the difference in color noticeable; especially in the *rotunda* female dun. The *dorothea* dun has a pale-yellowish body, whereas the *invaria* and *rotunda* body colorations are a deeper yellow influenced with brown and olive. Their wings are light gray, but noticeably darker than the pale wings of *dorothea*, yet the wings of the *rotunda* female may vary from creamy gray to cream. Moreover, there is a difference in size. *invaria* and *rotunda* average between 8-10 mm (#12, #14 hook size), while *dorothea* averages 7 mm (#16 hook size).

A. B.

Average actual size comparison of A, *invaria/rotunda* and B, *dorothea.*

The seasonal emergences of *invaria* and *rotunda* and those of *dorothea* occur at different times. However, on most waters that have each type, the hatching periods may overlap. For example, in western Pennsylvania and the Poconos, the best *invaria* and *rotunda* activity takes place from May 15 until the 1st of June, while *dorothea* usually hatches in good number during the last week in May and continues through most of June, an overlap of about a week. This is also true on our home rivers in the Delaware system.

Normally, all three are common to the same trout streams, so caution must be maintained to determine which species are hatching, *invaria, rotunda* or *dorothea,* especially during an overlap. If emergence takes place in the afternoon in the faster currents, chances are that the hatching activity will be that of *invaria* and *rotunda.* If it occurs in the slower currents during the early evening hours, it's possible that the activity may be caused by *dorothea* or *invaria* and *rotunda* or all three, especially if the water temperature is above 60°F., which is not uncommon during this overlap period.

Trout are very selective to the size and color of the naturals, so selection of the proper imitation is imperative. This selectivity was emphatically demonstrated to us one day on a long, flat stretch of Penn's Creek above Coburn.

It was a clear pleasant afternoon in late May, and I was fishing the faster water at the head of a very long, flat stretch, while Bob was about 200 yards downstream in the slower water. There were various species of Tricoptera (caddisflies) emerging and we decided to evaluate our caddis imitations during this activity before heading downstream to a favorite stretch in Poe Paddy State Park for the exciting Ephemera *guttulata* (Green Drake) activity that evening.

Around 2:30 P.M., sulphur-colored duns began to emerge in the faster runs that I was working, and the trout seemed to be taking every dun that popped through the surface film. "Dorothea", I thought excitedly, "but they do look a little big!" I finally captured a specimen and identified it not as *dorothea*, but as the larger *rotunda;* it was between a size #12 and a size #14. I could also see the slightly smaller (#14) *invaria* duns floating in the current. Annoyed with myself for not having a matching imitation, I rationalized that my *dorothea* patterns might suffice; they didn't. The flies were too small and the bodies were too light. Scrounging desperately through my fly box, I reluctantly settled for a #14 Light Cahill and finally took several trout between 8 and 10 inches. The #14 Canadense Compara-dun produced similar lackluster results. These makeshift imitations would not, however, dupe the larger, more selective fish who were now porpoising steadily on the *invaria* and *rotunda* duns. I was so preoccupied with my dilemma, that I almost missed Bob's hand motion downstream, indicating a nice fish. I figured he was successfully fishing the *invaria* hatch in the flatter stretch, so I stumbled my way down, hoping that Bob would have the correct *invaria* or *rotunda* patterns. As I approached him, he was carefully unhooking a good fish; a colorful 16-inch torpedo-shaped *brown.* I could see the #16 caddis pattern in the trout's jaw, as Bob explained that a dozen trout had fallen to his imitation that matched the emerging Hydropsche caddis perfectly. When I briefed him on the *invaria* activity in the faster water, he explained that only caddis were emerging so far in this slower stretch. Sensing my anxiousness, Bob quickly produced a few matching imitations that we had previously tied for our earlier trips to this area.

When we got back to my original spot in the faster runs and had changed our patterns, it was almost 4 P.M. The hatching and feeding activity had continued for over an hour and was now regretfully diminishing. Still, we counted five fish working on the final smattering of emerging duns. Where the riffles broke into the head of the pool, Bob took two on a skillfully manipulated #14 Hackled Compara-dun. My #14 Compara-dun, matching the *invaria* duns perfectly, was responsible for another pair. The last fish was a fat 15-inch Penn's Creek brown, whom I beached on pale amber gravel, beside a large limestone outcropping.

SPINNER

Our experience with the *invaria-rotunda* spinner-falls is that they are typical of the Ephemerella species, especially those within the subgenus. Mating takes place over the riffles. After mating, the females jettison their lemon-colored egg packets from above the stream's surface. The female imagoes sometimes fall to the surface or are blown there by puffs of wind. Their size (8-10mm-#12-#14, 2x long hook) and number generally instigates excellent feeding activity from the trout. Unfortunately, as in the hatching activity, the spinner-falls of our subject species are also confused with *dorothea.*

According to the feedback we've received, Eastern and Midwestern anglers habitually complain about the lack of success experienced during this activity. Fly-fishermen should note that the main reason these problems exist is because they have inadvertently grouped the individual problems of the *dorothea* and those of the *invaria* and *rotunda* species as one. This generalization, though seemingly convenient for the angler, ultimately leads to defeating compromises in fly pattern selection and presentation. We believe that the dilemma expressed by most knowledgeable *dorothea* anglers is a testimonial to treating each species specifically.

On streams where *invaria-rotunda* and *dorothea* populations co-exist, anglers must determine on which species the trout are feeding and present the correct size and color imitations that coincide with each hatch or spinner-fall. Anglers must not delude themselves into thinking that an easier approach is the answer.

The Invaria female imagoes are normally duplicated by a a #12 or #14 hook. Later in the season, when the Invaria populations diminish and the *dorothea* spinner-falls are more predominant, fly-fishermen should switch to the smaller #16 *dorothea* spinner pattern.

A good stretch of riffles for spinner-falls.

Ephemeralla dorothea
(Subgenus Ephemerella)

COMMON NAMES: Pale Evening Dun, Sulphur, Little Maryatt, Pale Watery Dun

SIZE RANGE: 6½ to 7½ mm

HOOK SIZES:
SURFACE (dry): #16, #18;
SUBSURFACE (wet): #16; std.

IMITATIONS:
NYMPH: Dorothea Compara-nymph
EMERGER: Little Marryat Wet, Pale Evening Dun Wet, Dorothea Deerhair Emerger
DUN: Little Maryatt, Pale Watery Dun, Dorothea Compara-dun, Dorothea Hackled Compara-dun
SPINNER: Dorothea Compara-spinner

dorothea is a member of the Ephemerella genus which belongs to the famous subgeneric Ephemerella group. The important activity associated with this hatch is known in fly-fishing circles as the"Sulphur Hatch". Although she gets all of the credit for this action, a major part of this "Sulphur" action can not be attributed to the *dorothea* species at all. Moreover, our research during the past three years indicates that the *invaria* and *rotunda* species is responsible for a great part of this so-called "Sulphur Hatch" (see Empemerella *invaria* and *rotunda* chapter).

It's really understandable why the *invaria* and *rotunda* species has been overlooked by most fly-fishermen. The close physical similarities in the nymph and adult stages and the similar hatching traits of these species and those of *dorothea* are probably major reasons for their being by-passed, the lack of available angling information on *invaria* and *rotunda* is probably the main cause.

The "Sulphur" activity on the limestone streams of western and southern Pennsylvania begins after the first week in May. Contrary to popular belief, this activity is caused by the *invaria* and *rotunda* species and not by *dorothea.* The *dorothea* hatches are normally later, when the *invaria* and *rotunda* activity wanes. *dorothea* emergence in northern and western Pennsylvania, including the Poconos, begins around May 19 and continues until the last week in June, with peak activity between May 28 and June 10.

In the Catskills, the best hatches are between May 30 and June 15, while the Adirondack and northern New England areas peak between June 10 and June 30. The Midwest-Great Lakes region has its general emergence between May 25 and July 3.

	May 7	May 14	May 21	June 7	June 14	June 21	July 7	July 14	July 21
N. and W. Penna. and Poconos									
S. N.Y. and Catskills									
N. New England and Adirondacks									
Midwest and Great Lakes region									

E. *dorothea,* nymph.

NYMPH

The *dorothea* nymphs are typical of their subgeneric group, having the same robust features supported by feeble legs.

The easily recognized differences between *dorothea* and other members of this subgeneric group are in size and color. We previously mentioned that the *invaria* and *rotunda* species are very similar to *dorothea* in both the nymph and adult stages. The easiest way to distinguish them is just prior to their hatching, when the size difference and thoracic markings become rather obvious, especially if you're on the look-out for it. *dorothea* averages 7 mm while *invaria* and *rotunda* are between 7.5 and 10.5 mm (a difference of almost 2 hook sizes). Closer scrutiny of the nymphal stage will show that *dorothea* is somewhat lighter and has different markings on the thorax. Under magnification it lacks the paired dorsal spines at the rear of each tergite segment.

Similar differences are also apparent in the dun stage, but the stick-out is that *invaria* duns are usually at least a hook size larger than those of *dorothea*.

Although the *dorothea* nymph is found in various habitats, it is essentially a quiet-water dweller. They flourish in limestone and other meandering streams and are of the remaining principal hatches on silt-ridden farmland streams of limestone quality where most mayfly populations have all but disappeared. Beside their abundance in alkaline waters, they are also plentiful in pools and other tranquil areas of freestone mountain streams. On the other hand, nymphs of the similar *invaria* and *rotunda* species are predominantly fast-water dwellers. Although the freshly emerged duns of

The light "V" pattern on the thorax of E. *dorothea.*

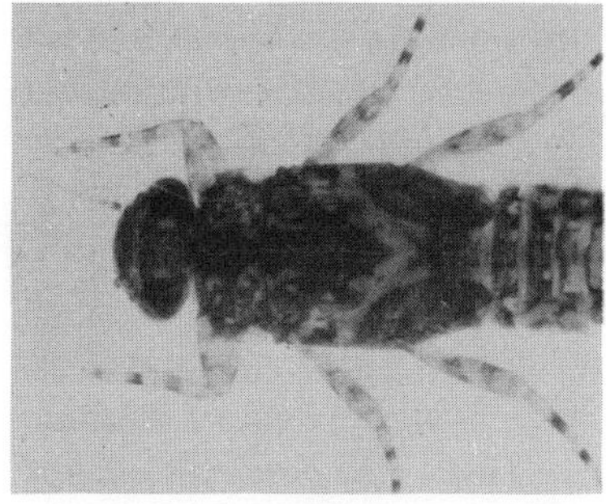

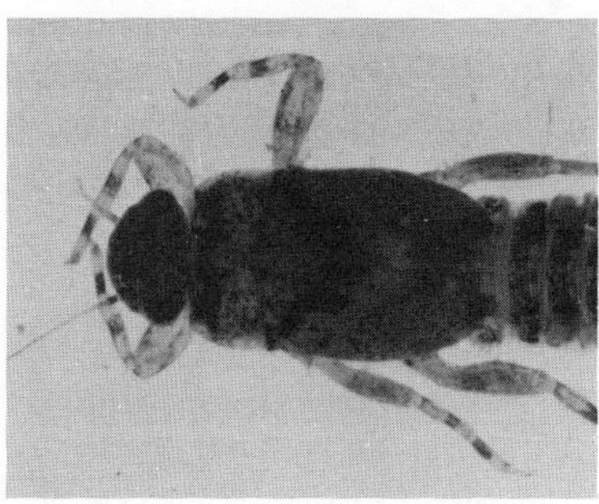

The very similar *invaria* nymph has a dark "V" pattern on its thorax.

these species may be flushed into the heads of pools where they mix with the hatching *dorothea* duns, the *invaria* and *rotunda* nymphs usually emerge in the faster rifles, runs and pocket waters requiring different angling tactics and imitations.

Prior to emergence, the nymphs become active and available to the trout. Like most Ephemerella nymphs, they wiggle temptingly when swimming to the surface in a manner that seems to entice trout into feeding. Nymph imitations should be fished in typical Ephemerella style—in and on the surface film during the hatch and on the bottom prior to emergence.

When the subimagoes are escaping their shucks, in or just under the surface film, they may drift with the current for some time before they pop through the surface as a dun. We use nymph and emerger imitations fished in or just under the surface film to imitate this action. As an alternate, nymph patterns with stiff hackle and pontoon tails should be tied and fished similar to a dry-fly. Favorite wet-fly patterns such as the Little Marryatt and Pale Evening Dun are also effective for this activity when fished downstream with twitches and jerks to simulate the naturals struggling in the surface film.

E. *dorothea,* male dun.

DUN

The local names for *dorothea* are Pale Evening Dun, Pale Watery Dun, Little Marryatt and Sulphur Dun. These small, yellowish mayflies make their debut when the weather is at its springtime best. The unpredictable days of early spring have given way to balmy, shirt-sleeve afternoons and intoxicating evenings filled with the anticipation of rising trout. During this season, streams are usually in ideal condition and are a pleasure to wade.

In the initial *Comparahatch* volumes, before our discovery of the *invaria* activity, we expressed our concern for the conflicting daily hatching activity associated with *dorothea* which kept anglers constantly off balance. Let's reflect on what was written in that chapter on *dorothea*.

> "Fly-fishers are kept constantly off balance by the ability of these insects to turn hatching activity on and off like a faucet. Blizzard-like hatching between 7 and 8 P.M. one evening might be followed the next day by a sporadic three-hour emergence in the afternoon.
>
> During the earlier hatches, emergence might take place in later afternoon or early evening, but will usually occur after 7 P.M. Later, as the weather gets warmer, hatches will most likely occur just before dusk except during cool, unseasonable weather when premature hatching might occur during the afternoon.
>
> There are, no doubt, many factors which contribute to the confusing emergence behavior of these mayflies . . ."

Armed with the new knowledge obtained from our *invaria* research, it's now understandable why we were confused in *Comparahatch* about the *dorothea* activity. We now realize that the hatches in the afternoon were those of *invaria* and *rotunda* and those "just before dusk, later in the season" were those of *dorothea*.

Continuing on this tack, we also mentioned in *Comparahatch* that we repeatedly came across situations where trout were selective to flies that were allowed to drag downstream in the faster water. We now believe that when the trout were consistently feeding in these faster stretches they were being selective to the struggling *invaria* and *rotunda* naturals—not to the slower water *dorothea* mayflies.

Toward the end of the *invaria* and *rotunda* hatching season, the summer Epeorus species may emerge with these stragglers. At that time anglers should be observant as the trout will normally feed on whatever species is the more prevalent.

Primary hatching of *dorothea* takes place in June when the afternoons are rather hot. At this time, hatching normally takes place between 7 P.M. and dusk, when the water cools to approximately 60° to 65°F. On unseasonably cool days, pre-emergence may occur in the late afternoon. During heat waves, hatching usually starts at dusk.

Trout are normally extra-selective to the size, silhouette and color of the *dorothea* imitations as the duns emerge in slower waters and pools. The Compara-dun, no hackle or parachute patterns, produce best during this activity. They should be cast with utmost caution. Trout usually feed very deliberately on these duns, so it pays to observe the rising pattern of your target trout before casting. *dorothea* hatches rarely last more than an hour and many are within a 30-minute period; hence, fly-fishermen should anticipate this action by preparing themselves ahead of time.

On blustry evenings, successful fishing becomes easier as the trout can be duped into taking less exacting imitations and the chances for spooking them become fewer due to the diffused stream surface. As discussed in the Ephemerella genus chapter, hackled patterns work best for these conditions. Two old-time favorites are the Little Marryat and the Pale Watery Dun. These patterns are also very effective when tied thorax style similar to our Hackled Comparaduns.

SPINNER

Shortly after the first hatches, the *dorothea* spinners will make their appearance above the riffles to mate in typical Ephemerella fashion. The female lays its eggs in a single cluster which is usually jettisoned from a safe distance above the stream. At times, however, some females will dip their sacs into the surface film or will themselves be blown into the water by a sudden gust of wind. When this occurs, trout favor these egg-laden spinners for their high protein content.

After mating and egg-laying, the spinners usually fall exhausted to the stream's surface in highly concentrated swarms. During the earlier hatches or on cloudy days, the spinner-falls may take place earlier (some time after 7 P.M.) but as the season continues, the falls become progressively later until they occur at dusk or after dark.

During the earlier spinner-falls (especially those that occur in late May and early June), anglers must again be extra-observant to determine whether the trout are taking the *dorothea* spinners or the larger *invaria* and *rotunda* species which, as with the case of the duns, have also historically been mistaken for *dorothea*. (See *invaria* chapter.) The size difference between these species is considerable. Anglers should capture a natural for evaluation before selecting an imitation. Extreme caution must also be taken to determine whether trout are feeding on duns or spinners of the respective species, as both may be on the water simultaneously. If a good fish is located and you are unable to determine what stage or species the trout are feeding on, try both the spinner and dun patterns of each of the species before throwing in the towel.

Ephemerella infrequens and inermis

(Subgenus Ephemerella)

COMMON NAME: Pale Morning Dun

SIZE RANGE: *infrequens*, 7 to 8 mm; *inermis*, 5½ to 6½ mm

HOOK SIZES:
SURFACE (dry): *infrequens*, #16; *inermis*, #18
SUBSURFACE (wet): *infrequens*, #14, #16; std. *inermis*, #16, #18; std.

IMITATIONS
NYMPH: Infrequens Compara-nymph
EMERGER: Infrequens Deerhair-emerger
DUN: Infrequens Compara-dun
SPINNER: Infrequens Compara-spinner

infrequens and *inermis* are two of the most important species of Ephemerella mayflies in the West. We found them in great abundance on Western rivers of various chemical make-up, but their abundance was really phenomenal on rich limestone spring creeks.

In *Biology of Mayflies,* Dr. Needham classifies only three Western species in the Invaria subgeneric group (now subgenus Ephemerella). Beside *infrequens* and *inermis,* he also listed the lesser-known *mollitia* species which, consequently, we found in good number. According to Doug Swisher and Carl Richards, Ephemerella *lacustris* is a very important Western species that also belongs to the subgenus Ephemerella.They give this species a "Super Hatch" stature in their book *Selective Trout* and claim that it is mostly found in lakes and limestone spring creeks. They also state that it starts to emerge early in July when most streams are unfishable due to the runoffs.

Thus far we have been unable to find any information about this species in our entomological reference materials nor have we captured the nymphs during our Western seine tests. Dr. Edmunds confirmed our negative findings in his book review of *Hatches* in Etonia. He said, "specimens that I have seen from creeks and rivers that have been identified as *lacustris* are *inermis.*"

These small, pale *infrequens* and *inermis* mayflies are the Western counterpart of the so called Eastern "sulphurs", E.*dorothea,* E. *invaria,* and E. *rotunda,* and the problems experienced during their emergence parallels those of the Eastern species (see these respective chapters).

The Western sulphurish mayflies of our subject species are geographically widespread and adaptable to the various habitats throughout the West. We witnessed good hatches and captured nymphs on most of the "blue ribbon" trout streams of the gigantic Yellowstone and Missouri River systems that drain most of Montana. We also found them in waters that make up the vast Snake River system which drains the northwestern section of Wyoming and most of Idaho. Ernie Schwiebert reports in his books *Nymphs* and *Matching the Hatch* that those insects are found throughout the Rocky Mountains as well as in the Pacific coast mountain ranges.

The emergence dates for these insects cannot be conveniently predicted over a broad geographic area, as can the hatching sequences of similar Midwestern and Eastern species, because of the remarkable variances of altitude in the

Al and Bob researching the *infrequens* and *inermis* hatches on the Boulder River in Montana.

GENERAL EMERGENCE:
General emergence occurs on Western freestone streams in July and August in accordance with altitude and other geological influences; on Western limestone and alkaline spring creeks or rivers, July through October.

Western mountain ranges and other geological influences such as thermal activity and subterranean springheads. Rivers influenced by the latter will normally reach ideal hatching temperatures much quicker than those which are influenced by the lofty snow fields of the more towering peaks.

Pinpointing emergences on individual Western rivers is much more reliable than trying to generalize hatching dates over a broad area, but even the most prolific angler would have to spend several lifetimes to compile sufficient information as to have a comprehensive record of this vast expanse of trout land.

infrequens and *inermis* activity is usually reliable on the beautiful Boulder River which drains the rugged Absarokas and joins the Yellowstone System at Big Timber, Montana from the second week in July through August. Normally, this activity does not begin on the main Boulder until the last week of July due to an exceptionally late and heavy runoff. We captured both the *infrequens* and *inermis* duns, however, on the smaller East Boulder during the 15th and 16th of July. We camped on a peninsula where these rivers joined and were able to observe trout dimpling for the *infrequens* and *inermis* duns on the little East Boulder (which was in normal condition), slightly upstream of where its waters mingle with the cold, swollen 48°F current of the Main Boulder which looked barren and was yet devoid of any hatching activity. When we returned to this confluence toward the end of the month, the *infrequens* and *inermis* duns activity was starting in earnest on the main Boulder and the water temperature was about 55°F.

Both species usually peak by mid-July on the Madison River below the town of West Yellowstone. Hatching on its alpine tributaries, the Gibbon River and the Firehole River, also expire early due to the hot spring influx of the Norris and Midway geyser basins which blend their boiling waters with these glacial meadow rivers within the Yellowstone Park boundary. Hatching on the main Yellowstone, within the Park boundary, usually starts during the third week in July. However, during seasons with less snow accumulation, this activity should begin after the first week in July and continue into August. The unique South Fork of the Madison in the same area is a cooler river system and emergence generally takes place several weeks after the Park-water hatches are underway.

Western alkaline rivers like the ideally-rich Henry's Fork of the Snake and Silver Creek in Idaho resemble the fullblown spring-head rivers of the Midwest. These streams have little or no influence from snow melt; water temperature is ideal and they are fishable most of the year. *infrequens* and *inermis* hatching occurs on these prolific streams during early July and the activity may continue through October when the first snow storms will drop the water temperature sufficiently to quell most of this hatching.

NYMPH

The *infrequens* nymphs are very similar to those of *inermis*, but closer observation will reveal their differences. *infrequens* (7-8 mm) is a darker and larger nymph than *inermis* (5 1/2-6 1/2mm). The mottlings on the pro-thorax and head of the *infrequens* nymph are less distinct than on those of *inermis*. The lateral extensions of its pro-thorax are not wholly pale as are the extensions on *inermis*. The latter also has a distinct dorsal stripe which is lacking on the *infrequens* nymph (see photo).

inermis also has pale dorsal spots or dots which are absent on *infrequens*. The light markings on the head of the *inermis* nymph is probably the most recognizable difference to the naked eye. Most differences between the nymphs are more difficult to detect, but they will become quite apparent if you use an 8X magnifying glass.

The less-important Ephemerella *mollitia* is approximately 8mm and the lightest of the three nymphs. Upon maturity, their dark wing pads become contrastingly obvious against their light background color. Its legs are less distinctly banded than those of *inermis* and *infrequens* and their lateral abdominal extensions are the best developed of the three species.

These nymphs can be found in a variety of habitats. We have captured them in riffles, moderate runs and slower eddies; especially along grassy banks where they hide in the foliage and debris that collects on the edge of the current.

Left: E. *infrequens,* nymph. *Right:* E. *inermis,* nymph.

Initial hatching can be expected when the water temperature reaches approximately 50°F. More reliable activity, which will cause a good rise of trout, takes place when the water temperature climbs to between 55° and 60°F.

The emergence characteristics of these nymphs parallel the "sulphur" Ephemerellas of the East and Midwest. They are very active prior to emergence and normally make several unsuccessful trips to the proximity of the surface film before hatching. Their enormous number prompt trout to feed on them at varying depths during this activity. Our observations on the stream and in our lab indicate that the dun leaves its shuck a few inches beneath the surface film and is then bouyed to the surface by gases as it floats helplessly in the current.

As the hatch beings, try bouncing a nymph imitation along the bottom or fish an emerger pattern at mid-depth. These patterns are best when fished across and downstream so that jerks and twitches can be added to duplicate the Ephemerella-like wiggle of the naturals. When the duns begin to pop through the surface film our "stiff-hackled" nymph and emerger patterns are excellent fished right in the film, a la dry-fly method. Trout are extremely selective to the size and color of these imitations, so selection of the correct pattern is essential.

E. *infrequens,* male dun. (Note that one tail is broken off.)

DUN

Doug Swisher and Carl Richard dubbed the small, yellowish mayflies of *infrequens* and *inermis* (also their species *lacustris*) as the "Pale Morning Duns" and recommended their imitations be tied on #16 through #22 hook sizes. Over a decade before their publication, Ernest Schwiebert, in *Matching* the *Hatch,* called the *infrequens* duns a Western version of the Hendricksons and likened their size and color to the eastern Hendricksons (E. *subvaria).* He recommends (even in his new book, *Nymphs)* #12 and #14 hooks for both *inermis* and *infrequens* imitations.

Our studies of the live nymphs and the adults, including scrutinization of our photographs, agree with the smaller size and coloration of Swisher/Richards' findings. However, we believe that the hook sizes for the *inermis* and *infrequens* duns (5 1/2mm-8mm) can be limited to two sizes, #16 and #18 (see hook size chart).

It should be mentioned that we have not found a smaller Ephemerella mayfly (5mm body-6mm wing) emerging with the duns of *infrequens* and *inermis.* Although we have made many attempts, we have not been able to identify this small mayfly despite wing venation and genitalia comparisons. To our knowledge, it is not described in any of our entomological reference materials. We have, therefore, simply labeled it, "Western Ephemerella No-Name". The point is, when this smaller mayfly is mixed in with the *inermis* and *infrequens* duns, a #20 imitation (somewhat darker) may be necessary.

The duns of *inermis* and *infrequens* resemble the various "sulphur" Ephemerella mayflies of the East and Midwest. The main difference is that they are slightly smaller and that their yellowish bodies have a definite olive cast. The wings are pale gray with a hint of yellow.

The earlier hatches on the gushing freestone streams may be ignored by the trout who usually stick it out on the bottom until the river subsides and the currents become more conducive to surface feeding. When the water temperature reaches 55°F, the run off is generally over and the trout are usually much more cooperative.

Like most Ephemerella species, the nymphs of these species seek out the quiet pockets, eddies and the moderate runs adjacent to the faster water for their emergence. We observed and collected hundreds of these duns one afternoon in a side slough about three feet deep. This miniature pool (7 feet wide by 20 feet long) was fed by a tiny channel which crossed an enormous bar of polished stones before it splashed into the little pond. This cold artery mingled the drifting emergers from the main current with those nymphs which had taken up permanent residence long before the

A rich Western spring creek where *infrequens* and *inermis* thrive.

main channel had receded. As we entered this pool with our equipment, we spooked a wise rainbow who obviously used this slough for his own, private eating place.

The daily hatching sequence of *infrequens* and *inermis* parallels the *invaria*, *rotunda* and *dorothea* species of the East and Midwest. When the water temperature reaches around 50°F, the hatch will normally take place around midday, between noon and 3 P.M. Later, when the temperature is in the 60's, hatching will occur intermittently throughout the afternoon, according to the weather conditions. During hot weather, emergence usually takes place in late afternoon and evening hours or in the morning hours when the water temperature is more favorable.

The hatching process, from nymph to dun, is exceptionally lengthy, especially when the water temperature is around 50° F or lower. When the duns evacuate their nymphal shucks a few inches beneath the film and finally reach the surface, they slowly unfold their wet, sailboat-like wings from their thoracic structure to dry. We have studied this activity on the stream and in aquariums and have observed that it often takes several minutes for these duns to dry their wings before they take off. When the waters warmed to between 55° and 62°F the hatching and takeoff time was reduced considerably. Yet, it still took surprisingly long even on spring-fed rivers of ideal temperature such as the Henry's Fork of the Snake.

Due to their hatching traits, a good percentage of the dun population are cripples. These helpless duns ride the current until they are eaten by the trout or are drowned. The majority, however, are healthy and usually struggle to get airborne. There being both cripples and normal duns, it is necessary to use both hackleless and hackled patterns if the angler is to fish this hatch successfully. When the water temperature is low and the duns have exceptional difficulty thawing their wing muscles, or if there are a considerable number of cripples, the Compara-dun generally works better when fished dead-drift. On warm, sunny days, when the duns are more active and leave the water sooner, a hackled pattern may be better. Try fishing it downstream with occasional twitches and skittering to duplicate the struggle of the duns. Correct imitation size and color is imperative if success is to be obtained during this fantastic hatch. Twitching and skittering is seldom effective on larger, wild fish.

SPINNER

The spinner-falls of *infrequens* and *inermis* are typical of the smaller Eastern and Midwestern Ephemerella mayflies.

The imagoes are attracted to the riffles and rapid-water sections. On gently flowing rivers, look for their concentrations above the scarce patches of broken water. After copulation it appears that the females jettison their single egg packet from the air. Both sexes then fall to the surface, spent.

The spinner flights we witnessed took place toward dusk, when the wind died down. We sometimes spotted sporadic spinner activity during the day, but not enough to compete with the heavier dun activity. During hot spells, the spinner-flights took place in the morning.

One evening I was working a wide, relatively flat stretch of the Henry's Fork on the famous Last Chance Ranch water. The best mayfly activity had taken place during the day, but I was still able to pick up some nice-sized rainbows which were feeding on sporadic hatches of Siphlonurus (Gray Drakes) which were mixed in with a smattering of tiny Baetis flies (B. *devinctus* and B. *parvus*.)

Toward dusk, my eyes scanned the sky above for signs of spinner formations. When none materialized I made my way upstream where Bob's silhouette indicated he was into something on a broken-water stretch. He was stationed in one of the few sections of riffles on the entire stretch of the river. It was impossible to converse above the gentle roar of the wide river, but after a few hand signals and some sign language, I dipped my fine-mesh aquarium net into the surface film momentarily and accumulated several *infrequens* imagoes which were still struggling. I detected the subtle blips in the surface caused by the deliberate rises of the trout and I knew we were into a good spinner-fall.

The fall lasted around 45 minutes and we scored heavily on #16 and #18 yellowish-olive Compara-spinners. When the last of the spinners had fallen, the feeding turned off like a faucet. We believe that *infrequens* spinners were mixed in with those of the smaller *inermis*, which probably accounted for the success of the #18 Compara-spinners.

Ephemerella cornuta
(Subgenus Drunella)

COMMON NAMES:
Blue-winged olive

SIZE RANGE: 9 to 10 mm

HOOK SIZES:
SURFACE (dry): #16, #14
SUBSURFACE (wet): #14, #12; std.

IMITATIONS:
NYMPH: Cornuta Compara-nymph
EMERGER: Cornuta Deerhair Emerger
DUN: Blue-winged Olive, Cornuta Compara-dun, Cornuta Hackled Compara-dun
SPINNER: Cornuta Compara-spinner

The prolific hatching and feeding activity associated with Ephemerella *cornuta* was practically unknown in American fly-fishing circles prior to release of *Hatches* (1975). It's doubtful that even the most serious fly-fishing addicts had realized the great action surrounding this important mayfly which we've found to be so common throughout the East and Midwest. Our stream research indicates that the *cornuta* hatches are on par with the more famous and celebrated mayfly hatches. In many cases their importance surpasses those mayflies of literary fame that fail to produce consistent hatches and angling opportunities. We hope with the publication of this chapter, that the angler's interest will be stimulated to experiment with the *cornuta* hatch. We are confident that fly-fishermen will enjoy the excellent angling opportunities and challenges that this hatch provides.

cornuta hatching takes place on northern and western Pennsylvania streams between mid-May and early June, but the best activity occurs between May 25 and June 3. During the 1973 and '74 seasons, we gathered many specimens for photography on the famous Penn's Creek at Coburn, as well as on the legendary Brodheads. During our collections we also experienced excellent angling and feeding activity on these streams during the last week in May.

Catskill emergence lags by a week or two. We photographed Beaverkill specimens on June 15th while we camped at Wagon-Tracks Pool with two good friends, Paul Dickes and Jack Davis. During that memorable weekend we evaluated our *cornuta* patterns and kept score of their effectiveness on those choosey Beaverkill Browns.

Northern streams, like those in the Adirondacks and northern New England, continue hatching throughout June. General emergence in the Midwest is from late May to the beginning of July, while emergence in northern Minnesota, Wisconsin and the Upper Peninsula of Michigan usually continues until the second week in July. We found mature nymph specimens as late as July 12 on certain sections of

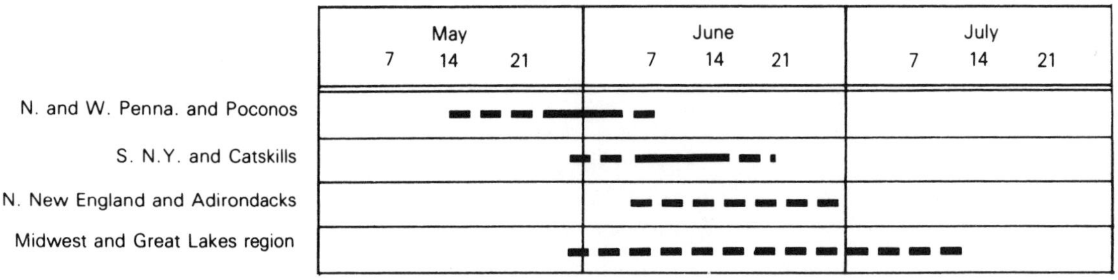

	May			June			July		
	7	14	21	7	14	21	7	14	21
N. and W. Penna. and Poconos									
S. N.Y. and Catskills									
N. New England and Adirondacks									
Midwest and Great Lakes region									

the Au Sable River in Michigan. Our Western research showed no evidence of *cornuta*. These findings coincide with the entomological information available on this species.

NYMPH

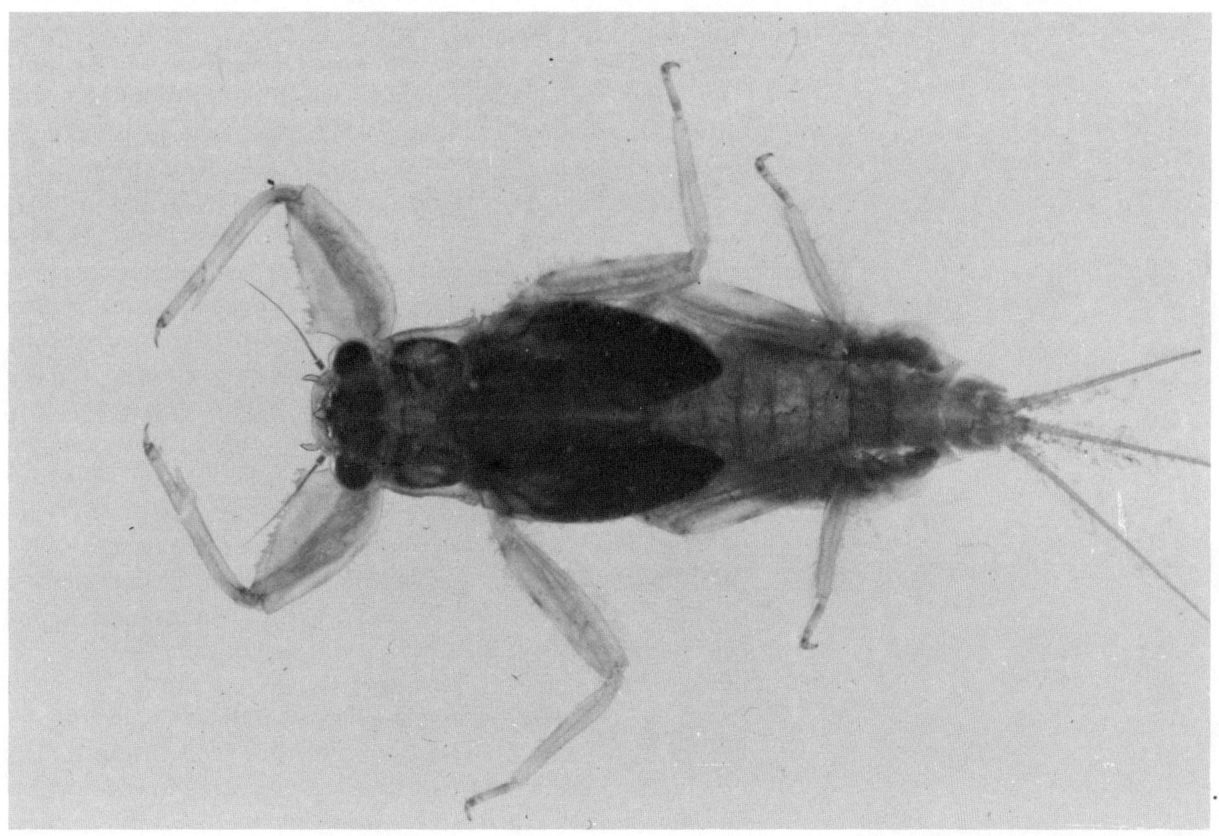

Fully mature E. *cornuta* nymph, ready to hatch. The soon-to-be-a-dun's legs are clearly visible beneath the chitin legs of the nymph.

Like the closely related Ephemerella *lata* species, *cornuta* belongs to the subgenus Drunella—one of 8 subgeneric groups in the super Ephemerella genus. The nymphs of the Drunella subgenus are often much different than those of other Ephemerella subgeneric groups, having much flatter body configurations accentuated by powerful femora in the forelegs which resemble the clinging Epeorus and Stenonema nymphs. Although *cornuta* nymphs are found in slower waters, their flattened profile, which is typical of the Drunella subgenus, extends their habitat to runs and riffles and eddies of pocket-water.

The wider front femora of *cornuta* have irregular, tubercle-like spines on the leading edge, giving them a fearsome appearance. This is quite a contrast to those nymphs of the more famous subgenus Ephemerella, which have rounded bodies and feeblish legs; i.e., *dorothea, subvaria, invaria*. The *cornuta* nymphs and those of the closely related Midwestern *lata* species have similar body configura-

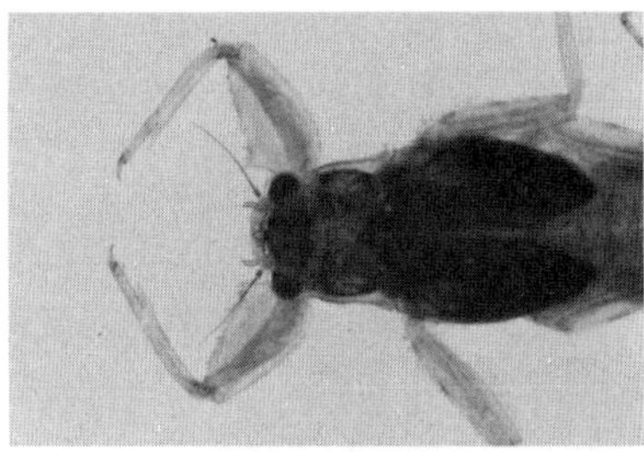

Top: Incurved horns of E. *cornuta* nymph. *Bottom:* Barely visible horns of E. *lata* nymph.

tions; yet they are readily distinguishable by their size, color and horns. *cornuta* is lighter in color and about 10 mm in length, while *lata* averages 7 mm, a difference of almost two hook sizes. Another distinctive characteristic is the pair of conspicuous in-curved horns that protrude from *cornuta's* head between the bases of the antennae, while the semblance of horns on *lata* are subtle; almost non existent. Aside from *cornuta's* in-curved horns, another unique physical characteristic is the horn-like tubercle which extends from the middle of the frontal shelf of its head.

cornuta nymphs live in medium-to-fast riffles having gravel, pebble or medium-sized rock bottoms. During emergence they may migrate to slower sections and eddies. As do most Ephemerella nymphs, they make several trips to the surface during emergence. During this activity, trout are enticed into taking these wiggley nymphs and the partially emerged duns as well as the fully winged insects.

In the case of the Cornuta hatch, the nymphs are extremely vulnerable once they leave their hiding places on the bottom. They swim and float enticingly, and clumsily, to the surface. Our autopsies over the past ten years reveal that the fish will take these nymphs early in the hatch when they start to leave their hiding places on the bottom. However, the peak of vulnerability is when the majority of nymphs are near the surface film. The nymphs, in most cases, seem to split their shucks several inches below the film or right in or beneath the film. The trout key in on the emerging nymphs or freshly emerged duns—they know instinctively that the insect in the state of emergence are

E. *cornuta,* male dun.

much more vulnerable than the surface duns, which may flutter off at any moment. On rivers that have abundant fly hatches, this selectivity will be the rule rather than the exception.

Although the emergence antics of Cornuta are typical of the subgenus, there is an additional problem; that being, the color of the emerging insect. Unlike most Ephemerella species, the body of the dun changes its color drastically once it hits the atmosphere. As the duns hatch in or beneath the surface film, their body is a pale greenish yellow color (almost chartruse). Within seconds after emergence (when the duns are floating on the surface) the bodies turn a medium olive. By the time they fly to the nearest shrubbery, they are a dark dirty olive. To be really successful during this hatch the angler must use an emerger pattern fished dead drift in the surface film or slightly under. The imitation should have a pale greenish yellow body.

DUN

Examining the circumstances, it becomes easy to understand why even the most serious angling students have thus far overlooked the important activity associated with the *cornuta* hatch. The main reason is that *cornuta* was never been covered in earlier angling literature nor in associated entomological texts, except for a few brief and vague references prior to the first printing of *Hatches*. The Leonards cover *cornuta* in *Mayflies of Michigan Trout Streams* insofar as physical identification of the nymph and adult are concerned. They included an excellent drawing of the nymph which helped us in our initial identification of this species.

Beside the lack of angling literature to provide incentive for anglers to explore the *cornuta* hatches, we also believe that this hatch was by-passed because they emerge in the morning, at a time when the peak of other mayfly activity occurs during the evening hours and at dusk. Hence, most serious anglers (those who might normally spot this prolific morning activity) plan their day, instead, to include the afternoon and evening activity associated with the heralded mayflies of Stenonema, Isonychia, Ephermerella and Ephemera—especially the *guttulata* (Green Drake) and *dorothea* ("Sulphur") hatches.

Finally, we believe that *cornuta's* obscurity was also due to a simple case of mistaken identity. We are convinced that even the most serious experts have mistaken the activity of *cornuta* for that of Ephemerella *attenuata*. Both are typical of the Blue-Winged Olive varieties that hatch in the morning hours during this season. To get to the base of the angler's identification problem, let's scrutinize these similar-

A. B.

Average actual size comparison of A, *cornuta* and B, *attenuata*.

ities. To the untrained eye, *cornuta* and *attenuata* look alike; especially on the water. Yet, up close, they are physically different and they have different emergence traits. The *cornuta* dun is larger, averaging about 9 mm, while *attenuata* averages around 7 mm (a difference of one hook size). Although the wings are identical in color, the olive body hues of each are different.

These differences along with the contrasting subsurface emergence traits of *attenuata* and *cornuta* causes trout to exercise extreme selectivity to the respective naturals. This selectivity probably explains the lack of success most anglers report during alleged *attenuata* hatches. Our stream research indicates, surprisingly, that *cornuta* is much more prolific on Eastern streams than is the more publicized *attenuata*. Therefore, in most cases when anglers believe that trout are rising to *attenuata* duns, they are in reality probably taking the larger and darker *cornuta* mayflies.

Our first experience with this hatch was in early May when they hatched from our aquariums. At first I thought they were *attenuata* duns, but the darkening body color and size indicated otherwise. When Bob arrived he was equally excited and went immediately to work photographing the duns. Our subsequent observations indicated which nymphs were responsible for these "oversized *attenuatas*". These observations led to positive identification of all of the stages, but, equally important, the hatches from our aquariums also indicated from which streams they were hatching. Penn's Creek, Brodheads Creek, the famous Beaverkill and others were represented by our tanks.

Our familiarity with premature hatching in aquariums enabled us to calculate when these nymphs would emerge on the streams that these aquariums represented. During subsequent fishing trips, we arrived early in the mornings and anxiously anticipated the *cornuta* hatching activity. We weren't disappointed. The hatching was prolific and reliable for more than a week.

Our experience with *cornuta* indicates that they will hatch anytime between 8 A.M. and mid-day, that emergence usually lasts from 60 to 90 minutes and that the best hatching activity takes place when water temperature is between 50° and 60°F.

The *cornuta* duns hatch in riffles and medium-to-fast runs as well as in eddies and back-waters adjacent to these areas. After emergence, they ride the current momentarily before they become airborne. On abnormally cooler mornings, the duns may linger on the surface making several attempts at takeoff. Trout are usually choosey about the size and color of the naturals, so imitations and their line of drift must be right on.

As previously mentioned over the last ten years we've found the most effective imitation for this hatch is a sparsely tied Deerhair Compara-emerger with a greenish yellow body (almost a chartreuse), fished in the surface film. If refusals persist, the emerger should be tucked under the film.

SPINNER

The glassy-winged imagoes are still somewhat of a mystery to us although we have sighted them many times over the riffles about an hour before dusk. Thus far we have found their significance questionable, as most spinners seem to drop their eggs a safe distance above the stream. Their significance is even further detracted from by the competition they receive from the awesome dun and spinner activity of *guttulata, dorothea* and several species of the Stenonema and Isonychia flies.

Toward the end of the *cornuta* hatching period, when the action of the peak mayfly season has subsided, they become more important although they must still compete with the dun and spinner activity of Isonychia *bicolor*, Stenonema *fuscum* and the mid-summer Epeorus flies. If the concentrated spinner-falls occur prior to (or after) these larger mayfly ovipositing flights, they may become extremely important and account for a rise of good fish.

A stretch of medium-fast *cornuta* water.

Ephemerella lata
(Subgenus Drunella)

COMMON NAME: Blue-winged Olive

SIZE RANGE: 6 to 8 mm

HOOK SIZES:
SURFACE (dry): #16, #18;
SUBSURFACE (wet): #16; std.

IMITATIONS:
NYMPH: Lata Compara-nymph
EMERGER: Blue-winged Olive Wet, Lata Deerhair Emerger.
DUN: Blue-winged Olive, Dun Variant, Lata Compara-dun
SPINNER: Lata Compara-spinner

lata is an important species within the enormous and productive Ephemerella genus. It belongs to the Drunella subgenus which consists of no less than 17 species; many of which are important to the angler. Aside from our Midwestern subject species, *cornuta* is a great Drunella hatch in the East, while E. *grandis,* E. *glacialis* and E. *flavilinea* are par excellence in the West.

lata is a first-rate hatch in the Midwest. General emergence in Minnesota, Wisconsin and Michigan is from the end of June to mid-August. Best hatching on Northern rivers, like Michigan's Au Sable and Wisconsin's Wolf, is from mid-July through the first week in August.

Reportedly, there are local populations of *lata* in the East. We believe these reports had their genisis in the 1935 Comstock publication, *Biology of Mayflies* by Needham, Traver & Hsu. In his book, Dr. Needham explains that his descriptions of *lata* are taken from preserved nymph specimens of the Cornell University collection, collected by several entomologists between 1900 and 1930. Over the years, we have never experienced a *lata* hatch in the East, nor have we ever noticed nymph specimens in our thousands of seine tests. It is our belief that what are thought to be *lata* are truly other closely related nymphs of the Drunella subgenus; mainly *cornuta, cornutella, depressa* (now synonym of *cornuta*) and *longicornis. attenuata,* previously covered in *Comparahatch,* is quite similar to *lata* in size and color in its subimago stage, as are the important and slightly larger *cornuta* duns.

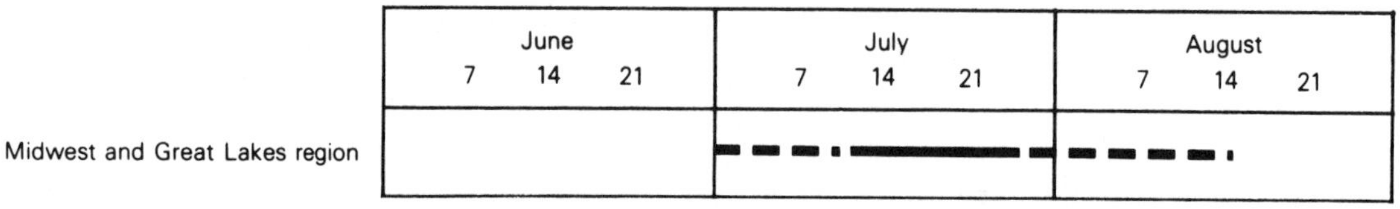

	June 7	June 14	June 21	July 7	July 14	July 21	August 7	August 14	August 21
Midwest and Great Lakes region									

NYMPH

We have collected, reared and photographed *lata* nymphs in three color phases. They are: 1) dark brown with an olive cast. The forelegs, head and thorax are lighter, 2) dark brown (almost black) with a contrasting, mottled appearance on the thorax and abdomen. All legs are distinctly banded, 3) almost the same as 1), except lighter. The ground color is a dull reddish-brown with an amber cast. In spite of the color differences among the nymphs, their physical charac-

Left: E. *lata,* nymph. *Right:* E. *lata,* male dun.

teristics are identical. In the dun and spinner stages, it is almost impossible for the angler to distinguish a difference in physical characteristics.

Unlike the more feeble-legged Ephemerella nymphs, these flattened nymphs live in faster stretches, especially those with gravel bottoms. Typical of the Drunella nymphs, *lata* can be readily identified at streamside by their unusually wide, crab-like femora which are not found on the species of other subgeneric groups. The emergence characteristics of these nymphs are typical of the entire genus. They wiggle enticingly to the surface, often making several attempts to break through the surface tension. In the Drunella subgenus, they have a tendency to hatch 6 to 12 inches below the surface and float to the top, buoyed by gases previously released by the nymph. During hatching, the nymphs and prematurely emerged duns drift helplessly in the current, making them easy prey for the trout.

Prior to hatching, when the nymphs move about nervously on the stream bed, they become more available to the trout. At this time, nymph patterns fished on the bottom will pay off. During hatching activity, nymph and emerger patterns are best, fished dead-drift in or slightly under the surface film.

DUN

The *lata* duns are commonly called "Blue-Winged Olives" as are scores of unrelated mayflies that have grayish wings and olive bodies. These Midwestern duns closely resemble those of the Eastern *attenuata* species and the larger subimagoes of the *cornuta* species. They have dark gray wings with abnormally stocky bodies of dark brownish-olive. The bodies average 7 mm in length. The oversized wings (about

8 or 9 mm) are helpful during takeoff, compensating for their extra-thick bodies.

In early July, before the hatch is in full swing, emergence may occur in the afternoon, especially on cloudy days. During this period, there is little other activity during the day, so trout may feed on the sparse emergence of duns if they float by convenient lies. The point is, trout will rarely go out of their way unless the insects are present in good number.

In mid-July when the water gets warmer, good hatching normally takes place in the morning when the water is still cool. During this time, emergence can occur anytime between 6 A.M. and noon, but the best hatching and feeding activity will usually take place between 7 and 10A.M.

lata duns are sporadic emergers which usually hatch over a four-hour period. This intermittent hatching can provide excellent opportunities for the dry-fly enthusiast, who can cast leisurely over rising trout throughout the morning. The best time for these ideal fly-fishing sessions is generally the 3rd and 4th weeks of July. At this time, the *lata* duns are not competing with other more prolific species for the trout's attention.

Prior to this period, the abundant Pseudocloeon *anoka* emerges in the morning. These concentrated hatches may divert attention from the more sporadic emerging *lata*. Toward the end of the month, the *lata* duns must compete with the overwhelmingly dense Tricorythodes duns and spinners which blanket the river daily until 11 A.M.

Due to their frequent subsurface emergence, the hatched *lata* duns normally float complacently, drying their wet wings before takeoff. This characteristic, and the fact that they are often funneled into pools and backwaters having smooth surfaces, makes them ideal for the Compara-dun application. The advantage of the distinct silhouette and the upright attitude for which the Compara-dun was originally designed are homogeneous with the natural. Imitations tied on #16 hooks, are about the right size for these duns, but one should take the time to capture a natural as refusals can be experienced if your imitation is at odds with the natural by even one or two mm.

Lata Compara-dun.

On breezy days, when duns are skittered across the current by puffs of wind, or on broken water which causes the trout's view of the natural to be diffused, a delicate, hackled pattern may be a better choice. Beside the Hackled Compara-duns, the traditional Blue-Winged Olive and the Dun variant tied on #16 hooks are also good bets for this activity.

SPINNER

The spinner flights are both impressive and productive. About an hour before dusk, the male spinners will usually appear over the riffles.

On Midwestern waters, these spinner-falls usually precipitate some of the best feeding activity of the year. The accumulated duns that have hatched sporadically throughout the morning fall in heavy concentrations toward dark. The spinner-fall and subsequent feeding activity will last about an hour; usually between twilight and dark.

During the earlier spinner flights, these imagoes may compete with those of Isonychia *sadleri,* Hexagenia *limbata* and several species of the Stenonema and Siphlonurus genera. However, in later July, these species are usually exhausted, leaving the *lata* spinners as the primary meal for trout feeding at dusk.

When the angler first spots the undulating males above the riffles during their nuptial flights, he should prepare himself for the eventual spinner-falls by selecting the most advantageous stream positions.

A riffle with good trout-holding capacity and one that also has good lighting conditions (preferably to the angler's rear) is of primary importance. If the angler is forced to cast into the waning light, he should make additional preparations by practice-casting, gradually lengthening his line, until his eyes become accustomed to the dark silhouette of his small fly floating in the glare of the reflected light.

These preparations are necessary as spinner imitations should be cast upstream, over broken water, and allowed to float dead-drift over the spinner-selective trout. Timing is very critical; hence, it is imperative that the angler see his imitation on the water and the subsequent rises of the trout.

If the trout seem to be slashing at the ovipositing imagoes we often start out with full-hackled spinner patterns and manipulate them to imitate the dipping spinners. Later, we use spent patterns to imitate the flush-floating spent spinners.

Evening spinner fishing is one of the most exciting and challenging aspects of fly fishing, requiring intense concentration and relentless practice of technique. Once the angler has accepted this challenge and mastered the necessary methods, he will often leave the stream as he should, fulfilled and content.

Ephemerella glacialis *(synonym to grandis ingens)*, *grandis ingens and doddsi.* *(Subgenus Drunella)*

COMMON NAMES: Western Green Drake

SIZE RANGE: *glacialis*, 13 to 15 mm; *grandis*, 12 to 13 mm; *doddsi*, 14 to 16 mm

HOOK SIZES:
SURFACE (dry): *glacialis*, #12, #10, #12, 4x long. *grandis*, #12, #10; *doddsi*, #10, #8.
SUBSURFACE (wet): *glacialis*, #10; *grandis*, #10 *doddsi*, #10, 3x long.

IMITATIONS
NYMPH: Glacialis Compara-nymph
EMERGER: Glacialis Compara-emerger, Glacialis deerhair emerger
SPINNER: Glacialis Compara-spinner

GENERAL EMERGENCE: General Western emergence of these overlapping hatches occurs from early July through mid-August on freestone streams in accordance with various geographic influences that affect water temperature and weather. Limestone or alkaline spring creeks emerge Mid June-mid July.

The important Western mayflies of *glacialis*, *grandis* and *doddsi* belong to the subgenus Drunella group and they are the largest mayflies in the entire Ephemerella genus. These uncommonly large, fat Ephemerellas constitute major fishing hatches throughout the West. There are several obscure species in this subgeneric group that approach or exceed the size of these mayflies. However, we have found no real evidence yet of their importance to the American angler.

The activity associated with these great fishing hatches has always been credited to the *grandis* hatch alone. Our intensive Western research on these species revealed that all three species commonly inhabit the same streams, are similar in size and resemble each other in the nymph, dun and spinner stages.

The emergence of these species overlap closely, but our records indicate *grandis* generally hatches first, then *glacialis*, followed by *doddsi*.

The seasonal emergence periods of these insects are, of course, determined by water temperature and it is, therefore, quite difficult to foretell Western hatching activity on a wide geographic basis. Unlike the predictable mayfly emergences of the Eastern and Midwestern streams, the endless mountain ranges in this vast Western country have so many intangible geological influences that hatching predictions (even from one valley to the next) can be virtually impossible. There are angling texts that stress altitude as the key for the wide scale prediction of hatching activity. We have found this criterion alone to be an unreliable factor. In reality there are many factors which determine the timing of emergence on the various rivers. Southerly exposures of high peaks, permanent glacial influences, thermal geyser activity and cold subterranian springs are only a few of the forces that will determine when water temperature will be right for hatching. Any one of these influences or a combination of several will determine if hatches will coincide on certain rivers or whether they will be weeks or even months apart.

The fabulous Yellowstone River system is a good example of how these variable forces, not altitude alone, affect hatching periods. We caught the tail end of the *grandis-glacialis-doddsi* activity on the Yellowstone River (at an altitude of approximately 8000 ft.) on July 17, 18 and 19 between the Grand Canyon of the Yellowstone and the headwaters where the river spills out of Yellowstone Lake; a distance of about

20 miles. This section of the Yellowstone is influenced by many factors, especially thermal activity and a galaxy of spring-heads which warmed the water to between 58° and 62°F in spite of the high altitude. Several weeks later, in the vicinity of Livingston, Montana (altitude, only 4500 ft.), the water temperature was just getting into the 50's and the *glacialis, grandis* and *doddsi* hatches were just beginning to develop. Apparently the icy flows that drain the primitive Absaroka and Beartooth mountains, as well as the streams that pour out of the rugged Bridger and Crazy Mountain ranges, reduced the temperature of this river so severely that hatching in these lower altitudes lagged by at least three weeks.

We caught the initial sporadic activity of the *grandis* duns on the Boulder River above McLoed on July 14 and 15. Although it was mid-July, the river ran cold (48-50°F) due to the extra snow that had accumulated in the high peaks during an extremely harsh winter. Toward the end of the month we rolled our motor home upriver again past McLoed, above Natural Bridge. Although the weather was in the 90's, the water temperature was only 55°F and the *grandis* duns along with those of *glacialis* and *doddsi* were starting to hatch in earnest. The Boulder was lower now and fishable, yet the water was numbing against our waders as we collected duns under the chilling stare of Mt. Contact.

On the other hand, hatching on the Henry's Fork of the Snake, Buffalo River and most of the other spring creeks in the Targee Forest area of Idaho had started during the first week of July. Our seine tests during the third week of July revealed excellent nymph populations of the smaller Ephemerella, Baetis and Pseudocloeon species, but apparently *glacialis, grandis* and *doddsi* were gone for another year.

Emergence occured on the Upper Madison (above Hebgen Lake) and on the Gibbon and the Firehole Rivers, which are also influenced by thermal geysers, at the beginning of July, but we did manage to catch dwindling activity below Hebgen Lake and Quake Lake on the roaring Madison River around July 20 and 21.

We have experienced good hatches of *glacialis* on this stretch of the Boulder River in Montana.

NOTE: In recent years entomologists have renamed and reclassified two of these three large Ephemerella mayflies:
grandis is now *grandis ingens*.
glacialis is now a synonym to *grandis ingens*.
doddsi: remains the same

We chose to live with our original manuscript for this chapter and treat these insects individually per Needman, Traver, Hsu because our hands-on research convinced us that these insects are sufficiently unique.

NYMPH

The *grandis* and *glacialis* nymphs are similar except for the following differences: 1) The pair of tubercles on the back of the head are larger and conical in *glacialis,* 2) Both species have paired abdominal spines on tergite segments 2 through 9. They are erect, finger-like and are directed backwards, gradually increasing in size. The chief difference between the species is that in *glacialis,* these spines are proportionately larger on segments 8 and 9, 3) The *glacialis*

E. *grandis*, nymph.

nymphs, when mature, are a deep blackish-brown while those of *grandis* are a lighter reddish-brown.

The nymphs of Ephemerella *doddsi* are similar to both *glacialis* and *grandis* in size and configuration. *doddsi* averages around 15mm in length, while *grandis* averages 13mm and *glacialis* 14mm. The obvious difference between the *doddsi* nymphs and those of *grandis* and *glacialis* are that the femora on all of the legs are thick and equal in size. *grandis* and *glacialis* nymphs have more slender femora on the middle and rear leg pairs. Other obvious differences are that the *doddsi* nymph lacks the thoracic and abdominal tubercles and spines that are present in the other species and that its head has a distinctive frontal shelf.

The nymphs of all three species are flattened and strong; perfect for the fast habitat in which they live. We found them in medium-to-fast riffles and runs. Prior to hatching they seek out quiet eddies and pockets or they may migrate to slower pools (similar to the fast-water Eastern Stenonema clinging nymphs). Luckily, nature mercifully triggers this migration urge in these nymphs as they are among the clumsiest hatching types in the whole Ephemeroptera order and their species would surely be in trouble if they hatched in the faster riffles where they normally live.

As is typical with many of the Ephemerella species, these nymphs make several seemingly aimless trips to the surface before hatching. Somewhere between the bottom and the surface film they evacuate their shucks and are buoyed to the surface.

When the emergers reach the surface, their wings are folded in a mass (like a neatly folded tent) on top of their thoracic structure. After what seems like an eternity (from 30 seconds to several minutes), the wings unfold and the

E. *doddsi,* nymph.

cumbersome ritual of getting airborne begins. Needless to say, the whole awkward emergence sequence is tailor-made for the trout who relish them.

When nymphing, concentrate on the calm pockets adjacent to the runs and riffles. Fish your nymphs deep so that they tumble to these spots prior to the hatch or as the activity begins. As the fat emergers pop through the surface film, switch to an emerger pattern. We use two versions of the Compara-emerger for this work. One is tied similar to a wet fly; the other a deerhair emerger with pontoon tails. The across-and-downstream-method, with plenty of imaginative twitches, is killing for this hatch. The upstream cast, followed by a dead-drift float, will also account for smashing rises, especially if the trout are feeding in faster currents.

DUN

The duns of these species are very popular with Western fly-fishermen as they bring large fish to the surface when they hatch in good number. They are big and plump and will entice trout even when the water is still high from the mid-summer snow melts. On spring creeks, which are usually not affected by the runoff, these species create an excitement which parallels the Hexagenia *limbata* madness in the Midwest and the Ephemera *guttulata* hysteria of the East. Consequently, Westerners refer to these duns as the "Green Drakes," which is the exact term used by Eastern anglers for the E. *guttulata* subimagoes.

Although *grandis* is given credit for this excitment, our initial studies and photographs show that the emergence of the *glacialis* and *doddsi* duns overlap those of *grandis* and that all of these duns are similar in size, color, and emer-

E. *glacialis*, female dun

gence characteristics. Our studies on these Western species indicate that there is still much to learn. We look forward to future projects in the West with great enthusiasm and believe that many new challenges and discoveries regarding the whole order of Ephemeroptera lie within the geological wonders of this overwhelming Western territory.

The *glacialis* duns have a dark greenish-brown body and slate gray wings as compared to the more brilliant green body of the *grandis* duns.

When the water temperature hovers around the 50°F mark, initial hatching activity will usually take place. If the river is too high and turbid during this earlier action, the trout may ignore the floating duns. By the time the temperature climbs to between 55° and 60° F the streams should be quite clear and fishable and the hatches of these large olive flies should be at their peak.

The *grandis*, *glacialis* and *doddsi* hatches overlap in that order. This lapped hatching activity (from the first showing of the *grandis* mayflies until the last dwindling duns of-*doddsi* are exhausted) usually lasts from 3 to 4 weeks on streams which have populations of all three types.

During the first week of emergence, the duns usually hatch at midday; between 11:30 A.M. and 2:30 P.M. As the water returns to its normal, clear state (after the runnoff) and its temperature climbs to between 55 and 60°F, hatching will normally be delayed until late afternoon when the last hatches take place between early evening and dusk. On cloudy days, hatching may occur sporadically throughout the afternoon.

The duns usually emerge in quiet eddies adjacent to fast-water stretches. They take so long to unfold their wings and take off that their distribution may be all over the river, especially during a heavy hatch. During a sparse hatch, however, it pays to seek out pockets or sloughs within the rapid-water sections where most of the duns hatch. The trout lurk here and make an easy meal of the awkward duns. We have timed individual emergences of these duns at up to 3 or 4 minutes when the water was between 50 and 55°F. This performance did improve, however, when the water temperature reached 60° F.

One season, in mid-July, I boulder-hopped a treacherous stretch of the Madison where it roared through a canyon below Hebgen Lake. There were a small number of caddisflies emerging and ovipositing plus a few Pteronarcys *californica* stoneflies (Salmon Fly) hatching here and there. We were not expecting any mayfly activity since seine tests an hour before had indicated only small, immature populations of late-season Ephemerellas, some Epeorus and scattered Heptagenia mayflies. So we decided to relax and log in some wonderful fishing time. Although there were very few rises, I managed to coax a half-dozen rainbows up to 16" to my caddis and stonefly imitations.

The fast water was tiring against my body and as I rested, my attention was drawn to the abstract shapes and colors that the fading light created on the awesome canyon walls. When I snapped back to reality, I made my way upriver to join Bob and John Hicks who hails from Chicago and had joined our Western expedition at Big Timber, Montana. His little V-W camper served as our satellite vehicle and it got us into some tight areas that the enormous 31-foot motor home we had rented could never go. A retired airline pilot, John developed a rare interest in entomology at the young age of 64.

When I approached the flat rock where they were sitting it was too dark for any further casting and I, too, flopped down beside them and started to disassemble my gear. Bob explained that while I was gone a sparse hatch of *glacialis* mayflies had developed in the lee of an island which split the Madison in two about 50 yards upstream from where we sat. Apparently we had overlooked this patch of calm when we made our tests earlier. The hatch lasted less than an hour, but John and Bob managed to split our normal duties of pattern evaluation. Bob scored well with nymph and

Al discusses mayflies on the Madison with John Hicks, our 64-year old convert to fishing the hatches.

emerger patterns using the dead-drift approach at the very edge of the current and a twitching return in the calmer water. John didn't fare nearly as well with the hackled imitations.

I performed autopsies on the two trout Bob had killed for this purpose and on a rainbow from the lower water which I kept for the same reason. We examined the stomach contents and found that Bob's fish were stuffed with nymphs and partially emerged duns (those with their wings still collapsed). My fish had a variety of caddis, two large Pteronarcys stoneflies and several *glacialis* duns. When we analyzed what had happened it was all very logical. Due to the lengthy emergence of the *glacialis* nymphs, most had floated slowly out of the calm water before they popped through the film as subimagoes. Hence, the trout who were drawn to the pool for an easy meal were greedily taking the sluggish nymphs and partially emerged duns before they were whisked through the rapids, downstream.

Popular Western ties for this hatch are the Goofus Bug and the Grey and Grizzly Wulffs. These patterns float well and are used extensively by the fast-water fisherman. Actually the Compara-dun, with or without hackle, is excellent for this rough application. When the duns are hatching in the calm pockets or on quiet flats it is a deadly imitation of the natural which sits flush in the surface film.

SPINNER

The initial spinner flights of these species may occur at midday. As the weather climbs into the 80's and 90's, they will progressively fall later until they occur at dusk.

In August, the spinner flight may take place during midmorning because the evening air temperature is too low and the afternoon temperature too high for effective mating flights.

We witnessed a dusk spinner-flight one evening in July. The spinners gathered in swarms around 8:30 p.m. high above the riffles—it was almost dark when they finally fell spent to the surface. When they floated by obvious trout lies they were gobbled up in good fashion. A spent Compara-spinner is a winner during this action. It should be used for all three species as they are all similar in size, shape and color.

Ephemerella flavilinea

(Subgenus Drunella)

E. *flavilinea* is yet another important mayfly in the Subgenus Drunella.

We found these nymphs in good number on the smaller, more gentle spring creeks such as Armstrong Creek in Livingston, Montana, but the populations were much better on the bigger rivers like the Henry's Fork of the Snake and the Yellowstone River. Our records indicate that they are well distributed on streams of all characteristics. The Yellowstone, Madison, Gallatin and Snake River systems and their connecting rivers are some of the streams that seem to have good populations of this insect. As described in other chapters of Western Ephemerella species, the emergence of these insects are dependent on water temperature which is directly linked to the erratic and complicated geological influences acting on each river and stream. The *flavilinea* duns will usually make their showing a week or so after the "big three" (E. *grandis,* E. *glacialis* and E. *doddsi)* mayflies have all but disappeared.

COMMON NAMES: Slate-winged Olive, Dark Slate-winged Olive, Western Slate Olive Dun

SIZE RANGE: 8 to 10 mm

HOOK SIZES:
SURFACE (dry): #12, #14;
SUBSURFACE (wet): #12, #14; std.

IMITATIONS:
NYMPH: Flavilinea Compara-nymph
EMERGER: Flavilinea Compara-emerger, Flavilinea Deerhair emerger
DUN: Blue-winged Olive, Flavilinea Compara-dun, Flavilinea Hackled Compara-dun
SPINNER: Flavilinea Compara-spinner

Left: E *flavilinea* nymph. Notice the similarity to the smaller E. *lata*.

NYMPH

The nymphs of *flavilinea* are typical of the Drunella group. They are almost replicas of the smaller Midwestern Ephemerella *lata* as well as the larger *grandis, glacialis* and *doddsi* Ephemerella nymphs. They are normally fast-water dwellers, as their body characteristics indicate, but they migrate to quieter sections when ready to emerge.

When the nymphs are ready to emerge, the midday water temperature is normally in the 60's and the weather in the 80's and 90's; hence, hatching activity usually takes place between late afternoon and dusk. On cloudy days, hatching may start at midday and continue throughout the afternoon. On exceptionally warm days which carry on through the evening, the angler can expect hatching in the morning.

Prior to and during emergence, anglers should apply the same patterns and technique given for the *grandis, glacialis* and *doddsi* hatches, except that the nymph patterns should be dressed on #14 hook sizes.

DUN

The duns also resemble those of *grandis, glacialis* and *doddsi,* but their bodies are deeper olive and the wings a darker gray. The most noticeable difference, excluding size, is that these duns lack the prominent wing venations and body segmental markings that are quite obvious in the "big three" western species.

These smaller duns get off the water quicker than the larger "big three" because the water and air temperatures are much higher when they hatch; however, they still linger on the stream's surface longer than most Eastern and Midwestern mid-summer mayflies.

The Compara-dun and hackled patterns are both applicable for this hatch. The *flavilinea* duns also resemble their subgeneric Eastern and Midwestern relatives E. *lata,* E. *cornuta,* and E. *attenuata.* So if you don't tie your own flies, store-bought Blue-Winged Olive patterns in size #14 will usually fill the bill when hackled patterns are required.

SPINNER

The spinner-falls of *flavilinea* are typical of their Ephemerella genus and will normally cause great spinner fishing. Seek out the moderate runs directly below riffled sections or the pockets of calm within the rapid water.

When evening air temperature is pleasant (if it does not drop suddenly), the spinner-falls will occur between early evening and twilight and during warmer weather, at dusk. If the air temperature drops suddenly during the evening, which is not uncommon in August in the Rockies, the spinner flights will normally be delayed until the air temperature is ideal the next morning. On cloudy days, the falls may occur during late afternoon.

The imagoes release their eggs en masse, a good distance above the stream, unless they are prematurely blown to the water. The upstream dead-drift method, using a spent spinner pattern is normally the best tactic. If gusts do blow the spinners to the surface before egg-laying, they may struggle to regain their airborne status. When this is the case, anglers may find that a full-hackled pattern is better if it is twitched and fluttered to imitate the vigorous attempts of the imagoes, however, the dead-drift method using a spent spinner is usually best.

GENERAL EMERGENCE:
Follows *glacialis, grandis,* and *doddsi.* Freestone Western rivers: mid-July through August. Limestone or alkaline spring creeks and rivers: July and August.

Ephemerella attenuata
(Subgenus Attenella)

COMMON NAMES: Blue-winged Olive, Tiny Dun Variant

SIZE RANGE: 6 to 8 mm

HOOK SIZES:
SURFACE (dry): #16, #18;
SUBSURFACE (wet): #16; std.

IMITATIONS:
NYMPH: Blue-winged Olive Wet-fly, Attenuata Compara-nymph
EMERGER: Attenuata Deerhair emerger
DUN: Blue-winged Olive, Attenuata Compara-dun, Attenuata Hackled Compara-dun
SPINNER: Attenuata Compara-spinner

Ephemerella *attenuata* belongs to the Subgenus Attenella. Considered an Eastern species, it is generally known as the Blue-Winged Olive, a term borrowed from our British cousins. This same name has been indiscriminately applied to over twenty mayflies species which fall under several unrelated genera causing confusion wherever anglers discuss these hatches.

In recent years, *attenuata* has gained a reputation as a major fishing hatch. It was first introduced to angling circles in 1955 by Ernest Schwiebert in his classic *Matching the Hatch* wherein he labeled *attenuata* as one of the important daytime summer hatches in the East.

In 1969, an updated edition of Art Flick's *Streamside Guide to Naturals and their Imitations* was republished featuring a major chapter on *attenuata*. In it, Art mentions that *attenuata* had always been important on the Schoharie where his research was conducted. Specifically, he said, "This very important fly was left out of the original streamside guide because we could not get it identified. Apparently Dr. Spieth, who did the identification work for me, did not recognize this one, so he did not include it in the collecting record."

Art also goes on to say, "It has a distinct olive body with very dark wings. As the insect is exposed to the air the bright olive color changes to a darker shade. Like the Quill Gordon, this fly emerges underwater and trout seem to feed on it mostly just as it reaches the surface, after having shed its shuck, with the wings still closed."

In regard to the subsurface emergence and color changes, our findings are identical to Mr. Flick's. We also experienced subsurface emergence in our aquariums and the rather quick color change phenomenom. We had some difficulty in photographing the duns before their body color darkened.

Two years later, Doug Swisher and Carl Richards covered *attenuata* in their excellent book, *Selective Trout,* and labeled it as an Eastern superhatch.

We treated *attenuata* as a major species in 1973 when we published *Comparahatch*. Our decision to cover *attenuata* was made on the basis of our aquarium research and stream experience. The fact that the distinguished authors cited above had covered *attenuata* as a major hatch in their respective works, added even more credence to our decision.

During our continuing research after the publication of *Comparahatch,* we discovered the prolific nymph populations of the Ephemerella *cornuta* species (see the separate chapter on this species). To our surprise, the *cornuta*

Art Flick, Master of the Schoharie.

duns closely resembled those of *attenuata* except for the difference in size. Attenuata averages 7 mm (#16 hook size) while cornuta averages 9 mm (#14 hook size). The fact that their hatching seasons overlapped and that their daily emergence periods were practically identical gave us second thoughts about the heavy hatching activity we had previously associated with *attenuata*. These doubts prompted further stream research which revealed that much of the action that we had previously assumed belonged to *attenuata* was instead, accountable to the plentiful *cornuta* species.

In retrospect, we still believe that *attenuata* can be an important hatch on many streams but we would be less than candid if we continued to perpetuate the theory that this species is generally on a par with the more important Ephemerella species; i.e., *subvaria, invaria, cornuta, dorothea, lata, grandis, inermis,* etc.

attenuata hatching activity can be expected in the Poconos from early June until the end of the month. Best emergence in the Catskill and Adirondack regions takes place from mid-June through early July.

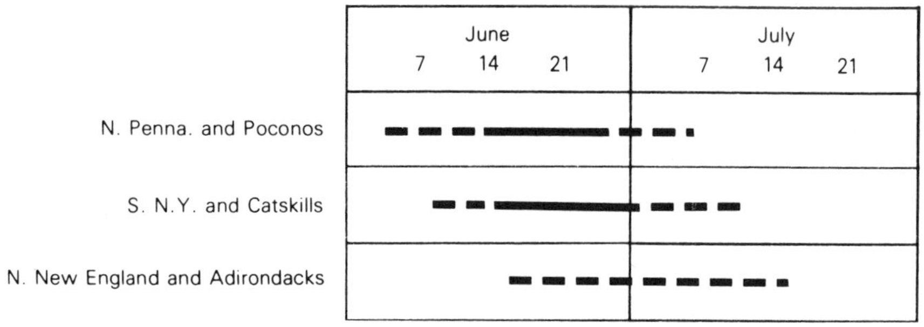

June
7 14 21
July
7 14 21
N. Penna. and Poconos
S. N.Y. and Catskills
N. New England and Adirondacks

NYMPH

Like the early-season Epeorus species, *attenuata* emerges subsurface. The nymph splits its shuck on the stream's bottom and rises to the surface as a dun. Our aquarium studies show that they are buoyed to the surface by gases that are released when the nymph leaves its case.

Autopsies show that trout favor the emerging duns as well as those which are floating. Thus, emerger patterns should be fished to simulate the ascent of the naturals. This pattern should also be tried right in the surface film dead-drift. A few days before emergence, the nymphs become active and congregate in quiet stretches. At this time, a Comparanymph, fished slow and deep may pay off handsomely.

DUN

Hatching usually takes place between 9 A.M. and noon, depending on the water temperature. During hot spells, emergence could take place very early in the morning or at early evening. The freshly hatched duns have slate gray wings and bright olive bodies that turn darker as they are exposed to the air.

During this season, most Eastern anglers are anticipating the exciting afternoon and evening hatches of Stenonema, Isonychia and other Ephemerella mayflies as well as the lingering Ephemera *guttulata* activity. Hence, they arrive at streamside too late for this hatch. Fly-fishermen who arrive at the stream early can catch the *attenuata* hatch in the morning as well as the afternoon and evening action of the others, including their respective spinner-falls.

Anglers must remember that Ephemerella *cornuta* hatches during the same hours as *attenuata* and that the seasonal emergences of both species normally overlap. Their contrasting size and individual emergence characteristics prompt trout to feed selectively on the species that is predominant at the time, so anglers must be extra-observant. The *cornuta* mayflies are normally much more prevalent, so

E. *attenuata*, male dun.

chances are that even if both species are hatching simultaneously, the trout will usually prefer *cornuta*. Unless, of course, the stream has an exceptional *attenuata* population.

On streams having good *attenuata* populations, the trout may feed eagerly on the emerging duns but they are also quite fond of the fully emerged mayflies. The subimagoes drift with the current while they dry their wings. Hot spots

An ideal slow-water *attenuata* emergence site.

for this activity are slow pools and back-waters. Anglers should be alert as fish may be feeding beneath the surface, in the surface film, or right on top. During this period, riseforms will usually indicate on which stage the trout are feeding. When trout are bulging or flashing they are usually taking the ascending duns beneath the surface. The dimple-rise and splash-rise are indications of feeding on top or in the surface film.

On windy days, when duns are being blown about, hackled patterns work well; however we've found the best all-around pattern for this hatch to be the Compara-dun. This hackleless flush-floating pattern with its prominent wing imitates the partially emerged dun and the fully developed mayfly with equal effectiveness. Patterns should be no larger than a #16. Occasionally #18's may be needed. Originally, in *Comparahatch* we also recommended #14's. As explained, this initial recommendation resulted from our confusing the activity of the larger *cornuta* duns with those of *attenuata* during our research for *Comparahatch*.

SPINNER

These glassy-winged, dark-bodied imagoes return to the riffles within a 24-hour period. After mating, the females deposit their eggs over the faster water. The spinner-flights may be inconsequential on most streams as they may compete with the larger, more prolific spinner action of the Isonychia, Epeorus and Stenonema species as well as E. *dorothea* activity. On streams with good *attenuata* populations, that lack this other mayfly activity, the *attenuata* spinners can be important. In any event the Attenuata Compara-spinner, though somewhat darker, is identical in size to the *dorothea* imitation, so, if you want to play the percentages, success could still be obtained by sticking with the *dorothea* imitation.

Family Leptophlebiidae
(The Feeble-legged Crawlers)

There are two genera of mayflies, of importance to the angler, that conform to the scientific criteria of this family. They are Paraleptophlebia and those of the Leptophlebia genus.

We believe that the importance of the Leptophlebia mayflies has been overplayed in angling literature in relationship to its existing populations on prime trout waters and that its status is questionable on the majority of rivers of the modern-day fly-fisherman. On the other hand, the small mayflies of Paraleptophlebia are extremely important to the economy of most trout streams during the early season when their number is highly concentrated, causing trout to feed on them selectively.

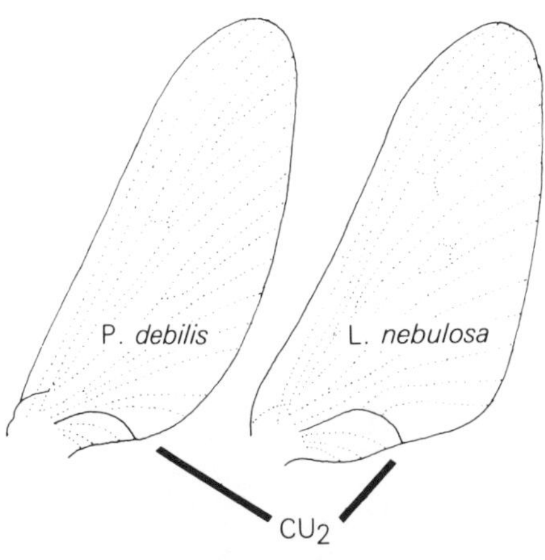

Above: Wings of Paraleptophlebia and Leptoplebia showing in detail the sharply bent course of CU_2 in the forewing.

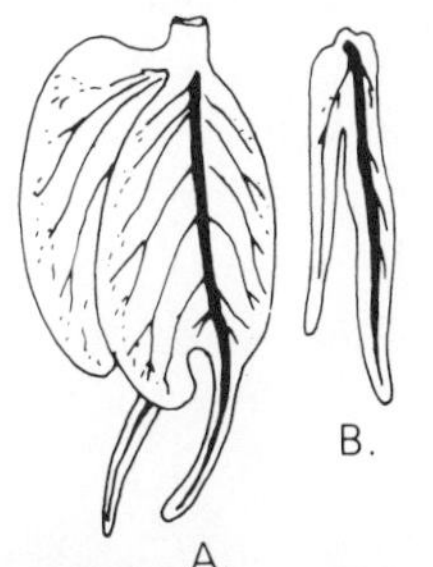

Left; Leptophlebia gills. A, double plate-like gills. Note the long filamentous apical extension stemming from the median trachea. B, the first pair of gills are smaller and are forked; similar to Paraleptophlebia gills. *Right:* Paraleptophlebia gills. All pairs are forked.

Below is a good stretch of medium current, ideal for the Paraleptophlebia hatches.

Genus Paraleptophlebia

The squarish head of a Paraleptophlebia nymph.

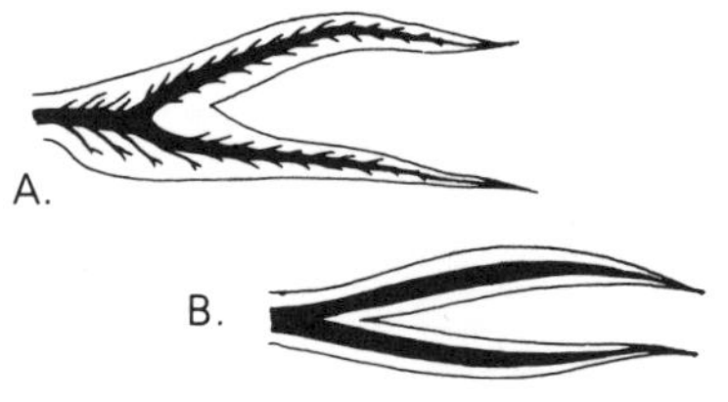

A, Detail of the 4th gill of *adoptiva* with tracheal branches. B, Detail of the 4th gill of *debilis* without tracheal branches.

The smallish mayflies of Paraleptophlebia have a special place in our hearts, especially those of the early-season *adoptiva* species. The heavy April hatches of these delicate creatures are of the first to greet the anxious angler and instill new life into his winter bones. Our memories are bright with their balmy midday hatching in a moody season of forsythia and unexpected afternoon snow flurries.

The general appearance of these nymphs is very similar to Baetis and Pseudocloeon. They are slender, and somewhat streamlined; however, their fragile legs and tails reveal shortcomings in mobility. The heads are squarish-looking when the paired mandibles (jaws) are in their normal position. They are most easily recognized by their size (6 to 8mm long) and their relatively long and delicate "forked" gills.

The nymphs prefer slow-to-moderate water types and their habitat is in leaf-drifts, on sticks and other debris.

Fishermen can easily recognize the duns during a hatch by their size (6-8mm), dark brown or mahogany bodies and pale-to-medium gray wings, which seem solid in color (lacking conspicuous venation or mottling found in other species). Although they may be on the water with the early-season Baetis mayflies, anglers should have little problem in segregating the 3-tailed Paraleptophlebia duns from the 2-tailed duns of Baetis, even regardless of their size similarity. The small hind wings are distinctly ovoid in shape and are easily separated from the minute hind wings of Baetis.

The various species of Paraleptophlebia, thirty-four in all (most from the West Coast and Rockies), start hatching in the early spring and continue through October on most waters throughout the continent, but the most important species to the fly-fisherman are those which bridge the prime mayfly season. Those occurring in late spring and summer must compete with the larger and more abundant mayflies and, generally speaking, they are usually less important. Paraleptophlebia *adoptiva* is extremely important in the East and Midwest during the early-season and we have paid homage to this "king" of the genus by pampering it with an individual chapter.

The sporadic mid-season *mollis* hatches have never been reliable for us as they are usually outclassed by more significant mayfly and caddisfly hatches, but the surprising clouds of their spinners have caused excellent angling for us in the pocket-waters over which they hover and fall in the evening. Although the female spinners conform to the typical coloration of the genus, the male *mollis* spinner looks like an entirely different species. The thorax is very dark, while the abdomen is translucently white.

P. *mollis,* female dun. Note the small, ovoid hind wings.

P. *debilis* nymphs resemble those of *adoptiva* and they are fairly common throughout the East and Midwest. Although most of their hatches occur in the summer, the best occur sporadically during September and October afternoons. If you can locate streams with good populations, be sure to list them in your "little black book" and return when midday water temperature is around 55°F. These September and October hatches (which will occur with those of the late-season Baetis hatches) is a wonderful way to cap the season.

NYMPH

SPECIES	DIST.	SIZE	LATERAL TRACHEAL BRANCHLETS ON GILLS	LATERAL ABDOMINAL SPINES
adoptiva	E, M	7-8	yes	segment 9
debilis	E, M	7-8	no	segments 8, 9
mollis	E, M	7-8	yes	segments 8, 9
**packi*	W	9½-11	no	segments 8, 9
**bicornuta*	W	9-11	yes	segments 8, 9

The general coloration of the nymph is chiefly brown, varying from chocolate brown to amber brown. The legs and tails are generally pale, predominantly amber.

*conspicuous sicklelike tusks

MALE SPINNER

SPECIES	DIST.	SIZE	MIDDLE ABDOMINAL SEGMENTS*	TAIL	GENERAL EMERGENCE PERIOD
adoptiva	E, M	6-8	same color as anterior and posterior	pale smoky brown	early spring
bicornuta	W	9-11	as much brown as white		fall
debilis	E, M, W	6-8	whitish hyaline	whitish	summer-fall
mollis	E, M	6-8	whitish hyaline	white	mid spring-early summer
packi	W	9-11	same color as anterior and posterior	– – –	late summer-early fall

*Females lack the paler middle segments and are of a uniform color.

DUNS

adoptiva: Body: brown. Wings: medium gray. Legs and tails: slightly paler than body.
bicornuta: Body: blackish brown. Wings: dark gray.
debilis: Body: dark brown; middle segments paler than base and apex. Wings: dark gray. Legs and tails: pale.
mollis: similar to *debilis*.
packi: Body: brownish. Largest species in genus.

Paraleptophlebia adoptiva

COMMON NAMES: Blue Quill, Dark Blue Quill, Blue Dun, Iron Blue Dun, Slate-winged Mahogany Dun

SIZE RANGE: 6 to 8 mm

HOOK SIZES:
SURFACE (dry): #16, #18;
SUBSURFACE (wet): #14. #16; std.

IMITATIONS:
NYMPH: Adoptiva Compara-nymph
EMERGER: Adoptiva Deerhair emerger
DUN: Dark Blue Quill, Adoptiva Compara-dun, Adoptiva Hackled Compara-dun
SPINNER: Adoptiva Compara-spinner

One of the season's most interesting but underrated hatches is that of Paraleptophlebia *adoptiva*. This prolific little mayfly is extremely abundant in the East and Midwest and is usually referred to as the Blue Quill, Blue Dun or Slate-wing Mahogany Dun. *adoptiva* emerges in the early-season with peak activity usually concentrated in a five to seven day period at any given geographic location.

This mayfly makes its showing in Southern Appalachia in early April and can also be on the water as late as early June in the Upper Peninsula of Michigan as well as northern Minnesota, Wisconsin and upper New England. Peak emergence in the Poconos and northern Pennsylvania can be expected somewhat earlier. The Catskills are best during the second week in May, while the Adirondacks and northern New England are usually good a week later. The prime hatching activity in the Mio, Grayling, Manistee and Traverse City areas of Michigan and in Northern Wisconsin is between April 25 and May 5, but the northern tips of these states, as well as the Upper Peninsula of Michigan may have this activity until June 1.

Like the early Epeorus flies, water temperature is the key to hatching. When the water has been above 50‘ F. for a few days, the sky will be pocked with thousands of these smallish duns. Once hatching has started, it will usually continue daily even though a sudden cold snap may drop the water temperature back into the low forties again.

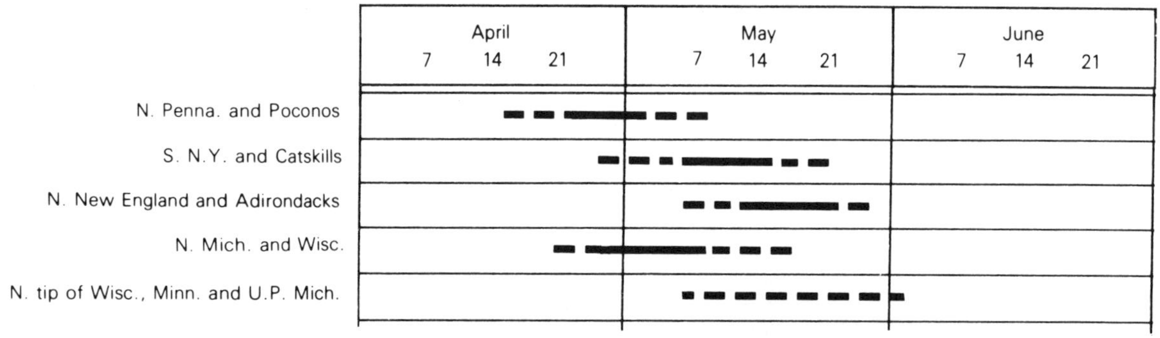

	April 7 14 21	May 7 14 21	June 7 14 21
N. Penna. and Poconos			
S. N.Y. and Catskills			
N. New England and Adirondacks			
N. Mich. and Wisc.			
N. tip of Wisc., Minn. and U.P. Mich.			

NYMPH

adoptiva nymphs, easily identified by their forked gills, are of the feeble-legged crawling variety which usually prefer quieter water such as pools and side currents. They may also be found in eddies of faster water and moderate, gravelly runs. Look for them where detritus has accumulated which serves as an excellent hiding place with a built in food supply.

Although activity may start as early as 10 A.M., hatching usually begins in earnest around eleven and continues well past 2 P.M. with midday being the peak. However, on warm spring days, when water temperature remains favorable, sporadic hatching may take place throughout the afternoon. During the earlier hatches, the emerging nymphs may compete with those of Baetis *vagans* for the trout's favor. This is usually the case in more alkaline waters (those with a ph factor above 7.4) where *vagans* seems to thrive. In more acid or freestone waters, *adoptiva* seems to be the more prevalent of the two.

Over the years, we have accumulated and recorded much data on the relative populations of these two species, and perhaps we should pause here to reflect on a curious aspect of our findings. On streams or stretches of rivers where borderline ph factors exist (7.0-7.4), both the *adoptiva* and *vagans* nymphs prefer the same habitats and compete for the same food supply. Hence, we've found that the establishment of, or foothold gained by, one of these species in a particular stream or stretch of river will usually result in a population decline of the other species. Thus, the declining species are ultimately reduced to something less than a fishing hatch.

When zero hour arrives, the *adoptiva* nymphs swim clumsily to the surface. From the moment they leave their hiding place on the bottom, they are at the complete mercy

A mature *adoptiva* nymph with its feeble legs and tails and its distinctive forked gills.

of the silken currents and eager trout, who love these nymphs, and often show a preference to them over several larger species which might be hatching at this time of year.

The tendency of trout to gorge themselves on these emerging insects make the nymph patterns very deadly. During the first hour of activity, our Compara-nymph, dressed on a heavy wire hook, fished dead-drift through medium runs, slow pockets and side eddies is extremely effective. This type of fishing demands intense concentration and one should strike at the slightest indication of a take. A pause of the leader or a subtle flash in the current is usually the key. Later, when duns are emerging and trout are starting to rise, the same pattern on a fine wire hook, fished dead-drift in the surface film will sometimes score more consistently than if you had switched to a dry-fly.

DUN

During those warm days of early spring, *adoptiva* can be one of the most pleasant, yet demanding hatches of the year as trout can be ultraselective, ignoring patterns larger than a #16. Although sporadic hatching may begin around 11 A.M., the best emergence usually occurs around noon, the warm-

P. *adoptiva,* male dun. The elliptical hind wing is noticeably paler than the fore wings.

est part of the day. Trout should be rising consistently then, and good sport with the dry-fly is at hand.

A good method for fishing this hatch on a medium-sized stream is to select a pool with a moderate current, and take a position near the tail and approximately midstream. This will give you the opportunity to cast to rising trout upstream and to the eddies on both sides. When resting the water above, you will be in perfect position to work the runs and eddies directly downstream, where the cripples are swept.

On larger rivers, the angler must scrutinize the water more carefully to determine which runs or lanes the trout have selected as their feeding stations. In this early, cold-water season, the efficient trout seldom cruise from their lies, and a fly presented a few inches from his feeding lane will usually be ignored. This behavior is typical on larger streams (where the food supply is generally more abundant). This is especially true during a hatch of small flies like *adoptiva* as the trout instinctively senses the futility of chasing such a small mouthful.

In warm weather, the duns struggle to take flight as soon as they reach the surface. At this time, a bushy, hackled fly, fished with timely twitches, is usually very productive. Its impressionistic appearance when manipulated subtly, characterizes the fluttering effort of these duns.

When adverse conditions prevail, and cold temperature retards the delicate subimago's ability to get airborne, the duns will usually ride the currents placidly. Good-sized trout will station themselves in optimum feeding lanes and methodically gorge themselves on these smallish duns. At this time, when bad lighting conditions are common, the Compara-dun is a dynamic imitation. It is easier for the angler to see, and affords a more distinct silhouette for the trout.

SPINNER

A few days after the first hatches, the spinners will make their nuptial flights around midday. The males gather in swarms above the riffles and females dart into the swarms to secure a mate. Copulation and ovipositing follow. They then dip their posteriors into the water time and time again, until the last of their eggs have filtered to the stream's bottom.

Although the subimagoes usually emerge in a one-week period, the spinners are usually on the water for approximately two weeks. Spinner-flights occur progressively later as the hatches wane, until some of the best flights occur toward early evening. Occasionally a heat wave (coupled with a dry spell) may occur in this early part of the season. When this is the case, the spinner-flights will usually occur at or during the morning hours when the air temperature is more conducive to the mating flights.

Fishing the ovipositing spinner and the subsequent spinner-fall can be challenging and productive even at midday if spinner activity takes place when hatching activity is sparse. The heads of pools, white water pockets and medium riffles are the best spots to look for feeding fish during this activity. They sip these imagoes inconspicuously and anglers must be extra-observant to locate a feeding trout. Once a fish is located, a drag-free float over his lair with a flush-floating spinner pattern is almost certain to produce a confident rise followed by an exciting fight in this white water habitat.

Fishing the waning spinner-falls toward evening has proven to be a most economic endeavor. The convenient midday hatches usually subside around 3 or 4 P.M. Before unstringing your rod, consider fishing the waning spinner-falls in that stretch of rapids and pocket-water usually reserved for streamer and bait fishermen. The stream will probably be deserted by this time and you'll have it all to yourself.

These white water pockets demand the respect of a 3x or 4x tippet and a lot of clever maneuvers and scampering to keep your hooked fish upstream. Trying to play a trout that has zoomed below you will almost certainly mean a parted leader. Be prepared to lose half of your hooked fish, as a 12-inch trout in this water is equivalent to a much larger fish in more placid water.

The Compara-spinner is a good representation of the spent swimmer. The same pattern tied with a full hackle and used in a twitching manner imitates the dipping female.

Genus Leptophlebia

This genus was first classified under the old generic key, Blasturus, but has since been integrated and reclassified with the Leptophlebia genus.

The importance of Leptophlebia mayflies is rather questionable as far as the trout angler is concerned. Their environment is not synonomous with the swift-flowing mountain streams and the heavy runs of the high valley rivers nor even the cold-flowing limestone streams that signify "trout" to the fly fisherman.

The Leptophlebia nymphs thrive instead on more sluggish lowland, coastal waters; those between the high country and the tidal rivers, which at one time (before deforestation, urbanization and industrialization) were also prime trout waters; even to the brook trout.

Our stream research and studies in entomology seem to bear this observation out. For example, there are nine species listed in *Mayflies of North and Central America* by Edmunds, Jensen, Berner. Four of these species, those most commonly related to trout fishing, i.e., *cupida, nebulosa, johnsoni* and *pacifica,* were collected and studied by entomologists between 1823 and 1923. *cupida* and *nebulosa,* the most commonly referred to, as far as trout are concerned, were collected between 1823 and 1862, on the Ohio River in Cincinnati. Jay Traver, who conducted her research on this genus in the 1920's and 30's collected her specimens from lowland ponds, lakes and on tributaries of the swamp-like Cape Fear River in North Carolina. The point is, that it's very difficult to conceive of trout fishing on these bottomland or metropolis rivers, where these mayflies thrive or once thrived especially in this day and age.

The general appearance of these nymphs is unique. The most outstanding feature is their gills, which are located on abdominal segments 2 through 7. They are double plate-like, having a feathery appearance caused by a distinctive

A typical flat coastal Leptophlebia stream.

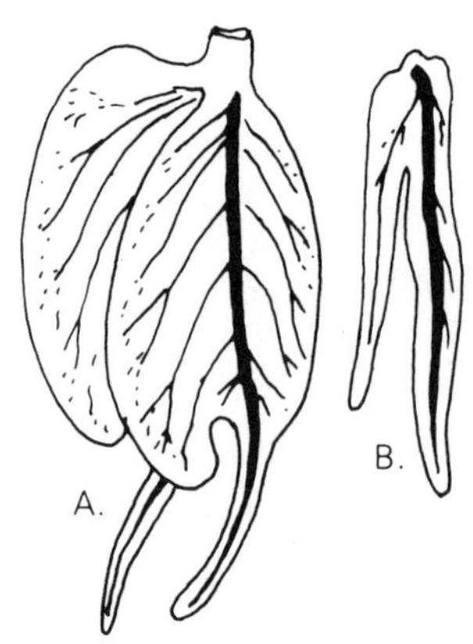

A, Double plate-like gills on segments 2-7. B, single forked gills on segment 1 only.

long, thread-like apical extension on the median tracheal vein of each gill. The first pair of gills on segment 1 is deeply forked as in those of their sister genus, Paraleptophlebia. Like the latter, they lack plumage or fringe hairs on their tails, which are 3 in number and equal in size. The general color of the body is chestnut brown and there are well developed lateral spines on segments 8 and 9. We believe that the double gills reveal the necessity for manufacturing and extracting more oxygen from their still-water habitat.

NYMPH

SPECIES	DIST	SIZE	PECTINATE SPINES BELOW CROWN OF MAXILLA	SPINE ON 8 vs. 9	MISC.
pacifica	W	13-14	5-6	shorter	---
gravastella	W	10-12	---	---	---
cupida	E, M	10-13	6-7	shorter	Almost indistinguishable from *nebulosa*
nebulosa	E, M, W	10-13	10-11	shorter	Almost indistinguishable from *cupida*
johnsoni	E	10-11	---	---	---

MALE SPINNER

SPECIES	DIST.	SIZE	CLOUD ON FOREWING	TAILS	TAIL JOININGS	GENERAL EMERGENCE PERIOD
pacifica	W	13-14	⅔ of tip	brown	obscure	---
cupida	E, M	10-12½	stigmatic area and base	gray	dark brown	mid spring, sporadic through summer
nebulosa	E, M, W	10-12½	⅓ of tip	gray	dark brown	mid spring
gravastella	W	9-12	stigmatic area	brown	obscure	---
johnsoni	E	9-11	faint in stigmatic area	---	bright reddish-brown	---

General coloration of duns is brownish to blackish; wings, dark gray.

Letophlebia species

COMMON NAMES: Black Quill, Whirling Dun, Borcher's Drake

SIZE RANGE: 10 to 13 mm

HOOK SIZES:
SURFACE (dry): #10, #12, #14;
SUBSURFACE (wet): #10, #12; std.

IMITATIONS:
NYMPH: Leptophlebia Compara-nymph
EMERGER: Leptophlebia Deerhair emerger
DUN Black Quill, Whirling Dun, Leptophlebia Compara-dun, Leptophlebia Hackled Compara-dun
SPINNER: Leptophlebia Compara-spinner

As mentioned in the genus section, we have never found these mayflies to be a major hatch of concern to trout fishermen. Several decades of combined diary notes have confirmed only a few hatches of a these species on bonified trout streams.

In our earlier research we have searched relentlessly for populations of these nymphs that would convince us that they could cause major hatching activity. We focused our research on streams in March, April and May when the *cupida* and *nebulosa* nymphs are supposed to be in concentration; i.e., nymphs of these species are reported to travel and migrate in schools. We even designed special underwater nets, fabricated from long-handled landing nets so we could intercept the swimming nymphs in the sluggish, still water that is their environment. When our field trips failed to produce even one nymph from prime trout waters, we concentrated our efforts on the lower reaches of these rivers and finally went into the marginal sections where the bass, pickerel and sunfish dominate.

Although we found an odd nymph here and there on these lower waters, we can say without reservation, that we never found populations of these insects that would cause a significant hatch on legitimate trout waters. The specimen photographs in this book are from the lower Scoharie in the vicinity of the Gilboa Reservoir.

L. *cupida* nymph.

Our failure to find populations of these nymphs is not to say that the Leptophlebia mayflies are not consequential on those coastal or bottom land rivers that walk the tightrope between marginal and legitimate trout streams. Ernie Schwiebert in his intriguing book, *Nymphs,* writes 'The Nissequogue had excellent hatches of these agile swimming nymphs and their imitations are deadly there. The little river holds many memories for me, fishing in April hatches of Leptophlebia with my good friends, Lester Brion and Tony Coe.' The Nissequogue is on Long Island, New York, a stones throw from New York City.

More recently two fly-fishermen from Massachusetts, Phelps Laszlo and Wally Blanchard, wrote an interesting article which was entitled, "The Alewife Fly," that was published in the April, 1974 edition of Fly Fisherman magazine. This article is an informative account of the importance of this hatch on the sluggish coastal Parker River, which the authors claim is really a marginal trout stream that is typical of the Northeast coastal rivers. For those who are fortunate enough to be within proximity of these uncommon, rare streams during April and May, we understand excellent fly-fishing can be experienced to all three stages of these insects. In recent years we have found good population of

L. *cupida,* female spinner.

Leptophlebia on the West Branch of the Delaware and the main river. There were enough insects to cause fishable hatches.

NYMPH

The chestnut-colored nymphs inhabit the slow or slack currents. They clamber and hide in the leaf-drift, silt and rotting sticks and will cling to the skunk cabbage sprouts and eel grass that parallel the banks of the rivers where they reside. Hatching can be expected after the water temperature reaches 55°F. The nymphs are sluggish during emergence which takes place on the surface. When available, they will climb onto vegetation or debris to emerge. Peak emergence usually occurs between midday and 2 p.m., although this will vary in accordance with daily water temperature. Prior to hatching, weighted nymphs are deadly and during their awkward emergence, emerger patterns fished in the surface film dead-drift should account for plenty of action.

DUN

The duns have deep brown-colored bodies (10-13mm) and slate gray wings approximately one mm shorter than their bodies. They can be readily distinguished from similarly colored mayflies by their shorter middle tail. Due to their early-season emergence, the duns of these species, like those of Ephemerella *subvaria*, linger on the surface several minutes, seemingly unperturbed, while the trout gobble them up. Laszlo and Blanchard claim that the trout in the Parker River are extremely finicky to artificials on its mirror-like surfaces. They state in their article that this selectivity had puzzled them for a few years until they read our book, *Comparahatch*, and fashioned a Compara-dun to imitate the darkish subimagoes. We've found that this pattern, as well as the Deerhair emerger pattern, works well on our home rivers in the Delaware system.

The Compara-dun should be tied on #10, or #12 and #14 hooks according to the size of the species that is hatching. The Black Quill and the Whirling Dun are two standard dry-flies that work well for this hatch, but are best when applied to riffled or ruffled water situations.

SPINNER

The spinner flights are typical of the very-early-season mayflies and they occur at-midday. On streams where this action lingers into May, they may occur during the late afternoon.

After copulation, the spinners repeatedly dip their posteriors into the surface film to deposit their eggs. This action can be duplicated by full-hackled spinner patterns, fished downstream in a twitching, enticing manner. On large rivers that hold wild trout spent spinners work best, fished with the dead-drift method.

Families Tricorythidae and Caenidae

(The Tiny Crawlers)

The minute mayflies of these families range from 2 to 7mm, but average around 3-4mm in length and are divided into three genera. They are Tricorythodes, Caenis and Brachycercus. The Tricorythodes mayflies are extremely important to the angler from coast-to-coast; those of Caenis rank second. The significance of the Brachycercus mayflies is questionable. Through the years, our notebooks list little or nothing of their activity on trout streams—our coverage of this genus is given as a convenient cross reference to assist the angler in discerning it from the Tricorythodes and Caenis genera.

The nymphs of the miniature Tricorythidae and Caenidae mayflies resemble the larger Ephemerella nymphs. They are clothed in fine filamentous hairs which collect silt and debris, blending them with their habitat. The enlarged gill-plates or flaps on segment 2 covers the remaining gills on segments 3 through 6.

These insects are among the few mayfly species that hatch, moult in midair, mate and deposit their eggs within a short time period; between one and four hours. They have a single pair of whitish wings, completely lacking hind wings. The only other species, important to the angler, that have single pairs of wings are those of the Pseudocloeon and Cloeon genera, which belong to the swimming family of Baetidae. However, the Pseudocloeon and Cloeon insects have tiny marginal veinlets at the anterior portion of its wings, which are completely lacking in Tricorythodes, Caenis and Brachycercus. Another unusual characteristic of the tiny mayflies of the Tricorythidae and Caenidae family is that the male and female winged stages have the same small-sized compound eyes. These eyes are so small that they are usually about the same size as their ocelli (3 simple eyes), a rarity indeed.

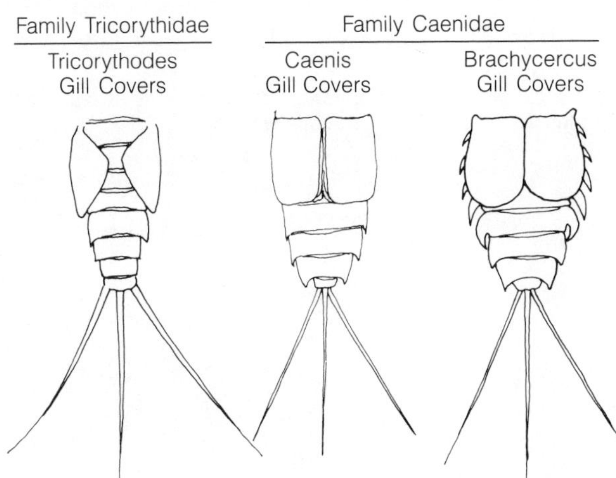

Detail of debris-laden Tricorythodidae nymph.

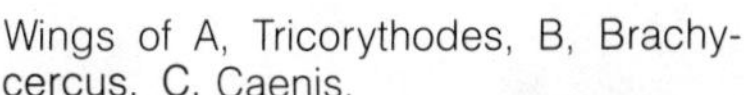

Wings of A, Tricorythodes, B, Brachycercus, C, Caenis.

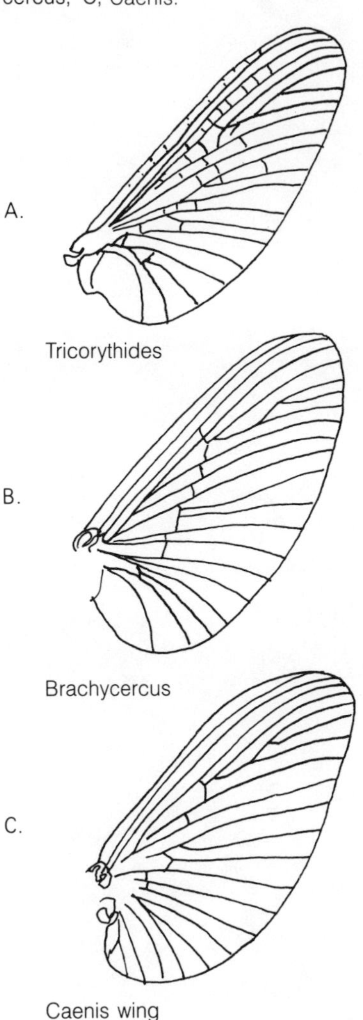

Genus Tricorythodes
(Family Tricorythidae)

Detail of Tricorythodes triangularly shaped gill plates.

The tiny mayflies of Tricorythodes rival those of the phenomenal Ephemerella genus, being widespread and most common throughout North America. They are the most reliable and perhaps the key fly-fishing hatch to the serious late-season angler.

There are 19 species now listed within the genus, eleven more than Needham listed in *Biology of Mayflies* in 1935. All are very similar in appearance to each other and important to the fly-fisher as their requirements for rich, cold water are synonymous with prime trout habitat.

The enlarged gill plates on body segment 2 cover the remaining gills on segments 3 through 6 and are distinctly triangular in shape. This characteristic is the main key in separating Tricorythodes nymphs from those of Caenis and Brachycercus. The three tails are relatively long; longer than the length of the abdomen.

The minute size of the duns and spinners make it difficult to discern the structural differences with the naked eye, but anglers should have little trouble distinguishing them from other genera by their tiny size, blackish bodies, the three light or whitish tails and the singular pair of whitish wings. Under magnification, a blunt pair of tubercules can be seen at the rear of the head. This conclusively separates them from Caenis and Brachycercus.

MALE SPINNER

SPECIES	DIST.	SIZE	FEMORA	THORAX
atratus	E, M	3	light gray	black
stygiatus	E M	3-3½	reddish black	black
fallax	W	5	reddish-brown	blackish-brown
minutus	E, M, W	3-3½	light brown	blackish brown
allectus	E	3½-4	yellow	brown

Identification of individual nymph species unknown. General body coloration of adults is blackish; dun bodies are somewhat paler.

Tricorythodes species

COMMON NAMES: Trico, Caenis Hatch, Tiny White-winged Black, Black Caenis

SIZE RANGE: 3 to 5 mm

HOOK SIZES:
SURFACE (dry): #20, #24, #26; turned-up eyes
SUBSURFACE (wet): #18 wet std. #24, #26; turned-up eyes

IMITATIONS
NYMPH: Tricorythodes Compara-nymph
DUN: Tricorythodes Compara-dun, Tricorythodes Hackled Compara-dun
SPINNER: Tricorythodes Figure 8 Compara-spinner

This chapter describes the extremely important activity associated with the minute mayflies of the Tricorythodes hatch and their relationship to the trout that feed on them.

Tricorythodes activity is not for the occasional angler who ventures forth to the stream, indifferent, with a "bakers dozen" of assorted traditional patterns. It is for the more serious angler who is dissatisfied in wrapping up his season prematurely after the traditional hatches have waned in June. For this serious fly-fisherman, the Tricorythodes hatch is an angling revelation, offering some of the most reliable, challenging and fulfilling angling of the year.

The mayflies of the Tricorythodes genus belong to the Tricorythidae family and those of the Caenis and Brachycercus belong to the Caenidae family. Nymphs of all three genera are quite similar in physical configuration, but most similarities end there.

Brachycercus is predominantly a silt-dweller, preferring lake bottoms and slow marginal trout rivers. Their impact on prime trout water seldom approaches that of the Tricorythodes activity.

Species of the varied and complex true Caenis genus differ with those of Tricorythodes in many ways. The most emphatic difference, as far as angling aspects go, is that, unlike the dependable early morning emergence of Tricorythodes, the true Caenis species normally hatch at twilight. Another surprising difference is that some very important species of Caenis are even smaller than the average Tricorythodes naturals (as small as 2mm), making them impractical to imitate on even the smallest hooks available today.

On streams where the Tricorythodes thrive, awesome hatches of these minute mayflies occur daily without fail from late June thru October. Hatching may also continue through November in milder zones where killing frosts hit later in the season.

The East is blessed with streams rich with Tricorythodes, from the Maritime Provinces of Canada to the drainages of southern Appalachia. The most famous waters are the pastoral limestone rivers that thread Pennsylvania's legendary Cumberland Valley. Here, magical names like the LeTort, Big Spring, Yellow Breeches and Falling Spring Run, steeped in American fishing lore, rival the English chalk streams of Halford, Skues and Sawyer.

Pennsylvania has many unpublicized waters that approach the celebrated waters of Vince Marinaro and Charlie Fox throughout the commonwealth. Some of our favorites are the little cosmopolitan rivers that flow through the Allentown-Bethlehem-Easton megalopolis. The spring creeks in this Lehigh Valley area offer excellent fishing to the Tricorythodes hatches. Some of the best angling, even to native browns, are well within some of the city's limits. Anglers and ecologists throughout the country should salute the conservation efforts of the embattled fly-fishermen of this area. The results of their efforts in stream conservation are living proof that the trout and his habitat *can* coexist with the urban population sprawl although the tables have turned on the Little Lehigh in Allentown during the last decade.

Western Pennsylvania limestone streams also offer excellent Tricorythodes angling, as do the slower stretches of the famous northern rivers like the Loyalsock and the upper Delaware river. The Paulinskill and the Musconetcong in neighboring New Jersey are also among those that offer good fly-fishing to the Tricorythodes hatch.

The spring creeks of southern New York offer excellent angling to these species as well as do the slower sections of the more rugged Catskill and Adirondack Rivers. New England rivers also offers good Tricorythodes activity; one of which is the fabled Battenkill in Vermont.

The midwest has ideal habitat for Tricorythodes. We believe that the best hatches in the entire country occur in Michigan and Wisconsin. Gigantic Michigan river systems like the Au Sable, Pere Marquette and Manistee support unbelievable populations of these tiny mayflies as do the Wolf, Brule, and Namekagon in Wisconsin. The best fly-fishing to these hatches, however, is usually located in the numerous feeders and branches of these large systems and in the upper third of the main river.

Western anglers in the Rocky Mountain regions and the Pacific coast drainages are also blessed with abundant Tricorythodes populations. Excellent angling to these tiny mayflies can be found in the plentiful, rich alkaline creeks of these regions as well as on the flat stretches of the larger rivers. The Yellowstone River system in Montana and the Henry's Fork of the Snake River in Idaho are excellent examples of large rivers that have good populations of Tricorythodes. The Missouri River in Montana is unsurpassed.

June 7	14	21	July 7	14	21	August 7	14	21	September 7	14	21	October 7	14	21
GENERAL EMERGENCE: On rich streams in the East, Midwest and West, where Tricorythodes thrive, hatching occurs daily from late June through October. On streams in milder zones, hatching may continue through November until killing frost lowers the water temperature.														

Edmunds, Jensen, and Berner, *Mayflies of North and Central America,* list 19 species of Tricorythodes, of which five are important to the trout angler. The most abundant species in the East and the Midwest are *stygiatus* and *atratus. minutus* is the most common species in the West *(fallacina* is considered synonymous with *minutus). fallax* is another important Western species. These Tricorythodes nymphs are almost identical to the naked eye, but closer scrutiny reveals differences in color and markings. As far as angling considerations are concerned, identification of the individual Tricorythodes species seems to be irrelevant.

Tricorythodes nymph. Notice the gills underneath the opened gill plates.

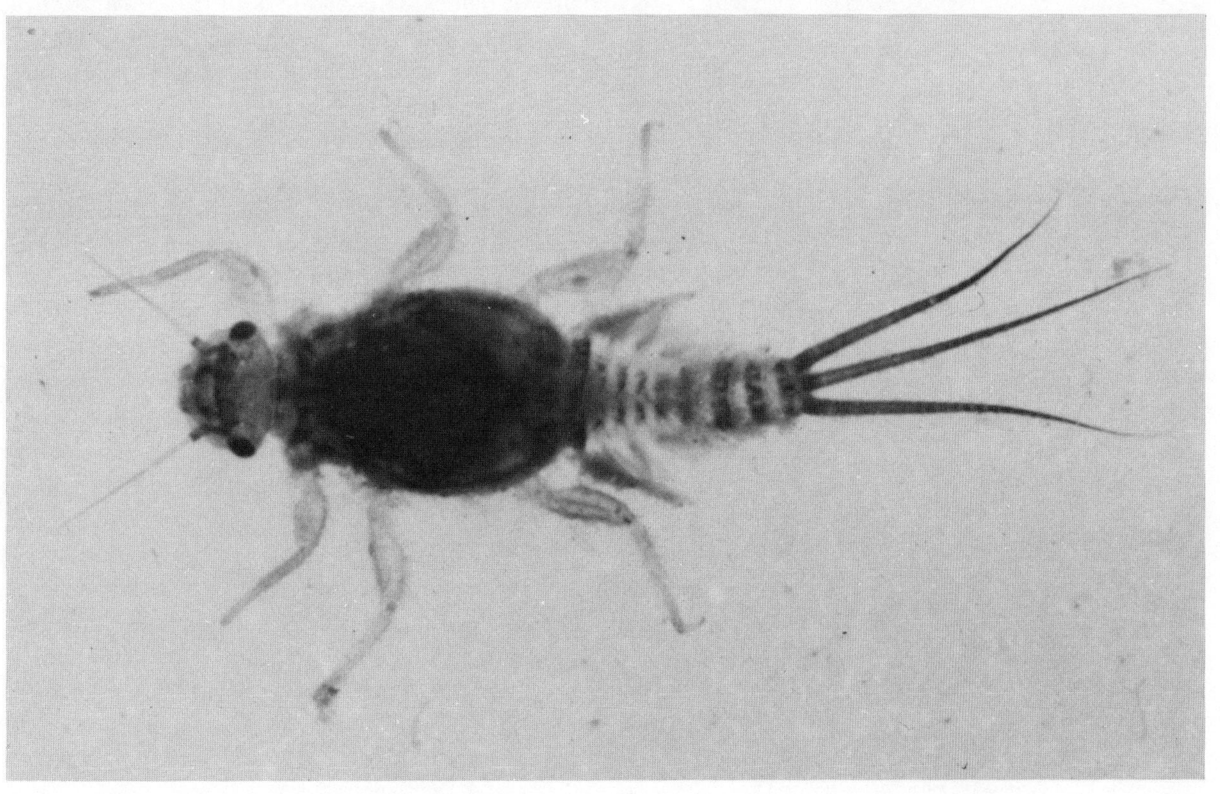

NYMPH

The Tricorythodes nymphs are found in streams of various chemical make-up, but the best populations are found in marl-rich streams that drain limestone areas. These streams are considered alkaline because they have high P.H. factors (normally over 7.5) and they also contain high contents of carbon dioxide (CO_2). The CO^2 is ideal in producing aquatic growth because it combines with the existing lime and calcium to create marl (calcium and magnesium carbonates). The marl then combines with the CO2 again to form the soluble bicarbonates which are so necessary in producing the prolific microaquatic life that the Tricorythodes nymphs require.

These nymphs subsist in the marl-rich silt, sand and gravel of the slow-to-medium currents. More often, we have found that the best populations are located in the subaquatic weed beds of limestone spring streams. The varieties of these underwater plants undulate mysteriously in these gentle, cold currents providing perfect camouflage for the tiny Tricorythodes nymphs, while they forage on the microorganisms that accumulate on the foliage.

Anglers can determine if populations exist on their favorite streams by shaking this foliage gently so that the current sweeps the nymphs into a receptacle such as an aquarium net. However, this check will seldom reveal the density of the populations (whether the members are sufficient to cause a good rise of trout). This factor is best determined by visual stream inspection during the actual spinner activity, which not only reveals the hatching density, but also the associated feeding activity of the trout.

The mature *stygiatus* and *atratus* nymphs range between 3 and 4 mm in body length, while the *minutus* nymphs range between 3 and 3 1/2mm. The brownish coloration of the nymph's bodies usually match their environment. The body and legs are normally covered with fine filamentous hairs, which accumulate specks of debris adding to their camouflage. A convenient key in identifying these Tricorythodes nymphs is the pair of operculate gills on the second abdominal segment which cover the remaining gills on segments 3 through 6. The gill-covers prevent the silt, which is common in their habitat, from smothering the function of the gills. The Brachycercus and Caenis nymphs have similar gill-covers but those of Tricorythodes are triangular in shape, unlike the squarish shape of Brachycercus and Caenis.

During emergence, the nymphs crawl or feebly struggle to the surface, and become easy prey for the trout. Large trout will often feed on them exclusively and autopsies have shown that individual trout may take several thousand of these nymphs during the course of a single hatch. Generally, larger fish will prefer the nymphs to the duns as they normally intercept them more efficiently. Of course, if a trout has an efficient lie adjacent to a current-tongue where the emerging duns are conveniently funneled to his station, the situation would be reversed. Stream-wise browns are instinctively efficient, so the angler must observe the feeding tactics of each fish and determine which stage they are taking before presenting his fly. This observation, and subsequent fishing to only those individuals who are feeding, is a common practice among Tricorythodes fishermen and we feel that this practice is necessary to obtain any degree of success during this hatch.

Few anglers fish the nymph during these hatches. Part of this neglect is traditionally oriented, but more legitimately it is often impractical to float a nymph properly on the smaller Tricorythodes waters that are common throughout the country. The short upstream cast and following natural drift, so essential in successful nymph fishing, becomes impractical on these smaller waters because they are typically low, clear limestone creeks which demand 40- to 50 foot casts with the finest of tippets. As you can imagine, maintaining control or even visual contact with your tiny subsurface fly under these circumstances is very difficult.

Tricorythodes, female dun. Notice the short, stubby forelegs.

Another problem related to nymphing tactics on these smaller creeks is that they are usually choked with aquatic growth and that they have marshy silt banks that telegraph the angler's presence many yards away. So, in most cases, on these smaller creeks, fishing downstream becomes equally impractical. In situations where downstream casting *is* practical, keep low by kneeling a safe distance from the stream while casting.

Standard nymphing tactics become practical again on larger limestone streams with firm bottoms of sand and gravel, because anglers can wade closer to the trout without spooking them. Thus, they can cast a shorter, more controlled line. These ideally large rivers are quite common throughout the country, but are more typically found in the Midwest, where they are typical.

During hatching activity, nymph and emerger patterns should be fished in the surface film, dead-drift, or several inches under the surface. When fishing the nymph upstream, try an indicator which will mark the approximate location of your sunken imitation. This indicator can be a piece of bright spun fur knotted above the bloodknot, where the tippet joins the leader.

DUN

The "tiniest of mayflies" and "the white curse" are terms referred to by Vincent C. Marinaro in his 1969 Outdoor Life article about these minutae which zoomed this important hatch into national focus. In his report, Mr. Marinaro identified these wee ephemerids with the aforementioned British terms and erroneously called them the "Caenis Hatch", instead of the correct Tricorythodes designation. Nevertheless, Mr. Marinaro's accurate account of this activity is accomplished with candor and an intense fervor that conveys his deep feeling for this hatch to the reader.

A #24 Tricorythodes pattern.

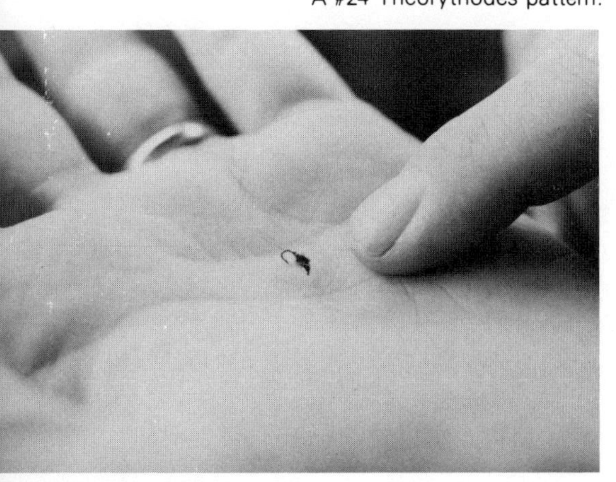

In recent years, this genus has steadily picked up a dedicated following. "Trico" or "Tric" is the term now used on the gentle Pennsylvania limestone waters of Carlisle and Allentown, as well as in the cracker barrel sessions at Harry Darbee's in the Catskills and at Francis Better's Adirondack Sport Shop. The popularity of this hatch is also picking up momentum in the Midwest, the Rockies and on the West Coast.

On large, rich systems, like the Au Sable in Michigan, hatching activity is heavy on the larger main river as well as in the river's upper section and tributaries. The best fishing, however, is in the upper sections where these tiny mayflies have more impact on the trout. The lower river is broader and swifter, so the trout usually hug the bottom eddies, feeding on the plentiful crustations, fish life and larger insect life. The quaint upper sections of the river are more intimate and offer more convenient lies for the trout. They lay poised in these areas beneath undercut banks and deadfalls, where they pick off hundreds of these tiny duns with little effort.

Unlike most mayflies, the male and female duns of Tricorythodes have the same size eyes. The shorter stub-like forelegs and heavier bodies of the females separate them from the more slender males. The darkish bodies of the duns are 3-4mm in length. Their single pair of wings are usually one mm larger and are pale-to-medium gray.

The Tricorythodes emergence season is probably the longest of all mayflies. On streams that hold good populations, the initial hatches may start in late June or in early July and continue, on a daily basis, until late October, especially if the water temperature remains favorable. On Pennsylvania limestone streams, where much of our "Trico" data has been accumulated, the duns hatch between 7:30 A.M. and 8:30 A.M. during July and August when the water temperature is between 52° and 56°F. The emergence periods on these alkaline spring creeks are consistent because the water temperature is stable. On the freestone streams that lack cool spring-heads, hatching may occur earlier in the morning when the ideal water temperature is reached.

In September and October, hatching usually occurs between 8:30 and 11 A.M., again coinciding with the ideal water temperature. During this period, hatching is less concentrated and sporadic hatches of duns may continue for several hours. Take advantage of these crisp autumn mornings, as the trout will normally feed during this sparse activity. Fewer big fish will rise at this time, due to the lack of concentrated spinner falls, but that will not cause the fishing to be less exciting.

According to the air temperature, the subimagoes may transform to spinners within several minutes after they leave the water or they may take several hours to moult. Moulting takes place in midair; thus, capturing the duns and preparing them for photography turned out to be "all work", cancelling out any fishing plans we might have contemplated for that late summer morning.

We selected a favorite limestone stream in the Lehigh Valley area for our photographic session. Bob assembled the camera equipment at streamside in one of the municipal park picnic shelters where electricity was available, while I organized a shuttle system so that the fresh "Trico" duns could be delivered to him for photography. Our recruits for the shuttle system were two good fishing pals; Paul Dickes and Jack Davis, a native of Allentown.

A crystalline Tricorythodes stream.

Around daybreak, I stationed myself in the cold current with a creel full of empty coffee cans, several hundred yards downstream from the shelter, where I knew good populations of duns would emerge. The first score of duns, scooped carefully from the stream's surface, were placed into a dry can and quickly delivered to Bob. Jack guarded the duns in Secret Service fashion as Bob finished setting up the camera. Meanwhile, Paul and I harvested more of the tiny critters from the stream's surface.

When Jack returned 30 minutes later, he shook his head negatively and explained that by the time Bob had the photographic gear arranged, they had moulted into spinners. As Jack eased himself into the stream to assist me, Paul Dickes was already on his way to the picnic shelter with two more cans of fresh duns. And so it went throughout the morning, back and forth, as early strollers stared in disbelief at the strange invasion of their park. The bizarre scene of three grown men armed with strainers and butterfly nets, splashing in their little river while swishing at invisible insects, combined with the equally peculiar sight of another, curled up in a tiny ball, squinting fitfully through a camera, was certainly not a normal occurrence in their neighborhood.

Sometime after the last duns had hatched, anticipating failure, we sulked back to join Bob and cry in our beer. As we stumbled into the shelter, we realized that his swearing and sweating had stopped. Instead, Bob was wearing his familiar victory grin. My spirits were instantly uplifted. He jiggled the Kodak can confidently in front of my nose. He winked nonchalantly and said, "Relax pal, it's in the can!" The sweat that drenched his head and clothing were the only evidence of his nerve-wracking ordeal. His forced blase manner caused us all to break up in uncontrollable laughter. We all went to Jack's for a delayed breakfast and celebrated with a strong pot of coffee.

Correct imitation size is imperative during the "Trico" activity. The duns are best imitated on a #24 hook, but #26's may be more accurate on some streams. Sometimes, #22's will be needed, especially if the water is high or dirty. It pays to capture a natural and to compare it with the imitation you intend to use. Remember, if your fly is just a single mm larger, its size is off by approximately 30%. This would be similar to using a #6 fly when a #14 is required. Leaders should terminate to 7x or 8x, as the ratio of the tippet diameter to the size (mass) of the fly is very critical.

Most of us are very happy with the realistic float that can be obtained when a #14 dry fly is used on a number 5x tippet (which is approximately .006 diameter). The leader seems to have little influence on the fly's floating ability if enough slack is present throughout the leader. The leader's influence on the dry-fly's float increases considerably if the fly size (mass) is reduced to a #24 hook, even if we reduce the tippet to 8x (.004 diameter). The reason is that when we reduce the fly size from a #14 to a #24, the *mass* of the fly is reduced many times over (over 1200%) while the reduction of the tippet from 5x (.006 dia.) to 8x (.004 diameter), reduces the diameter and mass of the tippet by less than *100%*. This lopsided increase of the tippet mass over that of the #24 fly mass creates an unbalanced relationship, causing the leader to have a detrimental influence on the natural buoyancy of the fly. Thus, the fly is now more susceptible to drag or "invisible drag" which is constantly acting on the tippet ("invisible drag" is caused by the galaxy of minicurrents and whirlpools that vary from inch to inch, even on the deceptively smooth currents which are typical on "Trico" water.) Finally, the disproportionately large tippet presses the tiny fly further into the surface film than it normally would. This would not be the case with the #14 fly on the 5x tippet, as the mass of the larger fly is sufficient to offset the influence of the tippet.

To help overcome the problems cited above, we normally refrain from using the Compara-dun during this hatch. Instead, generously hackled patterns are needed to compromise the problems associated with the proportionally larger tippet and "invisible drag". The hackled patterns are automatically skittered across the tiny cross currents when "invisible drag" tugs at the leader. This action is not unlike the struggling antics of the tiny duns who even somersault to get airborne. A hackleless pattern under these circumstances could never duplicate the action of the naturals. The Compara-dun can be effective, however, on mirror-like surfaces or back-waters where there is little or no current to cause "invisible drag".

Another helpful hint in combating "invisible drag", especially in relatively broken current, is to cast upstream and check your line's forward progress so that the leader and tippet fall in snakelike coils. These coils act like shock absorbers, reducing drag to the bare minimum. The old truism about turning your fly over, picture perfect, with a straight leader does not apply here! In fact, it's seldom applicable in dry-fly fishing when a natural float is required.

SPINNER

The Tricorythodes duns usually make their transformation to the imago stage within the hour of their emergence. They often cast their subimago skins in midair. If you look closely, you will see the white nymphal shucks drifting on the stream's surface like chaff. On summer days, this metamorphosis may take place within minutes, because the summer warmth stimulates quick moulting. During these earlier periods of July and August, spinner-falls are extremely concentrated as hatching, moulting, mating and ovipositing must take place quickly before the direct rays of the summer sun become too intense.

Late in September and October, the cooler weather and indirect rays of the autumn sun retard the metamorphosis and the subsequent ovipositing process; hence, the spinner falls become less spectacular and occur sporadically throughout the morning and early afternoon.

Prior to the spinner-fall, the moulting mayflies congregate in swarms (ball-like formations). These formations are attracted to any section of the stream that even resembles a riffle, including tiny side trickles. On large rivers, these swarms are usually along the bank. These early noticeable swarms are generally the males which undulate several feet up and down in unison.

Later, the swarms seem more confused as the females move in. The uniform undulation of the swarms then transforms into disorganized swirls. After mating, the females

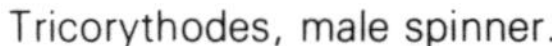

Tricorythodes, male spinner.

progressively lower themselves to the stream's surface, following the course of the river and using the direction of the wind for flight control. At this point, the females land and expel their eggs. Sometimes they will struggle off the water again and repeat the process.

A good Tricorythodes spinner-fall is a spectacular sight to witness. The water will be completely covered with the tiny struggling imagoes. Although miniscular in size, their sheer number prompts excellent feeding from most trout, even very large ones.

When the spinners blanket the surface, the trout are normally very selective. They often develop rhythmic feeding patterns, rising at predictable intervals, efficiently gulping dozens of naturals at one clip. If you are to realize even a glimmer of success at this time, you must anticipate this rhythm and time your casts so that your imitation is among those that will be gobbled up at the trout's next appearance.

Trout that feed in secondary currents, near undercut banks, deadfalls or other obstructions, are more prone to consider individual flies than are those rising in the thick of a spinner-fall. It still pays to observe their feeding traits carefully, however, if your batting average is to increase, as even these trout establish a feeding rhythm.

The streams are usually low and clear when these mayflies are on the water. So, whether you're fishing from the banks of smaller streams, or wading larger rivers, it's imperative that you keep low and stay out of the trout's sight. Crouching, kneeling or hiding behind stream obstacles will reduce the chances of spooking the trout as well as assist you in obtaining close casting positions. Closer casting positions are very important because they reduce the possibility of drag, the angler's worst enemy during this spinner-fall. False casts should be angled away from your target trout. Casts should be fished through so as to reduce the impulse to whip the fly off the water prematurely. Impatience in getting your fly back over the fish immediately after a bad cast or refusal will often cause disastrous surface commotion that will put the fish down. So fish your cast through, it will help you develop the discipline necessary to fool these "Trico"-eaters.

During the sporadic activity in late September and October, the number of feeding fish will taper off somewhat, so anglers should compensate by covering more territory. Walk the stream beats carefully to pinpoint feeding trout. Avoid wasting time by directing your attention to the riffled sections where the spinners congregate in their mating flights. Wise trout will generally hold in the first good hole or eddy below these riffles to feed on the spinners ultimately funneled there. During this late season, also watch for nonresident trout who have strayed from their normal homes to spawn. Fishing for these spawners is a pleasant diversion from the familiar rivalries with the resident trout you have faced so many times before.

We "figure 8" our Compara-spinner hackle to imitate these heavily thoraxed spinners. This is accomplished by separating the hackle with dubbing wound in figure 8 style, which creates a deep "V" splay of hackle for the wings. Jack Davis ties a similar pattern which he says was developed on the Bushkill Creek in Easton, Pa. This pattern is identical except for the addition of a few turns of bleached Peacock quill behind the humped thorax, which is more exacting of the abdominal rear segments of the female spinner. The hackle used for the wings and tails are of exceptionally long fibers (equivalent to a #18 size fly.) We've found that his extra long hackle is advantageous in defeating "invisible drag" and associated problems caused by the tippet-diameter-to-fly-size ratio previously discussed.

We use hooks with "turned up eyes" when dressing these tiny flies, because the larger hook gap accounts for more hooked fish. They also hold fish better as they bite more mouth tissue than do the much smaller-gapped "turned down eyed" hooks. If you must use the latter, be sure to open the gap slightly by bending the hook shank laterally until it makes about a 30' angle with the hook point. This can be accomplished in a few seconds with your finger while the hook is in the vice. After you hone the hook point with a small stone, you'll be ready for one of the most fascinating and challenging aspects of fly-fishing, the "Trico" hatch!

Our good friend, Eric Peper, in the thick of a limestone "Trico" hatch.

Genus Caenis
(Family Caenidae)

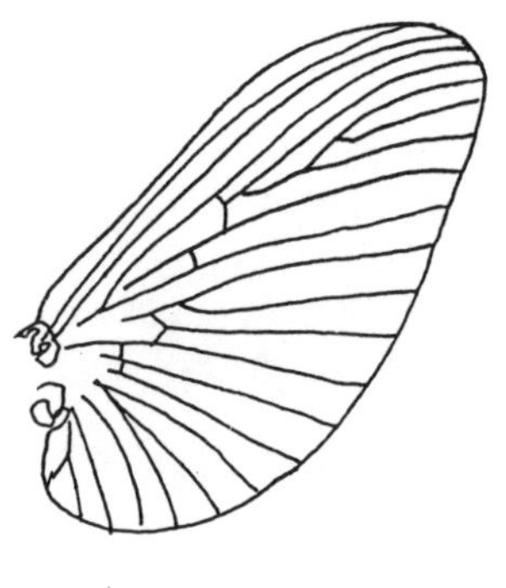

Caenis hilaris wing

We call these mayflies "true Caenis" as their name has been erroneously linked with the Tricorythodes mayflies in the past.

The Caenis species are truly the tiniest of mayflies. Most are much smaller than the minute Tricorythodes species which obviously presents an unprecedented size problem in their imitation.

Geographically widespread throughout the continent, these infinitesimal creatures prefer the back-waters and still pools of trout streams and lakes rather than the cold, constant flow of the rich alkaline streams where Tricorythodes species abound. They can be strained from the muck and silt of lake and pool bottoms as well as from still-water weeds.

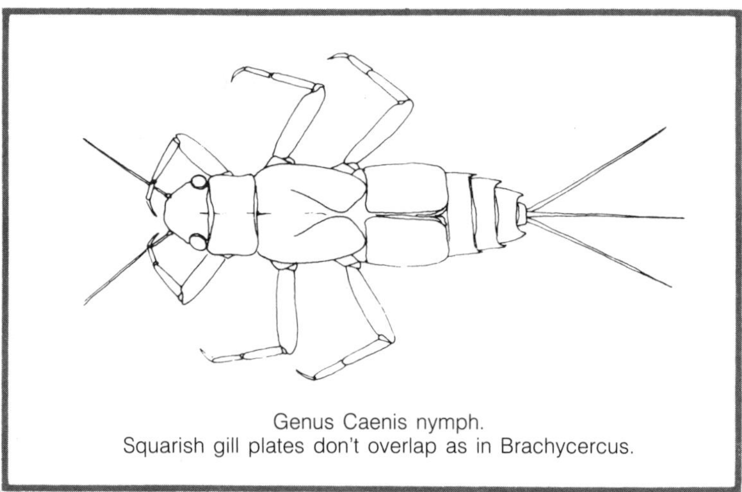

Genus Caenis nymph.
Squarish gill plates don't overlap as in Brachycercus.

The nymphs have "squared" or quadrangular gillplates rather than the triangular covers which describe the Tricorythodes nymphs. They also lack the 3 tubercles which adorn the anterior portion of the head of the Brachycercus nymph. Also, the flattened lateral spines are not upcurved nor sharply toothed as are those of Brachycercus.

The adults of this genus have whitish wings, similar to Tricorythodes and Brachycercus, but their body colors are light (buff to yellow) as compared to the blackish bodies of Tricorythodes adults. The single pair of wings are fairly wide and under magnification it becomes apparent that they have very few cross veins; averaging less than one cross vein to every longitudinal vein, which, in itself, is a very unusual characteristic.

The angling value of these mini-mayflies is usually limited because, unlike the late-season, early morning emergence of the Tricorythodes mayflies on limestone streams, the Caenis mayflies seem to hatch on still-water pools of freestone streams during the prime mayfly season; hence, their importance is overshadowed by the larger mayflies. Our notebooks show only a few cases during June and July evenings when trout fed on C. *amica* and C. *jocosa* selectively due to the lack of other significant insect activity. However, their size was so tiny (2mm) that our #24 Tricorythodes imitations looked like bass bugs in comparison to the naturals; even our 28's were obviously too large.

The important Caenis mayflies usually hatch in June and July, but some hatches will dwindle into early September. The June and July twilight hatches of Caenis coincide with requirements of ideal water temperature for the emerging nymphs coupled with perfect evening air temperatures, which are needed for the brief moulting, mating and egglaying process which follows within the hour. Those dwindling species which hatch in the late-season may emerge and mate during the morning hours. The exasperating problems that confront the angler during this activity are even more tedious than those surrounding Tricorythodes; hence, anglers should use the tactics recommended in the "Tricorythodes Species" chapter as a guide. Listed below are some of the important species found throughout the country.

This is the type of freestone pool where you are likely to see a Caenis hatch.

MALE SPINNER

SPECIES	DIST.	SIZE	REAR OF HEAD	DARK MARK ON REAR FEMORA	TERGITE SUFFUSED WITH BLACK
latipennis	E, W	4	pale	streak	yes
tardata	W	3	black	streak	yes
amica	E	2-2½	black	streak	yes
forcipita	E, M	4	pale	triangular	yes
hilaris	W, M, E	2-2½	pale	streak	no
jocosa	M, E	2½-3	pale	streak	yes
simulans	W, M, E	3½-4	black	streak	yes

Identification of individual nymph species unknown. General coloration of adults are pale yellowish-white with pale whitish wings.

Genus Brachycercus
(Family Caenidae)

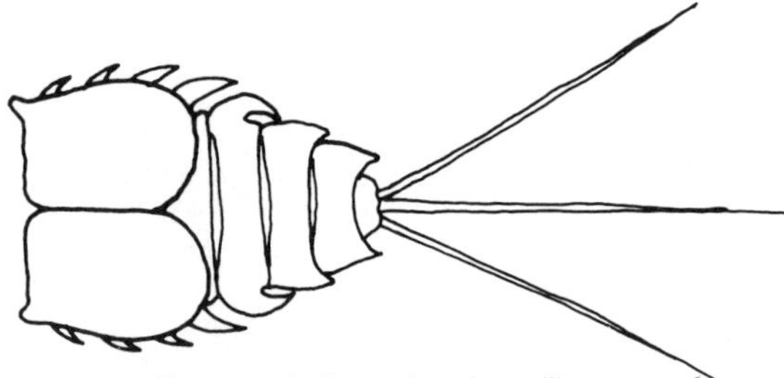
The rounded, overlapping gill covers of the Brachycercus nymph.

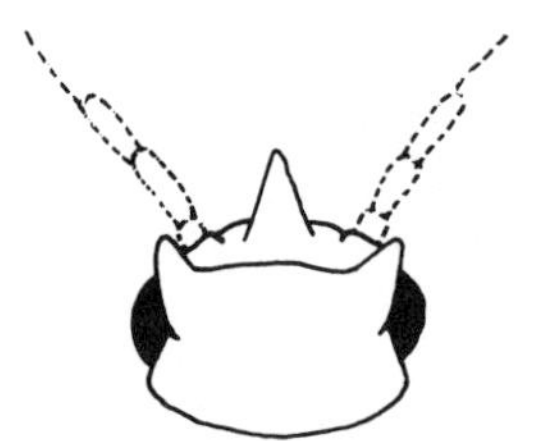
The head of a Brachycercus nymph with its three prominent tubercles.

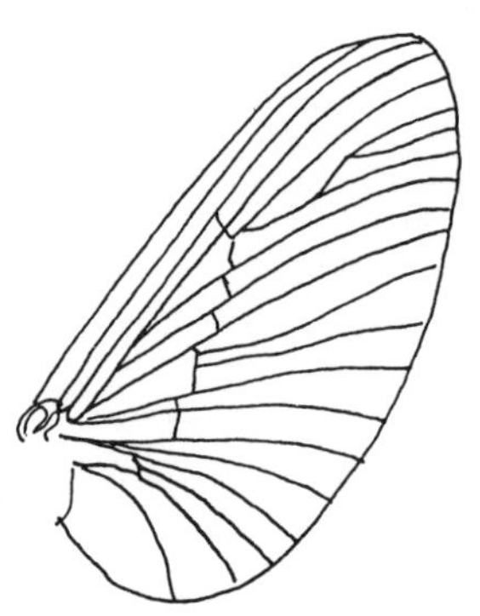
The wing of Brachycercus *lacustris.*

During our stream research we have never encountered important hatches of these insects that would even suggest that they are important to the trout angler. Their lack of importance is also evident in all the angling entomological literature that we have had the pleasure to read.

Of the species listed, *locustris, prudens* and *nitidus* seem to be the species most often mentioned. Reportedly, *lacustris* is found in the East and Midwest, *nitidus'* range is similar, but extends into North Carolina, while *prudens* is a Western species.

The gill plates of these nymphs are arranged on the same body segments as in Tricorythodes and Caenis. These gill covers are different from the triangular and squarish-shaped covers of Tricorythodes and Caenis, being rounded along the outer margins (see sketch). The best distinguishing characteristic, however, is the three obvious tubercles in the front portion of the head—Caenis and Tricorythodes lack these. Their larger size and general shape resemble the smaller Ephemerella species, but their feeble, spindly legs (especially the femora of the skinny forelegs) are more likened to the legs of Paraleptophlebia nymphs.

There are any number of ways to determine the Brachycercus adults from those of Caenis and Tricorythodes, but most of this evaluation usually requires high magnification and does nothing to help the squinting angler at streamside. Generally speaking, however, the adults can be separated from Tricorythodes and Caenis by their larger size (5-7mm), and by their medium to dark brown body color.

When they are important to the fly-fisherman, the angling problems and fishing tactics of Brachycercus parallel those of Tricorythodes; hence, anglers should refer to that chapter for this information.

NYMPH

SPECIES	DIST.	SIZE	LEGS	PRONOTUM
nitidus	E, M	5-6	not banded	2 tubercles
lacustris	E, M	6-7	banded	no tubercles
*prudens**	W	3-3½	---	---

*Nymph not known, but is the only Western species

MALE SPINNER

SPECIES	DIST.	SIZE	MESONOTUM	FORFEMORA	DUN
prudens	W	3-3½	brown	light gray	Body: entirely pale yellowish-white. Wings: pale gray. Legs and tails: Whitish.
nitidus	E, M	5	dark brown	olive-brown	Body: purplish gray-brown. Wings: pale gray. Legs: all have light brown femora and yellowish tibiae. Tails: yellow at base, amber-brown distally.
lacustris	E, M	5-6	medium to dark brown	pale gray tinged with light brown	Body: medium brown. Wings: pale gray. Legs and tails: pale amber to white.

Family Baetiscidae

(Genus Baetisca)

The unimportant family of Baetiscidae has but one genus, Baetisca. Isolated populations may be found in small, medium or large streams, or along the shoreline of lakes where there is sufficient wave action. They are mostly found in a habitat that is of a sand and silt mixture in quiet waters, or in fine gravel of moderate current.

In recent years, our research has turned up very little that would change our original findings in that these insects are uncommon in our cold water fisheries and are unimportant as trout food.

These insects are distributed through the East, Midwest and West, but are more commonly found in the southeastern United States. Chances are, the average angler will never come across this hatch during his lifetime.

The nymphs have a distinctively unique, enlarged thorax which forms a shield covering the entire thorax and abdominal segments 1-6. They also have short tails that are about as long as the visible portion of the abdomin when viewed from above.

The duns and spinners have a stout thorax and a thick abdomen which tapers dramatically from abdominal segments 6-10. It's fore wings have strong long-veins and numerous but almost invisible cross-veins. The rear edge of these wings are always at least slightly scalloped and its hind wings are almost perfectly round. The male imagoes have outer tails four-fifths the length of its body, with the middle tail being very short.

In the Southeast, the emergence of the adults starts in March and extends through early July, with the heaviest concentrations in April. The peak emergence time seems to be between 8:00 A.M. to 11:00 A.M. Species in the northern tier of the United States peak about mid May and June and extend into early July.

The nymphs crawl out of the water to hatch onto most anything protruding from the surface. Mating swarms are commonly five to ten feet above the waters surface.

COMMON NAMES: None

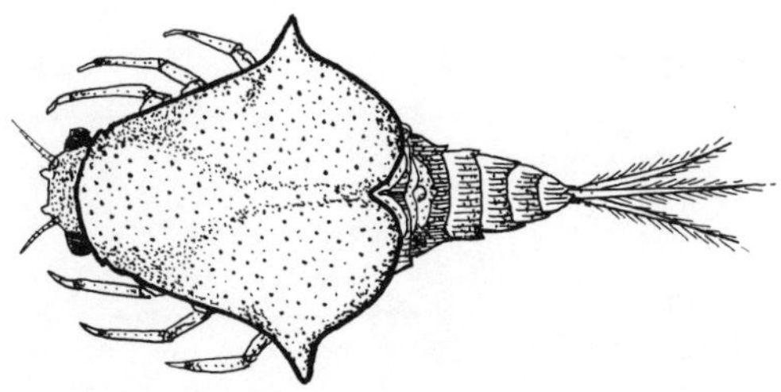

SIZE RANGE: 7-12 mm

HOOK SIZES: #16, #14, #12
GENERAL COLORATIONS: *NYMPHS* are generally olive brown with dark brown freckles and spots. *DUNS* have dark brown bodies with paler legs and tails. Wings are heavily spotted with black and white. *SPINNERS* have dark brown tergites with light brown underbody and legs. Tails are pale with narrow, brown bands.

SPECIES	DIST.	SIZE
obesa	E, M	12-14 mm
laurentina	M	12-14 mm
rogersi	SE	8-10 mm

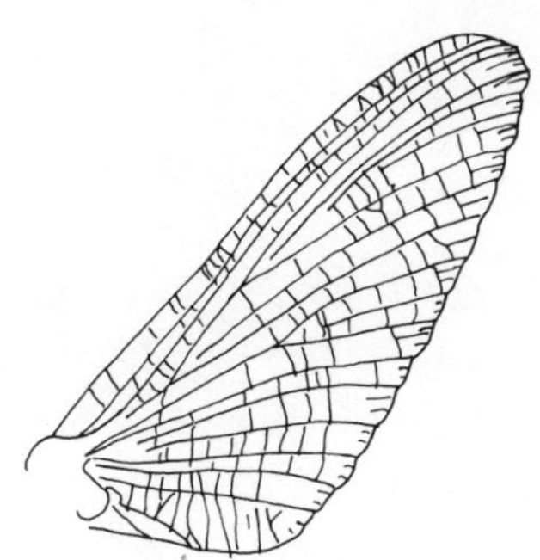

Baetisca forewing

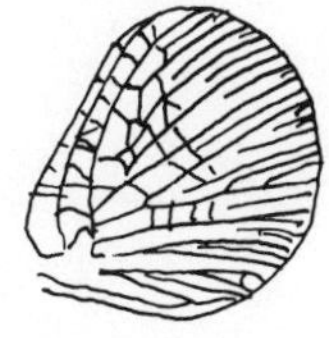

Baetisca hindwing

The Clingers

Family Heptageniidae
(The Fast-water Clingers)

The flattened nymphs of this important rapid-water family consists of five major genera; Epeorus, Stenonema, Stenacron, Heptagenia and Rhithrogena. Two additional genera in this family which are of little value to the trout fisherman in the east, but sometimes important in the west, are Cinygmula and the remote Cinygma.

The two most important genera are Epeorus and Stenonema. The Epeorus species are distributed more thoroughly (from coast to coast) than are the Stenonema varieties which are almost exclusively and Eastern and Midwestern genus. We also found ample populations of the Heptagenia mayflies throughout the country, but never in the number of its two more important sister genera. According to our research, Rithrogena is the least important of the five major genera within the Heptageniidae family. Over the years, we have found little evidence to support the theory that these insects are important in the east.

Our western research has shown more evidence of their importance, but nothing that approaches super hatch status. Western based entomologists and angling writers claim that Rithrogena is extremely important. For this reason, in the Rithrogena chapter, we have included the three species that were most written about.

The nymphs of this family are of the flattened, clinging variety. Their streamlined heads and bodies are designed to deflect the swift currents and riffles where they generally live. The heads are saucer-like and are normally as wide or wider than the thorax. The eyes sit on top and are situated along the lateral edge of the flattened head.

All of the genera of this family have three tails except the

The saucer-like head and clinging configuration of a Heptageniidae nymph.

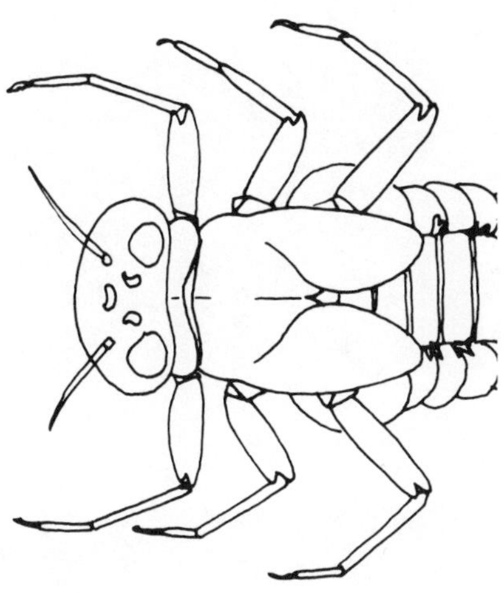

Typical habitat of the fast-water clingers. Look for the nymphs under the rocks in the white rooster tails.

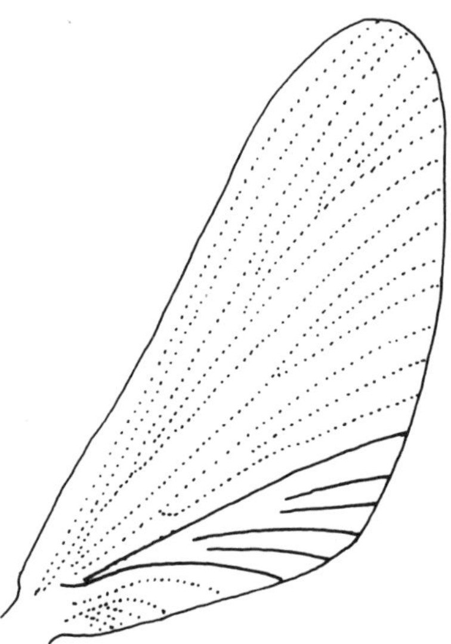

Detail of the four cubital intercalary veins of the forewing.

uniquely two-tailed Epeorus genus. It should be pointed out that the only other species in the entire mayfly order (of importance to the angler) that duplicates this two-tailed characteristic are the nymphs of the Pseudocloeon genus and three species of Baetis; *bicaudatus, propinquus* and *frivolus.*

The gills of all of the genera are plate-like. In Stenonema, gills 1 through 6 are plate-like and, unlike the others, undulate perceptibly (like Ephemerella) while the 7th gill is thread-like. Perhaps the ability of these gills to undulate and thereby extract more oxygen, explains how the Stenonema nymphs have extended their habitat to the quieter sections in addition to the faster currents. On the other hand, Epeorus and Rhithrogena genera have large platelike overlapping gills which act as suction cups, securing them to smooth stones at the bottom of white water rapids. The best place to collect them is right in the rooster tails of partially exposed boulders within the white water torrents.

The two-tailed adults of this family have five freely movable segments in the tarsi of the hind legs and the wings are heavily veined, having four cubital intercalary veins in the forewing. The eyes are large and semispherical in the males.

Genus Stenonema* and Stenacron

The very mention of the word "Stenonema" will most certainly produce reminiscent smiles across our faces. Memories of May browns slashing at fluttering Stenonema duns on long, sparkling Beaverkill and Esopus runs have special meaning to us. This is not to say that these rivers hold a special monopoly on these ideal dry-fly hatches, as we most certainly found excellent populations throughout their Eastern and Midwestern domain. Yet, there is a matrimony between Stenonema flies and Catskill rivers that is as synonymous as ham and eggs.

The Stenonema genus and that of Heptagenia have 34 and 36 species listed respectively. However, this circumstantial link has no relationship to the fact that both genera are very similar in appearance in the nymph and adult stages; many Heptagenia species look almost identical to those of Stenonema at first glance.

Stenonema nymphs can be distinguished from Epeorus by their three large, thick, rigid tails which are like a trade mark; however, these tails are nearly identical in the Heptagenia genus. Further separation from Epeorus and Rhithro-

Stenonema *rubrum*, nymph. Note its wide, flat femora.

*For simplification of this Genus text, both Stenonema and Stenacron are referred to as Stenonema.

Above: Detail of Stenonema's 7th thread-like gill.

Below: Detail of Heptagenia's 7th gill which is similar to gills 1-6

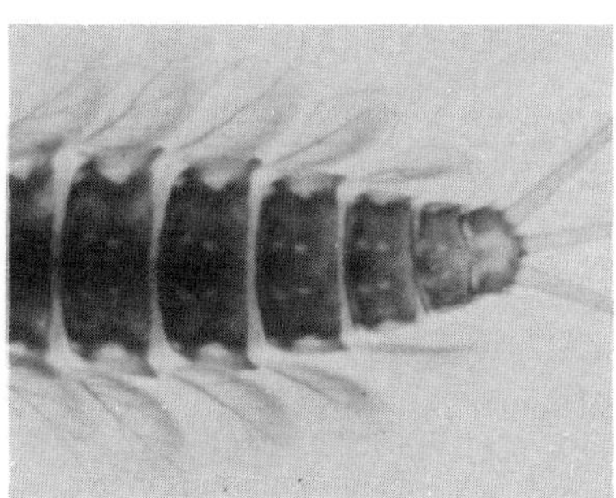

gena are by the gills which are slender, fringed and somewhat plate-like in Stenonema nymphs in comparison to large saucer-like plate gills of Epeorus and Rhithrogena, which act as suction cups on the surfaces to which they fasten. Although Stenonema and Heptagenia nymphs both bear similarly shaped gills on abdominal segments 1-7, the conclusive difference between these nymphs is that the gills on the 7th segment of Stenonema are thread-like. This feature, in most cases, is not readily visible with the naked eye, but, after the angler becomes familiar with the more prolific Stenonema species, he should be able to segregate them from Heptagenia by the subtle differences in their general appearance.

The Heptagenia nymphs are more slender and delicate-looking as compared to the crustacean look of the fatter Stenonema's. Another subtle feature that coincides with the general comparison of the nymphs is that the femora of Stenonema are wider (fatter) than in all the other genera of the family.

Stenonema and Stenacron mayflies are a fascinating group owing to the myriad of species within their genera which differ so in size and color. One peculiarity is the color of their compound eyes. Freshly emerged duns have dark brown or black eyes. However, as the duns are exposed to light, their eyes change to fluorescent colors of blue, green or yellow. This is due to the leaching out of fluorescent pigments located in the eye's interior. In the absence of light, the eyes return to their original color. Our aquarium studies and field expeditions revealed that this phenomenon was evident in most of the many duns handled and it is also common among other Heptigeniidae genera. The large elliptical eyes of the males do not touch (are noncontiguous) as they do in the Epeorus and Rhithrogena genera.

The winged stages of Stenonema have prominent cross veins in the wings, especially in the duns where they appear heavily mottled. We don't recommend identification by wing venation among the Stenonema species, as the venations vary within the species and can be quite confusing. Rather, we advise this separation through the genitalia which are surprisingly distinguishable in both the dun and spinner stages. All Stenonema penes are somewhat "L" shaped and the claspers are four-jointed. This general information concerning the genetalia can be convenient for separating them from other Heptageniidae genera.

GENUS STENACRON (was Interpunctatum group)

These nymphs have no pectinations on their claws. The apexes of their gills are distinctly pointed. The wings of the adult have a black dash at the bulla. The hind wing is dark on the outer margin.

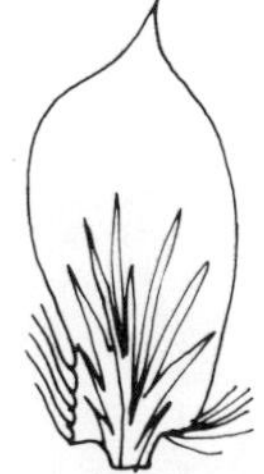

Pointed gills of the Genus Stenacron.

GENUS STENONEMA (was Tripunctatum and Pulchellum groups)

The pectinations in the claws of this genus are variable, but their truncate or rounded gills are quite reliable for identification.

The identifying features of the adults of this genus are variable, see charts below.

Rounded and truncate gills of the Genus Stenonema.

NYMPH

SPECIES	GENUS DESIG-NATION*	SIZE	GENERAL BODY COLOR	GILLS	SPINE 8 vs. 9	MISC.
vicarium	B	14-16	dark reddish-brown with amber	truncate	shorter	Legs and tails often orange. Abdomen: strongly banded.
fuscum	B	12-14	brown with amber	truncate	shorter	Similar to *vicarium,* but brown is more strongly influenced with amber.
ithaca	B	10-12	brown with amber	truncate	longer	Almost indistinguishable from *fuscum.* Usually more amber in color.
canadense (now *interpunctatum canadense)*	A	9-11	brown	pointed	– – –	Tails are more than twice as long as body.

*A, Genus Stenacron; B, Genus Stenonema

MALE SPINNER

SPECIES	SIZE	BODY COLOR	TAILS	DUN
vicarium	14-16	brownish-olive with purplish markings	brownish-gray with dark joinings	Tergites: brown. Sternites: tan. Wings: tan, mottled with dark brown. This is largest Stenonema species.
fuscum	12-14	amber brown above	brownish-gray with brown joinings	Tergites: amber brown. Sternites: yellowish-cream. Wings: pale gray mottled with darker gray.
ithaca	10-12	amber brown above	gray with darker joinings	Barely distinguishable from *fuscum.* Coloration and markings somewhat less intense than *fuscum.*
canadense (now *interpunctatum canadense*)	9-11	pale yellowish-olive with purple marking	pale whitish-yellow	Pale yellowish body with tinge of olive and purple markings. Wings: pale with slightly darker gray mottlings.

Stenonema vicarium

COMMON NAMES: American March Brown, March Brown, Ginger Quill

SIZE RANGE: 14 to 16 mm

HOOK SIZES:
SURFACE (dry): #10; #8; #12, 4x long
SUBSURFACE (wet): #10; #10, 3x long
IMITATIONS:
NYMPH: March Brown Nymph, Vicarium compara-nymph
EMERGER: Emerging March Brown Wet,
Vicarium Deerhair emerger
DUN: American March Brown, Vicarium Compara-dun, Vicarium Hackled
Compara-dun
SPINNER: Vicarium Compara-spinner

Vicarium is the largest and first of several important Stenonema species to emerge on Eastern and Midwestern trout streams. This species is commonly referred to as the March Brown, and is probably one of the most popular mayflies in the East. It is also of local significance on Midwestern waters. Most anglers love this hatch because the naturals usually emerge sporadically all day, providing a leisurely day on the stream. The absence of that pressure associated with the short emergence of early-season midday hatches is a welcome relief.

In the Poconos and northern counties of Pennsylvania, hatching begins in earnest around May 20 and continues to be excellent until June 1. On our home rivers in the Delaware system the flies will start to hatch during mid-May and continue into 2nd week of June. The Catskill region is best between May 24 and June 6 with the Beaverkill reaching its peak around Memorial Day weekend. The Adirondack area and northern New England have an emergence span from June 4 through June 23, with peak activity between June 6 and 17. Best activity on the Adirondack's Ausable is focused on the week encompassing June 10. We uncovered excellent populations of this insect on most Michigan and Wisconsin streams. Hatching and spinner-falls on the Au Sable, Pere Marquett, Manistee rivers as well as the Wolf, Namekagon, Peshtigo and Prairie River systems coincide with the activity on Pennsylvania and New York streams of the Catskill area. The uppermost parts of these states, including Minnesota and the Upper Peninsula of Michigan, should experience hatching activity between the first week in June and the second week in July.

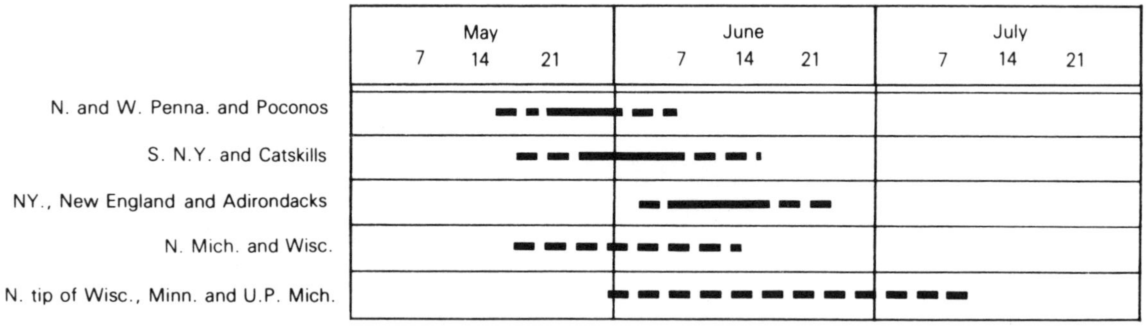

	May 7	May 14	May 21	June 7	June 14	June 21	July 7	July 14	July 21
N. and W. Penna. and Poconos									
S. N.Y. and Catskills									
NY., New England and Adirondacks									
N. Mich. and Wisc.									
N. tip of Wisc., Minn. and U.P. Mich.									

NYMPH

Nymphs of the Stenoema genus are easily recognized. Once the angler has made his initial confirmation, he will seldom mistake them for any other genus. The *vicarium* nymph like the nymphs of the Epeorus, Heptagenia and Rhithrogena genera are of the flattened, clinging variety. Their streamlined heads and bodies are designed to deflect

S. *vicarium,* nymph.

the swift currents of the rapids and riffles in which they live. *vicarium* is readily distinguished by its trademark of three long tails. These thick, rigid tails are approximately the same length as the overall body and are arranged almost 90° to each other, the outer tails being almost perpendicular to the abdomen.

All Stenonema nymphs closely resemble each other in appearance. The primary differences are those of size and color. *vicarium* is the largest of the genus (approximately 16 mm in body length) and is reddish-brown in coloration.

A few days prior to emergence, *vicarium* will usually migrate to pools, quiet eddies and side-rivulets of moderate-to-fast stretches. Examining the undersides of a few medium-sized rocks in ankle-deep water reveals their presence and indicates where the best hatches will take place. Anglers should be as stealthful as possible during these entomological expeditions as trout often lurk in these shallows, feeding on the nymphs.

Prior to emergence, when nymphs are migrating to the shallows or to other advantageous emergence sites, a weighted nymph pattern is potent. It should be fished on the bottom to imitate the swimming and crawling motions of the active nymphs.

During emergence, nymphs labor strenuously in or just under the surface film to escape their chitin shucks, causing a commotion that is irresistible to trout. The nymphs will often drift for long distances offering numerous opportun ities to their hungry predators. During this time a stiff-hackled nymph or emerger pattern, tied on a light wire hook and fished in or just under the surface film, usually provides plenty of action.

DUN

These magnificient duns can be readily identified by their large size and brownish appearance. The wings appear to slant back more than other mayflies; about 45°. Wings, legs and tails are tannish and marked with dark brown. The body is also tan with dark brown segment markings on the abdomen's top side. Species of this genus have three tails as a nymph, but only two in the adult stage.

Many anglers confuse *vicarium* with *fuscum*. This is mainly due to the vague descriptions given in most angling and entomological literature. When these duns are seen side by side they are rather contrasting and one wonders how this confusion ever began. *vicarium* is brownish, having a wing and body length averaging 15mm, while *fuscum* has an amber body with medium-gray, mottled wings averaging 13mm in length. On rare occasions we have collected duns with a dark, grayish look to the wings. Even these however, were much darker than the creamy gray wings of the *fuscum* duns.

On larger rivers, such as the Big Delaware in Pennsylvania and New York, the Beaverkill of New York and Pennsylvania's Penn's Creek, these duns will usually hatch sporadically all day, starting as early as 10 A.M. Smaller streams, like those prevalent in the Poconos, will usually have hatches in the evening after 6 P.M. As far as we can

Left: S. *vicarium,* female dun. *Right:* S. *vicarium,* female spinner.

determine, this variance is due to the more consistent daily water temperature of the larger streams as prompted by their greater volume. On smaller streams with greater fluctuation, nymphs seem to prefer the cooler temperature of late afternoon and early evening for hatching.

During emergence, these awkward duns have great difficulty in getting off the water. They flutter and flit in their attempts, creating disturbances which often incite trout into spectacular rises. Lunkers which were reluctant to rise during the earlier hatches of Epeorus *pleuralis,* Paraleptophlehia *adoptiva,* and Baetis *vagans* will often blast these meaty duns savagely.

This is not the case on very rich rivers that contain wild trout and prolific Ephemerella activity. On such rivers it is more common for wild trout, which are accustomed to dense hatching activity, to ignore the sporadic activity of the *vicarium* duns. This also holds true with other Stenonema and Stenacron species.

A tactic that works well for us during the *vicarium* hatch is to wade the middle of the stream. This offers the option of casting to the deep side while resting the shallow side and vice versa. Often the shallows will out-produce the more inviting deeper spots. Surprisingly, many a reluctant cast to water barely deep enough to cover a fish has resulted in a splashy rise followed by a spectacular fight.

Anglers should not limit themselves to pools during the *vicarium* and *fuscum* hatches. The hapless nymphs and duns have such a bad time clearing the water during emergence that many are swept from their original emergence pools to downstream locations. Look for them in heavy runs and pocket water. Often large trout lurk here (spooked from the pools by high fishing pressure) to pick off the struggling and crippled duns.

The far bank is a good example of *vicarium* habitat just prior to emergence, within migration distance of fast water.

When duns are fluttering in the shallows or are being blown about by the wind, a heavily hackled fly should be used. The American March Brown, originated by Preston Jennings and refined by Ernest G. Schwiebert, is a good imitation.

In recent years we've abandoned most patterns for the Hackled Compara-dun. It has all of the durability of the Compara-dun. The hackle can later be snipped off with a clipper at streamside when a hackleless fly is required. Hackled flies should be twitched intermittently to resemble the efforts of the dun.

SPINNER

Good mating flights start a few days after the first hatches occur. Around dusk, imago males will be seen rising and falling above the riffles, signifying the start of the mating ritual.

The spinner flights are very impressive, even on streams with marginal dun activity, as the sporadic duns which have hatched over several days make their brief, compact appearance as spinners, just prior to dusk. Mating complete, the female dips her posterior into the water time and time again until all of the eggs are deposited. This activity entices even the wisest trout. Ovipositing complete, the female falls spent to the stream's surface, joining her mate who has descended before her.

Unfortunately, the imagoes return to the riffles at a time when the spectacular Ephemerella *guttulata* and Ephemerella *dorothea* duns are hatching from the pools; hence, these spinners play second fiddle to the anglers who crowd to the pools for the more popular *guttulata* (Green Drake) hatches. This is especially true on public waters that receive high fishing pressure. Anglers who are tired of being hassled during this period should give the *vicarium* spinner activity a try in the riffles.

Our testimonial to the productive Stenomena spinner-falls happened one night years ago when our aesthetic senses were turned off while competing with a half-dozen fellow anglers for casting position at a well known *guttulata* pool.

Wanting no part of this, we moved on to a long stretch of riffles and pocket-water nearby that we knew had excellent Stenonema spinner-falls. Our reels screeched loudly that evening until the blackness of night made it unsafe for further wading. We lost count of the fish landed and lost that night on our flush-floating spinner patterns—but the vivid memory of the "16-inch plus" browns that sheared our leaders in the rapids still gives us second thoughts about catching the *guttulata* hatch on a pool when the Stenonema spinners are over the white waters.

For the spinner action we prefer Compara-spinners in spent and full-hackled versions. The full-hackled ones can be twitched to simulate the dipping females and can later be trimmed to represent a flush-floating spent spinner.

Stenonema fuscum

fuscum is the second Stenonema species to emerge following *vicarium* and is considered top-rate by most Eastern anglers. This mayfly is also very important to the Midwestern fly-fisherman. *fuscum* is usually referred to as the Grey Fox or Ginger Quill. The name Grey Fox is usually representative of the dun, while the Ginger Quill tag is associated with the spinner.

fuscum hatches generally follow S. *vicarium* by about a week, but it's not surprising to see a good hatch of both species on the water simultaneously. On some streams, where they are predominant, premature emergence may actually preceed *vicarium*, confusing those anglers who rigidly categorize hatches in chronological order.

Northern Pennsylvania, including the Poconos, has a general emergence span from mid-May to mid-June, but best hatching activity is between May 28 and June 6. The Catskill streams seem to have some of the very best *fuscum* hatches in the country, starting in mid-May and lasting until late June. Peak activity on the Beaverkill system is between June 1 and June 15, while the Schoharie generally produces good hatches until June 20. The Ausable and Saranac Rivers of the Adirondacks are best from June 7 through June 21, while northern New England states are generally good throughout the month of June.

COMMON NAMES: Grey Fox, Sand Drake, Ginger Quill

SIZE RANGE: 12 to 14 mm

HOOK SIZES:
SURFACE (dry): #8, #10;
SUBSURFACE (wet): #10; std. or 3x long

IMITATIONS.
NYMPH: Fuscum Compara-nymph
EMERGER: Fuscum Deerhair emerger
DUN: Grey Fox, Fuscum Compara-dun, Fuscum Hackled Compara-dun
SPINNER: Fuscum Compara-spinner

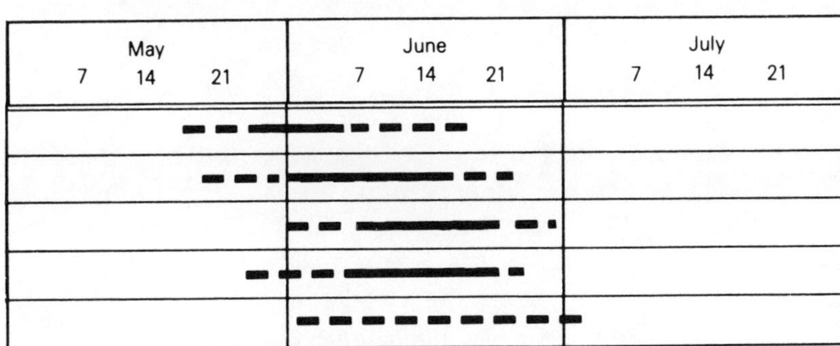

N. Penna. and Poconos
S. N.Y. and Catskills
N. New England and Adirondacks
N. Mich. and Wisc.
N. tip of Wisc., Minn. and U.P. Mich.

We found excellent populations of these insects on most Midwestern waters. The general emergence span starts in late May in more southerly waters and continues until July in the uppermost parts of Michigan and Wisconsin as well as in Minnesota and the Upper Peninsula of Michigan. Best hatching on the Au Sable River and Pere Marquette River in Michigan and on the Wolf River and Prairie Rivers in Wisconsin takes place around the first two weeks in June.

These nymphs, like those of *vicarium*, are of the clinging type whose flattened bodies enable them to withstand the pressure of their fast-water environment. *fuscum* and *vica-*

Left: These turtle-sized rocks are a favorite of Stenonema nymphs just prior to hatching. *Right:* S. *fuscum,* nymph.

rium nymphs are similar in appearance and may cause identification problems for the angler. However, when both species are seen side-by-side, the amber coloring of the *fuscum* nymph becomes contrastingly evident against the reddish-brown cast of the *vicarium* nymph. An important key to identification is that of size; *fuscum* nymphs measure about 13 mm, while *vicarium* averages 16 mm. Both species have the same migratory and emergence habits; hence, angling techniques run parallel. The large size of *fuscum* and *vicarium* and their early spring emergence set them apart from the smaller Stenonema species which hatch later in the summer. Only S. *ithaca* approaches this large size and it emerges after the prime *fuscum* hatches.

A few days before hatching, a great percentage of the nymphs leave the riffles and migrate to slower eddies and side-currents adjacent to their original habitats. It's interesting to note that the Stenonema nymphs crawl during these migrations. They can scurry faster than most nymphs can swim, crawling backwards and sideways with equal speed. When forced to swim, they make awkard attempts with their legs instead of using body undulations so typical of the burrowing, sprawling and swimming mayfly families. Observations in our tanks show that when they are dislodged from their crevices by the current, they prefer to float back to the bottom, motionless, like tiny kites descending softly to the earth on a quiet breeze.

After migration, the nymphs can be found under turtle-sized rocks along the shore. Both *vicarium* and *fuscum* nymphs ordinarily occupy the same rock, giving the angler an opportunity to determine which species will be predominant on any particular stretch. This opportunity also makes identification problems easy by the simple comparison of size and color.

S. *fuscum,* female dun.

During emergence, the nymphs abandon their hiding places beneath these rocks and crawl or struggle to the surface where they make several erratic attempts to break through the surface tension. Trout feed eagerly on these drifting nymphs and properly presented nymph or emerger imitations are deadly at this time. Imitations should be tied on fine wire hooks for floating in or just under the surface film, while heavy wire hooks should be used for subsurface fishing. Imagination should be utilized in simulating the erratic behavior of the emerging and migrating insects.

DUN

On larger streams of the northern tier that have less daily fluctuation of water temperature, these duns emerge sporadically throughout the day. On streams that tend to warm earlier in the season, the naturals usually hatch in the early evening when the water is cooler and continue hatching until dusk. The 42° parallel which separates Pennsylvania and New York seems to be a convenient border for daylight versus evening emergences in this area. However, such generalities should be taken lightly for more major criteria such as altitude and stream origin (spring fed vs. runoff) must be taken into consideration.

The light color and large size of these duns make them simple to detect on the water. Anglers can easily follow their course as they make clumsy attempts to get off the water. These disturbances stir the curiousity of the trout as well as their gastronomical senses. Many trout will cruise and take only those duns that are fluttering. More often, however, stream-wise browns will rise suddenly from their holding position conveniently located under choice feeding lanes in the faster runs.

During this hatch, the emergence activity of the mayfly and the subsequent pursuit of the trout are in plain view, giving the angler a chance to plan his strategy well in advance. When a feeding fish is located, an upstream cast followed by a drag-free float should be tried first, as this disturbs the water least. If the trout is slashing at the more active duns, the angler should simulate the commotion by twitching and skittering his fly. Fly-fishermen should bear in mind that the seemingly inconsequential shallow water along the stream's edge can offer dynamic dry-fly fishing during this hatch. As is the case with *vicarium*, most hatching originates in the shallows of pools and eddies, but many struggling or crippled duns are carried through the faster water downstream.

The Compara-dun is a first-rate imitation for the dun. Its floatability and silhouette makes it a potent deceiver. The Hackled Compara-dun is our choice when excessive twitching is necessary. Throughout the years, the popular pattern for this dun has been the Grey Fox, created by the meticulous angler entomologist, Preston Jennings in the 1920's. It is a proven pattern and will take fish during this hatch.

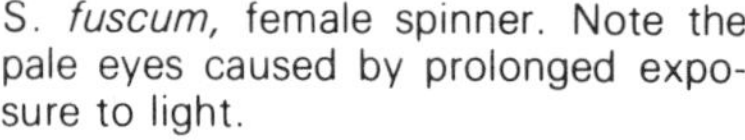

S. *fuscum*, female spinner. Note the pale eyes caused by prolonged exposure to light.

SPINNER

The *fuscum* spinner-falls are very similar to those of *vicarium* and the best falls occur over the riffles and white pocket-water. Before the females show, the males will be seen high above the stream in squadrons like dive bombers, their elongated forelegs extended straight forward while their lengthy imago tails trail, delta-like, behind.

This impressive display is the signal for the fly-fisherman to prepare himself for the exciting and challenging fishing of the spinner-falls to come. Within 20 to 30 minutes, the females will show, copulation will take place and the females will deposit their eggs into the stream with a repeated dipping action. Duty complete, both male and female will fall to the surface, spent, to be swept away or swallowed up by the trout.

When the male imagoes are first sighted in the air, the angler should use his 20-minute grace period to tie on an appropriate spinner pattern and to wade into an advantageous casting position. Good spots are within the white water pockets where productive casts can be made to adjacent pockets and eddies. Another is in the riffles, where the spinner-feeding browns hold behind hidden boulders. Short-line casting is a must during this dusk-to-dark period and final casts will usually be made in darkness when the angler's fly will be sensed rather than sighted. Leaders should be clipped down to 3x or 4x during this action in order to hold the fish in these treacherous pockets. Short casts should be checked so that line and leader fall in snake-like coils to prevent drag.

Those in quest of the spinner fishing should take heed that freestone streams hold no monopoly on the gratifying spinner activity of *fuscum*. We have found this species equally prevalent on smooth limestone waters. The necessary wading tactics are a bit less adventuresome on these waters, but the subsequent spinner activity is no less exciting.

The spinners on these alkiline streams will congregate above the moderate riffles or ruffled stretches between the long pools and silken runs that characterize these waters. As on freestone streams, fly-fishermen should make it a practice to wade into these stretches, among the fish, rather than cast to them from the bank or sidelines. This, of course, will present more opportunities for the angler to cast to more fish while reducing the chances of dragging his fly unnaturally.

When darkness approaches, the trout will sip in the spinners deliberately but inconspicuously, so trained reflexes, similar to those practiced in nymph fishing, must be developed to time the strike and send the hook home. The reel-screaming run of a fat limestone brown during these quiet evening hours can draw the curtain on your day astream on a sweet note.

Spinner patterns in both full and trimmed-hackle versions are our favorites during this action. When trout are slashing at the evasive, dipping spinners, full-hackled and semi-spent patterns should be twitched and skittered. If trout are sipping spent spinners in the surface film, the hackle should be trimmed top and bottom, so that the imitation rides flush in the film. The trimming operation can be performed at streamside with fly-tying scissors or nail clipper.

Stenonema ithaca and Stenacron interpunctatum canadense

COMMON NAMES: Light Cahill, Ginger Quill, Cahill

SIZE RANGE: *ithaca*, 10 to 12 mm; *canadense*, 9 to 11 mm

HOOK SIZES:
SURFACE (dry): *ithaca*, #10, #12; 2x long. *canadense*, #14; #10
SUBSURFACE (wet): *ithaca*, #10, #12; std. *canadense*, #14, #12; std.

IMITATIONS:
NYMPH: Light Stenonema Compara-nymph
EMERGER: Light Stenonema Deerhair emerger
DUN: Light Cahill, Cream Stenonema Compara-dun
SPINNER: Cream Stenonema Compara-spinner

If a coast-to-coast consensus were taken as to the one fly pattern considered to be the most indispensable, the overwhelming choice would no doubt be the Light Cahill. Few patterns have lived up to their advance billing as has this delicate cream-colored fly that represents the dun stage of the *ithaca* and *interpunctatum canadense* (was *canadense*) species as well as those of the late summer minor Stenonema species.

The popularity and success that this hatch enjoys is certainly not due to its abundance on the water, as hatching activity is usually very sporadic. Rather, its stature is primarily due to the lack of competition. The best emergence period for these duns is from the second week of June through early July, well past the peak mayfly activity in the East. Were it not for this timing, *canadense* and *ithaca* hatches would probably be rather inconsequential as compared to the prolific hatches of early-season and the blizzard-like hatches of mid-spring. Such is the case in the Midwest (especially in Michigan and Wisconsin) where the populations of these insects are on par with those of the East. However, due to the overshadowing activity of the more populous species (H. *limbata*, E. *lata*, I. *sadleri* and the Pseudocloen species during June and July), these Stenonema species play a minor role on most of these Midwestern trout streams.

The emergence of *ithaca* follows the peak hatches of S. *fuscum* by about a week or two. Probably everyone, at one time or another, has confused this activity with that of *fuscum* as discrimination between the duns is very difficult with the naked eye. Glancing back, we are quite confident that some of our early diary notes indicating lingering hatches of *fuscum* were in fact the peak activity of *ithaca*.

canadense is the first major Stenacron species to emerge, following the *ithaca* hatches by about a week. We have never witnessed concentrated hatching of this species;

	June 7	June 14	June 21	July 7	July 14	July 21	August 7	August 14	August 21
Northeast									
Midwest and Great Lakes region									

rather, their emergence is sporadic and dwindles into late August along with a variety of minor Stenonema species that closely resemble the *canadense* duns. Generally speaking, we have found them to be more prevalent in the Midwest, while *ithaca* seems to be dominant in the Eastern areas.

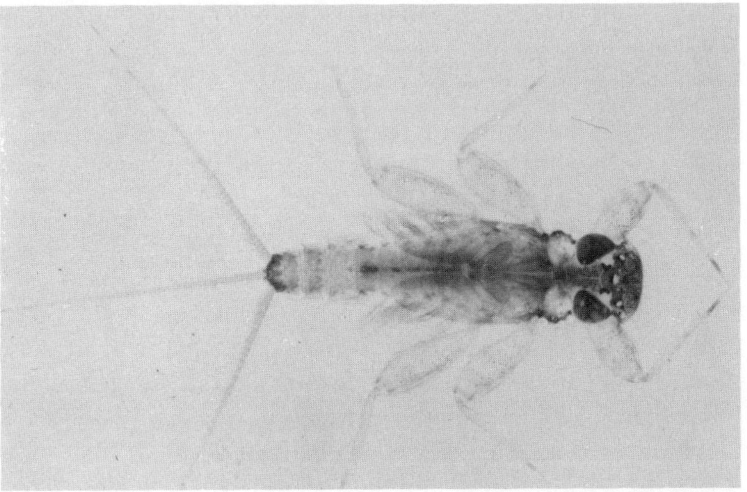

Stenonema *ithaca*, nymph.

NYMPH

The *ithaca* nymphs closely resemble those of *fuscum*, but are 3 to 4 mm (5/32") smaller, the difference of at least a full hook size. They can be separated from the *fuscum* nymphs by their lack of abdominal (tergite) bands on the underbelly. Closer observation will show that *ithaca* nymphs have softly blurred bands on the tibia section of the forelegs, while *fuscum* nymphs lack these bands.

canadense nymphs average slightly smaller than do *ithaca* nymphs, but the best way to distinguish them is by their gill shape and the length of their tails. The gills on abdominal segments 1 thru 6 on *canadense* nymphs are pointed and their tails are extremely long—over twice the length of the body. Stenacron *interpunctatum frontale* (a species of minor importance) is usually found with the *canadense* nymphs and they are almost indistinguishable from them.

Like S. *vicarium* and *fuscum*, the smaller clinging nymphs of the subject species live most of their life in the riffles and runs. Some seek quiet eddies a few days prior to emergence. During emergence, these nymphs swim to the surface and split their shucks much easier than do the other Stenonema species, causing much less commotion.

Prior to emergence, fish nymph patterns deep with occasional twitches to simulate the migratory crawling habits of the naturals. During emergence, imitations should be allowed to drift naturally in the surface film over feeding fish. Patterns should be tied on fine wire hooks to drift in the surface film and heavy wire hooks for bottom-bumping.

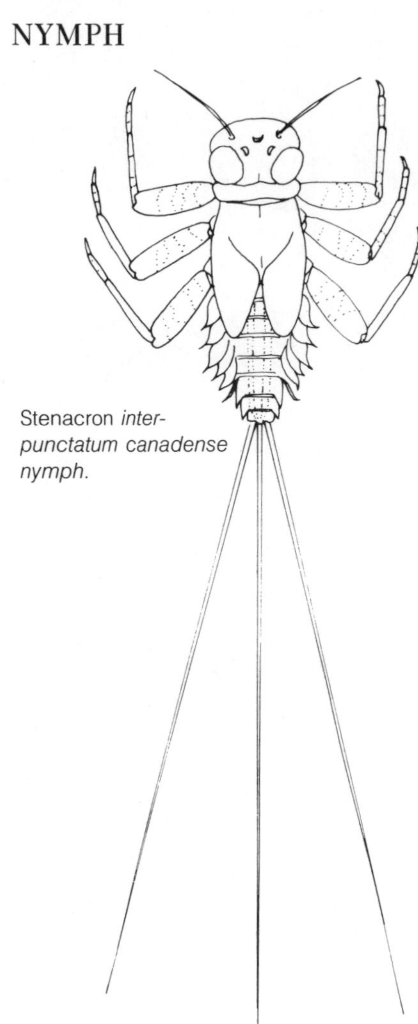

Stenacron *interpunctatum canadense nymph.*

The coloration of the nymphs of these species may vary from stream to stream. However, we seriously doubt the need for exact color imitation for each species. Instead, we recommend that all Stenonema nymphs be tied in only two shades; medium brown and dark brown. *vicarium, fuscum, ithaca,* and *canadense,* as well as the minor Stenonema nymphs, can be imitated in these two shades; sizes #8—#14.

DUN

Daily emergence activity of *canadense* and *ithaca* is usually related to water temperature. On Northern waters that remain cool, or on streams with cold spring-head origins, duns often hatch sporadically throughout the day. On the other hand, streams that warm earlier will usually have more concentrated hatches toward twilight.

During this hot, mid-summer season, anglers should pay special attention to chilly, overcast or rainy days, as inclement weather can drop water temperature sufficiently to produce ideal daytime hatching. Diary records show sporadic morning and aftenoon hatches under these conditions, during which trout fed eagerly. The lack of highly concentrated numbers and the likelihood of several Stenonema species emerging simultaneously, rarely causes trout to be too selective. Thus, even novices oblivious to hatching activity may score heavily with their Light Cahills.

The duns of *ithaca* are almost identical to those of *fuscum.* They do, however, have a tendency to be slightly larger and less intense in color in the darker areas of the wing and the tergite sections of the abdomen.

canadense duns are considerably paler than the *fuscum, vicarium,* and *ithaca* subimagoes. They average 2 mm's less than *ithaca* in wing and body length. The eyes of *canadense* are a purplish-black when freshly emerged. They turn bluish-gray when exposed to light—this feature is also typical in the spinner stage. Like *fuscum,* the freshly hatched duns of *ithaca* and *canadense* are easy to spot on the water, affording the angler the opportunity to observe hatching activity and the feeding characteristics of the trout.

Before takeoff, the duns drift with the current for reasonably long periods, though not as long as those of *fuscum* and *vicarium.* Although trout are fond of the emerging nymphs, they seem to switch over to the duns rather quickly. Records of autopsies taken over the years seem to verify this preference. Apparently, these duns escape their shucks much faster than *do fuscum* or *vicarium,* affording greater opportunity in the dun state.

During these mid-summer hatches the streams are usually low and crystal clear. Favorite side-currents and shallow flats that produced well for the *vicarium* hatch have been reduced to tiny, unfishable trickles—so attention must be turned to the deeper runs and pockets that have now, with the receeding waters, taken on new, secretive personalities.

Trout spook easily during these low-water conditions, so one must wade carefully. Leaders should be tapered to a fine tippet and casting must be accurate. When casting across or downstream, anglers should stay well hidden. After a fish has been raised, hooked, or landed, the water should be rested before casting is resumed.

The famous Light Cahill.

The all-time favorite for this hatch is the beloved Light Cahill. The Cahill was originated by Dan Cahill of Port Jervis, New York and modified by Theodore Gordon. Its present dressing was created by William Chandler on the legendary Neversink. Along with the Compara-duns and Hackled compara-duns, we also like the Light Cahill, but tied with creamish-gray mallard flank feathers instead of the traditional wood duck wing. The gray wing is much more descriptive of the natural and mallard flank feathers are a lot easier to come by these days.

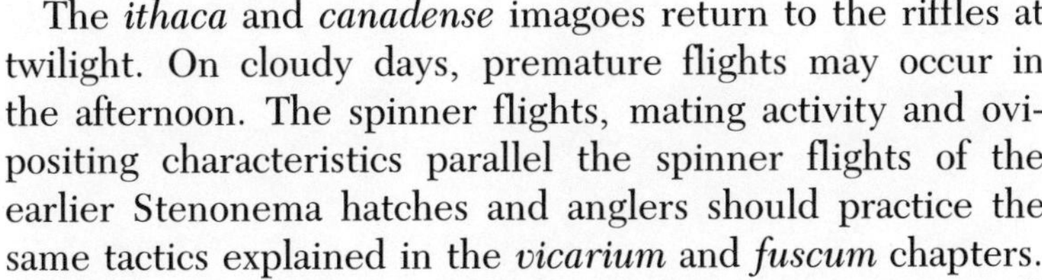

SPINNER

The *ithaca* and *canadense* imagoes return to the riffles at twilight. On cloudy days, premature flights may occur in the afternoon. The spinner flights, mating activity and ovipositing characteristics parallel the spinner flights of the earlier Stenonema hatches and anglers should practice the same tactics explained in the *vicarium* and *fuscum* chapters.

Anglers can expect good spinner-falls through June as well as the early part of July. On Eastern streams, these spinner-falls often account for feeding by nice-sized fish in the riffles and pocket-water. Trout dine on these spinners nightly for the brief 20 to 30 minutes that they fall and the chances for hooking a decent fish at this time are good.

In the Midwest, fishing to these spinner falls is less productive, as the spinner-falls are overshadowed by the awesome Hexagenia and Isonychia activity which occurs simultaneously with the dun emergence and spinner activity of these smaller Stenonema flies.

The Compara-spinner is an excellent imitation when the spinners fall en masse. On those occasions when imago and subimago activity are almost equal, some trout will prefer the spinners and others, the duns. At such times, we compromise with the Compara-dun. It floats flush in the film like a spent or ovipositing spinner and, of course, it resembles the dun perfectly. The durable, light-colored deer hair is also a great indicator of the location of your fly in the waning light.

LATE SEASON MINOR SPECIES OF STENONEMA AND STENACRON

The habits and related fly-fishing data of the key Stenonema and Stenacron species *(vicarium, fuscum, ithaca* and *canadense)* are covered comprehensively in the preceeding chapters. Once this activity has passed, the angler will find that the remaining late-summer Stenonema action will be less concentrated and that the multitude of species that will be hatching should be quite similar. This less concentrated and similar activity rarely causes trout to be selective. Therefore, a compromise in imitation size and color is suggested. We have found that just two nymph patterns (Light and dark Stenonema Compara-nymphs) in sizes #12 and #14 will suffice for all the Stenonema hatches except for the*vicarium* and *fuscum* species, where #8 and

NYMPH

SPECIES	GENUS DESIGNATION	SIZE	HOOK SIZE	GENERAL COLORATION	SECONDARY SHADE	BODY MARKING
nepotellum	Stenonema	9-11	12-14	dark brown	amber or olive	dark mottlings
rubrum	Stenonema	9-11	12-14	dark brown	amber or olive	dark, wide femoral bands
integrum (now *integrum integrum*)	Stenonema	8-10	12-14	dark brown	amber or olive	dark mottlings
luteum	Stenonema	8-10	12-14	dark brown	amber or olive	dark mottlings
pulchellum	Stenonema	8-10	12-14	light brown	olive	very pale
tripunctatum (now *tripunctatum tripunctatum*)	Stenonema	9-11	12-14	dark brown	olive	speckled
heterotarsale (now *interpunctatum heterotarsale*)	Stenacron	9-11	12-14	brown	olive	mid dorsal stripes
interpunctatum (now *interpunctatum interpunctatum*)	Stenacron	9-11	12-14	brown	olive	moderate mottlings

The above table is intended as more of a guide to imitation generalization than to identification.

DUN

SPECIES	GENUS DESIGNATION	SEASON	SIZE	HOOK SIZE	GENERAL COLORATION	SECONDARY SHADE
nepotellum	Stenonema	summer	9-11	12-14	yellow	green
rubrum	Stenonema	summer	9-11	12-14	pale amber	yellow
integrum (now *integrum integrum*)	Stenonema	summer	8-10	12-14	cream-white	amber
luteum	Stenonema	summer	8-10	12-14	pale yellow	green
pulchellum	Stenonema	summer	8-10	12-14	cream-white	greenish-yellow
tripunctatum (now *tripunctatum tripunctatum*)	Stenonema	spring and summer	9-11	12-14	cream	brown
heterotarsale (now *interpunctatum heterotarsale*)	Stenacron	summer	9-11	12-14	pale yellow	green
interpunctatum (now *interpunctatum interpunctatum*)	Stenacron	summer	9-11	12-14	pale yellow	green

The above table is intended as more of a guide to imitation generalization than to identification The wings of these species are generally pale gray or yellowish.

#10 hooks will also be required. The case is similar with dun and spinner patterns.

For the angler who relies on store-bought imitations, the ever-popular Light and Dark Cahills and the Ginger Quill are three time-tested patterns that work well for the dun stage of the Stenonema hatches. As in the case with the nymph imitation, the duns and spinners can also be covered with just four patterns; i.e., Cream Stenonema Compara-dun, Yellow-olive Stenonema Compara-dun, Cream Stenonema Compara-spinner and Yellow-brown Compara-spinner.

Genus Epeorus

The fast-water Epeorus nymphs can be immediately distinguished from all other mayfly nymphs by their unique two tails. As discussed under "Family Heptageniidae", only the tiny mayflies of the Pseudocloeon genus and three small Baetis species have this characteristic. There are many more subtle differences between the Epeorus nymphs and those of its sister genera, but the quick unmistakeable difference is the "two tails".

The obvious gills are plate-like and fanned out from abdominal segments 1 through 7, acting like suction cups. Each gill slightly overlaps the other. The total area that these gills cover is proportionately larger than or equal to the area of the bottom surface of the nymphs abdomen and thorax. Thus, the gills enable the nymphs to maintain their attitude even in the fastest of torrents. When trying to remove these nymphs from the sides of an aquarium or from buckets for photography, most were damaged before we were able to pry them loose until we developed several simple instruments and techniques.

Immature Epeorus nymph.

Another identification characteristic of Epeorus are the heart-like shaped markings in the centers of the femora.

The adults are not as readily distinguishable from their related genera as are the nymphs, but if you know what to look for you should be able to distinguish them easily from other mayflies with the naked eye. The wings in the dun stage are of a solid color ranging from dark to medium gray to light, creamy gray. They lack the mottlings found in the wings of the important Stenonema and Heptagenia mayflies. The basal costal cross veins on the forewing slant upwards and usually the cross veins are less conspicuous than are the longitudinal veins in both the spinner and the dun. The irregular heart-shaped leg band is normally located at the center of each femur. When present on the apical end of the femur they are usually less distinct. When this is the case, the bands are usually found only on the forefemora. The eyes of the males are more rounded than are those of Stenonema. The Epeorus eyes are contiguous (touch or meet) at the top of the male's head.

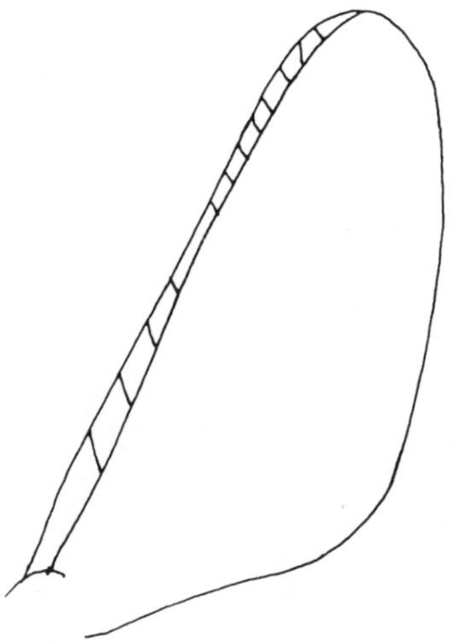

The upward slant of **Epeorus' basal** costal cross-vein.

There are 18 species listed under the Epeorus genus.

In our original publication of *Hatches*, we spelled *vitreus* as *"vitrea."* We picked up this error from George F. Edmunds. *Type Localities of the Ephemeroptera of North America, North of Mexico Vitreus* is also the valid designation for the *humeralis* species.

Another synonymn which has been treated as separate species throughout the years are *fraudator* and *confuscus*. These species are now considered synonymous with *pleuralis* which is given individual treatment in a following

A beautiful stretch of fast-water Epeorus habitat.

Epeorus chapter. Also described in detail are the habitat requirements of these nymphs, their emergence traits, imitations and angling tactics.

MALE SPINNER

SPECIES	DIST.	SIZE	VENATION	DARK MARKS PLEURA	TERGITES 2-7	DUNS
pleuralis	E, M	9-12	dark brown	no	dark brown	Body: yellowish-gray with dark brown tergites. Wings: medium to medium-dark gray.
vitreus	E, M	9-12	whitish	yes	whitish-yellow	Body: pale yellow with tinge of olive. Wings: medium pale gray.
punctatus	E, M	8-9	pale	no	whitish	
rubidus	E, M	8-9½	yellow	yes	whitish	
suffusus	E, M	9-12	pale	no	brown	
albertae	W	9-11	brown	no	grayish	
deceptivus	W	8-10	dark brown	no	brown	
longimanus	W	10-11	light brown	no	brown	

NYMPH

SPECIES	DIST.	SIZE	TEETH ON CLAW	FEMORAL FLANGE	GILLS, 1st PAIR	GENERAL COLOR
vitreus	E, M	10-12	5	sharp	remote	Body: reddish-brown with darker brown speckling. Legs: amber spotted with brown.
deceptivus	W	8-10	---	blunt	remote	---
pleuralis	E, M	9-12	3-4	blunt	approximate meeting	Body: dark brown with amber and olive highlights.
longimanus	W	10-11	3	blunt	meet	---
rubidus	E, M	8-9	5	sharp	remote	---

Epeorus pleuralis

As mentioned in the chapter "Genus Epeorus," due to the newly accepted synonymity among species names, Epeorus *fraudator* and Epeorus *confuscus* is now known only as Epeorus *pleuralis.* This legendary mayfly is on the water during mid-April in southern Pennsylvania and earlier in the less hostile clime of the southern Appalachians. In the Pocono mountains, excellent hatching activity takes place during the week embracing April 23. On the famous Brodhead and Paradise creeks, fantastic dry-fly fishing can be experienced as early as April 13. This also applies to the less famous, but equally productive streams of the Poconos having open public waters. *pleuralis* reaches its peak on New York's Beaverkill system around the second week in May and a little later in the more northern latitudes of New York and New England. According to geographic latitude and related water temperature, Midwestern hatching starts in late April and continues until mid-May. The best activity on Michigan's Au Sable River and Wisconsin's Wolf River occurs during the last week in April and the first week in May. Hatching will continue northward until the third week in May.

The key to hatching activity is water temperature. When the streams register 50°F for a few days in succession, hatching will usually commence. Once started, these mayflies seem to hatch daily in spite of the fickle, unpredictable days of early spring which may drop the water temperature back into the forties overnight.

The Eporus nymphs require fast, pure water with little or no pollution. Streams and feeders exploited by commercial development or dam-building which introduces silt, waste material and detergents usually causes the demise of this important aquatic insect. Generally speaking, good populations of Epeorus are an excellent indicator to the angler that the water quality of his stream is in good shape.

COMMON NAMES: Quill Gordon, Iron Dun

SIZE RANGE 9 to 12 mm

HOOK SIZES:
SURFACE (dry): #10, #12, #14
SUBSURFACE (wet): #10, #12; std.

IMITATIONS:
NYMPH: Dark Epeorus Compara-nymph
EMERGER: Hares Ear Wet, Quill Gordon Wet, Dark Epeorus Compara-emerger
DUN: Quill Gordon, Dark Epeorus Compara-dun, Dark Epeorus Hackled Compara-dun
SPINNER: Dark Epeorus Compara-spinner

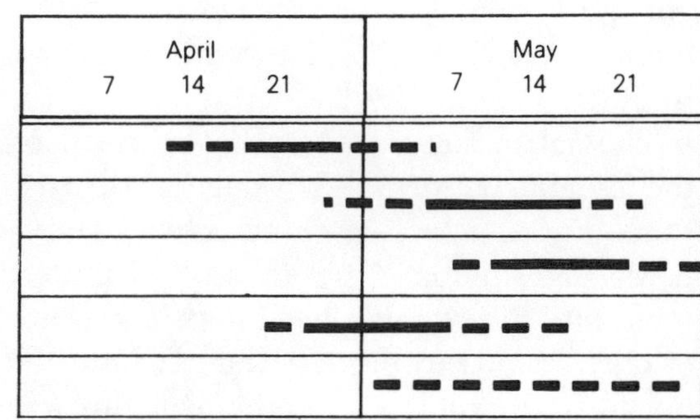

N. and W. Penna. and Poconos
S. N.Y. and Catskills
N. New England and Adirondacks
N. Mich. and Wisc.
N. tip of Wisc., Minn. and U.P. Mich.

The nymphs require vast amounts of oxygen which is generated by rapids, riffles and swift, gravelly runs. They

NYMPH

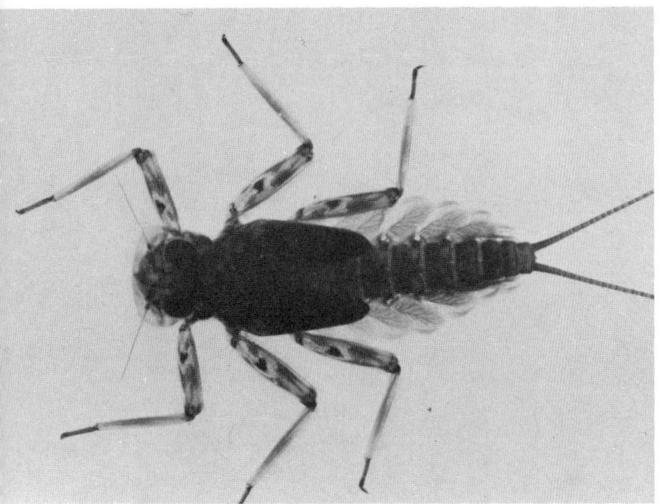

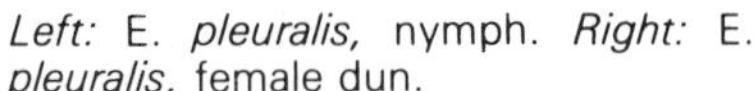

Left: E. *pleuralis,* nymph. *Right:* E. *pleuralis,* female dun.

cling to the bottoms of rocks and boulders, and their flat heads, bodies and disc-like gills enable them to retain their attitude in this turbulent environment.

A unique habit of this species is that they migrate to the downstream sides of rocks and boulders where they congregate a day or so prior to their emergence. At nature's signal, they escape their nymphal shucks on the streambed and rise to the surface. At this time they become quite vulnerable and patterns suggestive of the emerging duns are dynamic! Imitations should be fished to simulate the emerging duns. Cast across and downstream and allow the imitation to drift through feeding lanes. When the current starts to straighten the line, the fly should be pulled off of the bottom to imitate the ascending dun. When duns are being intercepted near or in the surface film, anglers should cast upstream and allow their imitation to float dead-drift to the feeding fish.

The Compara-emerger and the Hares Ear wet-fly are excellent imitations for this work. The Quill Gordon wet is a traditional favorite among early-season anglers and although not quite as imitative or suggestive as those formerly mentioned, it does account for good catches for those who stick by it.

A fine assortment of emerger patterns for the Epeorus subsurface emergence.

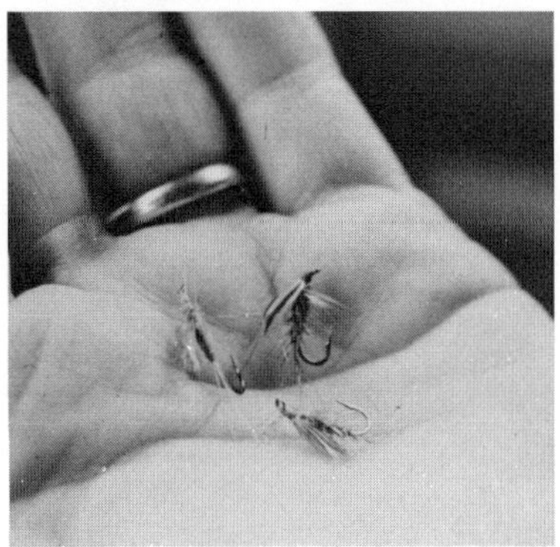

The subsurface emergence of the Epeorus nymphs make the nymph patterns less effective than the emerger imitations during actual hatching activity. However, between 10 A.M. and midday, the nymphs expose themselves while migrating to favorable hatching sites located on the lee side of obstructions in the fast water where they become available to trout who root for them in this area. At the time of this activity, a weighted nymph fished at the base of these hatching sites will often produce exceptional results.

DUN

Once the emerging duns pop through the surface film, they ride the current to dry their smoky-colored wings. These extra seconds of exposure on the stream's surface are enough to entice some nice fish into surface-feeding even though their metabolism may still be low due to the cold water temperature.

Although these subimago flies usually emerge in riffles and pocket-water, special attention should also be given to the heads of pools where duns are helplessly swept through the cascading white water and delivered to the trout in the pools and quiet water below. Even the most lethargic trout will congregate here to pick off the disturbed or crippled duns. Smaller or stocked trout may cruise these pools to intercept the duns, but the larger, stream-wise browns will usually occupy the most efficient lies through which the naturals are funneled; hence, anglers should study trout lies carefully instead of casting blindly. During these exciting moments of early-season dry-fly action, anglers must never delude themselves into thinking it's a duffer's holiday. We've found trout ultraselective in these slow-water stretches during this period offering an early challenge to the angler. Also, the possibility of several species being present on the water together adds to the complexity of the problem.

Al, fishing the head of a pool where the duns were carried down from the fast water above.

On warm spring days, when waters are below normal and clear, the duns dry their wings and are airborne much quicker, causing a more hurried feeding pattern, which may trigger slashing and showy-type rises. One of our favorite imitations for this type of fishing is the famous Quill Gordon in size #10, #12 or #14 tied with a generous amount of hackle. Anglers should not hesitate to twitch or skitter their imitation when it is apparent that the naturals are fluttering on the surface.

The Quill Gordon.

When adverse conditions prevail (which can be the following day), some of the season's best fishing is at your frozen fingertips. At such times, the ardent fly-fisherman has the advantage of having a whole stretch of his favorite stream to himself. The lighting is usually poor and the surface riffled, enabling him to move into advantageous casting positions without spooking the trout. The angler's most significant advantage lies in the inability of the duns to thaw and dry their chilled wing muscles sufficiently to get airborne. The trout, sensing that the helpless duns will not escape its gaping jaws, develops a subtle but deliberate feeding pattern, stuffing himself. At this time a Comparadun, delivered with a precise cast and followed by a dragless float, will usually turn the trick. This fly sticks out like a miniature sailboat, even in the worst of lighting conditions.

Its buoyancy, durability and distinct silhouette make it a killer when trout are rising to placid, floating duns.

Peak emergence is usually between 1 and 2:30 P.M. but on cloudy, cold and drizzly days, hatching usually takes place between 2 and 4 P.M. During unusually hot spells, when the air temperature registers around the 80°F mark, it is not unusual for these mayflies to hatch after 5 P.M. when the water cools.

SPINNER

Around 3 or 4 days after the first hatches occur, the imagoes make their appearance over the riffles. The males are an impressive sight, hovering in squadrons over the riffles. On typical, colder days, the falls generally occur during the warmest part of the day (generally between noon and 2 P.M.). During unusually warm springs (when weather is in the eighties), the spinners will normally return in late afternoon or early evening (between 5 and 7 P.M.).

In recent years we have come to love these spinner-falls. They are surprisingly reliable, producing eye-opening feeding activity during this unpredictable early season.

Anglers should remember that these imagoes mate, oviposit and fall spent in the white pocket-water or heavy runs. Trout lurk in the tiny eddies and mini pools within these torrents and sip the spinners inconspicuously. Hence, excellent feeding may be in progress, but if the angler isn't looking for this activity, chances are he'll by-pass it, completely unaware.

We mentioned in our initial *Comparahatch* volumes that the *pleuralis* spinner activity is "relatively unimportant when the duns are hatching" and "that they do become a principal food source for the trout when subimago activity is scarce." We still believe this to be generally true, but we believe a more detailed explanation is in order.

As explained, the dun activity is best fished from pools and runs located directly below rapid water sections where trout congregate to pick off the duns. When spinner-falls occur along with subimago hatching activity in slower stretches, the trout will usually ignore the spinners and feed on the duns. However, the case would be reversed in white-water sections where spinner activity usually overshadows the availability of the duns.

For this fast-water spinner activity we use the Compara-spinner in spent and semispent versions. Cast these imitations to eddies at the base of boulders and obstructions in these fast pockets and allow them to float drag-free. A full-hackled version is also useful when twitching and skittering are necessary to duplicate the ovipositing females.

Epeorus species

We believe that the most important Eastern and Midwestern Epeorus species (previously called *fraudator)* is *pleuralis,* because it hatches in an ideal season (April through May) and daily time period (midday) which makes them a perfect hatch for the fly-fisherman. We have, therefore, given it special treatment in an individual chapter (see Epeorus *pleuralis).* The remaining species in this unique two-tailed genus emerge in late spring, summer and fall, overlapping in the territories where they reside.

Among the Eastern and Midwestern species, those of *vitreus* loom as omnipresent. During our research in the East, and Midwest we have found their number sufficient to consider them an important angling hatch.

The greatest variety of Epeorus species are reportedly found in the West. However, our intensive seine tests on scores of Montana, Wyoming and Idaho rivers revealed disappointing populations of these nymphs although some did have populations that could approach a fishing hatch. An important factor that must be considered, however, is that almost all of our work was done after July 13 and it appears, at least initially, that the important Western Epeorus hatches probably preceded this date. If they did they certainly would not occur during the cold runoff that affects most streams during most of mid-June through early July.

This leaves a very important question to be answered: Do the important Western Epeorus flies (as well as those from other families) hatch in April, May or June, prior to the snow-melts? On streams that approach or surpass the 50°F. mark, we suspicion this to be the case. To our knowledge, almost nothing has been written in fishing books that would support this theory. But, then again, few authors have dealt with the specifics of angling entomology. Those who have, hailed from the East or Midwest and they naturally chose to write about the home streams, intimate to them, which were constantly available during their research. More recently a western based book confirmed this theory. Rick Hafele and Dave Hughes in their book *Western Hatches* states that. . . "Emergence begins in early spring and continues through the summer. We have witnessed excellent hatches in the Northwest in May. Emergence in the Rocky Mountains usually occur in June and July, depending on elevation. Some species are common at high elevations, where they emerge as late as August."

We have listed what appear to be the more populous Epeorus species throughout the country, but are placing special emphasis on *vitreus,* which we believe to be one of the most important Epeorus species in the East and Mid-

COMMON NAMES: Pale Evening Dun, Little Marryat, Sulphur

vitreus

SIZE RANGE: 9 to 12 mm

HOOK SIZES:
SURFACE (dry): #12, #14
SUBSURFACE (wet): #12, #14; std.

IMITATIONS:
NYMPH: Light Epeorus Compara-nymph
EMERGER: Little Marryat Wet, Light Epeorus Compara-emerger
Dun: Little Marrat, Light Epeorus Compara-dun, Light Epeorus Hackled Compara-dun, Pale Evening Dun

GENERAL EMERGENCE:
vitreus .... early June-early July
punctatus .... late June-late July
ribidus .... late June-late July
suffusus .... June
albertae .... early July-mid August
deceptivus .... July-September
longimanus .... mid-June-mid-July

west and typical of its genus in physical characteristics, size, color value, emergence characteristics and mating behavior; therefore, angling techniques and imitations for most of the species in this genus are similar.

We have experienced the hatches of *vitreus* on key Northeastern rivers like Penn's Creek, Brodheads Creek, Beaverkill River and the West Branch of the Au Sable from early June through early July. The emergence period is identical on most Michigan and Wisconsin streams. However, their populations are not on par with the East. We have witnessed fishable hatches in late July that were similar to *vitreus* and also some that were slightly smaller and darker. We identified the latter species as E. *rubidus* and E. *punctatus*.

SPECIES	SIZE mm	HOOK SIZE	PRIMARY DISTRIBUTION
vitreus	9-12	12-14	East-Midwest
punctatus	8-9	14	East-Midwest
rubidus	8-9½	14	East-Midwest
suffusus	9-12	12-14	East-Midwest
albertae	9-11	12-14	Rockies-West Coast
deceptivus	8-9	14	Rockies
longimanus	10-11	12	Rockies

NYMPH

The nymphs of these species require exacting specifications in water purity and a tremendously high concentration of oxygen to survive. Therefore, they are nearly always found in the fastest of rapids and riffles. When raising them in aquariums for photography and observation, it was necessary to create an unusual amount of turbulence through the use of air stones and pumps. Thus, we usually had to segregate them from nymphs of other families which would find this environment too trying. Our success in rearing them was about 50%. When the right combination of current and habitat was created, they matured and hatched.

All of the Epeorus nymphs are amazingly similar in shape and size and they are even similar in color. The color can be divided into two basic color groups; dark, as in *pleuralis*, and medium, as in *vitreus*.

Nymph patterns, as a rule, are relatively unimportant as the nymphs hatch on the stream's bottom and are buoyed to the surface and encapsulated in nymphal gas which is released when the subimago leaves its shuck. Thus, the subsurface feeding of the trout is concentrated on the emerging duns.

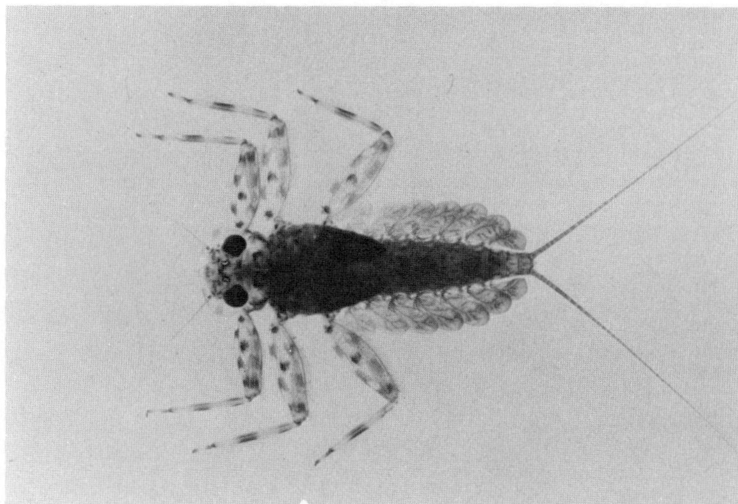

E. *vitreus*, nymph.

When these flies are emerging, a wet-fly or emerger pattern is exceptional and usually accounts for more fish than does the dry-fly. Popular patterns for this activity are the pale Little Maryatt and the brownish Hare's Ear wetflies in #12 and #14 hook sizes. We have enjoyed success with these patterns too, but have found that emerger patterns tied with short sprouts of wings or an enlarged fiberous thorax will account for more and better fish as they are more imitative of the subsurface dun whose wings are still collapsed on its thoracic structure. Across and downstream deliveries are usually best, but an upstream dead-drift presentation in the film or at mid-depth can also be deadly.

DUN

vitreus duns are considerably paler than those of the early *pleuralis* hatches, yet not as pale as the light Ephemerella and Stenonema flies that are also common in June and July respectively. The male body is a dull yellowish with a delicate olive cast; the female body is distinctly reddish or orange, due to the underlying bright red eggs. The wings are a medium gray.

These June hatches of Epeorus flies occur when the sulphur-colored Ephemerellas are hatching, so it's quite possible you will be casting over fish that are selective to a specific species. For instance, if the lighter, smaller (6-8mm, #16 hook) *dorothea* duns are emerging along with the somewhat darker *vitreus* subimagoes (9-12mm, #12 or #14 hook) the trout will normally prefer those which exist in greater number within the confines of his feeding station. Anglers must be alert during these situations and switch to the pattern which best duplicates the predominant species.

E. *vitreus* male dun.

A general rule which may be helpful during this situation is to use the Ephemerella *dorothea* pattern in quieter pools and flats where E. *dorothea* is common. When fishing the faster stretches synonymous with the Epeorus flies, use the larger *vitreus* imitations.

This rule, however, does not apply when the larger Ephemerellas (like *invaria* or *rotunda),* which hatch in the faster currents, are mingled with those of the Epeorus species. But, then again, neither does the problem, because the Ephemerella mayflies are about the same size (9-11mm) and their color is similar; hence, a common pattern can be selected that will imitate either group.

During the typically hot weather in June or July, the best hatching activity generally takes place whenever the water temperature is in the ideal range of 55°-60°F. During early July in the East and the Midwest, this may be in the afternoon or early evening. Toward the end of the month, hatching will normally occur at twilight. When the temperature remains high, as in heat waves, hatching will usually occur in the morning hours when the water temperature drops into the more favorable range.

Although the wet-fly scores heavily during this hatch due to the subsurface emergence of the duns, the dry-fly, too, is first class. It's hard to beat working a dry in the fast water and heavy runs. We use short (6- to 7-foot) fast-action rods for this work, because the fly moves so quickly in the fast current that quick, repetitive casts are necessary to place it precisely at the narrow ribbon of current where the frothing rapids and the patch of calm meet. This is also the perfect time to work your fly with twitches and to flutter it from a heavy run into the surprisingly calm pockets. You can almost anticipate every blast of the fish. Yet, when it comes, it invariably catches you off guard.

Another technique for this hatch, especially in the faster currents, is to allow your dry-fly to drag downstream into inaccessible spots where you previously spotted a rising trout. This procedure is similar to wet-fly fishing, but the action of the fast water against the hackled fly apparently creates a commotion which closely resembles the emergence activity of the subsurface Epeorus duns.

E. *vitreus*, female spinner.

SPINNER

Like most spinner-falls, the Epeorus imagoes will form their squadrons when the air temperature is most favorable (usually between 60° and 70°F.) In early June, they will take place between early evening and twilight; later in the month, it's usually a dusk situation. In July, when many evenings are too hot and muggy, the flights will be delayed until the following morning. On cloudy, cool days, the spinner activity may take place during the afternoon.

The spinners have an affinity for the faster rapids and riffles. After mating and copulation is complete, they fall into the swift torrents and swirl helplessly into the tiny pockets and backwaters. Trout lie here or at the tail of a rapid stretch that funnels into slower runs or into the head of a pool for the feast. Stalk these spots carefully and position yourself within casting distance of several good lies caused by large boulders, deadfalls or other obstructions.

On the hard-fished streams of the Northeast, especially in June, many of these ideal spots will be taken long before you are ready to wade into position. This has happened to us frequently on such hard-fished streams as the Beaverkill and the West Branch of the Ausable in New York state.

If it happens to you, don't despair, and by no means should you intrude on the angler who had the foresight to secure the spot first—this would only reduce the fishing for both of you. Instead, give him a wide berth and enter the white water upstream or the slower runs below him. Opportunities for this activity lie in both water-types. The spinners will fall in the fast water, so work the calm pockets where the trout are holding at the edge of the current. Most of the spinners will be whisked downstream into the slower runs where they will be gobbled up by deliberately feeding trout.

Spent spinners patterns in #12 and #14 hook sizes are the best bet for these falls, but full-hackled patterns will also pay off, especially in the faster current. The angler should not hesitate to cast across or downstream and manipulate his pattern by fluttering it into suspected pockets and eddies.

Genus Heptagenia

The Heptagenia species resemble closely those of Stenonema* and Stenacron but they are smaller, averaging 6-9mm. In fact, species of Heptagenia in the West are dead-ringers for the Stenonema nymphs.

Like Stenonema, the nymphs are streamlined and flattened, bearing three tails. The middle tail is lost during the transition from nymph to dun which is typical of the whole Heptageniidae family. Their habitats are identical to the Stenonema nymphs; they seem to like medium currents, but are equally at home in fast riffles and rapids. They can also be found around debris and detritus in eddies and quiet pockets to which they usually migrate prior to emergence. As in Stenonema, their gills undulate noticeably, which supports our theory of their ability to live in these quiet sections.

The gills on segment 7 are similar to the preceeding pairs on segments 1-6; the 7th pair on Stenonema nymphs are thread-like.

The differences in the gills are difficult to determine at streamside, but after some familiarity with the nymphs, the angler should be able to segregate them at a glance, as the Heptagenia specimens that we have studied are more slender and the abdominal tergites (top of abdomen) are generally dark brown or blackish with pale submedian streaks on each tergite (these give the appearance of twin longitudinal streaks on the dorsal area of the abdomen).

The male dun and spinner can be segregated from the Epeorus and Rhithrogena males as the large elliptical eyes do not touch at the top of the head (are not contiguous apically). Also, in the male, the forelegs are longer than the bodies, while the female's are 3/4 of the length of the body. The basal joint in the foretarsi are only 1/6 to 1/4 of the length of the second joint. Continuing on this tack, the hind legs of both sexes have tibia that are 3/4 of the length of the femur while the tarsi are about 1/2 of the length of the tibia.

Although this genus is geographically widespread, the Heptagenia species are of minor importance on Eastern and Midwestern rivers, because they lack sufficient populations for concentrated hatching and the best hatches are in June when larger and more prolific mayfly species are emerging. This is not the case in the West, however, where we found suprisingly good populations that rival the populations of the Stenonema species in the East and Midwest.

*For simplicity of text throughout this chapter, the similar genera of Stenonema and Stenacron will be referred to as Stenonema.

GENERAL EMERGENCE:

minerva	*June-July
juno	*June-July
hebe	*June-October
pulla	*August-October
elegantula	June-July
criddlei	June-July

*Best emergence

Heptagenia, male dun

Heptagenia nymph. Note that the 7th pair of gills are similar to the preceeding pairs and are not thread-like as in Stenonema.

SPECIES	DIST.	SIZE	PRONOTUM WIDEST AT	CLAW PECTINATE	FILAMENTS ON GILL 7	ABDOMINAL SPINES ON 8	ABDOMINAL SPINES ON 6-7	MISC.
pulla	E, M	10-12	front	no	yes	no	no	Body: brown to dark brown with pale spots on thorax and pale blotches on abdomen. Gills: purplish gray. Tails: light and dark bands.
hebe	E, M	6-8	middle	yes	no	yes	yes	Body: grayish-brown tergites, pale sternites. Liberally marked with pale spots.
juno	E	6-7	middle	yes	no	yes	yes	Body: dark markings at anterior margins of sternites 8 and 9 in median area. Gills: purplish-black, pale at tips.
elegantula	W	8-10	front	no	yes	no	no	Pronotum has pale median streak and pale lateral areas. Large pale blotch on tergites 8 and 9.
rosea	W	9-10	middle	yes	no	yes	yes	Distinct pale streaks and round spots on tergites. Large pale median area on tergites 8-9.
simplicioides	W	8-10	middle	yes	no	yes	yes?	

MALE SPINNER

SPECIES	DIST.	SIZE	VEINS	TERGITES 1-6	DUNS
criddlei	W	6-7	brown	pale	Body: reddish-brown w/chevron marks. Wings: medium gray.
pulla	E, M	9-12	brown	pale	Tergites: reddish-brown wth dark rear margins and a light spot on each side of mid-line. Sternites: pale olive. Wings: medium-dark gray.
hebe	E, M	6-8	dark	brown	Body: reddish-brown. Wings: pale, with light gray markings. Tails: pale. Thorax: pale olive.
juno	E	6-7	pale	whitish	– – –
minerva	E	6-7	dark	yellow	– – –
elegantula	W	8-10	black	brown	Body: orangish. Wings: light gray.
rosea	W	8-10	brown	pale	– – –
simplicioides	W	9-10	pale	whitish	Body: pale cream. Wings: tan.

Genus Rhithrogena

As previously stated in the family section of this genus, we have found little to support the claims that the Rhithrogena mayflies constitute important hatches for the trout fisherman in the East. The Leonards reported good populations during the '50's and '60's in the Pre-Cambrian area of Michigan's western Upper Peninsula. Regretfully, we've never had the chance to research this area. We did manage to uncover some of these nymphs over the years on western Pennsylvania streams, but never have we found populations sufficient to produce a fishing hatch. Our western research has shown more evidence of their importance. Western based entomologist and angling writers claim that Rhithrogena is extremely important.

These nymphs, like those of Epeorus, prefer the fastest of currents. Their large plate-like gills are located on body segments 1-7. The first and seventh pairs are enlarged and meet at the mid-line underneath the abdomen, creating complete suction-like cups.

Their three tails separate them from the Epeorus species, the only other genera with similar plate-like gills. The head is widest at the anterior portion of the eyes. The femora have ovoid spots in their centers. The large, roundish eyes of the male adults nearly touch at the top of the head (are contiguous—nearly so). The stigmatic area of the forewing is anastomosed (has a network branching of cross-veins) and is reliable for identification.

Edmunds lists 21 species of Rhithrogena in his *Mayflies of North and Central America.*

Since most Rhithrogena species were collected and identified between the 1880's and the 1930's, it is our guess that these mayfly populations require extreme specifications of pure water, oxygen and the exact combination of nitrates; even more so than the fragile Epeorus species. Therefore, it's conceivable that the slightest change in their eco-system created by civilization via thermal, organic, toxic and silt pollution could well have been their demise. There are still reports of good hatches in remote areas of Michigan's Upper Peninsula and in untouched portions of the Rockies. It's a sobering thought and one must not pass it by lightly.

In the East and Midwest, emergence reportedly takes place between late May and the beginning of July with the best activity coming in early June. This hatching season coincides with the prime mayfly, caddisfly and stonefly activity, so even if the populations were good, it's very doubtful that Rhithrogena flies could compete with the likes of the awesome mayfly hatches of the Ephemerellidae, Ephemeriidae and Baetidae families.

For those anglers fortunate enough to have fishable hatches of Rhithrogena close by, we hope the following information will be helpful.

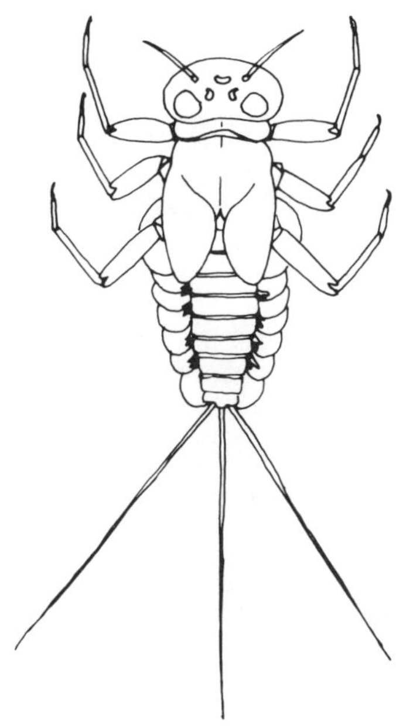

Above: Rhithrogena nymph. *Below:* Detail of suction cup-like gills underneath body.

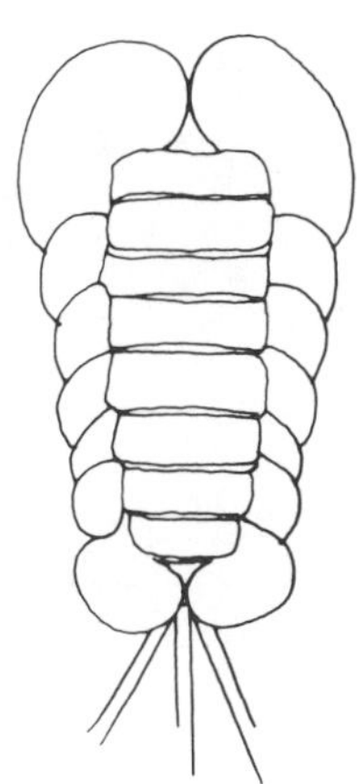

GENERAL EMERGENCE:

impersonata	late May-June
jejuna	May-early June
pellucida	June-July
sanguinea	June
hageni	July-August
morrisoni	April-May
undulata	July-August

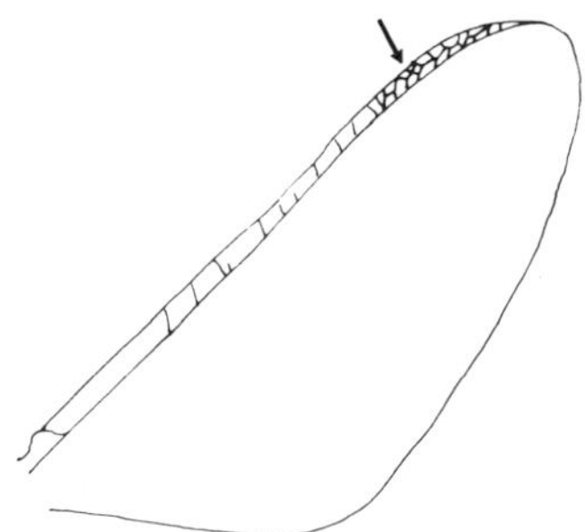

Note the anastomosed veins in the stigmatic area. Rhithrogena is the only genus in the Heptageniidae family of clingers to have them.

NYMPH

SPECIES	DIST.	SIZE	GILLS	GENERAL COLOR
pellucida	M, E	7-9	– – –	dark brown
jejuna	M, E	9-10	– – –	olive brown
impersonata	E, M	9-11	gray, with bluish-green trachae	brown or olive brown
sanguinea	M, E	8-10	bright red	medium to light brown
hageni	W	9-10	– – –	dark reddish brown
undulata	W	7-8	– – –	dark reddish brown

MALE SPINNER

SPECIES	DIST.	SIZE	MARK ON FEMORA	LONGITUDINAL VEINS	EYES	DUNS
jejuna	M, E	8-10	streak	dark brown	– – –	Similar to *impersonata* except wings tinged with brown and legs and tails are brown
impersonata	E, M	8-11	streak	blackish	dark reddish brown	Body: dark reddish-brown. Wings: medium gray. Legs: olive, fading to pale olive. Tails: pale olive, brown basally.
morrisoni	W	8-10	streak	brown	– – –	– – –
sanguinea	M, E	8-10	– – –	medium brown	bright reddish-brown	Body: reddish-brown tergites, pale brown sternites. Wings: medium gray.
pellucida	M, E	7-8	spot	nearly colorless	dark gray-green nearly black	Body: dark brown. Wings: dark gray.
hageni	W	9-10	– – –	– – –	– – –	Body: purplish black. Wings: mottled grayish brown.
undulata	W	7-8	streak	brown	– – –	Body: reddish brown. Wings: mottled grayish brown. Tails: speckled light brown.

Genus Cinygmula

Only one unimportant species, *subaequalis*, has been reported in the east by entomologists, and none in the midwest. Our research through the years in the east and midwest confirm these findings. We have yet to find one one single specimen.

Eight species have been reported in the west, mainly at 8,000 to 11,000 foot elevations in Utah and Colorado and in the redwood area of the coast ranges and Sierra Nevadas (re: Edmunds, Jensen and Berner, *Mayflies of North and Central America*, University of Minnesota Press).

We have not come across sufficient specimens of this genus in our research out west, thus we have few photographs to substantiate the information which was taken from entomological texts (see nymph shot in colorplate XIV). Until we come face to face with good numbers of these critters, we will continue to believe that they are relatively uncommon and unimportant as trout food. The same must be said of its sister genus, Cinygma, which is considered to be rare compared to Cinygmula.

The nymphs of this genus are typically flattened, although not as broadly flattened as in other genera in the Heptageniidae family. Their body configurations (in the specimens we have found) are similar to the Heptagena genus, except their colorations are more dramatic, having a broad, pale lateral band across the wing pads and pale areas in the abdomen. Gill pairs on abdominal segments 1-7 are all similar. Their mouth parts protrude like points from the edges of the head when viewed from above.

The duns and spinners have no markings on their wings. They have two tails and their femora is without bands. Positive identification can be made only from complicated entomological keys using a microscope.

SPECIES	EMERG.	DIST.	BODY SIZE	NYMPH DESCRIPTION	DUN DESCRIPTION	SPINNER DESCRIPTION
ramaleyi	Jun-Aug	W	7-8mm		Body: dk. olive brown. Wign: dk. gray.	Thorax: gray. Eyes: gray.
reticulata	Jun-Aug	W	8mm	lt. reddish brown, gills often red.	Body: orangish. Wing: yellow.	Thorax: reddish. Wing: has yellow venations.

The Burrowers

(Families Ephemeridae, Potamanthidae and Polymitarcyidae)

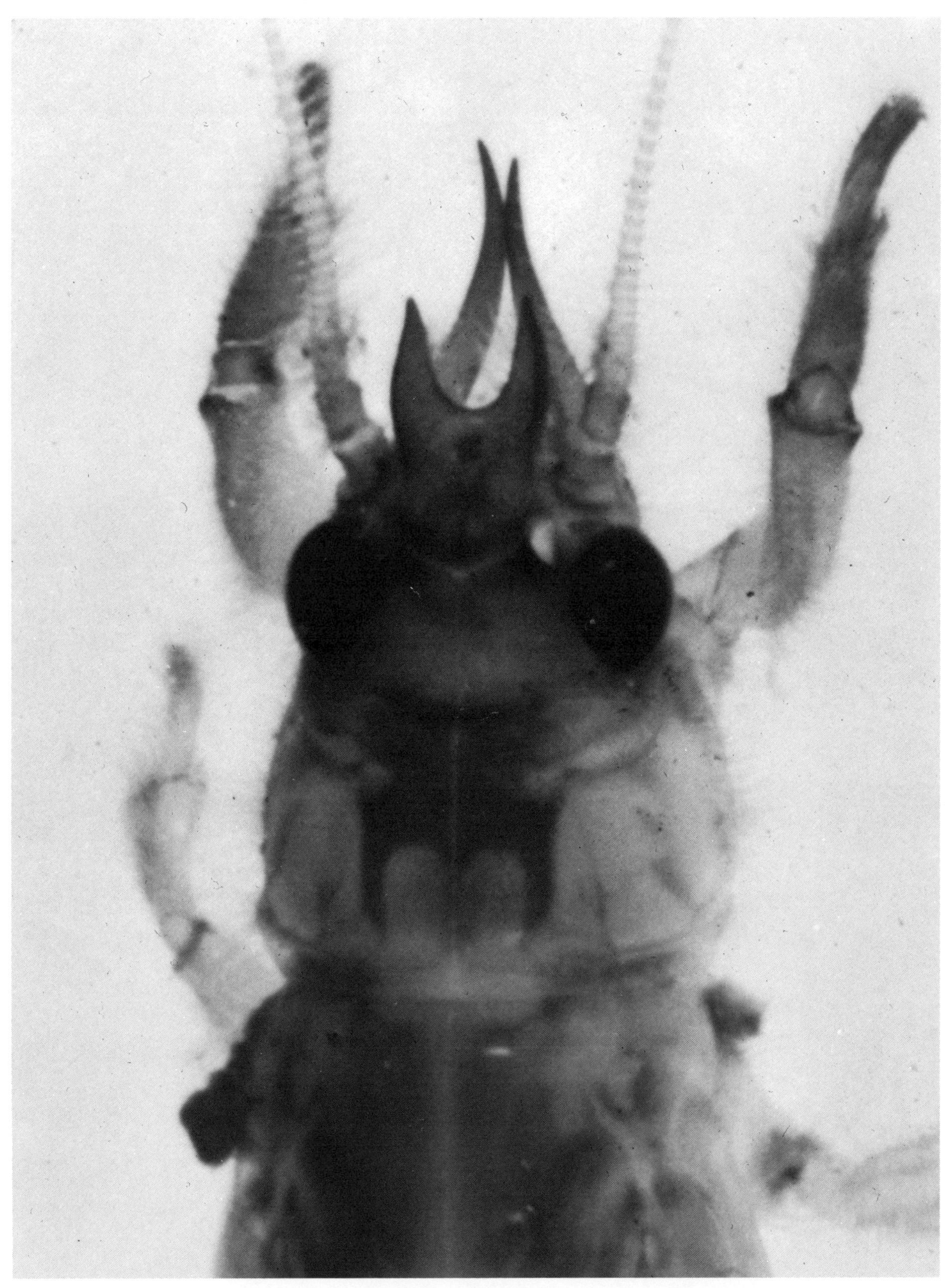

Families Ephemeridae, Potamanthidae and Polymitarcyidae
(The Silt-dwelling Burrowers)

The large, fascinating mayflies of these families are the most legendary in all of fly-fishing and they create the most thrilling and suspenseful angling experience of the year.

There are five genera in this exotic group that are important to the trout angler; Ephemera, Hexagenia, Litobrancha, Potamanthus and Ephoron. The Ephemera and Hexagenia species are superb fly-fishing hatches and their importance is extremely significant in the East and Midwest. Potamanthus is the third most important genus of this group to the fly-fisher, while the white flies of Ephoron are also surprisingly important, as is Litobrancha *recurvata* on rich chalk streams.

The nymphs are evasive due to their trait of burrowing in silt, sand and the fine gravel of our cold trout streams. The Potamanthus nymphs are really not burrowers at all, but they do crawl on the stream's bottom in the same siltaceous habitats as do their closely related burrowing cousins. Many species of Potamanthus and Ephoron are also quite at home in warmer waters that may be marginal for trout.

A silt-bottomed pool on the beloved Willowemoc in New York's Catskills.

The tusk-bearing mandibles of an Ephemeridae nymph.

The nymphs of these families are easily recognized by their long, tusk-bearing mandibles. They have three tails and their unique flanged* legs and shovel-like heads are ideally designed for burrowing into soft bottoms.

The wings of the Ephemera and Hexagenia adults are smaller than the bodies, and the hind wings are fairly large and well-developed as compared to mayflies of other families. Wing venations are prominent and well-developed (numerous) and are sometimes spotted.

*Potamanthus does not have flanged legs.

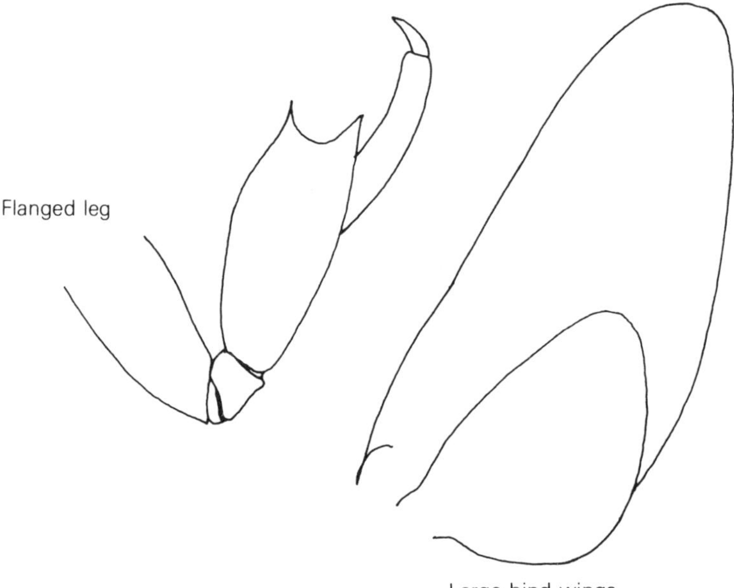

FAMILIES	EPHEMERIDAE	POTAMANTHIDAE	POLYMITARCYIDAE
Genera	Ephemera Hexagenia Litobrancha	Potamanthus	Ephoron

Genus Ephemera
(Family Ephemeridae)

Although the large mayflies of the Ephemera genus are renowned throughout the country, it is in the East where its premier species, E. *guttulata* (the Green Drake) marks the climax of the fly-fishing season. To many afflicted Eastern fishermen, the "Green Drake Hatch" is as irresistable and habit-forming as black jack, whiskey or easy women. Midwesterners are compensated for the Easterner's exclusivity of *guttulata* by the short but furious action of the *simulans* species, which warms them up for the awesome Hexagenia hatches that follow close behind. The *varia* species is extremely widespread and generally important to the Eastern and the Midwestern angler. The less-important warm-water species of *blanda*, *traverae* and *triplex* and the obscure Western *compar* species round out this genus of seven.

E. *varia*, nymph.

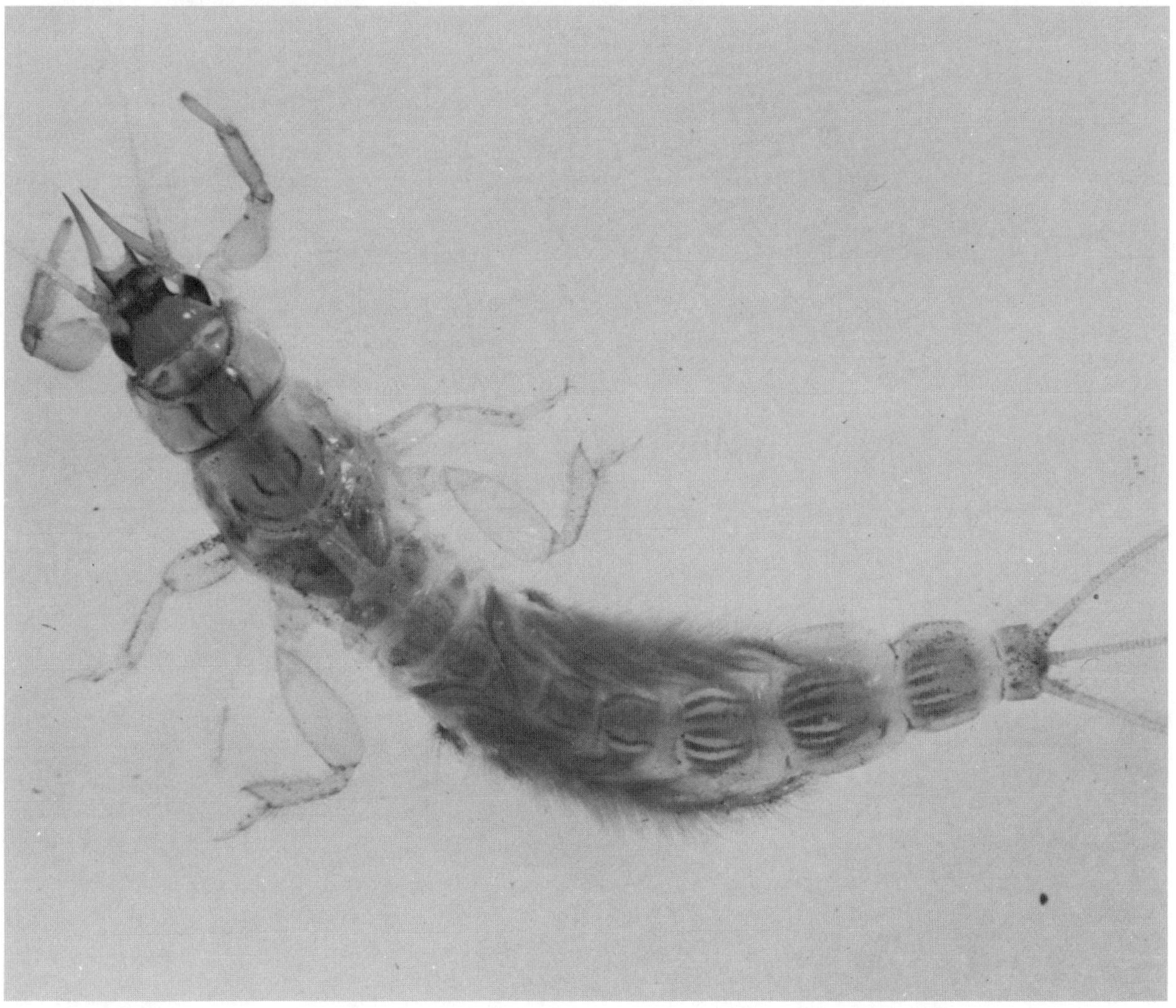

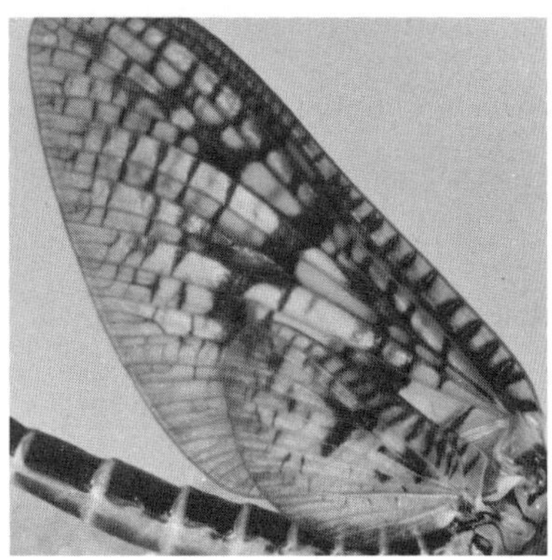

The heavily spotted wings of Ephemera.

The Ephemera nymphs have smooth, outcurved tusks and a deeply forked notch in the frontal prominence. The important *guttulata*, *simulans* and *varia* species can be distinguished by the length of their tusks and the configuration of the frontal notch. They have three relatively short tails and their fascinating plumage-like gills are arranged in dorsal fashion along their abdominal segments.

The duns and spinners have heavily spotted wings separating them from the larger Hexagenia adults. The forewings are noticeably shorter than the body. The eyes of the males are noticeably small, but slightly larger than are the females; hence, distinguishing the sexes is easier by the recognition of the male claspers. Their large size, spotted wings and three tails make the Ephemera duns and spinners readily distinguishable by the angler.

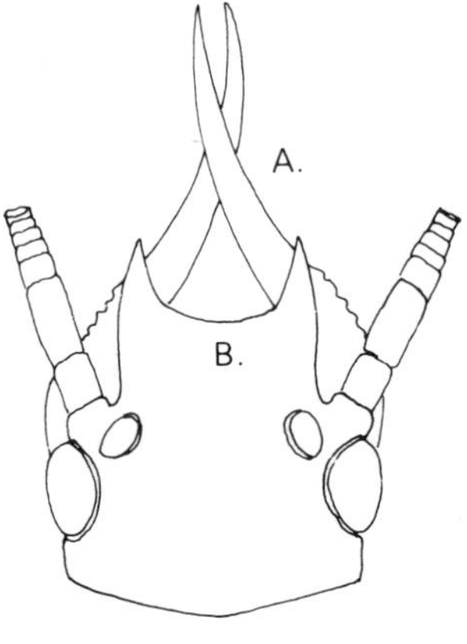

A, The outcurved tusks of Ephemera; B, its deeply forked frontal notch.

NYMPH

SPECIES	DIST.	SIZE	FRONTAL NOTCH	TUSK-BASE OUTER CURVE*	TUSK PROJECTION**
guttulata	E	18-30	rounded	outside	1x
varia	E, M	13-16	squarish	outside	1½x
simulans	M, W	11-14	rounded	outside	2x
blanda	SE	14-18	squarish	between	1½x

* Outer curve of base of tusk when viewed from above. Between: between antennae and frontal process. Outside: outside of base of antennae.

** Tusk projection beyond frontal process relative to length of process.

MALE SPINNER

SPECIES	DIST.	SIZE	FOREWING SPOTS	HIND WING SPOTS	TERGITES	DUN
guttulata	E	18-30	many	many	yellowish-white	Body: cream with dark tergites. Wings: cream, marked heavily with dark spots. Body and wings are suffused with yellow or green.
varia	E, M	13-16	moderate	none	cream	Body and wings: creamy. Tergites and wings are marked with purplish-brown.
simulans	E, M, W	11-14	many	many	dark brown	Body: dark brown. Wings: olive-brown, heavily spotted with dark brown.
compar	W	14-16	many	few	brownish-yellow	Body: yellowish-brown marked with blackish streaks. Wings: pale yellowish, heavily spotted with blackish dark brown.
triplex	SE	11-12	three	none	whitish	Body: very pale yellowish white with fine, dark markings. Wings: pale with almost no markings.
blanda	SE	14-18	few	none	yellowish	A yellowish-brown species. The wings have small dark spots instead of the typical blotches.

Ephemera guttulata

guttulata is one of the largest and most spectacular mayflys in the Eastern U.S. Its size is surpassed only by those of the Hexagenia and Litobrancha genera mainly L. *recurvata* and H. *limbata,* the famous Midwestern species. Local names for *guttulata* are Shad Fly, Shaddie, Mayfly, Green May and Green Drake, the latter being the most widely used and commonly accepted.

This species constitutes one of the most thrilling hatches of the year and is considered by many to be the climax of the Eastern mayfly season. Huge trout that ordinarily sit it out on the stream's bottom until nightfall will often rise with abandon in broad daylight to these struggling naturals.

Hatching activity begins in the more southerly reaches of Pennsylvania around the third week in May, while the big limestone streams of central Pennsylvania are best during the last week. The northern mountain regions of the state, including the Delaware System and the Poconos, peak between May 28 and June 6, with the Memorial Day weekend being the focal point. Emergence in the Catskills is usually between June 3 and June 12, with best hatching on the Beaverkill around June 7. Northern New York and New England are usually reliable between June 14 and 23, with peak activity on the Adirondack's west branch of the Ausable around June 18.

COMMON NAMES: Green Drake, Coffin Fly, Shad Fly, Shaddie, Mayfly, Green May

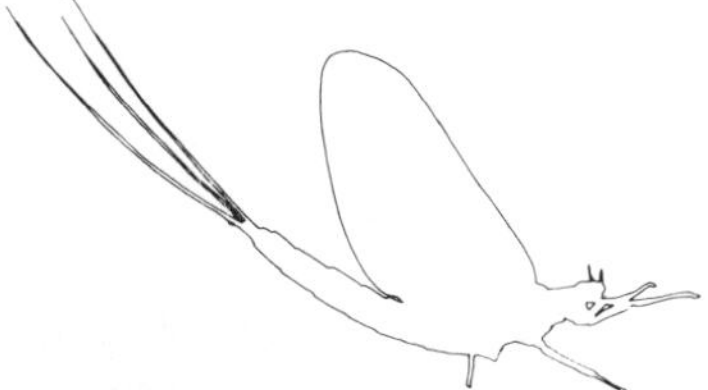

SIZE RANGE: 18 to 30 mm
HOOK SIZES:
SURFACE (dry): #8, #6, #8, 4x long
SUBSURFACE (wet): #10, #10, 3x long

IMITATIONS.
NYMPH: Guttulata Compara-nymph
EMERGER: Guttulata Deerhair emerger
DUN: Guttulata Compara-dun
SPINNER: Guttulata Compara-spinner

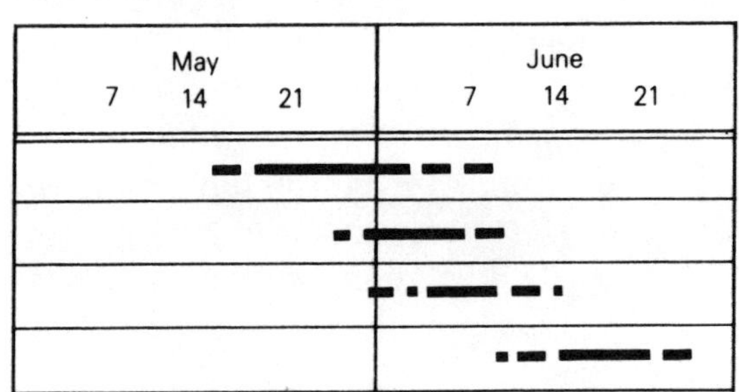

West. Penna. Limestones

N. Penna. and Poconos

S. N.Y. and Catskills

N. New England and Adirondacks

NYMPH

guttulata nymphs are burrowers and are usually found in rich, soft-bottomed pools and the mud banks of a river's slower sections. In predominantly fast-water streams, these insects inhabit the silt and debris that accumulates between large boulders and other obstructions. We've kicked them up here while seining for other species. On limestone streams they may also be found in fine, rich gravel.

Ephemera *varia,* a closely related species, will usually occupy the same haunts as *guttulata* and in its nymphal stage is quite similar in body characteristics. However, *guttulata* nymphs lack the distinctive markings which characterize the nymphs of *varia.* Yet, this difference isn't obvious

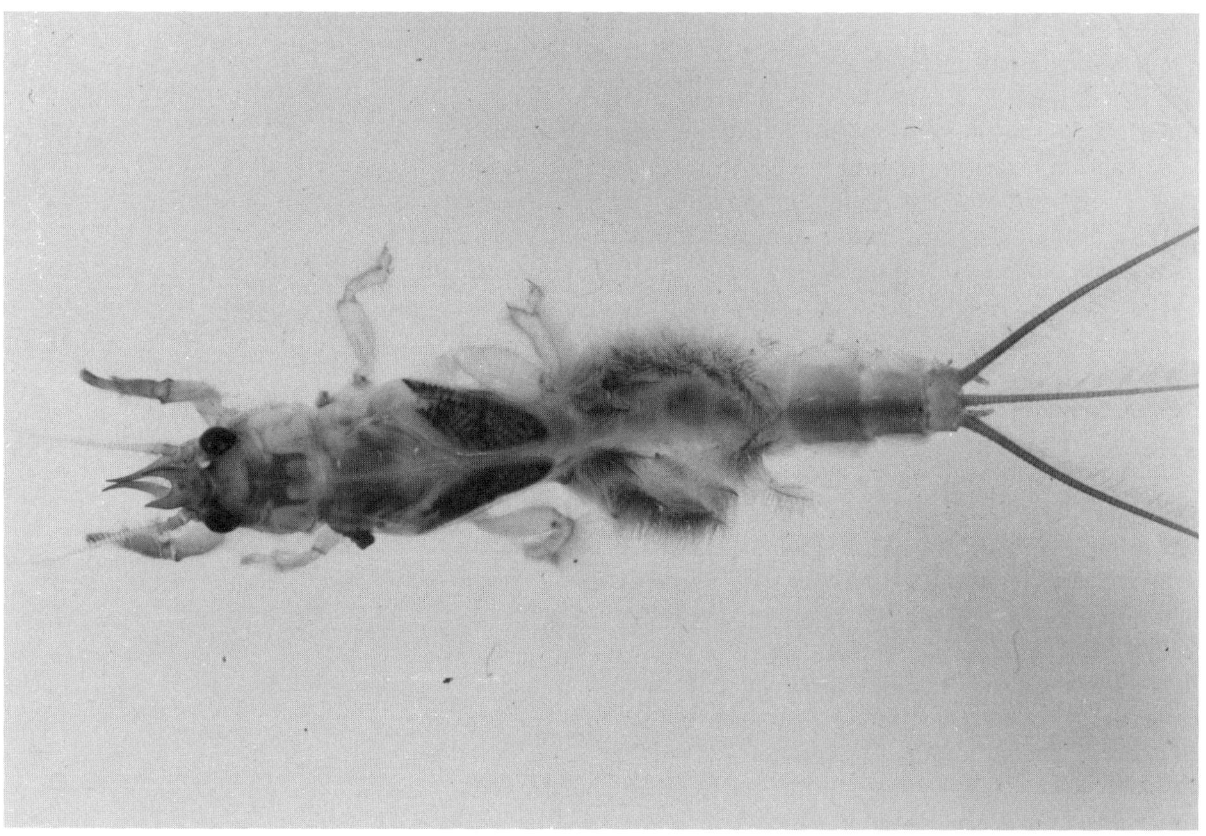

E. *guttulata,* male nymph.

enough for the average angler to make a confident streamside identification. A better method is to distinguish these nymphs by the frontal notches.

During our earlier stream research we sometimes mistook populations of *varia* for immature *guttulata* nymphs, especially on those field trips where time prohibited us from collecting samples for further study back at the lab. Later in the season, when we returned to those streams for some *guttulata* action, we were disappointed to find that they didn't exist on those streams.

When researching streams for future prospects of fishing these hatches, determination by size can be very misleading; especially if conducted in early spring or the fall. Ephemera nymphs take several seasons to mature; hence, comparing the dimensions of an immature *guttulata* nymph to a full grown *varia* can be very misleading. Unless positive identification is made by other means, confusion between the nymphs is probable. We made such a mistake in our original *Comparahatch* books. During the crazy schedule to meet our publishing deadline, we somehow failed to examine the *guttulata* and *varia* photographs properly. The result was that the nymph shown on the *guttulata* hatch plates, as well as the black-and-white photograph pictured in the chapter of the "reference volume" is really that of *varia*. For this error, though honest in its original intent, we humbly apologize.

guttulata nymphs, like most burrowers, are repelled by light and prefer to live most of their lives burrowed into the mud and silt of the streambed. It is estimated that thirty moults will take place before emergence and adulthood. During moults, the nymphs leave the safety of their burrows to shed their outgrown shucks. At this time they range about freely, thus becoming available to the trout. Nymphs also become vulnerable during freshets, when the streambed is disturbed, exposing the larvae temporarily until they relocate in other siltbeds.

The trout's greatest incentive for feeding on the nymph stage is provided during emergence when the nymphs leave their burrows and propel themselves to the stream's surface where they hatch rather quickly. Emergence often takes place sporadically all day with a concentrated burst after 7 P.M. On unusually cool and cloudy days, heavy hatching activity may occur anytime in the afternoon.

Our experience with *guttulata* indicates that most trout prefer the easy pickings of the awkward, struggling duns and spinners to chasing the deceptively quick, emerging nymphs. Autopsies of trout caught during this time tend to substantiate this.

However, we have, at times, realized successful nymph fishing during this hatch; especially on waters with steady currents lacking boulders and obstructions which create eddies where the trout can hold close to the surface. In such stretches it's more convenient for the trout to hold on the bottom and pick off the emerging nymphs.

For nymphing, we like the Guttulata Compara-nymph. It should be fished with jerks and twitches to simulate the quick ascent of the nymphs. When trout are rising or bulging under the surface, this pattern, dressed on a light wire hook, fished in or just under the surface film will sometimes produce excellent results.

DUN

There are many puzzling aspects to fishing the spine tingling Green Drake hatch. On freestone streams, where hatching is relatively sparse, these duns usually bring on a reliable feeding splurge of large trout unprecendented by any other mayfly. Yet, on Pennsylvania's big limestone streams, where the Green Drake has become synonymous with blizzard-like hatches, fishing to these overfed trout will often be a cause for disappointment and frustration.

On freestone streams, where populations are relatively

E. *guttulata,* male dun. Known as the Green Drake.

sparse as a rule, trout often gobble up every dun that pops to the surface. During this lighter hatching activity, trout are normally less selective. The fluttering antics of these duns during their labor to take flight seems to raise the ire of even the most satiated lunker.

On the other hand, the reluctance of trout to feed on prolific *guttulata* streams, when a great number of these giant mayflies are floundering helplessly on the surface, parallels the behavior of Midwestern trout during the Hexagenia *limbata* hatches—especially if the trout populations consist of more selective native or holdover fish. Often these stream-wise browns will gorge themselves during the first few days of a hatch. At this time they are easier to fool and anglers may score heavily. However, once the trout are initially satisfied and sense that this tremendous food supply will be available daily, they start to ignore the fluttering duns during the day and the premature spinner-falls prior to dusk. Instead, they become wary and choose their own feeding time; around dusk or after dark. If the feeding behavior of the trout sounds familiar and is typical of the streams you fish, perhaps you should consider the following methods.

Catch the initial day or two of the hatch, when trout are

less selective, and follow the action as it progresses upstream. This action can also be monitored on other nearby watersheds, thereby locating you over less complacent and more cooperative trout for a considerable period.

If you're of the hard-nosed variety and insist on taking difficult trout during the peak of the hatch, a good tactic is to stalk one (or two) fish for the night's work. Stealth is the criterion here, and a good casting position should be obtained well in advance of the trout's brief feeding period. Smaller trout will start rising well before your fish does, but casting restraint must be maintained. When your fish starts to work, further restraint is necessary until he has established a greedy feeding rhythm. If your pattern is right and the first few casts are true, your patience will be properly rewarded with an angry, screeching reel as your prize makes awesome, rod buckling runs into the darkness.

A peculiarity that has puzzled anglers over the years is that tremendous hatches of *guttulata* may occur on one river, while a neighboring stream bearing the same ecological characteristics may be completely devoid of this species. Water pollution and subaquatic habitat are, of course, prime factors in whether populations of *guttulata* will flourish. Another very important criterion for the perpetuation of prolific hatches (seldom mentioned) is the presence of ideal streamside habitat. Remember, these large insects are extremely vulnerable from the time they escape their burrows on the stream's bottom until they return as spinners to lay their eggs. The nymphs and duns that have escaped the trout and other fish must survive the further onslaught of swooping birds, predacious insects and rooting animals; hence, the survival rate is directly related to the distance the duns must travel to obtain proper cover after leaving the water.

On large, rich limestone streams which wind through unspoiled forested valleys, the water flow fluctuates only slightly throughout the year, encouraging the growth of large trees at the waters edge. On streams with these ideal tree lines, the subimagoes can obtain safety with just a few flaps of their wings; hence, their survival rate is astonishing when compared to streams with wide barren beds caused by runoffs and frequent flooding. These have inadequate foliage to hide the enormous *guttulata* duns.

Penn's Creek has one of the best populations of *guttulata* in the country and we consider it classic with regard to streamside habitat. It flows rich and unspoiled through many miles of friendly yet relatively inaccessible country in central Pennsylvania. Its streamside tree lines are abundant with tulip trees which have enormous leaves (approx. 8"x6") to serve as perfect tents for the moulting *guttulata* duns.

Federal and State conservation and fisheries officials should consider the importance of sufficient streamside cover and encourage planting programs. This factor is essential to the survival of all mayfly species.

Perfect large-leafed cover for moulting duns and resting spinners. This male spinner was disturbed from underneath the large leaf on which it was resting just before the shot was taken.

guttulata duns vary in color and size according to the stream or area in which they live. On the rivers of central and western Pennsylvania having limestone origins, the females average close to 30mm (approx. 1 1/4") in body length, while the males run considerably smaller. Here they have a yellow or greenish appearance; especially in flight. On Eastern freestone streams, the duns are more grayish with blackish or dull brown markings. The females average around 20mm on these streams; considerably smaller than the limestone variety. In spite of the variations in color and size, these duns are quite unique and, once identified, one will seldom mistake them for any other species.

During this hatch, anglers should fish their imitations creatively. Some individual fish will take only insects that are fluttering. Where this is the case, cast your fly above the take area. After it has sat awhile, simulate these fluttering movements. This is heart pumping business and once the angler has hooked a lunker under these circumstances he usually becomes afflicted with Green Drake Mania, an incurable disease.

At times, when the duns are floating placidly, a properly presented fly, followed by a drag-free float, will often turn the trick.

Trout are super-selective to this hatch and presenting an acceptable imitation can be a problem. The imitations that works best for us are the Compara-dun and emerger tied on #6, #8 and #8, 4x long hooks. When hackled patterns are needed for twitching or skittering to imitate the fluttering insects, we tie hackle fore-and-aft of the Compara-dun emerger wing. These patterns can be fished well into dusk as they are quite visible in the fading light.

SPINNER

This spinner is known as the Coffin Fly, owing to its funeral coloration of black and white. Many anglers consider the dun and spinner of *guttulata* to be two distinct species due to their radical difference in coloration. These great spinners are one of the very few species that can be confidently identified in mid-flight. Even the males and females are distinguishable on the wing, as the females are almost twice the size of the males, whose extremely long, black forelegs and tails make them a further stick-out.

About three days after the first hatches appear, the spinners will make their showing. An hour or so before dusk, the male imagoes can be sighted high above the stream. As they descend lower and lower, the air may become so thick with them, it resembles a raging snow storm. This fall is truly one of nature's premier events and yet the finale is still to come.

Prior to the appearance of the egg-laden females, squadrons of males will be seen hovering erratically just over the stream's surface awaiting females for copulation. Periodically, males will land on the water to rest, causing a premature rise of smaller fish. Soon males are airborne again. When the females finally show, the mating begins, followed by the fall of spent male spinners.

On freestone streams, where hatching and subsequent spinner-falls are of lesser density than those of the more prolific limestone streams, nice trout may rise to these male falls. But more often than not, only smaller trout will rise prematurely to them. On prolific limestone streams and large rich rivers these male falls almost always are ignored.

On cloudy days, the male spinners may make their appearance several hours early. This premature mating flight exhausts the impatient males who fall to the water frequently to rest—only to struggle to take flight again. At such times, we have watched in amused astonishment as the desperate males attacked freshly hatched female duns in their frustration to mate. Sometimes as many as three males would clumsily clasp an uncooperative female dun, causing her to fall to the water. Often, the commotion of the four connected bodies would instigate a blasting rise that would curl the hair on your back. It should be noted, however, that although many males die prematurely, the number of males is so great that when the female spinners finally do

E. *guttulata,* female spinner. Known as the Coffin Fly.

arrive, there are still sufficient numbers to service them.

Eggs fertilized, the females begin to make their final descent. As they land on the water, the eggs are extruded as they lay semi-spent on the surface film. The oviposting act is so irresistable that even the most sophisticated trout are driven into a feeding frenzy that borders on the bizarre.

During frantic spinner activity, many anglers delude themselves into thinking that hooking a good fish will be relatively simple—most go home very disappointed. Trout are very critical of the imitations presented, primarily because these larger flies are easily examined by the trout. Also, trout are keen to notice how the fly lands and moves on the surface. Often, premature casting to smaller fish, before the bulk of the spinners fall, will ruin the chances of hooking a good fish later. Another disadvantage is that the peak feeding activity takes place in the short period just before dark, leaving little room for error. During this period, and even after dark, the duns may start to emerge again in concentrated numbers; trout take them readily along with the female spinners. Our autopsies show that there is little preference between duns and spinners, however they do indicate that the trout prefer the bigger and fatter females over the males, almost exclusively.

While we're on the subject of autopsies, it's probably noteworthy to mention that almost all post-mortem operations revealed stomachs that were stuffed like sausages. One ten-inch fish had over sixty female duns and spinners in its stomach, which was so stretched that we could identify the insects through the stomach walls which had become almost transparent.

The point here is that although many duns and spinners seem to go unmolested on prolific waters, it's definitely not because the trout don't care for them. Rather, it's a situation where the food supply is more abundant than the need.

Anglers should understand that a show of spinners at treetop level does not necessarily guarantee a spinner-fall. The sudden appearance of lightning, mist or wind will usually drive the imagoes back into the safety of the brush for the night.

The spinner-falls represent the most challenging aspect of the *guttulata* activity and presenting a spinner imitation that works consistently has been one of our biggest problems. We have tested scores of patterns during this action. Among those evaluated with extended body types were Vince Marinaro's porcupine quill-body spinner, the unique "Lively Coffin Fly", designed by Chauncy Lively and what we call Eric Peper's "Salt and Peper", and black-and-white deer hair extended body type, featuring grizzly wings created by winding 2 or 3 oversized grizzly hackles tied about 2/5 of the hook shank distance from the eye. These wings are separated and formed by wrapping black dubbing in "figure 8" fashion to form the thorax. Eric explained that he could not accept credit for this creation as the basic design was developed by someone else.

The above patterns have proven effective for us on many ocasions, yet, none scored consistently over more selective fish. We would like to say that we have found the answer to this problem, but unfortunately we haven't. However, our batting average over selective trout did increase considerably when we switched to Compara-dun patterns tied on #6 and #8 hooks, 4x long.

The reasoning behind this is that the natural's long body rides well in the surface film—this is true of the duns as well as the spinners. Both use their tails for leverage against the surface tension; whether it's the dun attempting flight or the spinner writhing to extrude its eggs.

The Compara-dun design, with its flush-floating 4x long body and outrigger tails splayed in the surface film, maintains an attitude very similar to the *guttulata* naturals. Although we're not completely satisfied with the results of this fly, it works much better than those types whose extended bodies and tails curve away from the surface film. The flush-floating Compara-spinners on long-shanked hooks are also a good bet when only spinners are evident, but generally duns and spinners are on the water simultaneously, so the Compara-dun usually gets the nod.

During spinner activity, lunker trout will take up feeding positions as discussed in the dun section. Remember, the greatest factor in contributing to success is to concentrate on a few good fish and forget about trying to catch every fish in the pool. If you have stalked your fish, waited patiently, matched the natural with a good imitation and kept the water relatively undisturbed, the odds for hooking a dandy will be in your favor.

Bob scores with a Guttulata Compara-dun.

Ephemera varia

The creamish mayflies of Ephemera *varia* are very important to the late summer angler and should be considered a major hatch. *varia* is abundant on both Eastern and Midwestern waters. However, its importance is more significant in the East where it represents a good percentage of the trout's summer diet.

The general emergence span in the East and Midwest is similar to that of Potamanthus *distinctus;* from mid-June to early August. Hatching begins on Pocono and western Pennsylvania streams around June 17 and continues through mid-July. The Catskills are best from late June thru early August, while the Adirondacks and New England's streams are generally reliable from mid-July through mid-August. Midwestern emergence is best in July, but hatching often lingers through mid-August.

We have found this species equally abundant in streams of contrasting geographic makeup, as well as those of varying chemical composition. Awesome, swift mountain streams, cold, crystalline chalkstreams and pastoral, meandering valley rivers are all considered home to *varia.* Therefore, our nymph collections were taken from streams with these varying characteristics like intimate little streams in the Poconos and famous western Pennsylvania chalk streams like Penn's Creek, Spruce Creek and Fishing Creek. The sparkling Beaverkill and Willowemoc of Catskill fame have excellent populations, as does the awesome West Branch of the Ausable in the Adirondacks. Look for them on New England rivers like the Battenkill in Vermont as well as the brawling Kennebec of Maine. The giant Manistee, Pere Marquette and Au Sable river systems of Michigan have prolific populations of *varia* as do the rich Wolf and Brule Rivers of Wisconsin and the limestone rivers of Minnesota.

COMMON NAMES: Yellow Drake, Yellow Dun, Cream Variant, White Dun

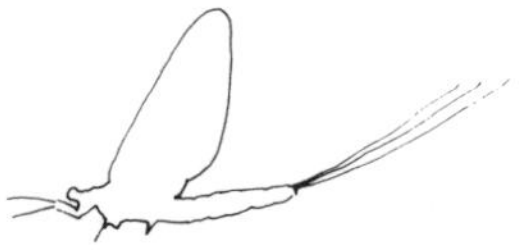

SIZE RANGE: 13 to 16 mm

HOOK SIZES:
SURFACE (dry): #10, #8
SUBSURFACE (wet): #10, #10, 3x long

IMITATIONS:
NYMPH: Varia Compara-nymph
EMERGER: Varia Deerhair emerger
DUN: Paulinskill, Varia Compara-dun, Varia Hackled Compara-dun
SPINNER: Varia Compara-spinner

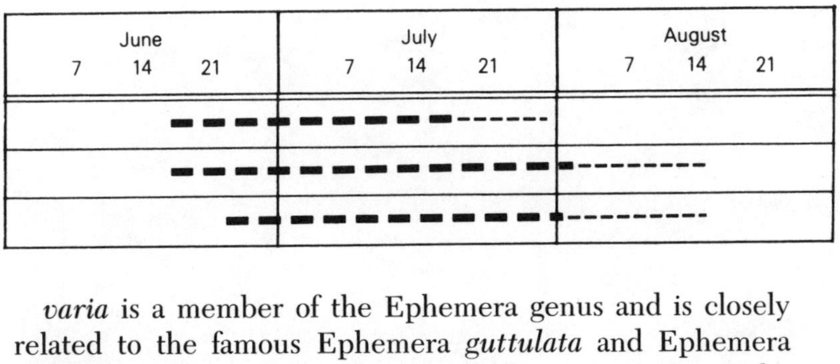

June			July			August		
7	14	21	7	14	21	7	14	21

NYMPH

varia is a member of the Ephemera genus and is closely related to the famous Ephemera *guttulata* and Ephemera *simulans* species. There are a total of seven species in the Ephemera genus. The remaining three, *compar, blanda* and *triplex,* are lesser known to the trout angler. *compar* is a

Western species and is of local importance in the Rocky Mountain drainage systems. *blanda* and *triplex* are limited to the Southeast, mainly the southern Appalachians. Their range is from West Virginia to the Smokies of northern Georgia.

The nymphs of this genus are almost identical, which makes individual identification rather difficult for the average angler. As previously described in the *guttulata* chapter, the Ephemera burrowing nymph forms have plumage-like gills arranged dorsally in two rows on their abdomen and their heads are adorned with fearsome tusks which encompass the deeply forked frontispiece. They are also long, relatively slender and resemble the fish-like swimming mayfly families rather than the sprawling or clinging families.

Trout anglers should be capable of distinguishing the difference between the more important *guttulata*, *varia* and *simulans* species if they intend to research their favorite streams for future prospects of fishing these hatches. The subtle and varying differences in color and markings on these nymphs make this criterion difficult for use in quick identification. Size is also inconclusive, as Ephemera nymphs take several seasons to mature and anglers will often uncover undersized, immature specimens during their stream research. The best way to identify these nymphs is through the deeply forked frontal notch and tuck lengths.

E. *varia,* nymph.

In the Ephemera genus, there are two types of frontal notch; squared and rounded. The inner and outer periphery of *varia's* notch is squarish, while that of *guttulata* and *simulans* is rounded. The differences between *guttulata* and *simulans* can be distinguished by the length of the tusks. The tusks of *guttulata* protrude beyond the frontal process by a length equal to that of the process, while *simulan's* tusks extend twice the length of the frontal process.

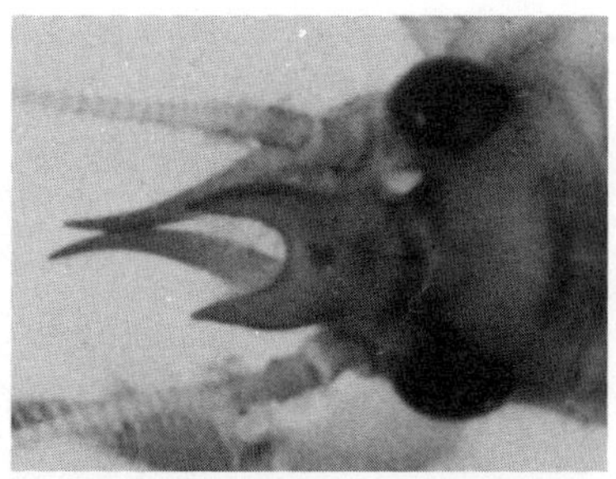

Rounded frontal notch of *guttulata*.

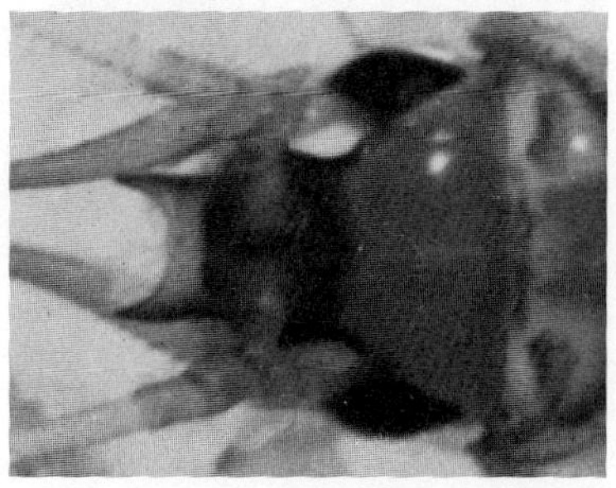

Squared frontal notch of *varia*.

The *varia* nymphs burrow into the same silt beds and mud banks as do those of *guttulata* and *simulans*, but they are also equally abundant in the faster runs and riffles; especially those with sand and gravel bottoms. On faster streams, we have often accumulated collections of them while seining for the nonburrowing types. This indicates that along with their capacity to subsist in rich silt, they also have the ability to clamber about in the gravel in search of food and they use the convenient sand and silt deposits behind the rocks in this faster water to burrow and hide.

During emergence, the *varia* nymphs wiggle to the surface enticingly and rather swiftly. At this time, anglers should utilize as much imagination as possible when manipulating their imitations. During ultra-low-water conditions, more subtle twitches will suggest less urgent emergences and tempt the more wary fish in quieter pools. Developing effective nymph patterns to imitate the complicated body characteristics and swimming motions of this burrowing nymph was a problem that needed constant revision. Our present dressing for this nymph has been very effective for us but we realize there's plenty of room for improvement.

We tie this pattern with Ostrich herl ribbing, which, when activated by the current, duplicates the movements of the plumage-like gills of the natural. Patterns should be dressed on #8 and #10 hooks.

DUN

varia is another important Ephemera species in the East to the fly-fisherman. The cream-colored *varia* duns are erroneously referred to as the Yellow Drake and Yellow Dun in most angling literature. Oddly enough, the yellowish P. *distinctus* mayflies are commonly called Cream Duns and Cream Variants. This is a good reason to always use the less confusing scientific names to promote better communication.

The body of the *varia* dun ranges from 13 to 16mm, with 15mm being about average. The wings are usually 1 or 2mm smaller. Like Potamanthus *distinctus*, *varia* emergence usually takes place around dusk, but on overcast or exceptionally cool days, sporadic hatching may start as early as 6 P.M.

Left: E. *varia,* female dun. *Right:* E. *varia,* female spinner. Their lighter color, smaller size and the absence of blotches in the hind wings easily separates them from E. *guttulata.*

Best hatching takes place on days of low humidity and when water temperature is below 70°F. During hot, humid weather, emergence may take place after dark, when the water cools.

varia duns emerge in all water types; from fast riffles to deep, still pools. At this time, the inviting riffles and runs of the early season on freestone streams are usually reduced to mere trickles, so anglers will do well to select a stretch that is deep enough to provide sufficient cover for the trout and is cool enough (below 70°F) to precipitate a hatch. Pools that are located near the influence of cold springs or stretches located downstream of a cold feeder are usually the most favorable. The use of a thermometer is indispensible during this hot summer period. Anglers should be mobile, probing various stretches of the stream they intend to fish, prior to stringing a rod for the evening hatch.

Once a stretch having the above qualities is selected, anglers should determine the most advantageous casting spot and proceed to their station with extreme caution. Stealth is a requisite to success during the dog days of summer; a thoughtless, splashy entrance to the stream during this time will often put the trout down for the night.

Our pattern evaluation experiences indicate that the Compara-dun is the best producer for this hatch. The upright attitude and wing silhouette are absolutely necessary; especially on slow-flowing, mirror-like pools. On diffused currents, a Hackled Compara-dun may produce better results. As the *varia* and P. *distinctus* naturals often emerge together, have the same hatching characteristics and are of similar size, we sometimes compromise on a common pattern which is tied with a tinge of yellow on the dubbed body and blondish deer hair for the Compara-dun wing. This compromise pattern will usually turn the trick with most trout, but it's wise to have both the cream-colored Varia Compara-dun and the yellowish Distinctus Comparadun on hand for more critical trout. When hackled versions are necessary, we like the Hackled Compara-dun. The Paulinskill is also a good imitation. It was created by the late fly-fishing naturalist, Ray Bergman, author of *Trout;* one of the historic milestones of fly-fishing literature.

SPINNER

Unlike the *guttulata* spinners that appear above the trees in swarms prior to ovipositing, the *varia* imagoes appear much more subtly and are usually first sighted at shoulder height. The males often fall to the surface prematurely to rest, and take off again to complete their copulation act with the females. During a good spinner-fall, many male spinners will rest intermittently on the surface film. Their struggle to regain altitude often prompts smaller fish into splashy rises. Habitual casting for these fish at this time will often spoil your chances for a larger trout later, when the female spinners land en masse and extrude their eggs.

My baptism into *varia* spinner activity (and also to that of Potamanthus) started many years ago on the cascading Pocono streams of northeastern Pennsylvania. During those nostalgic summer evenings, the surface of mysterious rhodedendron-lined pools would often churn with feeding fish, as I unsuccessfully cast my high-riding Light Cahill to exhaustion. During those years it became apparent that closer scrunity of spinner-fall activity and more exacting imitations would be needed if any semblance of success during these spinner-falls was to be obtained.

During the research for our first book, *Comparahatch,* Bob and I vigorously attacked the challenge of these spinner-falls. We conducted comprehensive entomological experiments and pattern evaluations which proved to be so necessary in solving the problems. Many evenings our rods remained reluctantly unstrung as we took up stations in the stream with butterfly nets, tape recorders and other paraphanelia in order to observe the mating flights and collect specimens for photography. Subsequent recording of this mating and oviposting activity became part of our streamside routine for all species. Those fishless nights rewarded us with a wealth of knowledge on overall imago activity which ultimately led to effective pattern development and fishing techniques. Had we instead diverted our attention to tempting, myopic casting over the countless evening rises, it would have certainly taken us many more years to develop the patterns and fishing techniques put forth in this text.

Our imago observations conclude that the Varia Compara-spinner in semispent and fully-spent versions are usually necessary for successful *varia* spinner fishing. The Hackled Compara-dun is excellent when resting males and females are fluttering, attempting to regain their airborne status. Also, this pattern is a good compromise when spinners and duns are on the water simultaneously. The silhouette of the deer hair wing provides an excellent imitation of the emerging duns. Later on, when a flush-floating pattern is needed, the underside hackle can be snipped with clippers.

Semispent spinner patterns are effective when females are on the water struggling to extrude their eggs. When the mating ritual has ended, the spent imitations are deadly for spinner-sipping trout. Anglers should note that *varia* spinner techniques parallel those used during the P. *distinctus* and E. *guttulata* spinner-falls and they should compare these techniques often.

Ephemera simulans

COMMON NAMES: Brown Drake, Chocolate Dun, March Brown

SIZE RANGE: 11 to 14 mm

HOOK SIZES:
SURFACE (dry): #8, #10;
SUBSURFACE (wet): #10; std. or 3x long

IMITATIONS
NYMPH: Simulans Compara-nymph
EMERGER: Simulans Deerhair emerger
DUN: Simulans Compara-dun
SPINNER: Simulans Compara-spinner

This large mayfly is known in angling literature as the Brown Drake. Much has been written over the years to glamorize the *simulans* species, resulting in the elevation of this mayfly to legendary status.

After 4 years of intense stream research on Pennsylvania, New Jersey, New York and New England trout streams, we had to conclude that the *simulans* species doesn't approach being a super hatch on many of these streams. We utilized more time in search of this insect than we did for any other species. Most of our effort was concentrated on western Pennsylvania streams where the initial reports of their importance seem to have originated. We found fantastic numbers of the related Ephemera *guttulata* and Ephemera *varia* on these rich rivers, but nothing in the way of great *simulans* populations.

We did, however, find very good populations on larger rivers such as the East and West Branches of the Delaware River, as well as the main Delaware just below the town of Hancock, N.Y. The Delaware system has produced blizzard-like hatches, but of very short duration (3-5 days). Unfortunately for the weekend angler, it is very possible to miss this hatch completely if hatching takes place during the week.

This is not the case in the Midwest, where the *simulans* activity does approach a fishing hatch of major importance. We have discussed the *simulans* hatch with Gary Schnicke (our Midwestern trips bridged the time period of this hatch), the District Fisheries Biologist from Mio, Michigan who is very knowledgeable on hatches of the Au Sable River system.

Gary claims that *simulans* hatches on the Au Sable and neighboring systems are heavy, but very short in duration. Peak activity on most of the Au Sable is usually during the first five days of June—the latest activity occuring on the "quality water" below Mio Dam on June 10, 11 and 12. He explains that these hatches offer only a few days of angling in any given location. This ultrashort hatching period causes

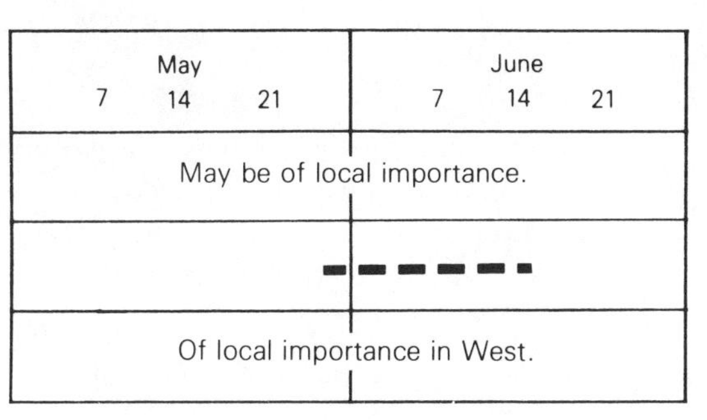

May 7	14	21	June 7	14	21	
May be of local importance.						East
		▬	▬ ▬	▬ ▬		N. Mich. and Wisc.
Of local importance in West.						West

fits among Michigan trout fisherman trying to hit the proper location. He adds that the geographic emergence sequence is similar to that of H. *limbata,* but due to its brief duration, this "sequence" is naturally, less distinct.

Although our initial probes for this species in the West were negative, this should by no means be construed as conclusive as the tests were conducted during the last three weeks in July. Reportedly, there are populations in the Rockies and according to Doug Swisher and Carl Richards, they are supposed to take place after the Ephemerella *grandis* activity.

NYMPH

The *simulans* nymphs are quite similar to those of *varia* in shape and even in color, but there are subtle differences in their characteristics. The most easily recognized difference is in the frontal process and tusks. The tusks of *simulans* are about twice the length of its deeply forked frontal prominence, while those of *varia* are only 1½ times as long. The base of these tusks, when viewed from the top, stem from slightly outside of the base of its antennae.

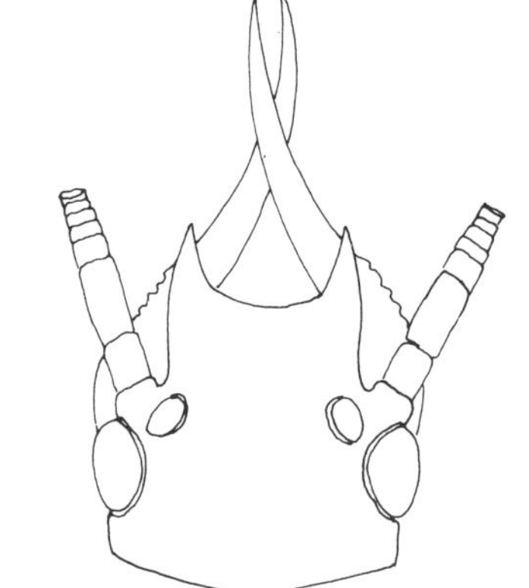

Head of E. *simulans* nymph.

simulans nymphs are equipped to burrow in the silt, but their normal habitat is a mixture of fine sand and gravel similar to the habitat of *varia.*

Typical of most Ephemera nymphs, those of *simulans* emerge rather quickly and wiggle to the surface as soon as they leave their hiding place on the bottom. Anglers should duplicate this ascent by jerking their imitation from the bottom and twitching it vigorously to the surface prior to and during the hatch. Emerger patterns fished in the film should be tried during the hatch.

DUN

The three-tailed duns of Ephemera can be separated from the two-tailed duns of Hexagenia by the typical dark blotches in Ephemera wings.

The dark duns of *simulans* can be distinguished from the lighter subimagoes of *guttulata* by size (its body averages only about half the size of *guttulata)* and by its hind wings which are proportionately smaller (about 35% of the size of the forewings) than those of *guttulata* (almost 50% the size of forewings). The size of the *simulans* duns is similar to *varia.* However, *varia* is a much paler, cream-like species which lacks any blotches on its hind wings. The wings of the *simulans* duns are blotched with dark brown on an olive background. Its body is dark brown influenced with yellow.

In the Midwest, where this species seems to thrive,

emergence takes place between 7 P.M. and dark, according to weather conditions, but will normally occur at dusk. The duns usually emerge from medium runs and pools, but will hatch from all types of water, even fast stretches.

simulans is the first really large mayfly (#8 to #10 hook size) of the season to hatch on Midwestern waters and it is usually greeted by the frenzied feeding of trout, even large ones.

Gary Schnicke has experimented with many patterns over the years, but has assured us that the Compara-dun is extremely deadly during this hatch and that it has become his favorite for most Midwestern hatches. Our favorite imitation is the Simulans Deerhair Emerger fished dead drift in the surface film.

SPINNER

The spinner flights, which are similar to those of *guttulata* and *varia,* usually form prior to twilight and the falls take place at dusk. Often, the spinners and duns will be on the water simultaneously and the trout will normally be selective to those in the greater number; especially the females of either stage. Anglers after big fish should be extremely cautious and stalk these lunkers using the tactics described in the H. *limbata* chapter.

The wing membrane of the spinners is hyaline, but heavily spotted with brown and the body is predominantly dark brown above and yellowish underneath. In view of these characteristics and also the fact that the size range is between 11 and 14mm, these spinners closely resemble the dun stage of the Stenonema *vicarium* in appearance, so anglers should capture a natural to confirm the 3-tailed species; the S. *vicarium* duns have only two.

Genus Hexagenia and Litobrancha

(Family Ephemeridae)

The enormous Hexagenia and Litobrancha mayflies are the largest in America. Although they are found throughout the East and Midwest, their importance is paramount in the Great Lakes region. Hexagenia *limbata* is by far the most widespread and prolific species of the genus and triggers unprecedented feeding sprees by the trout. Michigan natives erroneously call the "hair raising" dusk activity associated with *limbata* the "Caddis Hatch".

Needham lists 18 species of Hexagenia in the 1935 publication *Biology of Mayflies*. This number, however, is now 13 species. Other important Hexagenia and Litobrancha mayflies in both the East and the Midwest are L. *recurvata*, H. *rigida* and H. *atrocaudata*.

These three-tailed nymphs are primarily slow-water types and subsist in the rich marl bottoms of cold lakes, lazy rivers and the backwaters and flats of faster streams. They are easily recognized by their outlandish size and the rounded frontal process located between the tusks, segregating them from the Ephemera genus which has a deeply forked frontal process. The tusks are upcurved, smooth and more slender than those found on the Ephemera nymphs.

Hexagenia habitat on the beautiful Au Sable River in Michigan.

The enormous duns and spinners can be immediately segregated from the large Ephemera adults by their two tails—Ephemera has three. Also, the wings are not spotted; they are prominently veined and margined. The wings are smaller than the body as in Ephemera, but the eyes, especially in the males, are much larger. The upper portion of the eyes are different in color from the lower portion in both sexes although this characteristic is less noticeable in the L. *recurvata* species.

The rounded frontal process of a Hexagenia nymph.

NYMPHS

SPECIES	DIST.	SIZE	FRONTAL PROCESS	FIRST GILL
limbata (now *limbata limbata*)	E, M, W	16-35	dome-shaped	double
recurvata	E, M	16-38	angular	single
atrocaudata	E, M	16-26	truncate	double
*rigida**	E, M	20-30	conical	double

*claw of middle leg is longer and more slender than in closely related species

MALE SPINNER

SPECIES	DIST.	SIZE	ABDOMEN	ABDOMINAL MARKS	DUNS
limbata (now *limbata limbata*)	E, M, W	16-35	yellow	reddish-brown	Body: yellowish, marked with purplish-brown. Wings: medium gray.
recurvata	E, M	16-38	dark yellowish-brown	yellow	Body: dark reddish-brown, almost black, ringed with yellow. Wings: blackish-brown.
atrocaudata	E, M	15-24	blackish	olive	Body: blackish. Legs: dark brown. Wings dark slate.
rigida	E, M	18-28	brown	yellow	Body: yellowish-olive with reddish-brown markings. Wings: pale yellowish gray; the costal margin of forewing and outer margin of hind wing, smoky reddish-brown. Veins: dark.

Hexagenia limbata

COMMON NAMES: Michigan Caddis, Sandfly, Fishfly

SIZE RANGE: 16 to 35 mm

HOOK SIZES:
SURFACE (dry): #6, #8; 4x long
SUBSURFACE (wet): #4, #6, 3x long

IMITATIONS:
NYMPH: Limbata Compara-nymph
EMERGER: Limbata Deerhair emerger
DUN: Nelm's Caddis, Limbata Compara-dun
SPINNER: Limbata Compara-spinner

The legend of the Michigan Caddis can only be equalled by that of the Giant Salmon Fly (Pteronarcys *californica)* of the West, really a stonefly, and the fabulous Green Drake (Ephemera *guttulata)* of the East.

This colossal mayfly is also known as the Sandfly, Fishfly and Mayfly; names commonly used along the beats of the famous Midwestern rivers.

We have captured female duns and spinners of this species with body lengths up to 35mm (1³/₈"). It is reasonable to assume that some are even larger. This outrageous size is only slightly smaller than the giant species of Litobrancha *recurvata*, which can reach lengths of 38mm (1½ inches).

Minnesota, Wisconsin and Michigan are blessed with great *limbata* hatches, but the latter has grown to be synonymous with the Caddis Hatch, an erroneous label given to the *limbata* hatch many years ago.

General hatching in the Midwest begins in early June and dwindles through September, but prime hatching on famous Michigan Rivers usually takes place between June 20 and July 18. The lower Pere Marquette and Manistee River systems, along with the Little Manistee River, White River and Betsie River are usually reliable around the last week in June and the first week in July. Northern rivers like the Boardman, Platte and the upper stretches of the Manistee and Pere Marquette rivers are best the second and third weeks of July. The cold Jordan River has good hatching into August.

Wisconsin Rivers like the magnificent Wolf and Peshtigo Rivers should have good hatching during the last week of June and the first week of July. The eastern Brule and Namekagon Rivers lag by a week. The northernmost rivers that feed Lake Superior like the Bois Brule, Iron and White Rivers are reportedly best in late July and early August.

Emergence in northern Minnesota and the Upper Peninsula of Michigan is similar to the uppermost Wisconsin streams; generally between late July and mid-August. New England, New York and northern Pennsylvania, as well as Quebec, Ontario, Manitoba, British Columbia and some of the Canadian Maritime Provinces have good sporadic emergences of *limbata* in July and August. However, these are usually restricted to cold water lakes and ponds with firm, siltaceous bottoms.

Many Midwestern rivers have a complex sequence of *limbata* emergence. Michigan's classic Au Sable River, the granddaddy of all *limbata* Rivers, is a perfect example of this complexity.

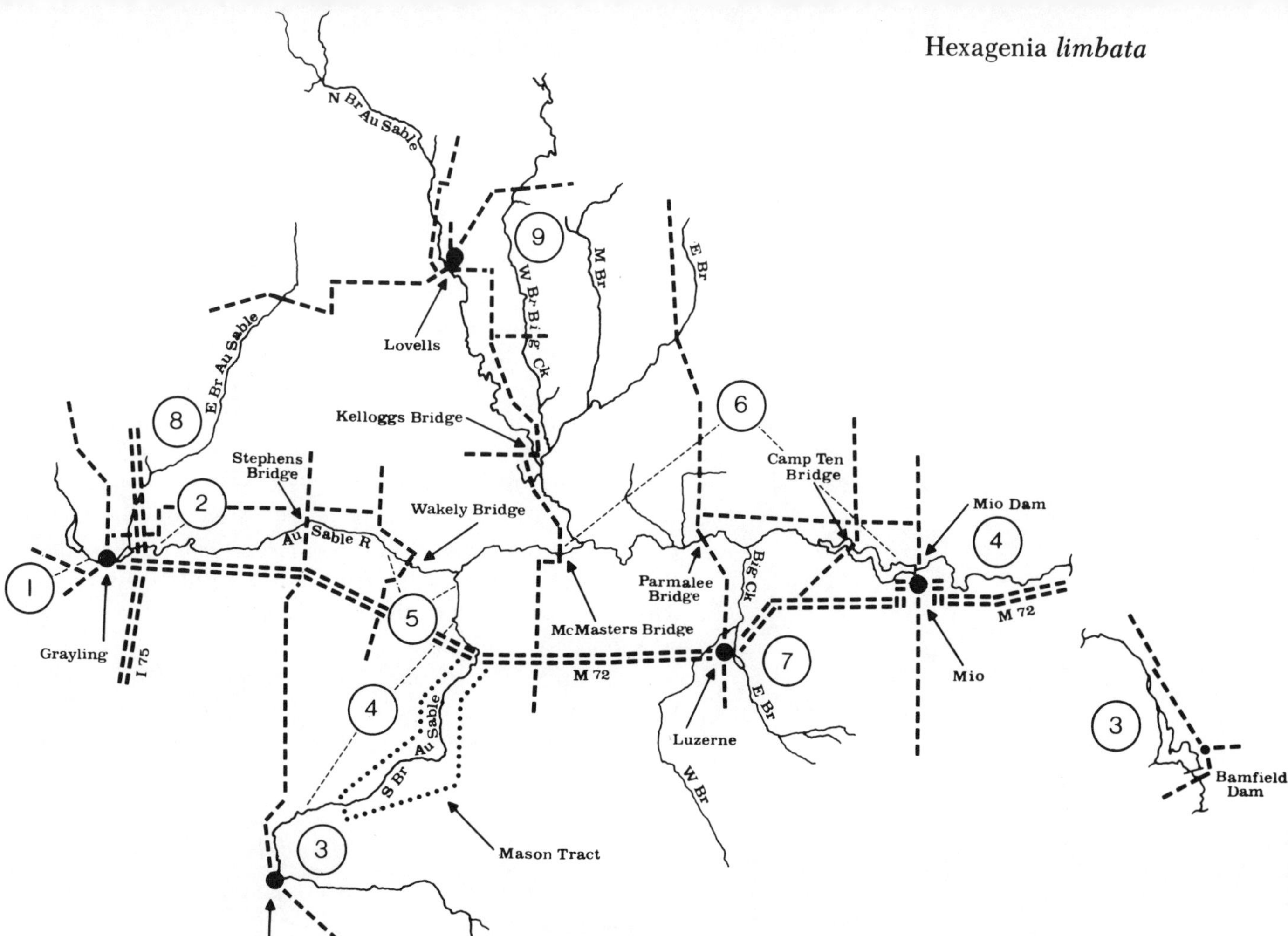

1. June 11 or 12
Between the two impoundments at Grayling—Standard from year to year with very little deviation.

2. June 13 or 14
The swamp 2-4 miles below Grayling—silt and marl beds.

3. June 15.
In the vicinity of Rosscommon. Still water—sand and silt bottom. Also June 15, 16 and 17 above Bamfield Dam—10 to 15 miles downstream of Mio. This is a good fishing hatch for large fish.

4. June 16, 17, 18
Below Mio to McKinley Bridge has very limited Hexagenia—few fishing hatches.
Mason Tract equals more generalized hatching.

5. June 15-20
Between Wakely Bridge and mouth of S. Branch Au Sable River. Not much actual hatching between Wakely Bridge and Burtons Landing (upstream).

6. June 20-22
Magic date 20, for heaviest fished part of Au Sable system—between Mio and McMasters Bridge. Also heaviest population of *limbata* and heaviest fishing pressure.

7. June 25-28
East branch of Big Cr. at Luzerne.

8. June 30-July 1
East branch Au Sable above Grayling.
Good hatches and good feeding activity with nice fish for a small stream.

9. After July 4
Big Cr. (North of Main Au Sable) relatively good hatches of Limbata—lasts 10 to 14 days. (Tributary) Best below Lovells. North branch of Au Sable—just before Big Creek—starting July 1. Only lower N. branch (Kelloggs Bridge and down) has Hexagenia.

Throughout the text we have repeatedly stressed that mayfly hatches are controlled mainly by water temperature. Normally, hatching starts in a stream's lower sections and moves progressively upstream as the water warms—not so with the Au Sable. The Au Sable varies greatly in temperature throughout its length, especially in traditional trout waters above Mio Dam. There are approximately 300 to 400 miles of prime trout water in the upper third of the river system which will vary alternately in terms of reaching ideal water temperature for hatching. This temperature is controlled largely by ground water influx. Stretches with a large number of spring-heads will of course be colder than those areas without them. These cold water influxs are located downstream as well as at the headwaters. Conversely, headwaters or tributaries may also be influenced by lakes or impoundments which allow the water to warm sooner; hence, hatching may take place 60 miles upstream, weeks before emergence begins in the lower stretches (see map).

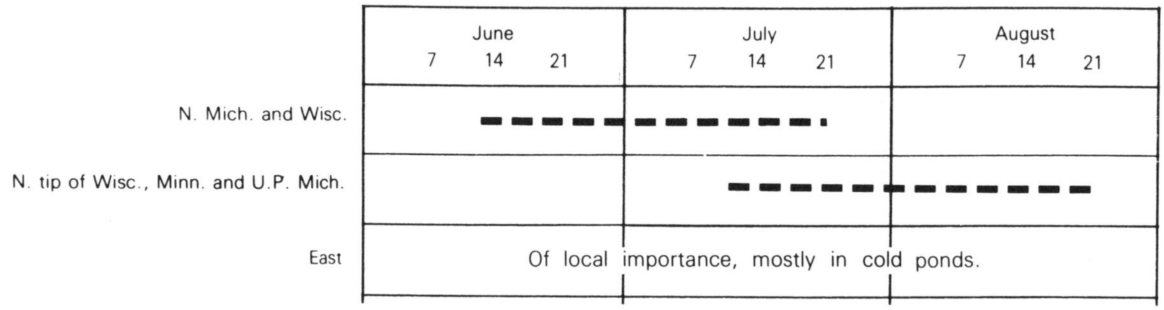

	June 7	June 14	June 21	July 7	July 14	July 21	August 7	August 14	August 21
N. Mich. and Wisc.		▬ ▬	▬ ▬ ▬	▬ ▬ ▬	▬ ▬	▬			
N. tip of Wisc., Minn. and U.P. Mich.					▬ ▬	▬ ▬ ▬	▬ ▬ ▬	▬ ▬	▬
East	Of local importance, mostly in cold ponds.								

NYMPH

The nymphs of the genus Hexagenia (and Litobrancha *recurvata*) are the largest mayflies in North America. The species *limbata* and *recurvata* are the largest of those which constitute a major fishing hatch, while *rigida* is a close third followed by *atrocaudata*. We have captured mature H. *limbata* and L. *recurvata* nymphs up to 35mm (1³/₈″) and 38mm (1¹/₂″) respectively.

The species of the Hexagenia genus belong to the Ephemeridae family, as do all true burrowing mayflies. Most anglers confuse Hexagenia with the burrowing Ephemera genus, especially Ephemera *guttulata* (Green Drake) whose size almost approaches that of some of the smaller Hexagenia nymphs.

Fortunately, nature has provided the angler with an unmistakeable identification characteristic in the nymphal state. The frontispiece of all of the Ephemera species is deeply forked between the tusks, while in Hexagenia it is extended and rounded.

Identification of the individual Hexagenia species is much

H. *limbata*, nymph.

more difficult than determining the differences between genera. But, when one combines the subtle differences in body characteristics, coloration, size and geographic distribution, he can usually differentiate among the species.

H. *limbata* and L. *recurvata* are similar in size and distribution range but *limbata* is more common in streams. The main differences are in the gills, general coloration, body configuration and tusks. The first pair of abdominal gills on *limbata* are doubles, while *recurvata's* are singular. *limbata* is usually a brownish-gray in appearance with purplish highlights, while the general coloration of *recurvata* is that of reddish-brown with amber highlights. Also, *limbata* is more slender in the thorax and abdomen than is *recurvata*. For differences in the tusks, see illustration.

The fascinating *limbata* nymph thrives on marl-rich, siltaceous bottoms laden with detritous. In these slow-moving stretches, they obtain life-giving oxygen by undulating their bodies and plumage-like gills which are arranged in dorsal fashion on each side of their abdomen.

These nymphs are extremely hardy, as are most of the burrowers, especially as they become mature. Maturity usually takes two years in trout streams, but in some lakes and ultra-rich areas of streams, adulthood can be achieved in one year.

Our exploratory diggings have revealed that the best nymph populations are usually found in 3 to 6 inches of silt firm enough to support their U-shaped burrows.

Reportedly, the nymphs seldom leave their burrows, yet Justin and Fannie Leonard state in their informative volume, *Mayflies of Michigan Trout Streams*, that autopsies of fish taken in the fall and winter months reveal that fish feed on nymphs regularly. Our aquarium studies have shown that

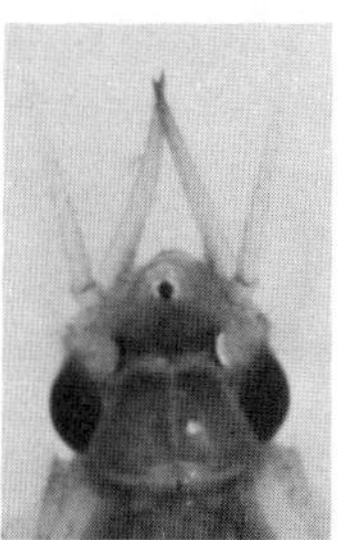

Left: limbata tusks. *Right: recurvata* tusks. Note the rounded frontispiece of both compared to the forked frontispiece of Ephemera below.

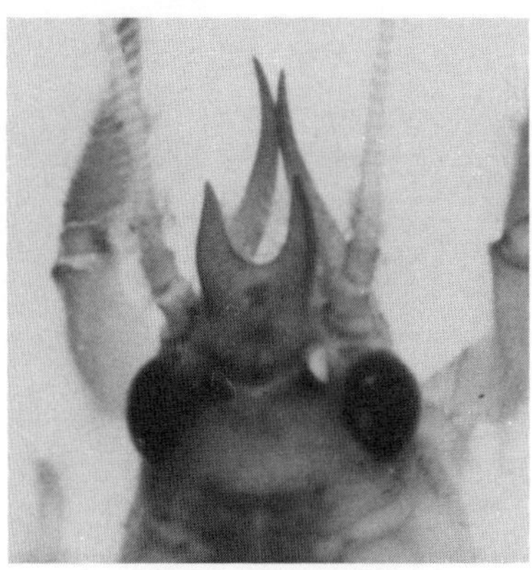

the nymphs seldom leave their burrows. However, we feel that our experiments were inconclusive due to the confined environment.

Perhaps the answer to this perplexity lies in the moulting periods. Like E. *guttulata*, the *limbata* nymphs moult more than 30 times (approximately once every 24 days) before they become adults. In a rich stream with optimum conditions, Leonard notes that as many as 500 nymphs can be supported per square foot of stream bottom. If a trout's domain is a 10 ft. x 10 ft. area, then it is conceivable that every 24 days, 50,000 nymphs (100 sq. ft. x 500 nymphs per sq. ft.) would be exposed to the trout, or a possible 2000 nymphs per day. These calculations are based on maturity occuring in two years in optimum water conditions. Considering these circumstances, *limbata* nymphs are probably a staple food in the trout's diet all year round.

During emergence, nymphs evacuate their burrows and wiggle enticingly to the surface, creating easy opportunities for the trout. Their ascent is reasonably fast considering their poor swimming capabilities.

To imitate the ascending nymphs, we like the weighted Limbata Compara-nymph in sizes #6 and #8. Patterns should be allowed to sink to the bottom and then be fished with pulsating jerks to imitate the ascent. All patterns should be tied on 3x long hooks.

Once in the surface film, the nymphs usually have great difficulty escaping their shucks and sometimes float for 10 or 15 minutes in the surface film as a struggling nymph or a partially emerged dun. This was dramatically demonstrated to us one cloudy evening on a flat stretch of the Au Sable River, several miles above Mio in the vicinity of Camp Ten Bridge.

We had purposely left our rods unstrung in the station wagon. It was 7 P.M. when we reached the river. Our arms were filled with butterfly nets, silt strainers and various containers to hold the duns and nymphs that we would photograph.

Several large trout were swirling and porpoising for what we thought were *limbata* duns. After some predictable mumbling about not having our tackle with us, we stealthfully eased ourselves into the river to get a better look. Although there were sprinklings of duns on the surface, they were greatly outnumbered by struggling *limbata* nymphs wiggling provocatively in the surface film. It took most emergers up to 10 minutes and sometimes longer to slither out of their shucks. Nymphs that weren't sucked in by the feeding trout, or picked off by swifts and waxwings, floated out of sight before they became duns.

Although our movements were cautious, the fish sensed our presence and soon stopped feeding. When we returned with our gear, the nymphs were still emerging, but the trout were through feeding for the night. It was 9 P.M. and twilight had not yet arrived.

Some of the lessons learned that evening were that trout are quite fond of these helpless emergers, that they become satiated quickly and that they spook very easily.

On long, flat stretches and in back-waters, trout will usually cruise, gulping the hapless emergers. In this situation, anglers must anticipate the path of the individual feeding fish and cast his fly 5 to 10 feet above where he expects him to reappear. A slight vibration or quiver added to the floating emerger pattern is deadly here. For this kind of work we like the deerhair compara-emerger tied on light wire hooks. This extremely bouyant fly, with shortened deerhair wings is an excellent imitation of the partially sprouted wings of the natural emerger.

In slow-to-medium currents, this pattern should be presented to the trout a la dry-fly, dead-drift method. Extreme caution must be exercised as most *limbata* streams have good wild-fish populations which spook easily.

On faster stretches, trout usually lurk in eddies of deadfalls and in the dark crevices of undercut banks. Here they pick the nymphs off as they drift by their convenient lies. Again, the angler should use the upstream dead-drift method.

DUN

To many anglers, the *limbata* hatch is the single-most explosive fishing hatch in North America. To others, it remains one of the most controversial fishing hatches in all fly-fishingdom.

We have been on the classic Midwestern rivers when the big flies blanketed the water and nary a fish rose. We have also been there during the hatch when the resounding thrashes of large rising fish echoed down the river, amplified in the darkness.

The trout's fickle behavior during this hatch and the angler's potential for success can usually be determined by the timing of the emergence sequence and the stealth utilized by the angler.

The timing of the emergence is critical and is more productive in the earlier phase of this hatch, usually during the first week. At this time, large fish surface-feed noisily on the enormous, struggling duns which seem to lack the ability to get off the water. The much-publicized feeding orgies usually take place at this time.

The Au Sable River system in Michigan typifies the complex emergence sequence on many Midwestern *limbata* rivers (see map on p. 223). Anglers should accumulate similar data on their favorite rivers as to realize the potential the *limbata* activity has to offer. According to the "sequence", the angler can experience the dynamic "early phase" of the hatch for more than a month if he plans his activity within an area of a 20-mile radius.

After the early phase, the orgiastic feeding sprees subside as the satiated lunkers sense the regular availability of insects which blanket the river daily from dusk until late in the evening.

During this secondary, more cautious feeding phase, productive fishing gets tougher, but the chances of taking several big fish in an evening's work are still good. The trout will usually surface for a brief period between dusk and midnight. At this time, the river resembles a conveyor belt full of live, quivering insects. Under these conditions, it takes a brief time for even the largest fish to fill up on the mammoth-sized *limbatas*. Satisfied, these fish will stop feeding until the next pangs of hunger urge them to resurface either later that night or again the following night.

During the secondary phase, anglers should, prior to dusk, stealthfully position themselves within casting range of a few known risers. Earlier, during the daylight hours, time should be taken to explore the river's bottom as a mishap can abruptly conclude the evening's fishing on a very wet and cold basis.

After stationing himself appropriately, the angler should refrain from casting until fish are rising freely. Repeated casting is usually necessary at this time as the imitation must compete with the galaxy of floating naturals. Extreme caution must be taken to avoid stumbling or splashing as most trout in *limbata* waters are usually wild fish that spook easily.

Tactics used in the earlier hatches, when trout are feeding greedily, parallel those used in the East during the E. *guttulata* hatch. Artificials should be cast and allowed to float naturally over feeding fish. Some individual fish will take only those insects that are struggling. Where this is the case, imitations must be twitched and fluttered to simulate the natural. Anglers should try both methods before giving up on a fish. During this time, when fish are slashing everywhere, the angler should concentrate on a few good fish instead of trying to catch every fish in the pool to avoid spooking even the most avid feeders.

Artificials used during this hatch make up the wildest assortment of sizes, colors and configurations used anywhere in trout fishing. Some concoctions rival those used for large-mouthed bass on Southern rivers. Each river system has its own local favorites.

Most of these favorites are relatively successful because of the tremendous size variance of the naturals and the contorted positions that they assume on the stream's surface. Insect sizes may range from 16 to 35mm, a difference of more than 100%.

We prefer to use the smaller #6 or #8, 4x long, sizes as they are more representative of the naturals and are much easier to cast. Our favorites for the dun and sometimes the spinner is the Limbata Hackled Compara-dun which is tied with several turns of gray dun hackle forward and aft of the deer hair wing.

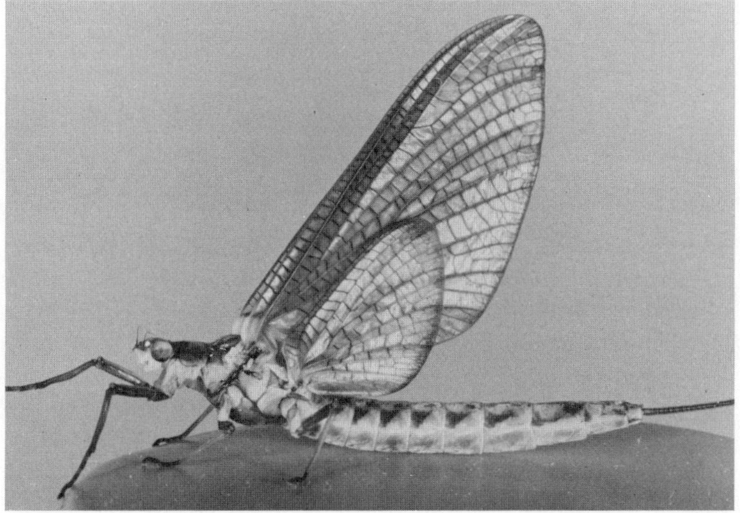

H. *limbata,* female dun.

H. *limbata,* female spinner.

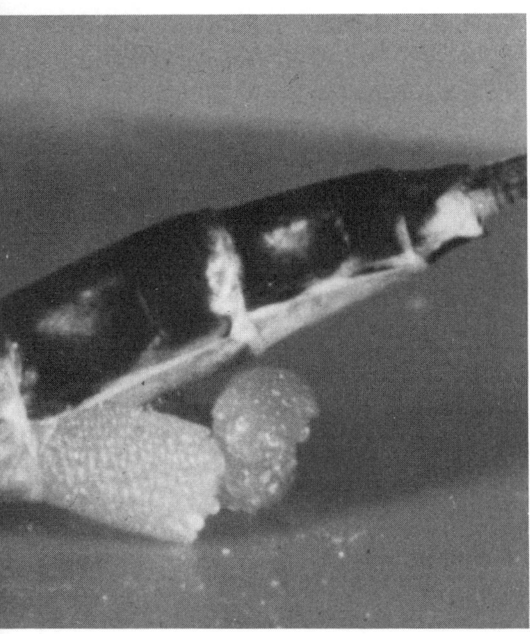

Double egg packets

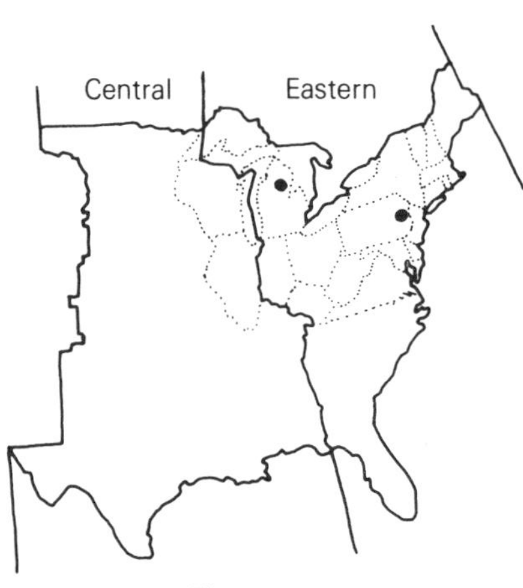

Time zones

SPINNER

Final moulting usually takes place between 24 and 72 hours after emergence. Imagoes are then ready to join the cloud-like spinner flights and subsequent mating ritual.

After nuptial flights and copulation, the females drop to the stream's surface to extrude their twin yellowish egg packets containing about 3,000 eggs. During ovipositing, the female lays prone on the surface film, quivering and convulsing as she squeezes the egg pellets from the double oviducts located on the 7th segment of her body. The eggs sink to the bottom and settle in crevices of gravel where they hatch in about two weeks.

Though spinner-falls are common on all types of water, imagoes seem to have a preference for riffled areas.

While imago flights are fairly regular, a sudden cold spell will usually retard moulting. Rain or mist will cancel out spinner flights for the evening.

The mating flights and following spinner-falls usually take place between 9 and 11 P.M. On cloudy days, spinner activity may take place several hours before dusk. Occasionally, spinner activity may last beyond midnight.

The times discussed here may be misleading to some Eastern anglers who relate 9 P.M. to dusk conditions. In northern Michigan, which has the best *limbata* hatches, the transition from daylight to dark is a long and smooth process. This is caused by Michigan's northern latitude, the absence of shadowy mountains and the fact that Michigan is located on the western edge of the eastern time zone. All of these factors add up to about an hour and one-half of light advantage. Hence, visability at 10:30 P.M. on a northern Michigan stream is relative to 9 P.M. conditions on a rugged mountain stream in New York or Pennsylvania.

On the larger river sections, awesome spinner flights of *limbata* are both spectacular and mysterious. The spent spinners blanket the river almost nightly. Yet, catching the actual spinner-falls (which usually produce better angling) can be quite evasive.

We have spent unproductive evenings when tremendous masses of spent spinners flushed past our waders for almost two hours, creating only sporadic, distant feeding. On other evenings, when we were fortunate enough to guess the location of actual spinner-falls, fishing was much more exciting and productive.

The *limbata* spinners create much more impact on smaller river stretches and tributaries. Here, fishing both the actual spinner-falls and the drifts of ovipositing spent spinners is usually very productive. However, as mentioned in the dun section, and pinpointed on the emergence sequence map, the initial spinner flights that arrive during the first week are the most productive and stimulate the best feeding activity.

On large rivers like the main branches of the Au Sable and the Manistee, it's usually customary to use very heavy tackle during the *limbata* hatch. We find this practice tiresome, cumbersome and unnecessary, as, prior to the action created by the *limbata* spinners, excellent and challenging angling for smaller trout can be enjoyed. These fish move out into open water to feed on the various spinner stages of Ephemerella *lata,* Isonychia *sadleri,* Psuedocoen *anoka* and spinners of the Siphlonurus and Stenonema species.

Fine tackle, for delicate presentation, is needed as these trout are usually ultra-selective. Since the refinement of graphite in the past decade, we use 8 to 9 foot rods and 6 and 7 weight lines for this work. Prior to the arrival of the *limbata* spinners we cut our 10½-foot leaders back to 2x or 3x depending on the size of the *limbata* imitation used. We've taken large fish easily on this gear and we have never had to quit prematurely due to a tired, aching casting arm.

During this preliminary activity, the angler should explore the stream's bottom carefully for safety purposes, while keeping a distant eye on deadfalls and undercut banks for signs of big fish feeding. As previously discussed, extreme caution must be utilized as these fish spook easily. It's best not to prematurely disturb those waters suspected of holding large fish until later.

When trout are taking the ovipositing spinners we like the Compara-spinner or Compara-dun tied on #6 or #8, 4x long hooks. The spinner pattern should be tied with full hackle and trimmed at streamside if this is needed. The pattern should be cast upstream and allowed to float over the trout dead-drift. Sometimes a timely twitch or jerk will take a wise brown that previously ignored your drag-free float. Another good imitation of local vintage is "Nelems Caddis". Our good friend, Gary Schnike, a knowledgeable fly-fisherman and fisheries Biologist from, Mio, Michigan, recommends this pattern. Gary knows the Au Sable intimately and takes big trout on a modified version of this pattern.

Fishing the *limbata* hatches on the classic, full-volume rivers of northern Michigan is truly one of America's great angling experiences. These congenial rivers coupled with the genuine friendship extended by the rugged natives make this double-barreled combination "tough to beat".

Litobrancha recurvata

(*was Hexagenia recurvata*)

COMMON NAMES: Dark Green Drake, Mayfly, Drakefly, Great Dark Green Drake

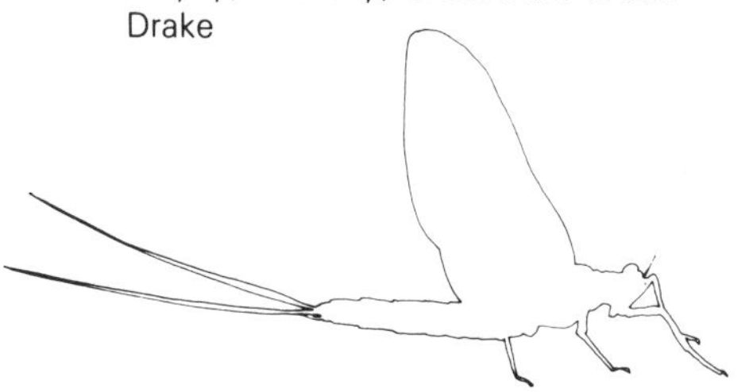

SIZE RANGE: 16 to 38 mm

HOOK SIZES:
SURFACE (dry): #8, #6, and #8; 4x long
SUBSURFACE (wet): #6, #4, #6; 3x long

IMITATIONS:
NYMPH: Recurvata Compara-nymph
EMERGER: Recurvata Deerhair emerger
DUN: Recurvata Compara-dun, Recurvata Hackled Compara-dun
SPINNER: Recurvata Compara-spinner

Hexagenia *recurvata* is one of the lesser-known mayfly species. However, on waters where they thrive, their impact on the trout community can approach that of H. *limbata.* This insect is found primarily on Northern and Midwestern lakes and streams having rich, firm silt bottoms. Good populations can also be found on Appalachian rivers from the Canadian Provinces to the Virginias; expecially those of cold limestone origin such as those found in western Pennsylvania, Michigan, Wisconsin and Minnesota.

Emergence on the limestone streams of western Pennsylvania usually occurs in late May. Hatching on the famous Fishing Creek above La Mar, Pa. usually centers around the 24th of May. Streams further north usually hatch throughout June. Emergence in the Midwest can start toward the end of May, but the best hatching takes place in June.

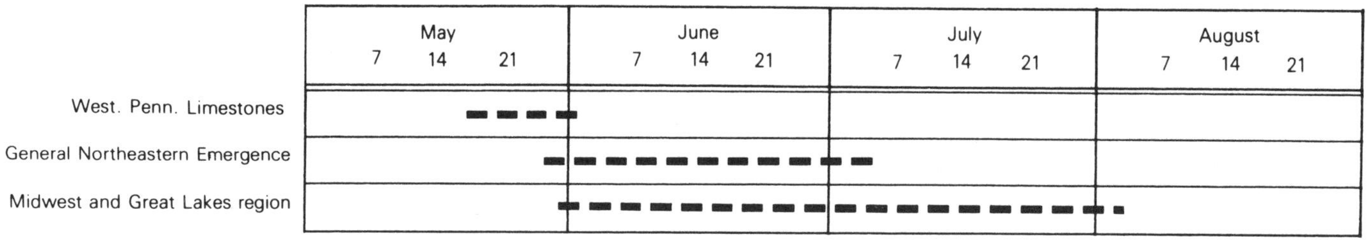

	May 7 14 21	June 7 14 21	July 7 14 21	August 7 14 21
West. Penn. Limestones	— — — —	—		
General Northeastern Emergence	—	— — — — — — — — — —	— —	
Midwest and Great Lakes region	—	— — — — — — — — —	— — — — — — — — —	—

NYMPH

recurvata has the distinction of being the largest mayfly of angling importance in North America. To the angler, it is also the second most important species of the large Litobrancha and Hexagenia genera.*limbata* is the most important, while H. *rigida* and *atrocaudata* can also be of importance. *rigida* is abundant on warmer, marginal trout rivers, while *atrocaudata* (which seldom reaches 1" [24mm] in body length) can be found in the same geographic areas as *recurvata* and *limbata.*

We found excellent populations of *recurvata* on the western Pennsylvania limestone streams. During the third week of May in 1973 we took collections of these nymphs from Fishing Creek at La Mar, Pa. and stocked our lab aquariums. It is interesting to note that although these nymphs were subjected to constant handling and extreme temperature differences during our photographic sessions and experiments, they hatched in our lab between the 22nd and the 26th of May. Amazingly, the hatching results were almost 100%. Like most species of the Hexagenia and Ephemera genera, *recurvata* nymphs are extremely hardy when they approach maturity. This is usually true of most species which take several years to develop.

Conversely, these same durable nymphs are most delicate during their critical embryonic and early nymphal stages, requiring close tolerance of environment and water temperature to exist. Hence, the best populations will only be found in rich, cold ecosystems free of toxic, thermal and other types of pollution.

recurvata nymphs thrive in rich silt firm enough to support their burrows, yet fertile enough to generate the minute life on which they feed.

Like *limbata,* these nymphs, on leaving their burrows, wiggle enticingly to the surface. Once within the surface tension they experience great difficulty in escaping their shucks. This situation presents easy opportunities for the trout, which sometimes relish the squirming emergers more than the duns.

Prior to emergence, when nymphs are swimming to the surface, a nymph pattern is a good bet. Your imitation should be allowed to sink above a suspected lair and be jigged off of the bottom with enticing jerks as it approaches the trout's position. The Recurvata Compara-nymph is excellent for this work. As nymph sizes vary about 100% (16 mm to 38 mm), patterns should be dressed on #4 through #6 hooks, 3x long.

When trout are taking the struggling emergers in the surface film, the compara-emerger dressed with dark deerhair, will often take those trout feeding on the surface or in

Left: L. *recurvata*, nymph. *Right:* L. *recurvata*, male dun.

the film. We tie this buoyant emerger pattern with stiff tails which act as pontoons. These patterns can be deadly when fished throughout the hatch and sometimes will prove to be more effective than if you had switched to a dry-fly.

DUN

This dun is known as the Dark Green Drake, Mayfly, Drake fly, or Great Dark Green Drake. Oddly enough, the most commonly accepted term for this dark, reddish-brown insect is Dark Green Drake. This erroneous term is typical of the serious problem of incorrect terminology that confronts the angler. The only logical answer to this confusion is for anglers to use scientific names such as *recurvata* and *limbata*. Soon they will roll off the tongue as easily as *gladiola*, the scientific name given to the popular flower.

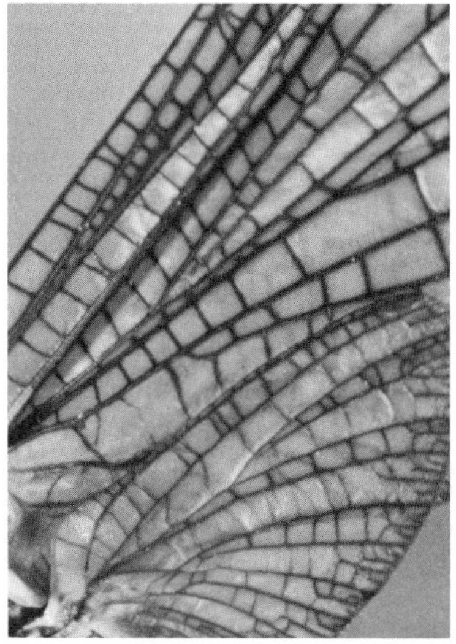

Top: Venation detail, female dun.
Bottom: Venation detail, male dun.

recurvata is widely distributed but seldom is it found in the same density as *limbata*. Where it is found in good number, the fishing aspects of this insect can approach that of its more famous *limbata* species.

These monstorous duns seem blackish on the wing and are so large that they resemble small birds in flight. When scrutinized at close range, the wings of the female are a medium tannish-gray with dark brown (almost black) venations. The male wings are of the same general coloration, except that the venations are more heavily margined, reducing the size of the "panes" between venations, thus resembling stained glass windows. The bodies are a dull, dark blackish-brown with yellow segmental markings.

A remorseful characteristic of this hatch is its short emergence period; usually only four days at any location. Therefore, if hatching should start at the beginning of a week, it is quite doubtful that the majority of weekend anglers would even be aware of its having passed.

Emergence usually begins at dusk and continues after dark. It's not unusual to witness sporadic hatching in daylight hours during dark, cloudy days. The awkward duns, handicapped by their enormous bodies, struggle visibly on the stream's surface. Like *limbata*, they seem to float eternally in their attempt to take flight. On the more rugged mountainous limestone streams, these long floats result in many cripples. Repeated attempts at flight and tarrying cripples create easy meals for the predacious trout.

For all dry-fly work, we recommend the Recurvata Compara-dun, with and without hackle. On faster stretches, the silhouette of the natural is diffused by the broken currents. Therefore, we tie in several turns of very dark gray hackle fore-and-aft of the deer hair wing. This enables the angler to activate his imitation, thus duplicating the struggling movement of the natural. For slower, flatter stretches, we reduce or sometimes eliminate the hackle in accordance with the behavior of the duns.

Like the nymphs, the size variation of the duns are extreme (16 to 38 mm), so we favor smaller size hooks (#6 or #8) with longer shanks. They are easier to cast and are more acceptable to very selective trout. Sometimes an outrageously sized imitation will be the undoing of a curious feeder.

Charles Wetzel treated these duns as a major hatch in his book, *"Trout Flies."* This 1955 publication recommended the Dark Green Drake for the male dun imitation tied on a #8 hook. No mention was made of the female dun.

SPINNER

In the East, spinner-falls are usually overlooked by anglers as they may occur simultaneously with Ephemera *guttulata* activity. Like *limbata,* final moulting takes place in 24 to 72 hours.

A unique characteristic of this species is that it is very difficult to determine the difference between the dun and spinner stages. The angler must capture a specimen and scrutinize it very carefully before he can actually distinguish between the stages. In the case of the male spinner, however, the giveaway is the elongated forelegs and tails, typical of most imagoes. The body of the female is reddish-brown as opposed to the dull, dark brown body color of the dun.

Spinners usually fall at dusk and their number can be rather staggering. Even streams that have seemingly inconsequential hatching activity can produce surprising spinner-falls. The accumulation of duns which have hatched throughout the emergence period gather in concentrated mating swarms creating heavy spinner-falls which may occur for only a few nights.

After the mating ritual, the female extrudes its egg packets onto the surface, conforming to the ovipositing habits of the similar Hexagenia genera. They usually die here, spent in the throes of a quivering death struggle. Some spent spinners, however, tarry in eddies and back-waters until morning. The wise angler will take advantage of trout feeding on these early-morning stragglers.

Imitations for the spinners are identical to those used for the dun, except that when trout are taking spent spinners in the surface film, the Recurvata Compara-spinner is more imitative. Angling tactics for *recurvata* spinner activity border on those used during the *limbata* falls, except that due to the short appearance of these imagoes, anglers may find the trout in a more cooperative mood.

Genus Potamanthus
(Family Potamanthidae)

Bull-like horns of P. *distinctus.*

The midsummer hatches of the yellowish Potamanthus mayflies are surprisingly important to the late-season Eastern angler. Although they are widely distributed throughout the Eastern and Central United States, their impact is greatest on the freestone streams of the Northeast and in the southern Appalachians from Maryland to North Carolina where they constitute the ultimate low-water challenge for the fly-fisherman. This interesting dusk activity comes at a time when most fishermen have swapped streamside activity for baseball and backyard barbecues; thus, the persistent angler who pursues this Potamanthus action will be rewarded by fishing over sophisticated holdover or native fish in an atmosphere of rare solitude.

Needham listed 8 species of Potamanthus in 1935. More recently, entomologists have synonymized the *medius* species under that of *myops*, but another species, *walkeri* which was added after Needham's list, still brings the total to 8 species.

The striking Potamanthus nymphs are of moderate size. Unlike the filamentous semidorsal gills of the Ephemera nymphs, those of Potamanthus have wholly lateral gills on

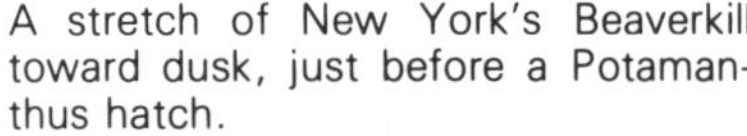

A stretch of New York's Beaverkill toward dusk, just before a Potamanthus hatch.

segments 2-7 which are forked and have a distinct appearance of paired hackle feathers. They also have three tails and the femora are flat and wide, resembling those of the fast-water clinging nymphs. Unlike the Ephemera, Ephoron, Hexagenia and Litobrancha genera, the tusks of Potamanthus nymphs have spines located dorsally and hairs on their outer margins near the base. The tusks are proportionally thicker at the base and have a pincer-like configuration much like the horns of a bull.

The adults wings are not spotted as in Ephemera, nor heavily veined as in Hexagenia; rather, they are pale yellow or whitish with pale longitudinal veins. The cross-veins are often fine or narrow, yet dark in most species. The adults have three tails, the middle tail being somewhat shorter than the outer tail. The eyes of both sexes are almost equal in size and surprisingly small.

Unique, dark cross-veins highlight the otherwise pale wings.

MALE SPINNER

SPECIES	DIST.	SIZE (mm)	CROSS-VEINS MALE	CROSS-VEINS FEMALE	ABDOMINAL MARKS (sides)	EYES	TAIL JOININGS	WING COLOR
distinctus	E, M	13-16	dark	dark	stripes	moderate	reddish-brown	yellow
rufous	E, M	14-15	pale	pale	spots	small	reddish	pale
neglectus	E, M	8-9	dark	dark	spots	small	black	mostly hyaline
diaphanus	E	8-10	pale	pale	none	large	faint	whitish
verticis	E, M	9-10	pale	dark	spots	large	yellowish-brown	white
inequalis	E	10-12	pale	–	none	small	faint	whitish hyaline

Species description of nymphs not known.

DUNS. *distinctus:* yellowish body, wings, legs and tails. Abdominal markings present. *rufous:* similar to *distinctus*. *neglectus:* creamy white body, wings, legs and tails. Abdominal markings present. *diaphanus:* pale yellowish-white body, wings, legs and tails. No abdominal marks. *verticis:* whitish body, wings, legs and tails. Abdominal marks present. *inequalis:* yellowish-white body, wings, legs and tails. Very faint brownish marks present.

Potamanthus distinctus

(Family Potamanthidae)

COMMON NAMES: Golden Drake, Cream Dun, Evening Dun, Cream Variant, Yellow Drake

SIZE RANGE: 13-16 mm

HOOK SIZES.
SURFACE (dry): #10, #8
SUBSURFACE (wet): #10, #10, 3x long

IMITATIONS:
NYMPH: Distinctus Compara-nymph
EMERGER: Light Cahill Wet, Distinctus Deerhair emerger
DUN: Distinctus Compara-dun, Distinctus Hackled Compara-dun
SPINNER: Distinctus Compara-spinner

The large yellow mayflies of Potamanthus *distinctus*, along with the cream duns of Ephemera *varia*, can constitute some of the best evening activity of the late summer season in the Northeast.

The general emergence span for the *distinctus* in the East and Midwest is from the latter part of June to mid-August. Although this species enjoys a large geographic distribution, it reaches its greatest importance in the Northeast, where its abundance makes it a primary food source for the dusk-feeding trout.

Catskill streams like the Schoharie, Esopus, and East Branch of the Delaware River are generally best in July, but we have caught good hatches on the neighboring Beaverkill system as early as June 15 and as late as August 14. The Adirondacks and the New England areas are reliable the last two weeks of July and the first two weeks of August. Best hatching in the Poconos and western Pennsylvania usually takes place between June 25 and July 17. Through the years, *distinctus* activity in the Poconos and Catskills has produced some heavy and selective feeding activity in the late summer season on small to medium size freestone streams.

	June 7	June 14	June 21	July 7	July 14	July 21	August 7	August 14	August 21
N. and W. Penna. and Poconos									
N.Y., New England, Catskills and Adirondacks									
Midwest and Great Lakes region									

NYMPH

The striking Potamanthus nymphs are very distinct and easy to recognize among other mayfly genera. Their most unique characteristic are their obvious gills which extend laterally from the body in pairs on abdominal segments 2 through 7. These forked gills resemble tiny pairs of ginger hackle-feathers. Other easily recognized characteristics are the large pincer-like tusks which protrude like a pair of bull's horns and the brown mosaic-like symmetrical body markings which are arranged dorsally over the amber colored body. The body length ranges from 13 to 16mm, with the average size being around 15mm.

Through the years, the Potamanthus nymph-forms were usually mistaken for burrowers. This is probably due to their original classification in the Ephemeridae family (which indicates all true burrowing insects). They have since then, been placed in their own family, Potamanthidae. However, these agile nymphs are not burrowers at all, but are of the crawling and slower swimming types of the Polymitarcidae family which inhabit the quiet stretches and medium runs as well as the eddies of faster pocket-water.

In the quiet stretches, the *distinctus* nymphs usually share the same gravel and siltacious habitats as those nymphs of the Hexagenia and Ephemera genera.

Prior to emergence, the nymphs move about nervously on the bottom, prompting the trout to feed. Around dusk, they usually make a quick ascent to the surface, lingering momentarily as they transform into the delicate duns, and fly off.

During this activity, nymph patterns should be allowed to sink toward the bottom. Trout will often take them as they drift by their lies, but the best results usually occur when the imitations are jerked off the bottom with erratic twitches.

A time-tested pattern that works well is the Light Cahill tied in wet-fly fashion. This pattern is a favorite with old-timers in the Pocono and Catskill areas during the late season and they score well with it tied on a #10 hook, or larger. This is not too surprising because the barred Wood duck wing and light gingerish hackle blended over the creamish body of this classic pattern is very impressionistic of the *distinctus* nymph. It's even more imitative when fished with twitching jerks in typical wet-fly fashion.

P. *distinctus,* nymph.

DUN

The yellow *distinctus* duns are commonly called Golden Drakes, Cream Duns and Evening Duns. They usually appear on quiet-to-medium stretches with the creamish-colored duns of Ephemera *varia*. Their differences are contrasting enough that observant anglers can usually discriminate them on the wing. However, this is a bad practice and we recommend the capture of a natural for final confirmation.

Needham lists eight species of Potamanthus; six of which are found in streams cold enough to support trout. Of these six species, *diaphanus*, *inequalis* and *rufous* have very pale cross-wing venations, while *distinctus*, *neglectus* and *verticis* have conspicuously dark (almost black) cross-wing venations. *distinctus* ranges between 13 and 16 mm in size (#8, #12, 4x long) while *neglectus* and *verticis* are relatively small, 8-10 mm (#14 and #16). Other easily recognized differences are that the *verticis* male has wholly white wings and *neglectus* has black tail joinings, while *distinctus* has yellow wings and reddish-brown tail joinings. Another interesting characteristic of *distinctus* is that, unlike most mayflies, males and females have the same size eyes. These dark eyes often turn a fluorescent green or yellow when exposed to

P. *distinctus,* male dun.

the light. This phenomenon is also prevalent in the Stenonema and Stenacron genera as was discussed in the *vicarium* chapter.

Perhaps we should pause here to reflect on the importance of Potamanthus *rufous;* one of those species with wholly pale wing venations. Although our experience with this species is limited, this mayfly seems to have great trout appeal. Ernie Schwiebert reports excellent fishing hatches of *rufous* take place on our larger Eastern and Midwestern rivers that remain cool throughout the summer. Systems that are inherently cool by their eco-characteristic or those influenced by the icy flows released from the tail gates of reservoirs seem to create ideal habitat for this species. The East and West branches of the Delaware River in New York are prime examples of the latter as well as the main stream that separates New York and Pennsylvania as far downstream as Callicoon.

The mayflies of *distinctus* and other Potamanthus species are common on large rivers which have marginal trout populations but they are also abundant on prime trout waters that remain relatively cool throughout the summer. When they are abundant on these waters, they become a major food source for the trout providing excellent sport for the fly-fisher.

Our records show that hatching is best during pleasant summer evenings of low humidity, when water temperature is below 70°F. During this time, premature emergence will usually start sporadically a few hours before dusk. Heavier hatching activity normally takes place around dusk. During hot, humid weather, emergence often takes place after dark when the water cools. These night hatches are a boon to night fishermen who cast large flies for lunker browns.

The *distinctus* hatch can present some of the most challenging angling of the year due to low water conditions and selective feeding by shy holdover or native trout. Another critical factor is that during these spooky conditions, trout are usually ultra-selective to imitations due to their comparatively large size.

The *distinctus* duns hatch in slow-to-medium currents where they maintain a relatively placid attitude prior to taking flight. At takeoff though, they do flutter somewhat clumsily. Their placid attitude after emergence usually makes them ideal for Distinctus Compara-dun application as the wing is not obscured by hackle. Hackled Compara-duns are a better choice on breezy nights when duns are being blown about on the surface or when trout seem to be taking those duns that are fluttering just at takeoff. These patterns should be manipulated to imitate the various dun movements.

SPINNER

These imagoes are known as the Golden Spinners on most Eastern waters. Mating takes place around twilight and ovipositing occurs around dusk and may often continue or even start after dark. Unlike more obvious mating swarms that form high above the stream, these imagoes often appear suddenly at shoulder height, giving the angler little time to react—so fly-fishermen must be prepared.

The *distinctus* spinners may be on the water with those of Ephemera *varia,* Isonychia *bicolor,* and several species of Baetis and Caenis as well as the respective duns of these species. The trout will usually prefer the species or stage that is predominant, so anglers must be alert and observe what the trout are feeding on. When the *distinctus* spinners are in good number, the trout usually relish them even though they may be outnumbered by the spinners of smaller species; however, they are extremely critical of these larger naturals. Occasionally, we lacked imitations that had the right size, color and silhouette combinations. During this time, we fared poorly and were often shut out. When we were prepared to match the natural with the correct imitation, we usually had strikes on every accurate cast.

Our experience indicates that the best imago action occurs when the last rays of light disappear from the skies. Feeding activity normally continues into the darkness. As darkness settles, casts must be shortened and controlled, similar to nymph fishing. Fish every cast thoroughly and just before pick up, allow your fly to drag erratically in the current adding a twitch or two. This imitates the struggle of the ovipositing females and often causes vicious strikes.

The Distinctus Compara-spinner is an excellent imitation for the imago in spent and semispent postures. This pattern may also suffice for the E. *varia* spinner activity which commonly occurs with the *distinctus* action; however, cream-colored *varia* imitations are usually required for picky trout. Full-hackle versions, trimmed to suit at streamside, are a good bet. It takes a good eye and a steady hand to trim at streamside in the fading light; especially when the exciting sound of big dusk-feeding trout quickens the pulse and reduces the dexterity of most anglers to bunglefingers.

P. *distinctus,* female spinner

Genus Ephoron
(Family Polymitarcyidae)

COMMON NAMES: White Fly

SIZE RANGE: 9-14 mm

HOOK SIZES
SURFACE (dry): #8, #10, #12, 2x long
SUBSURFACE (wet): #12, #10, #10, 3x long

IMITATIONS:
EMERGER: Ephoron Deerhair emerger
DUN: Ephoron Compara-dun
SPINNER: Polywing Spinner, Ephoron Compara-dun, Ephoron Compara-spinner

It's a strange paradox indeed, that one of the least known mayflies to the fly-fisherman would be that of Ephoron, the first American mayfly known to science.

In 1802, while Thomas Jefferson was still President of the American Philosophical Society, Dr. Hugh Williamson, physician and statesman, read a paper to that society which contained the first accepted description of an American mayfly (Ephoron *leukon)* and its habits. His interesting observations were as follows:

> "They begin to rise out of the [Passaic] river 35 or 40 minutes after the sun sets and continue rising about 15 minutes . . . The chrysalis deposits a thin white pellicle or skin on the surface of the water and rises a perfect insect. It continues on the wing an hour and perishes. Some of them, not one in a hundred, rise from the water in the form of a chrysalis. They fly immediately to the shore and in less than a minute they creep through the white pellicle that covered the trunk, abdomen and appendices, and rejoin their companions on the wing.
>
> In their flight they seldom rise more than six or eight feet above the water, but they usually skim or play near the surface.
>
> The female drops two clusters of eggs upon the water and perished immediately.
>
> The eggs are yellow. Each cluster is nearly one quarter of an inch in length and the thickness of a common pin, resembling the roe of a fish and containing about 100 eggs. They sink in the water.
>
> These flies are so numerous that they appear some evenings like thick driven snow in a cloud that is hardly transparent.
>
> Their first appearance every year is about the 20th of July, and they continue rising every evening, more or less, for about three weeks.
>
> They seek the light, for they fly in crowds to a lamp or candle, but they are supposed to be the only genus of winged insects that never see the sun.
>
> The insect of an hour, that is never at rest, might serve for a strong figure in the hands of a peevish philosopher."

These pale white mayflies are common on the warmer, marginal reaches as well as on the legitimate stretches of our top trout waters throughout the country. The nymphs are typically "burrowing" in form. They seem to thrive on unpolluted rivers with an ideal combination of pure water, a high p.h. factor and silt beds or banks where they burrow and subsist on rich diatomacous marl.

GENERAL EMERGENCE:
General hatching in the East and Midwest occurs during late August through September.

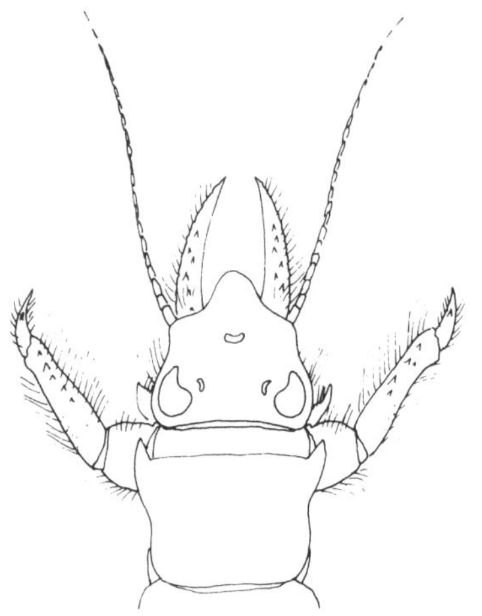

Ephoron nymph.

It's hardly necessary to segregate the duns and spinners during the hatch because they are so similar. Beside their pale white coloration, their curiously underdeveloped legs are an easily recognized feature of these mayflies. Only the extended forelegs of the male are developed to a functional state, as they are necessary for its mating duties.

There are only two species of Ephoron listed in Edmunds, Jensen and Berner's 1976 work those of E.*album* (Say, 1825 Winnipeg, Manitoba) and E. *leukon* (Williams 1802 Bellview, N.J.). We have examined specimens of *leukon* and *album* under magnification, as well as others which are obviously "species unknown" as their descriptions did not conform to *album* (11-12mm) or *leukon* (13-14mm). Unfortunately, we never did get to photograph these curious-looking mayflies, so the illustrations were made from entomological drawings, tempered by specimens sent to us by interested angling friends from the East and the Midwest.

The best hatches in the East and Midwest take place between late August and September. Rich streams of Pennsylvania's Cumberland Valley, like the Yellow Breeches are a challenge. Eric Peper describes the heavy hatching on the Breeches as "difficult at best" and claims these flies are so thick on its surface that arousing the interest of even a single trout amongst the carpet of naturals can at times be a full evening's work. Larger Pennsylvania streams, especially those that feed the mighty Susquehanna River system, have generous populations of these mayflies.

Del Mazza, one of the really skillful fly-tying perfectionists in the East, reports that the Ephoron mayflies are the principal September hatches on many of the great trout rivers that drain the southern and western slopes of New York's Adirondacks. He also describes similar difficulties in these hatches, as these rivers are generally blanketed with spent spinners. Although it doesn't come easy, he and his cronies usually manage to hook several browns in the 18" class during these hatches.

Michigan and Wisconsin rivers have great hatches of Ephoron and the spinner-falls are extremely heavy on the lower stretches of these famous trout rivers starting in mid-August and continuing into late September, if the weather holds out. Gary Schnicke confides that heavy hatches, big fish and the September solitude makes the Ephoron activity on his home rivers, "hard to beat". His favorite for this hatch is the Compara-dun.

The best hatches occur on warm nights when the water temperature is between 65° and 70°F. About an hour before dark, the nymphs leave their burrows and emerge very quickly. Once they reach the surface, they seem to leave their shucks in a wink. Moulting, mating and egg-laying takes place within the hour. When darkness settles, the surface of the river is literally covered with these spinners, which the trout gobble at their leisure.

During September, it's not unusual for the evening air temperature to drop into the 50s or 60s toward twilight—and the water temperature may also dip below 60°F. At such a time, duns may have difficulty taking off due to the relatively chilly temperature. The Compara-dun is normally deadly during this time as the trout have a good opportunity to feed on the placid floating duns.

The Poly-wing spinner and the Ephoron Compara-spinner on #8 through #14 hook sizes are excellent during the spinner-falls.

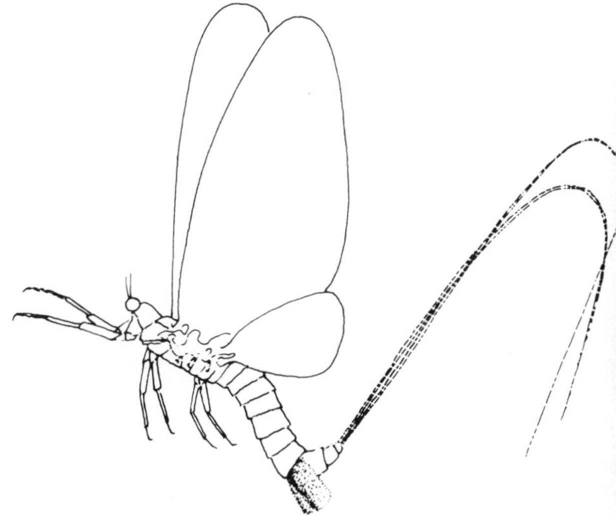

Ephoron *album,* female dun, carrying egg packets. The male moults into a spinner immediately after hatching; the female does not moult into a spinner at all.

MALE SPINNER

SPECIES	DIST.	SIZE	ABDOMEN	COSTAL VEINS	ANTERIOR VEINS
leukon	E, M	13-14	pale yellowish-white	dark purplish	purpish-gray
album	E, M, W	11-12	yellowish white	purplish gray	faint gray

Species description of nymph not known. Duns are similar to spinners, being whitish in wings and body.

A good stretch of Ephoron habitat.

The Swimmers

(Families Baetidae, Siphlonuridae and Metretopodidae)

Families Baetidae, Siphlonuridae and Metretopodidae

(The Darting Swimmers)

The mayflies of the the "Swimmer" families are the most variable group in the entire mayfly order in regard to physical size, distribution, habitat and seasonal emergence. Major hatches of the various species will occur from March through November in a diversity of water types, ranging from tumbling mountain streams to gentle, rich limestone creeks to still-water spring-fed ponds. Many species have as many as three broods in a single season; thus, winter hatching may occur on waters which remain relatively warm (above 45°F) throughout the winter.

All genera within the families are transcontinental, making them the most widely and evenly distributed of all mayflies; populations that constitute major fishing hatches are common throughout the country. The drastic size variance within the families range from 3mm (#26 hook size) to 17 mm (#10, 4x long hook size).

The duns and spinners are so variable in their physical characteristics that identification on the family level is impractical as well as unnecessary. Each genus is quite distinct and with some experience anglers should have little problem distinguishing these mayflies from those of other families and associated genera.

This is not the case, however, with the nymphs, which are quite similar throughout the families, from the tiny Pseudocloeon species to the large Isonychia nymphs, and consequently are quite easy to identify at a glance. All have

Left: detail of male Baetis eyes. *Right:* detail of male Siphlonurus eyes.

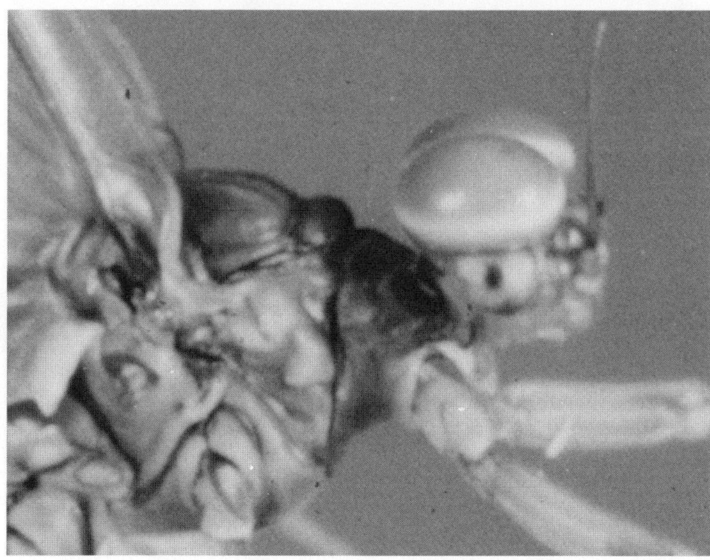

slender, streamlined bodies, long, slender legs and platelike gills on abdominal segments 1 through 7. Each gill plate is either round or ovoid and is usually singular. Some species have gills that are wholly or partially double. All genera have three tails except Pseudocloeon and a few Baetis species which have only two. The tails are heavily fringed and plumage-like in the larger Isonychia, Siphlonurus and Ameletus genera, but they are usually less prominent in the species of the smaller genera.

So that the angler will have a better understanding of the swimmer group, the families should be divided into two major groups; the *"tiny swimmers"* and the *"large swimmers"*.

Except for the nymphs of Callibaetis, which can be as large as 12mm, the "tiny swimmers" generally range in size from 3mm to 9mm, but average around 5mm; they are Baetis, Callibaetis, Centroptilum, Pseudocloeon and Cloeon. Found in practically every nook and cranny in the United States, and in every water type, these nymphs principally thrive on highly rich alkaline streams.

SMALL-SWIMMERS

Family Baetidae
- Genus Baetis
- Genus Pseudocloeon
- Genus Cloeon
- Genus Callibaetis
- Genus Centroptilum

LARGE SWIMMERS

Family Siphlonuridae
- Genus Isonychia
- Genus Siphlonuris
- Genus Ameletus

Family Metretopodidae
- Genus Siphloplecton

Genus Isonychia nymph.

Genus Siphlonurus nymph.

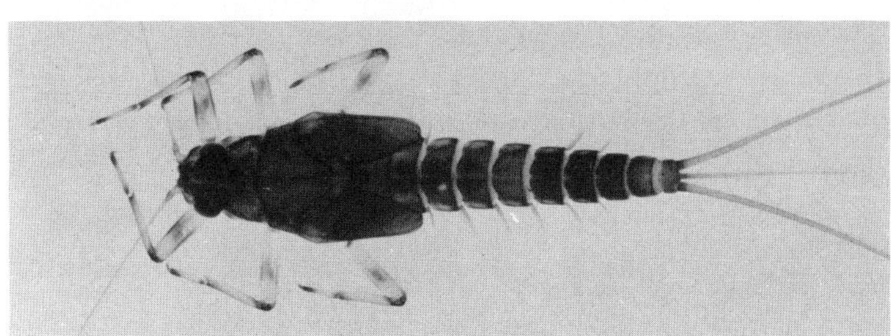

Genus Baetis nymph.

Genus Baetis

(Family Baetidae)

Detail of dwarfed hind wing of Baetis.

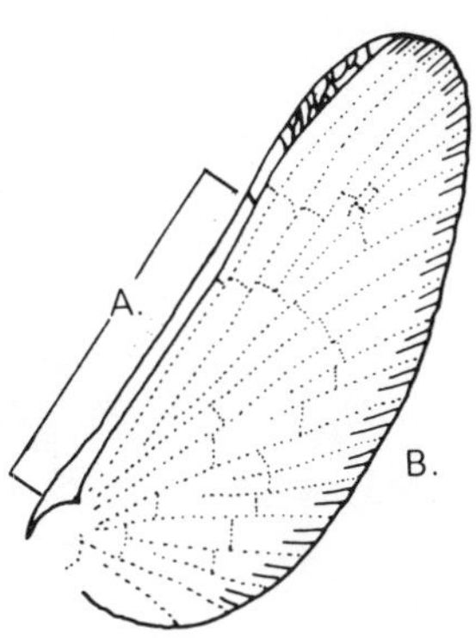

Forewing of Baetis: A, Lack of basal, costal cross-veins; B, paired marginal veinlets.

The importance of the Baetis genus is relatively unknown to most fly-fishermen. It has not enjoyed the literary popularity shared by most of the traditional hatches we have come to know over the past half-century. Yet, these tiny mayflies are of paramount importance to the angler who is familiar with their habitat and acquainted with their hatching traits. Alvin R. Grove warned of their importance in his classic, *Lore and Lure of Trout Fishing,* which was published in 1951. His accolades, however, were relatively ignored until 1970, when Doug Swisher and Carl Richards presented them as species of major importance in *Selective Trout.* But, even this welcomed treatment of the Baetis species was still short of its true magnitude.

In 1935, Needham, Traver and Hsu listed 41 species in their entomological standard, *Biology of Mayflies,* but today that total is 62. The size range of these species is relatively extreme—from the tiny 4 mm *levitans,* to the surprisingly large *hiemalis* species of the Midwest which reaches 10 mm. This scope represents a range of 6 hook sizes (#14 thru #24). Although this range is somewhat extreme, most Baetis of angling importance range from 5½ mm to 8 mm (#16 and #18 hook sizes).

The slender, streamlined nymphs of Baetis are perfectly designed for darting about in the underwater vegetation where they are mostly found. Their legs are very long and slender and the head is directed downward—ideal characteristics for perching on and foraging among blades of subaquatic foilage.

The gill plates are singular and are located on abdominal segments 1 through 7. Beside their respiratory function, they probably play an important part in locomotion. The quick mobility of these nymphs, however, is mainly due to rapid movement of the abdomen and the three tails which are heavily fringed; the middle tail is shorter than the outer tails. Three Western Baetis species have only 2 tails; the middle one vestigial.

The Baetis duns have wings which range in coloration from pale to dark gray; the bodies vary from dull grayish to olive to dark brown. The spinners have sparkling-clear hyaline wings and the body colorations are similar to the duns, except more vibrant.

One of the most outstanding features of the adults are the curious-looking eyes of the males which are turbinate and on stalks. The eyes of the females are small and not divided. The marginal veinlets of the forewings are in pairs and the costal cross veins at the base are entirely wanting.

An important characteristic in separating the adults from

those of the similar Pseudocloeon and Cloeon genera is that Baetis has tiny or dwarfed hind wings which are wholly absent in the others. The finger-like hind wings of Baetis, which usually have three longitudinal veins, differ from the similar and closely related Centroptilum genus, which usually have only two longitudinal veins.

NYMPHS

SPECIES	DIST.	SIZE	GILLS	TAILS	MISC.
vagans*	E, M	6½-8	colorless tracheae	Middle approx. ½ length of outer. Unbanded.	Body: yellowish-brown with dark brown markings. Tergites 5, 9 and 10, pale.
cingulatus* (now *quebecensus*)	E, M	5-6	colorless tracheae	Middle less than ½ length of outer	Ground color: light to medium olive-brown; head and thorax, darker mottlings. Tergtes 5 and 10: pale.
frivolus	E, M	5-6	– – –	2 tails	– – –
hiemalis*	E, M	9-10	dark tracheae dark margined gills	Middle approx. ¾ length of outer. Dark basally, fading to grayish-white. No bands.	Dark olive brown.
levitans	E, M	4-5	– – –	Band at mid-length and tips.	Abdomen: similar to *cingulatus*. Head: brown with pale patches on each side of mid-line.
***tricaudatus*†**	W	8-9	distinct tracheae	Middle approx. ½ length of outer.	Medium olive brown.
devinctus*	W	6-7		Band at tips	Body and thorax: dark brown.
propinquus	M, W	4-5	– – –	2 tails	– – –
bicaudatus	W	4-5	– – –	Two tails only	Tergites: 1-10 pale with dark markings; 3, 4 and 7, distinctly darker. Body: medium brown.
parvus	E, W	5-6	– – –	middle ¾ to ⅝ length of outer tails	Dark olive brown.
brunneicolor	E, M, W	6-7	– – –	middle ¾ to ⅝ length of outer tails	Body: dark olive brown with faint mid-dorsal stripe.

MALE SPINNER

SPECIES	SIZE	HIND WINGS VEINS	HIND WING COSTAL PROJECTION	ABDOMINAL TERGITES 2-6	DUN
vagans*	6½-8	3	acute, pointed	olive brown	Body: dull olive-brown. Legs: medium olive-gray. Wings and tails: medium-dark gray.
cingulatus* (now *quebecensus*)	5-6	3	acute, conical	yellow white	Body: olive-brown. Legs and tails: pale. Wings: smoky gray.
frivolus	5-6	2	absent	deep brown	– – –
hiemalis*	9-10	3	acute, truncate	med. dark brown	Body: blackish-brown. Legs and tails: pale. Wings: dark gray.
levitans	4-5	3	acute	yellow white	– – –
***tricaudatus*†**	8-9	3	acute, well developed	– – –	– – –
devinctus*	6-7	3	acute, small	whitish	Body: reddish-brown. Legs and tails: paler. Wings: medium-dark gray.
propinquus	4-5	2	absent	whitish	– – –
bicaudatus	4-5	2	acute	med. dark brown	– – –
parvus	5-6	3	acute	– – –	Body: dark olive brown. Wings: dark gray.
brunneicolor	6-7	3	acute	– – –	Body: dark brown. Wings: almost black.

*Important species high lighted in the following Baetis Species chapter.

†**Note:** Entomologists Morihara and MacCafferty regard B. *vagans* and B. *tricaudatus* as identical species. However, B. *tricaudatus* duns are considerably different in color.

Color Plate I

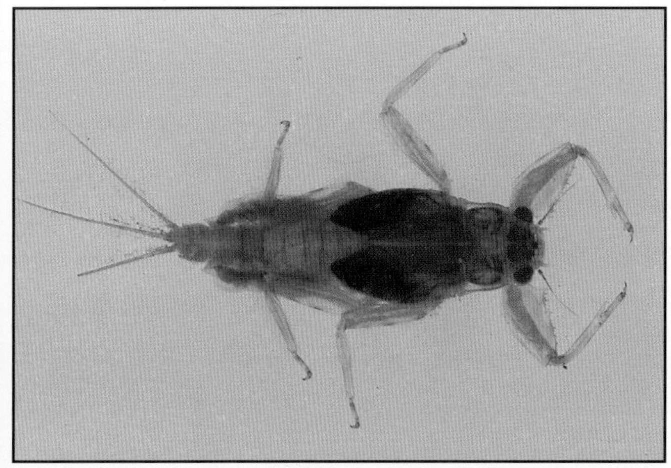

Ephemerella *cornuta*, nymph

Ephemerella *subvaria*, nymph

Ephemerella *cornuta*, male dun

Ephemerella *subvaria*, male dun

Ephemerella *cornuta*, male spinner

Ephemerella *subvaria*, female spinner

Color Plate II

Ephemerella *dorothea*, male dun

Ephemerella *dorothea*, nymph

Ephemerella *rotunda*, female dun

Ephemerella *rotunda*, nymph

Ephemerella *attenuata*, male dun

Ephemerella *needhami*, male dun

Color Plate III

Ephemerella *invaria*, female dun

Ephemerella *invaria*, nymph

Ephemerella *glacialis*, female dun

Ephemerella *glacialis*, nymph

Ephemerella *infrequens*, male dun

Ephemerella *infrequens*, nymph

Color Plate IV

Left and Right: Ephemerella *lata* nymphs in different color phases

Ephemerella *mollitia,* nymph

Ephemerella *lata,* male dun

Ephemerella *flavilinea,* nymph

Ephemerella *lata,* male spinner

Color Plate V

Ephemerella *inermis*, female dun

Ephemerella *inermis*, nymph

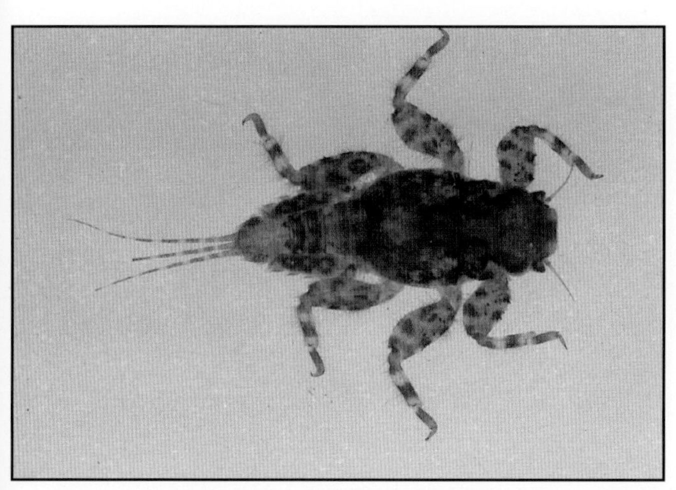

Ephemerella *walkeri*, nymph

Ephemerella *doddsi*, nymph

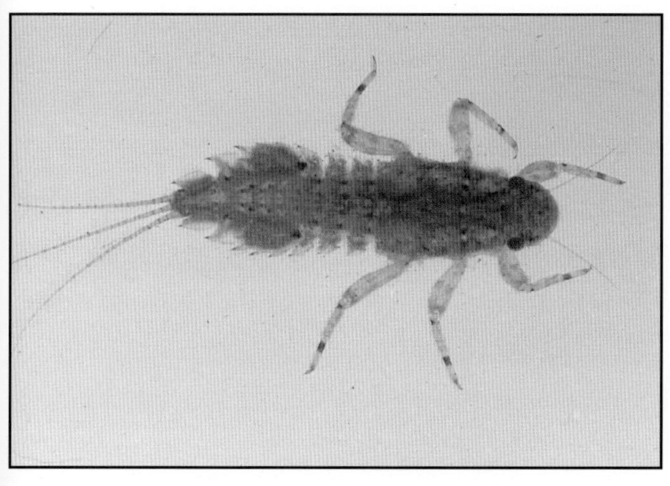

Ephemerella *simplex*, nymph

Ephemerella *doris*, nymph

Color Plate VI

Paraleptophlebia *adoptiva*, male dun

Paraleptophlebia *adoptiva*, nymph

Paraleptophlebia *adoptiva*, female dun

Paraleptophlebia *adoptiva*, female spinner

Leptophlebia *cupida*, female spinner

Leptophlebia *cupida*, nymph

Color Plate VII

Paraleptophlebia *mollis*, female dun

Paraleptophlebia *mollis*, nymph

Paraleptophlebia *mollis*, male spinner

Paraleptophlebia *mollis*, male dun

Paraleptophlebia nymph

Paraleptophlebia *debilis*, nymph

Color Plate VIII

Tricorythodes nymph (Midwestern species)

Tricorythodes *stygiatus*, nymph

Tricorythodes *stygiatus*, female dun

Tricorythodes nymph (Western species)

Tricorythodes *stygiatus*, male spinner

Tricorythodes *stygiatus*, male dun

COLOR PLATE IX

Stenonema *fuscum*, nymph

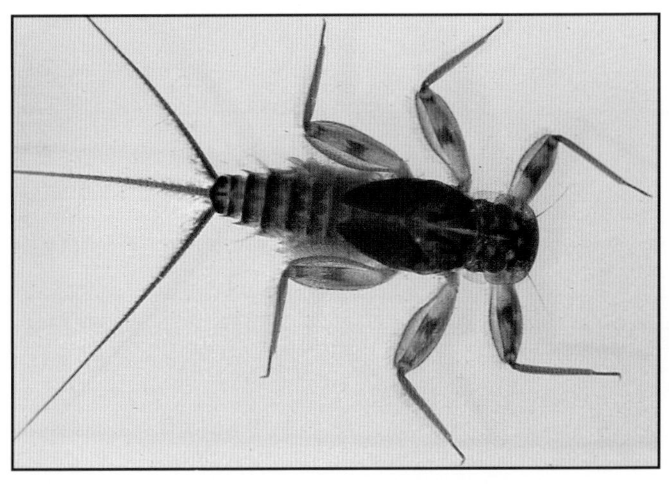

Stenonema *vicarium*, nymph

Stenonema nymph (Eastern species)

Stenonema *ithaca*, nymph (immature specimen)

Stenonema *canadense,* nymph

Stenonema *rubrum*, nymph

COLOR PLATE X

Stenonema *fuscum*, female dun

Stenonema *vicarium*, female dun

Stenonema *fuscum*, male dun

Stenonema *vicarium*, male dun

Stenonema *fuscum*, female spinner

Stenonema *vicarium*, female spinner

Color Plate XI

Stenonema female spinner (typical whitish late-season species)

Stenonema *ithaca*, male dun

Stenonema female spinner (typical yellowish late-season species)

Stenonema *heterotarsale*, female dun

Stenonema *rubrum*, male spinner

Stenonema *heterotarsale*, male dun

Color Plate XII

Epeorus *pleuralis,* female dun

Epeorus *pleuralis,* nymph

Epeorus *pleuralis,* female spinner

Epeorus *pleuralis,* male spinner

Epeorus *vitreus,* female dun

Epeorus *vitreus,* male dun

Color Plate XIII

Epeorus male dun (Western species)

Epeorus *vitreus*, female spinner

Epeorus male dun (Midwestern species)

Epeorus female dun (Eastern species)

Heptagenia *hebe*, male dun

Epeorus male dun (Eastern species)

Color Plate XIV

Epeorus nymph (Eastern species)

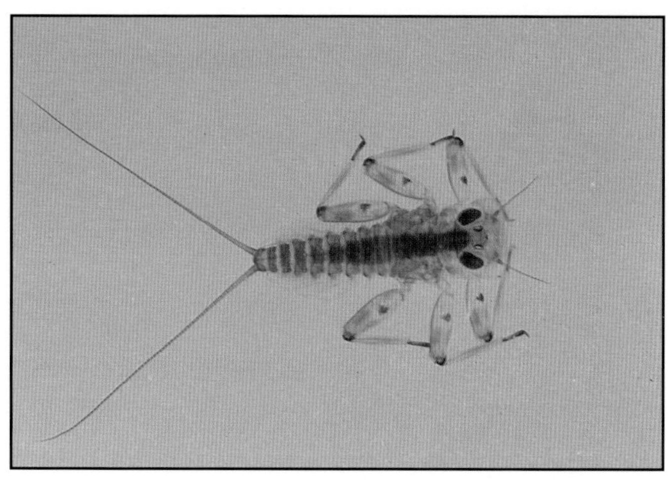

Epeorus nymph (Western species)

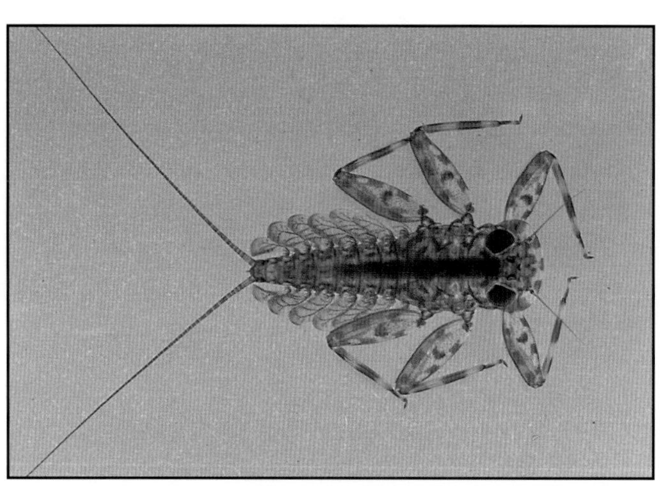

Epeorus nymph (Eastern species)

Epeorus *vitreus*, nymph

Cinygmula nymph

Heptagenia *hebe*

Color Plate XV

Ephemera *guttulata*, nymph (freestone specimen)

Ephemera *guttulata*, nymph (limestone specimen)

Potamanthus *distinctus*, nymph

Ephemera *varia*, nymph

Litobrancha *recurvata*, nymph

Hexagenia *limbata*, nymph

COLOR PLATE XVI

Ephemera *varia,* male dun

Ephemera *guttulata,* male dun

Ephemera *varia,* female dun

Ephemera *guttulata,* male spinner

Ephemera *varia,* female spinner

Ephemera *guttulata,* female spinner

Color Plate XVII

Potamanthus *distinctus*, female dun

Ephemera *varia*, male spinner

Potamanthus *distinctus*, female spinner

Potamanthus *distinctus*, male dun

Hexagenia *limbata*, female dun

Hexagenia *limbata*, male dun

Color Plate XVIII

Hexagenia *limbata,* female spinner

Hexagenia *limbata,* male spinner

Litrobrancha *recurvata,* female spinner

Litrobrancha *recurvata,* male spinner

Litrobrancha *recurvata,* male dun

Litrobrancha *recurvata,* female dun

Color Plate XIX

Baetis nymph (Eastern species)

Baetis *vagans,* nymph

Baetis nymph (Midwestern species)

Baetis *quebecensis,* nymph

Baetis *divinctus,* nymph

Baetis nymph (Western species)

Color Plate XX

Baetis *vagans*, female dun

Baetis *vagans*, male dun

Baetis *vagans*, female spinner

Baetis *vagans*, male spinner

Callibaetis female spinner

Callibaetis female dun

Color Plate XXI

Baetis female dun (Midwestern species)

Baetis *divinctus,* male dun

Baetis male spinner (Midwestern species)

Baetis *divinctus,* female dun

Baetis female spinner (Midwestern species)

Baetis *divinctus,* male spinner

Color Plate XXII

Pseudocloeon nymph

Siphlonurus *quebecensis*, nymph

Pseudocloeon *carolina*, female dun

Pseudocloeon *carolina*, male dun

Cloeon female dun

Siphlonurus *alternatus*, male spinner

Color Plate XXIII

Isonychia *sadleri*, nymph

Isonychia *bicolor*, nymph

Isonychia nymph (Eastern species)

Isonychia nymph (Midwestern species)

Siphlonurus *alternatus*, nymph

Ameletus nymph (Western species)

Color Plate XXIV

Isonychia *sadleri*, male dun

Isonychia *bicolor*, male dun

Isonychia *sadleri*, female dun

Isonychia *bicolor*, female dun

Isonychia *sadleri*, male spinner

Isonychia *bicolor*, female spinner

Baetis species

COMMON NAME: Blue-winged Olive

SIZE RANGE: 6 to 9 mm

HOOK SIZES:
SURFACE (dry): #14, #16, #18
SUBSURFACE (wet): #14, #16, #18, std.

IMITATIONS:
NYMPH: Baetis Compara-nymph
EMERGER: Baetis Deerhair emerger
DUN: Dark Blue Quill, Blue-Winged Olive, Baetis Compara-dun, Baetis Hackled Compara-dun
SPINNER: Baetis Compara-spinner

The Baetis species are without question of paramount importance to the angler, as they represent a valuable year-round food source for the trout. These agile, streamlined swimmers approach the importance of the hardy Ephemerella genus being geographically widespread and adaptable to waters of various chemical makeup. They are multi-brooded and favorable habitats may support as many as three generations in a single year. The Baetis mayflies commonly emerge from March until November, but on streams where the temperature remains suitable, they may continue to hatch sporadically throughout the winter.

Although individual Baetis species are somewhat variable in the scope of their size, distribution and season of emergence, we feel they are still best treated as a group. This convenience of treatment can be accomplished without compromising pertinent entomological or angling information. Their habitat, physical characteristics, coloration and emergence traits are all so similar that individual treatment would result in much repetition.

The bold type in the table on page 252 are what we believe to be the more important Baetis species found on our continental trout waters. As they generally represent the best fishing hatches, special emphasis is given to the *cingulatus*, (now *quebecensus*) *devinctus*, *hiemalis*, *brunneicolor*, *tricaudatus* and *vagans* species. Their emergence comes at the most opportune time for the angler in their respective locales; before and after the principal mayfly, caddisfly and stonefly hatches.

vagans is the first major mayfly hatch of the year, appearing on Pennsylvania's limestone waters like the Little Lehigh River in Allentown, as well as on other chalkstreams in the southern part of the state, around the 24th of March, well before the start of the regular fishing season. Pennsylvania, a pioneer in the "put'em back alive" theory, has scores of "Fish For Fun" stretches which have no closed season. These stretches are very popular with the early-season fly-caster, who can enjoy excellent dry-fly activity to this early *vagans* activity. On more southerly Pennsylvania, New Jersey and Maryland chalkstreams, as well as those in southern Appalachia, browns rise well to this hatch from mid-March until mid-April. By the second week in April, the *vagans* activity is in full swing further north in the Poconos as well as in Allegheny drainages in the central and western part of the state. The earliest hatches to prompt decent fishing in the Catskills and southern New York occur in mid-April, but the best action occurs toward the end of the month and continues until mid-May. The Adirondacks and northern New England also have good hatching which lags the Catskill activity by about two weeks.

A typical limestone stretch of Baetis water. Look for the nymphs under the submerged rocks at the tail of the pool.

In the East and the Midwest, *quebecensus* emergence follows *vagans* by about 2 or 3 weeks, progressing northward much like the *vagans* sequence. Gary Schnicke, a fisheries Biologist friend from Mio, Michigan, who is also a crack angler, states that these species create exciting angling on Michigan rivers like the Au Sable and the Pere Marquette systems from mid-April to mid-May. He explained that the trout feed well on these hatches until their attention is diverted by the prolific Emphemerella *subvaria* hatches which begin in late April.

Our stream research on Wisconsin Rivers did not reveal the early-season Baetis *vagans* or *quebecensus* nymphs. It should be noted, however, that this work was done after May 3, when the emergence activity of these species was probably over. Entomologists indicate that these species *are* common in this area, as well as in Minnesota. Thus, it appears that these important hatches had expired before May 3, opening day in Wisconsin in 1974.

Baetis *quebecensus* hatching follows *vagans* activity by about 3 weeks and progresses northward much like the *vagans* sequence. These hatches seldom reach the importance of *vagans* as they are overshadowed by the prolific early-season action of the Ephemerella, Epeorus and Paraleptophlebia genera.

tricaudatus and *divinctus* are important Western Baetis hatches, especially on the limestone streams and the richer freestone streams that drain the Rockies. The most significant hatching, as far as the angler is concerned, takes place before and after the principal mayfly, caddisfly and stonefly season; between April and May and then again from September through October. On rich, cool, high-altitude streams, like those that drain the alpine meadows of Yellowstone Park, water temperature and clarity will usually remain ideal for July and August hatches.

	March 7 14 21	April 7 14 21	May 7 14 21
S. Penna., N.J. and Md. limestones	— —	— — — — —	
N. and W. Penna. and Poconos		— — — — —	
N.Y., New England, Catskills and Adirondacks		— — — — —	— — — —
Midwest and Great Lakes region		— — — — — — — —	— — — —

NYMPH

The nymphs of the Baetis species are quite similar in appearance, having bodies which range in coloration from dark olive (as in *hiemalis*) to pale olive (as in *quebecensus*).

B. *vagans,* nymph.

tricaudatus and *vagans* have medium-dark olive bodies; *vagans* having contrasting chocolate-brown wing pads at maturity. These striking pads are a convenient key in separating them from *quebecensus,* as both usually inhabit the same waters and have similar emergence periods.

Another member of the Baetis group is *levitans.* It is the palest of all of the species, and, unlike the late and early-season species, it hatches in incredible number during the summer on Midwestern and Eastern chalkstreams.

Baetis nymphs subsist in a variety of water types, ranging from fast gravel runs and riffles to slow runs choked with aquatic vegetation. Some species, however, prefer specific habitats. *hiemalis* and *levitans* prefer slower currents, while *vagans* and *quebecensus* will usually be found among the detritus and debris that accummulates between rocks or around deadfalls in medium-to-fast runs and riffles. *tricaudatus* and *devinctus,* the western species, can usually be found in all current speeds.

The greatest populations of Baetis nymphs are usually found in alkaline waters; those with a ph factor exceeding 7.5 (7.0 is neutral). We have also found good populations in freestone streams that are neutral or slightly alkaline (7.0 to 7.5). In mountain streams that are slightly acid (below 7.0), good populations exist in the slower stretches having sufficient aquatic growth which provides the required amounts of oxygen and carbon dioxide to induce prolific plankton growth so necessary to these species.

Anglers can predetermine Baetis populations by vigorously shaking the subaquatic grasses and cresses so that the current sweeps them into a fine mesh receptacle. A small aquarium net is ideal for this. On sections lacking plants, the angler should concentrate on the submerged rocks at the tail of a pool. Detritus accummulations between these rocks can be removed by hand. A few quick shakes of this debris, holding your net in the current, will reveal whether good populations of Baetis exist.

Our aquarium studies show that the emergence characteristics of Baetis are analogous to the closely related Pseudocloeon, Cloeon, and Centroptilum genera. Prior to emergence, the Baetis nymphs seem to lose their agility and crawl clumsily and feebly to the surface via plants, deadfalls and rocks. When these convenient perches are absent, they are buoyed to the surface from the safety of crevices and chinks on the stream's bottom by gases within their nymphal skins.

During a heavy emergence, the trout pick off the emerging nymphs at an alarming rate. The best fish usually select stations near the most productive lines of drift, while the smaller trout often cruise, flashing their sides, as they intercept the emerging nymphs. During this exciting period, trout often bulge or break the surface with their tails, causing fly-fishermen to believe they are taking the surface duns, when in fact they are feeding on the ascending nymphs or on the partially emerged duns in the surface film.

Nymph or emerger patterns fished upstream, dead-drift, a la the dry-fly method, are killing during this period. Therefore, anglers will hook more fish if they wade steathfully close to the trout and cast a short line. Another tactic that works well is the across-and-downstream method, where, after the imitation is allowed to sink, it is subtly twitched off of the bottom and into the surface film, duplicating the ascent of the natural.

For this hatch, we use the Compara-nymph and Compara-emerger dressed on hook sizes #16 thru #22. The angler should capture a natural so that the exact size and color can be duplicated. Sizes #12 and #14 may be needed in the autumn on Midwestern streams when the larger *hiemalis* is emerging. Nymph patterns should be tied with dubbed bodies ranging from medium to dark olive. As an alternate, bodies should be dressed with dubbed fur or fine textured polypropolene for surface film nymphing. The Pseudocloeon, Cloeon and Baetis nymph and emerger patterns are so similar that anglers may consider them the same.

During high-water conditions or spates, which are quite common in the early season, emergence may not take place. However, many nymphs will be dislodged from their perches, prompting the trout to selective feeding. Nymph behavior at this time is totally unlike that of the emerging nymphs during a hatch. They dart minnow-like with quick jack rabbit bursts, rest awhile, then duplicate these movements until they can secure themselves to a suitable obstacle. At this time, fly-fishermen should duplicate these movements after letting their imitation sink, concentrating on eddies and undercut banks where the trout usually hang, away from the tiring current.

B. *vagans,* male dun.

DUN

The Baetis species are among the scores of mayflies commonly called Blue-Winged Olives.

The male duns are a curious lot, having conspicuous eye structures which rise from the head on conical or cylindrical shafts. The large compound eyes are set on top of these shafts much like a cap or beanie. The various Baetis duns have body colorations ranging from dull grayish-brown to dark brown and wings ranging from a light gray color to a dark slate. *(tricaudatus* and *quebecensus* have pale-to-medium colored bodies and wings; *vagans,* medium to dark; and *hiemalis,* dark.) The majority of the Baetis species fall into the medium color classification.

Initially, we carried a myriad of multi-colored patterns to match the colors and hues of the slightly varied naturals. Moreover, we alternated these various shades of dubbing fur with extensive assortments of quills to obtain the segmental appearance of the subimago bodies. When compared to the minimal differences obtained in test results, our Baetis pattern evaluations show that exact duplication of these closely resembling species is both unnecessary and impractical, especially for the average fly-fisherman and nontyer. A Baetis Compara-dun pattern having a body of medium brown fur with a touch of olive, together with wing and tails of medium gray dun color was over 90% as effective as the more imitative patterns. When we added an alternate version consisting of darker fur and darker wings and tails, the cumulative comparative result increased to almost 100%.

In respect to pattern evaluation, it should be mentioned that the best and most conclusive results are usually obtained by several persons evaluating the subject patterns simultaneously on the water, during the same hatch, over the same trout, using similar techniques and tackle. Since the inception of our studies for the *Comparahatch,* Bob and I have conducted countless such experiments, often ending in measurable, eye-opening results. As individuals, it undoubtedly would have taken many years for comparable results. Although analyses such as these are sometimes offensive to our angling solitude and traditional senses, the conclusions drawn from them are quite satisfying and fulfilling. In regard to further quantitative testing, we have always made it a point to supply our fishing cronies joining us on field trips with a supply of patterns to be tested. All results were carefully recorded, adding more credibility to our pattern evaluations.

Emergence during the early season (March and April) usually takes place between 11 A.M. and 4 P.M., which coincides with the warmest and brightest part of the day. Best hatching occurs when the water temperature climbs into the high 40's. During the summer months, hatching activity may start late in the afternoon, but more often it will occur around dusk. In the fall, hatching will again be best between late morning and late afternoon. Our experience indicates that emergence activity is rarely good when the water temperature exceeds the mid 60's.

On colder days in both the early and late season, the duns have great difficulty thawing their wing muscles. Thus, they ride the currents for extremely long periods, presenting easy meals for the trout. On warmer days, throughout the season, duns again have problems when faced with turbulent water conditions. (Our aquarium experiments, as well as stream observations, show that the duns of the Baetis species, like those of Pseudocloeon and Cloeon, experience difficulty in escaping the surface film and in drying their wings should they emerge on a surface that is even slightly turbulent.)

On those occasions when the duns float on the surface for long periods, we have found the Compara-dun unparalleled as a fish-getter, especially on smooth surfaces where the distinct wing silhouette of the imitation is of paramount importance. The proven durability of this pattern is also essential to success, as sometimes the peak surface activity of these species may be as short as 30 minutes, leaving little time for pattern changes due to fly deterioration. We use this pattern in sizes #14 through #24 and tie an alternate, darker pattern for darker species like *vagans* and *hiemalis*.

In riffles, where many duns float half-drowned owing to their difficulty in drying their wings, an emerger pattern is usually more effective, especially when fished upstream and allowed to float dead-drift. Hackled versions such as the famous Dark Blue Quill and the traditional Blue-Winged Olive usually produce well on windy days when the duns are skittered across the surface, or on rough waters where delicate surface contact is more important than the wing silhouette. All patterns should be tied in the sizes previously mentioned and anglers should always capture a natural to insure exact size duplication.

SPINNER

According to the habits of individual species and the prevailing seasonal temperature, the Baetis duns may take several hours or several days to moult. The male imagoes then appear above the riffles in swarms. Females dart into the squadrons to secure mates. Copulation and egg-laying follows. After copulation, the females of many species alight on rocks, plants or obstacles protruding from the water and crawl down under the surface of the water where they lay their eggs in rows. This procedure takes place on the downstream side, away from the turbulent current.

The early season Baetis spinner-flights usually conflict with the peak emergence periods of the dun stage as well as other early mayflies such as Paraleptophlebia *adoptiva* and Epeorus *pleuralis*.

Genus, Pseudocloeon and Cloeon *(Family Baetidae)*

COMMON NAME: Blue-Winged Olive

SIZE RANGE: 3 to 5 mm

HOOK SIZES:
SURFACE (dry): #20 through #28; turned-up eyes
SUBSURFACE (wet): #20 through #28; turned-up eyes

IMITATIONS:
NYMPH: Pseudocloeon Compara-nymph
DUN: Blue-winged Olive, Dark Blue Quill, Pseudocloeon Compara-dun, Pseudocloeon Hackled Compara-dun.
SPINNER: Pseudocloeon Figure 8 Compara-spinner

GENERAL EMERGENCE:

P. *carolina*	May, Aug., and Oct.
P. *anoka*	June 20-July 20, and Oct.
P. *edmundsi*	late summer
P. *dubium*	summer
P. *futile*	late summer
C. *rubropictum*	sporadic summer
C. *simplex*	mid-summer
C. *mendax*	summer
C. *insignificans*	summer
C. *ingens*	summer

There are 23 species of Psuedocloeon, Cloeon and Neocloeon listed in Needham's classic, *Biology of Mayflies,* which was increased to 31 in Edmund's latest listing. In our original edition of hatches, we included the genus Neocloean in this chapter. Since then, the Neocloeon genus became a synonym to Cloeon.

Pseudocloeon *anoka* is one of the newly introduced species. This significant mayfly was formally introduced by the Leonards in their famous work, *Mayflies of MichiganTrout Streams.* It was also singled out as a Midwestern superhatch by Doug Swisher and Carl Richards in their angling milestone, *Selective Trout.*

We have taken the liberty to list what we consider to be the more important species of our subject genera. Heading this list are four species from the Pseudocloeon genus. They are *carolina* (of the East), *anoka* (of the Midwest) and *edmundsi* and *futile* (of the West). Anglers should note that some of the seemingly remote species of these genera may in fact be the most significant on some waters.

GENERA	SPECIES	SIZE	DIST.
Pseudocloeon	*carolina*	4-5	E
Pseudocloeon	*anoka*	4-5	M
Pseudocloeon	*edmundsi*	4-5	W
Pseudocloeon	*dubium*	3-4	E, M, W
Pseudocloeon	*futile*	3-3½	W
Cloeon	*rubropictum*	4-5	E, M,
Cloeon	*simplex*	4-5	E
Cloeon	*mendax*	4-5	E, M
Cloeon	*insignificans*	3-3½	E, M
Cloeon	*ingens*	8-9	W

NYMPH

The Pseudocloeon and Cloeon nymphs are quite similar and resemble those of the prolific and enormous Baetis genus. A quick way to tell the nymphs of Pseudocloeon from those of Baetis is by their two tails. The Baetis species have three tails except for the dual-tailed *bicaudatus,propinquus* and *frivolus.* These two-tailed Baetis species, however, are indigenous to Western streams, so the Eastern and the Midwestern angler should have little problem in making a quick identification. Another identifying feature which will be helpful to all anglers is that Pseudocloeon and Cloeon nymphs have a wider and stockier thorax than those of Baetis. This difference becomes quite evident when the nymphs are compared, side-by-side. Cloeon nymphs have three tails like those of Baetis, but they are of equal length and can be differentiated by the double plate-like gills which protrude in pairs from the body segments.

The principal species of this chapter, mainly P. *anoka* and P. *carolina,* along with the major Western species, P. *edmundsi* are a tiny 4 to 5mm (3/6″); the Western species, *futile,* is even smaller at 3mm. (1/8″). These minutiae parallel the diminutive Tricorythodes and Caenis mayflies and are usually found in the same eco-systems. Anglers should not confuse their seemingly insignificant size with their importance. When good populations exist, trout will feed consistently on these tiny nymphs, consuming hundreds and sometimes thousands during a single hatch.

Although we have collected these nymphs in rivers of varied characteristics, geographic location and chemical makeup, their real importance as a fishing hatch is usually restricted to cold, rich alkaline streams, where they abound in staggering number among the luxurious subaquatic grasses, cresses and sheltering gravel.

3-tailed Baetis nymph.
(middle tail shorter)

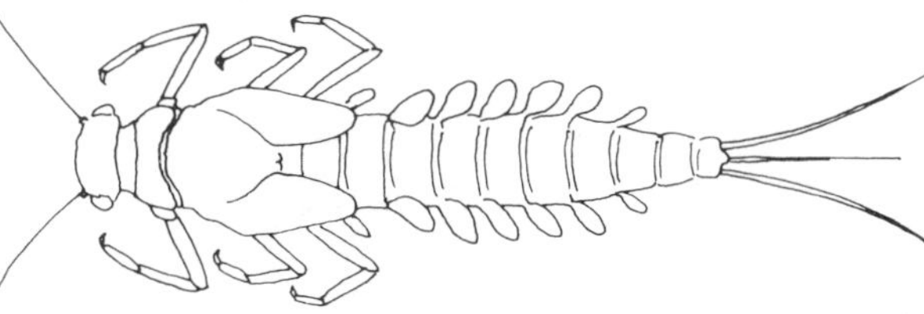

2-tailed Pseudocloeon nymph.

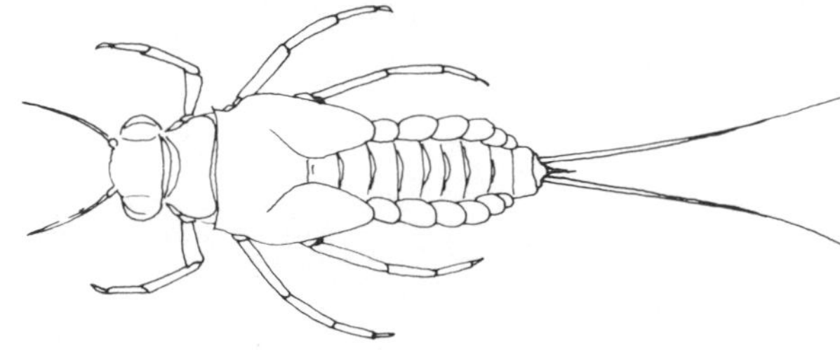

3-tailed Cloeon nymph.
Note that the middle tail is equal in length to the outer tails.

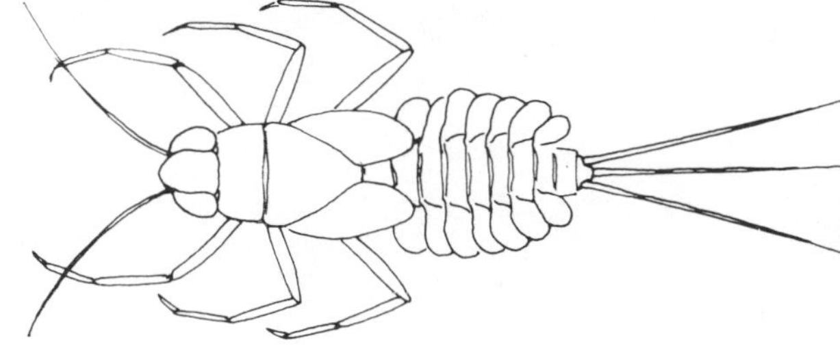

Pseudocloeon, nymph.

The emergence characteristics of these nymphs have been a curiosity to us ever since our initial aquarium observance of their peculiar ascent and hatching traits. Their quickness and surprising agility during normal swimming activity had led us to expect explosively swift ascents followed by a similar quickness during the hatching and takeoff sequence. However, over the past several seasons, Bob and I have observed in wonderment as these nymphs crawled feebly up the blades and leaves of aquatic plants, or inched their way up the glass walls of our aquariums to emerge slowly and uneventfully in the surface tension of the tank. Once hatched, many duns had to be assisted in escaping the mild turbulence caused by the aquarium's filtration and aeration systems.

At streamside, the case was similar. Instead of swimming to the surface, the nymphs would crawl slowly up the swaying foliage and release gases at the proper time to insure flotation through their hatching process.

The nymphs that reside in gravel runs and riffles were also buoyed to the surface by these gases which are released from the nymphal skins on the stream's bottom. When emergence is imminent, the gases are released, seemingly involuntarily, committing the nymphs to a helpless, slow, drifting ascent.

During the emergence process, the trout usually feed at various depths, intercepting the helpless ascending nymphs in the most advantageous line of drift. Anglers should cast their imitation across and downstream, allowing the currents to raise the pattern subtly from the bottom, duplicating the ascent of the naturals. A good hot-spot for this tactic is downstream of extensive weed beds.

Left: Pseudocloeon, female dun. *Right:* Pseudocloeon, male dun. The lack of hind wings separates them from the similar Baetis.

Our subject genera are multi-brooded and as many as three generations may evolve during a single season. Like most of the gray-winged, olive-bodied mayflies, the duns of these genera are called Blue-Winged Olives.

These subimagoes are often mistaken for the duns of the various Baetis species, as they, too, have two tails, olive bodies and blue-gray wings. The males have large, curious, turbinate eyes as in Baetis. On closer examination, however, the angler will be able to distinguish these duns from those of the Baetis genera. Pseudocloeon and Cloeon have a single pair of wings, lacking the tiny hind wings found in Baetis and the closely related Centroptilum genus.

These tiny duns are found on most streams throughout the country, but their populations reach significant angling importance only on the rich limestone waters of the East and Midwest and the alkaline spring creeks of the West. The Eastern species Pseudocloeon *carolina* hatches prolifically on Pennsylvania chalkstreams; especially those of the western slopes of the Appalachians such as Penn's Creek, Elk Creek and Fishing Creek where we have witnessed excellent hatching and have collected many aquarium specimens. We also stocked our aquariums with Pseudocloeon *anoka* nymphs from Michigan's Au Sable River system, later observing the similarities in emergence of this Midwestern species to its Eastern and Western counterparts. The Western Pseudocloeon species *edmundsi* and *futile,* hatch on the pristine spring creeks of the Rocky Mountain states. These calcium-rich streams, like Idaho's Silver Creek and the Henry's Fork of the Snake as well as the fertile Yellowstone Park waters produce superior hatches of these species.

Prior to emergence, the nymphs of Pseudocloeon are usually found on submerged plants and rocks in proximity to smooth runs or shallow gravelly riffles where they float to the surface and complete their metamorphosis. When the freshly emerged duns are evident on the stream's surface, anglers should switch from the nymphal imitations to dryfly patterns.

Primarily, emergence takes place a few hours before dark (7 P.M.), but on overcast and cloudy days, when the water temperature remains low, hatching may begin as early as 11 A.M. and continue sporadically throughout the day. In either case, Mother Nature has provided the fly-fisher with an ample time period in which to enjoy this challenging hatch.

The duns usually float serenely for a short period, drying their wings before takeoff. Due to their small size, the duns are susceptible to the slightest breeze, which skitters them across the smooth currents or riffles. At this time, when trout are licking up the duns like candy, anglers should

DUNS

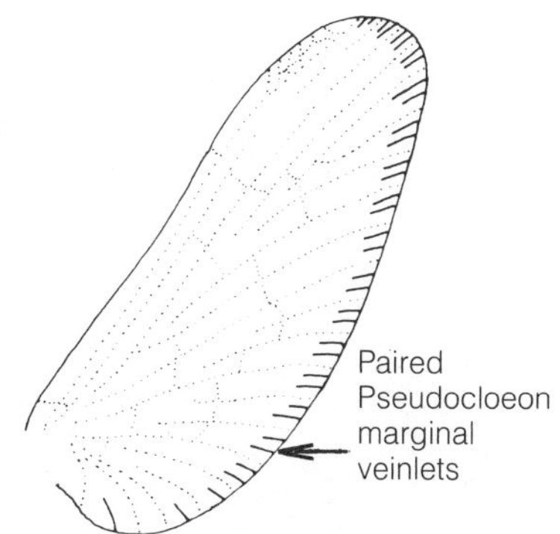

The wings of Pseudocloeon are a dead ringer for Baetis except that they lack entirely a hind wing; Baetis has a dwarfed hind wing. Note the paired marginal veinlets. The veinlets of cloeon, below, are single.

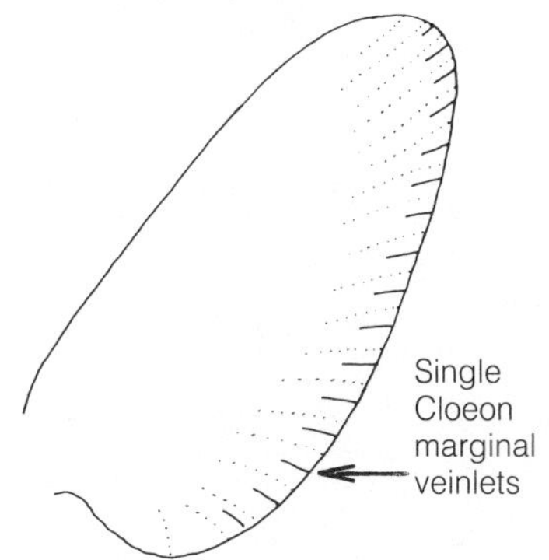

concentrate on the lines of maximum drift, as the larger, more selective trout seldom cruise for these tiny duns, preferring instead, to rise efficiently from their selected stations.

The Pseudocloeon Compara-dun is our favorite for this hatch. We dress this pattern on light wire #20, #22 and #24 hooks with turned-up eyes. When hackle is needed to suggest the subtle fluttering movements made by the duns during wind gusts, or when delicate hackle barbules are required to respond to the tiny whirlpools and wavelets on riffled surfaces, we simply add a few turns of dark blue dun hackle fore-and-aft of the wing. Standard dry-fly patterns like the Blue-Winged Olive and the Dark Blue Quill also work well for this hatch.

SPINNER

The spinner stage provides the best opportunity to identify the Pseudocloeon species from the species of its sister genus, Cloeon. With the aid of an 8x magnifying glass, the angler will be able to detect the double veinlets located on the outer or anterior margin of Psuedocloeon's wing. Cloeon's marginal veinlets are singular.

The final moult usually takes place in close proximity to the stream, within a few hours after the duns emerge. Many duns moult, mate and oviposit during the same evening.

Spinners return en masse at dusk in cloud-like formations that are usually difficult to observe in the fading light. Subimago activity usually continues simultaneously with the spinner-falls and the angler must be alert to spot which stage is being taken. If the rises seem extra-subtle, more like a sip, the trout will usually be taking the ovipositing or spent spinners. Another way to determine the stage on which trout are feeding is to invest about 5 minutes to determine if the dun activity has decreased or ceased. A small aquarium net or a piece of cheesecloth will help you to determine this rather quickly. If the duns collected are in the minority, it's usually best to switch to a spinner pattern.

For spinner activity, we use the "Figure 8" Compara-spinner exclusively. This pattern differs from our typical spinner imitation because we dub a "Figure 8" thorax over the wound hackle instead of trimming it. This procedure separates the hackle, creating a deep "V" outline when observed from the front. When further trimming is necessary, we use our nail clippers to snip off more hackle, leaving an excellent spent-wing version that floats flush in the surface film. We also use this "Figure 8" method on the Tricorythodes Compara-spinner, as these tiny mayflies, like those of Pseudocloeon have a relatively robust thorax. Both patterns are identical except for the slightest variation in color; hence, anglers may use the same pattern for both hatches.

NYMPHS Pseudocloeon

SPECIES	DIST.	SIZE	TAILS	MISC.
anoka	M	4-5	– – –	Ground color: pale grass-green. Tergites 2 and 6 bear a rounded black spot on mid-line; tergite 7, a somewhat smaller dot.
carolina	E	4-5	unbanded	Tergites 1-8 almost entirely dark.
dubium	E, M, W	3-4	median band, dark	Tergites 3, 4, 8-10 are mostly pale; others are dark. 9 has dark lateral dash.
futile	W	3-3½	– – –	– – –

MALE SPINNER Pseudocloeon

SPECIES	DIST.	SIZE	EYES	FORE FEMORA	TERGITE MARKINGS 2-6	TERGITES 2-6	TERGITES 7-10*
anoka	M	4-5	orange	light gray	yes	hyaline white	med. brown
carolina	E	4-5	brown	brown	no	brown	brown
dubium	E, M, W	3-4	reddish-brown	pale reddish-brown	no	white	dark brown
futile	W	3-3½	greenish-brown	whitish	no	clay brown	yellowish-brown

*The female abdomen is a uniform color, similar to the color of tergites 7-10.

The duns of this genus are generally similar to Baetis, though sometimes paler. The body colors range from olive-brown to yellowish or light reddish-brown. The legs and tails are usually paler than the body color. There are no markings on their grayish wings.

MALE SPINNER Cloeon

SPECIES	DIST.	SIZE	THORAX	TERGITES 2-6	TERGITE MARKINGS 2-6	TERGITES 7-10
insignificans	E, M	3-3½	brown	hyaline	yes	yellowish-brown
mendax	E, M	4-5	rust	rust	no	rust
rubropictum	E, M	4-5	dark brown	yellowish-white	yes	reddish-brown
simplex	E	4-5	blackish-brown	whitish	no	dark brown
ingens	W	8-9	blackish	olive brown	no	brown

The duns of this genus are generally pale. Their bodies, light in color, range from yellowish to orange to reddish-brown The legs and tails are likewise pale. There are no markings on their palish-gray wings.

Genus Callibaetis
(Family Baetidae)

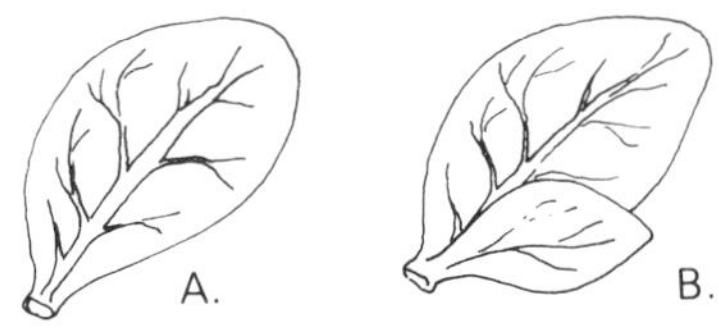

A, Single gills of Baetis nymph; B, Pointed, double gills of Callibaetis nymph.

The uniquely winged mayflies of this genus are primarily found in lakes and ponds throughout the Rockies and the West Coast. Of the twenty-eight species listed by Edmunds, only three are considered to be important to the Eastern and Midwestern fly-fishing specialist who frequent the spring ponds and calm, flat stretches of the rich, highly alkaline spring creeks and rivers. We have fished to sporadic hatches of these species, when they were present on trout streams, during our hot pursuit of the more prominent and popular mayflies; i.e., Tricorythodes, Baetis, Pseudocloeon, Hexagenia *limbata*, etc.

The nymphs are highly specialized and dart minnow-like in the calm water when not perched on the shafts of vegetation or on the slowly undulating filamentous foliage of subaquatic growth. They are very similar to Baetis, but can be quickly segregated by their three tails of equal length and by their larger size. Most of the important species range from 7 to 12mm in body length, while those of Baetis, who prefer riffles and faster currents, average between 5 and 8mm, except for the Midwestern species Baetis *hiemalis* which approaches the size of the Callibaetis nymphs.

Closer inspection will also show that the gills of Callibaetis are quite different from those of Baetis. Although they are present on body segments 1-7 like Baetis, they differ as follows: 1. They are pointed at the tips in a "heartlike" fashion compared to the oval shape of Baetis gills; 2. the gills are double rather than single as is Baetis. The secondary gills are quite small and are best viewed under at least an 8x magnification; 3. Their three tails are of equal length. It is not uncommon for a broad, dark band to be present at the apical portions of the "hairy", plumage-like sector of the tails.

Left: Callibaetis, female dun. *Right:* Callibaetis, female spinner. These uniquely marked wings easily separate them from the Baetis species.

The Callibaetis mayflies are multi-brooded and three generations may hatch during a single season where habitats are favorable. Those hatches of the various species that bridge the principal mayfly, stonefly and caddisfly season in each geographic area are worthy of attention by the fly-fisherman. This activity will vary from species to species and the hatching period of each brood will also vary according to whether the environment is harsh or favorable in each geographic area.

The adults of this genus are immediately recognizable by their uniquely freckled bodies and fancy wings. Also, they lose their middle tail in the transition from nymph to dun. In the dun stage, the wings are attractively mottled in appearance. The venations are wholly pale or white against a darker background, resembling the bared flank-feathers of a teal. An excellent standard dry-fly pattern for this species is the Grey Quill which features the imitative teal wing.

In the spinner stage, the wings are contrastingly spotted and splotched, having a delicate lace-like appearance; the bodies are attractively freckled. Both the dun and the spinner can be readily identified on the wing or on the water; however, it still pays to capture a natural to determine the correct size, as trout are usually ultraselective on smooth waters where these insects live.

MALE SPINNER

SPECIES	DIST.	SIZE	CROSS-VEINS	MARGINAL VEINLETS
ferrugineus	E, M	7-9	many (35-60)	paired
coloradensis	W	7-9	many (35-60)	paired?
fluctuans	E, M	6-7	few (15-25)	single
nigritus	W	8-10	many	paired?

species description of nymph not known.

Genus Centroptilum
(Family Baetidae)

GENERAL EMERGENCE:

album .... June-Oct.
convexum .... throughout Summer
elsa .... June-Oct.
rufostrigatum .... June-Oct.
walshi .... throughout Summer

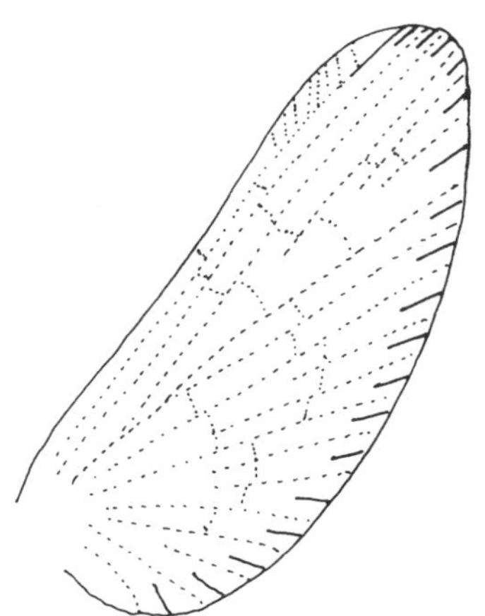

Single marginal veinlets of Centroptilum forewing

Our research on this genus had a negative outcome, as we have never found populations of these nymphs that could cause even minor hatching. The Leonards report similarly lean findings on Midwestern limestone streams in their definitive book, *Mayflies of Michigan Trout Streams* where they state:

> "We have found members of this genus of very infrequent occurence in Michigan trout streams; they are more plentiful in warm-water streams of slow to moderate current, and in lakes.
>
> Like other species of genus, Centroptilum *album* appears to be of little importance to the trout fisherman."

The Centropitilum nymphs are remarkably similar to those of Baetis, except their three tails are equal in length. They are thicker in the thorax as in Pseudocloeon and the claws are not pectinate as they are in Baetis. The plate-like gills on segments 1 through 7 are variable in shape from species to species and some have recurved dorsal flaps on most or all of the segments, giving the appearance of double gills.

The duns can be separated from similar Baetis mayflies by their thread-like hind wings, which are even narrower than the finger-like secondary wings of Baetis. They usually have only two longitudinal veins as compared to three in Baetis. The marginal veinlets of the pale forewing are singular, compared to the double veinlets in Baetis.

The spinners have hyaline wings and the bodies of the males are pale yellow or whitish in color with reddish-brown or brown markings. The females have even paler markings and are similar to the Pseudocloeon and Cloeon imagoes.

MALE SPINNER

SPECIES	DIST.	SIZE	EYES	TERGITES	THORAX
album	E, M	5-6	orange-brown	whitish	yellow-brown
convexum	E, M, W	5-6	dark brown	whitish	brown
rufostrigatum	E, M, W	5-6	blackish-brown	brown	blackish-brown
walshi	M	6-7	reddish	cream	yellow-brown
elsa	W	6-7	pinkish	yellow-brown	reddish-brown

Basal abdominal segments of the male are yellowish or whitish; females lack these paler segments and, in most species, are often uniformly light reddish-brown.

The descriptions of the nymphs and duns of this genus are not known, but are generally considered simllar to the Baetis species.

Genus Isonychia
(Family Siphlonuridae)

The powerful "large swimmers" of the Isonychia genus are very important to the Eastern and Midwestern angler, especially the concentrated, heavy evening spinner flights. These flights parallel those of the Stenonema genus and we have come to respect them as one of the more reliable stream activities that produce exceptional fly-fishing.

The Isonychia nymphs are well distributed throughout the country, but their impact on the trout community and the angler is best in the East and the Midwest. Unlike the "tiny swimmers", who prefer rich alkaline streams, these "large swimmers" are equally abundant on freestone mountain streams. Actually, they seem to like these tumbling streams even better; perhaps it's because these swifter currents bring more food to their basket-like forelegs. Like many of the stoneflys of the Plecoptera order, these nymphs are predacious and will feed on minute Diptera and caddis larvae as well as tiny mayfly nymphs.

These swift, highly streamlined nymphs are among the easiest to recognize. They are usually large (12mm-16mm), brownish-black, with a whitish mid-dorsal stripe and have explosive starts when swimming which reminds one of sleek "Indy" racing cars.

The gills are similar, being ovoid or plate-like and are located on abdominal segments 1 through 7. Each pair of plate-like gills has a second, filamentous portion that is partially obscured beneath it. In addition, these nymphs have gill-tufts present under the thorax, at the bases of the fore-coxae (similar to the gills of a stonefly). The forelegs have basket-like, long spine-like hairs on the femur and tibia, which are most noticeable on the tibia. The nymphs have three heavily fringed tails; fringed on both sides of the middle tail as well as the inner sides of the two outer tails. The plumage is usually dark basally and lighter apically.

Basket-like forelegs of Isonychia nymph.

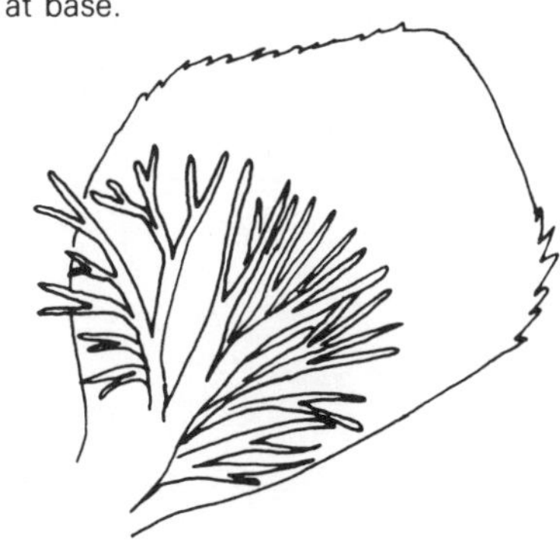

Isonychia gill with filamentous portion at base.

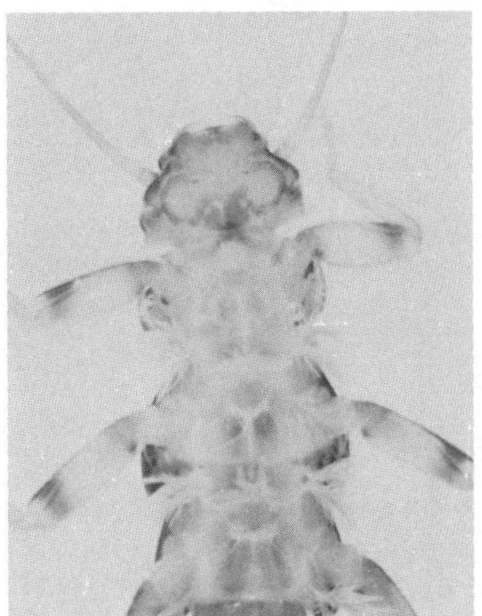

The unusual gill tufts of Isonychia (left) are similar to the gills of a stonefly (right).

The duns and spinners have reddish-brown bodies. The wings of the dun are dark gray with milky-soft areas in the lower center portion of the fore and hind wings. After moulting, they are sparkling-clear (hyaline). The large eyes of the male are contiguous at the top of the head in the imago state, but not quite in the dun stage. Both male and female eyes have an oblique stripe which is noticeable after the specimen is exposed to light. The middle tail is lost in the transition from nymph to dun and the remaining tails are pale cream or white, as are the middle and rear pairs of legs. The dark forelegs are similar in color to the body.

NYMPH

SPECIES	DIST.	SIZE	DORSAL STRIPE
bicolor	E, M	13-16	Head to basal abdominal segments.
sadleri	E, M	13-16	Head to segment 9; less distinct on 7-9.
harperi	E, M	13-15	– – –
velma	W	13-16	Anterior halves of tergites.
campestris	W	10-12	– – –
sicca	W	9-11	– – –

MALE SPINNER

SPECIES	DIST.	SIZE	GENERAL EMERGENCE	VENATION	FORE-TARSI	DUNS
bicolor	E, M	13-16	1st Week June Mid-July	pale	whitish	Body: dark reddish-brown. Wings: dark gray with milky cloud. Forelegs: dark; middle and hind, pale yellowish.
sadleri	E, M	13-16	Mid-June Mid-July	pale brown	brown	same as *bicolor*
harperi	E, M	12-14	Sept.	pale brown	brown	Similar to *bicolor* and *sadleri*, but anterior portions of abdominal segments are paler than the posterior.
velma	W	13-16	June-July September-October	dark brown	reddish	Dark reddish-brown insect with dark gray wings.
campestris	W	9-11	September-October	dark	light reddish	Dark reddish-brown insect with dark gray wings.
sicca	W	9-11	June-July	brown	smoky brown	Same as *bicolor* and *sadleri*.

Isonychia bicolor

The strange name Isonychia *bicolor* so befits these unusual and exotic members of the Ephemereoptera (mayfly) order. The characteristics which establish this mayfly among the unique are its bicolor legs, carnivorous nature and long emergence span (late May to September). Another strange trait is that it emerges on rocks and logs, completely out of the water.

There are several species of the Isonychia genus in the East that cause a good rise of trout. Among these, *sadleri* seems to be the most important. All are similar to *bicolor* in appearance and habits; therefore, fly fishermen should treat them alike. It should be mentioned that *albomonicata* which was singled out as a major species in many angling texts, is now considered synonymous with *bicolor.*

bicolor is known as the Leadwing Coachman, Slate Drake, Dun Variant and Mahogany Dun. In most locations, after the initial, heavier hatches, the emergence of this species dwindles, sporadically, throughout the summer; hence, it probably hatches on more calendar days than most mayflys. Although *bicolor* is mainly an Eastern species, good hatches are not uncommon in the Midwest, where the more important Isonychia species is *sadleri.* Heaviest activity in Pennsylvania, including the Poconos, is June 7 through the end of the month. The Catskill region is best between June 10 and July 7, while the Adirondacks and upper New England peak between June 19 and July 21. Best hatching on Michigan's Au Sable River starts around June 12. Wisconsin rivers like the Prarie and the Wolf hatch around the same time, while the rivers of the northern tier of these states and Minnesota hatch a bit later.

COMMON NAMES: Leadwing Coachman, Slate Drake, Dun Variant, Mahogany Dun

SIZE RANGE: 13 to 16 mm

HOOK SIZES:
SURFACE (dry): #10, #8
SUBSURFACE (wet): #10, #10, 3x long

IMITATIONS:
NYMPH: Zug Bug, Bicolor Compara-nymph
DUN: Dun variant, Bicolor Compara-dun, Bicolor Hackled Compara-dun
SPINNER: Bicolor Compara-spinner

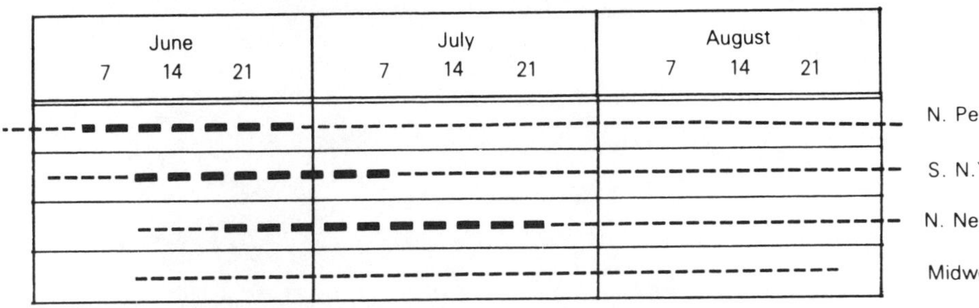

N. Penna. and Poconos

S. N.Y. and Catskills

N. New England and Adirondacks

Midwest and Great Lakes region

The rushing mountain streams of the Northeast are the principle domain of *bicolor,* but the rich alkaline streams of the Midwest also offer excellent hatches. This strong, sleek, minnow-like swimmer darts about in the current foraging on larvae, plankton and other minute organisms. When at rest it maintains an attitude similar to the dun; forelegs extended while being supported by the middle and hind legs. These extraordinary forelegs are fringed with hairs forming miniature webs which are utilized as food-gathering baskets.

Our aquarium observations show that these nymphs rank among the swiftest of all mayfly niads. Aside from being quick, they are also among the shyest, streaking for the cover of crevices as soon as the aquarium is disturbed. In spite of their lightning speed, these nymphs are extremely agile and can change direction as quickly and unpredictably as a mexican jumping bean.

A few days before emergence, these fast-water-swimming nymphs migrate to the shallows where they congregate in a stream's quieter sections. As emergence approaches, the nymphs crawl out of the water to hatch like a stonefly. As evidence of this emergence, their empty shucks may be found on sticks, logs, banks, and, most commonly, rocks.

On quieter stretches, such as long, wide flats with a steady current, look for emergence activity around undercut banks, deadfalls or man-made abutments. This is also a great hangout for lunker trout who take advantage of the nymphs hatching traits.

On streams with miles of pocket-water, look for the empty shucks on the lee side of protruding boulders. These boulders create tiny pools within these turbulent white water stretches where the nymphs can emerge safely. They also provide ideal holding stations for trout who take full advantage of the nymph's launching sites.

Trout are very concious of all Isonychia migrations and follow the nymphs into these shallow areas when safety permits. Anglers should exhibit extreme caution in the shallows by casting softly and keeping out of sight.

The Compara-nymph is very effective during the nymphing period. Casts should be directed to the base of large

Left: I. *bicolor,* nymph. *Right:* I. *bicolor,* female dun.

boulders and rocks where trout usually hide. The pattern should drift naturally over these suspected hideouts. Nymphing in clear, shallow pockets is exciting business, especially when a streaking rainbow charges your fly with his shimmering dorsal completely out of the water.

Another pattern that has had a history of success during this activity is the Leadwing Coachman wet-fly. The good fortune this fly enjoys is probably due to the irridescent quality of its peacock-herl body which is not unlike the natural. An even better imitation is the popular Zug Bug which is available in most fly shops.

DUN

These large smoky-winged mayflies have three tails as a nymph and only two in the adult stage. The middle and hind legs are yellowish, while the extended forelegs are reddish-brown, the same color as their elongated bodies. These features make this handsome, dark-winged dun easy to recognize at streamside.

Hatching usually takes place in late afternoon or evening, but during cloudy or rainy days, they may emerge sporadically throughout the day. This is primarily due to cooler water temperature resulting from the lack of sunlight.

Although the naturals generally crawl out of the water to emerge, enough of them awkwardly flop back into the stream or are blown in by gusts as to make them a great favorite with trout, especially rainbows. However, not all duns reach the trout in this manner. Occasionally, high water conditions will submerge those convenient locations where nymphs would normally crawl out, forcing them to emerge on the stream's surface. When this is the case, they emerge quite efficiently. After escaping its shuck, the dun

I. *bicolor,* female spinner.

floats with the current for exceptionally long periods, struggling to get its extra-long body airborne.

When duns are drifting motionless, the Compara-dun is hard to beat, but when naturals are struggling, our choice is a hackled pattern. Art Flick, master of the Schoharie, originated the Dun Variant for this hatch—it's a proven fishgetter.

The Compara-dun should be allowed to drift naturally over feeding fish while the high-riding Variant is best when manipulated. A well-tied Variant lands like a feather upon the shallows.

SPINNER

This sparkling imago was dubbed by Charles Wetzel as the White-Gloved Howdy owing to its extended brown forelegs, capped with tiny white feet (tarsi) held in the gesture of a handshake. The wings are glassy-clear and the body reddish-brown.

Spinner flights are quite impressive and take place around dusk. Trout love these imagoes when they are on the water in goodly number. Often spinner-falls occur when duns are hatching, creating a situation where, to be successful, the angler must first determine on which stage trout are feed-

These anglers are in good position for a late-season Isonychia spinner-fall. Look for them at dusk.

ing. These spinner-falls are practically identical to those of *sadleri* and anglers should also refer to that chapter for spinner-fall characteristics and angling tactics.

A clever choice for the spinner-fall is the Compara-dun. This amazing floater serves a dual purpose when duns and spinners are both on the water due to its flush-in-the-film floating quality (like the spinner) and its high wing silhouette (like the dun).

When duns aren't hatching and trout are feeding only on flitting or spent spinners, the Compara-spinner is an accurate imitation. A popular and traditional imitation for this spinner fail is the White-Gloved Howdy, created by the Pennsylvania writer-angler, Charles Wetzel.

Through the years, we have found the spinner-falls (those which take place in the late season) to be more reliable than the hatching activity of the duns. After the initial heavy hatching in late spring, the duns hatch sporadically throughout the season—but only when the water temperature is ideal (below 70°F). During this late season, the spinner activity is more consistent owing to the concentrated flights which form just prior to darkness. During those warm nights, when trout might ignore other sporadic insect activity prior to dusk, they seldom pass up the *bicolor* spinner-falls. Rather, a stretch that seemed almost dead one moment will almost always errupt with feeding trout once the Isonychia spinners fall ovipositing and spent to the surface.

Isonychia sadleri

COMMON NAMES: Maroon Drake, Mahogany Dun, Mahogany Drake

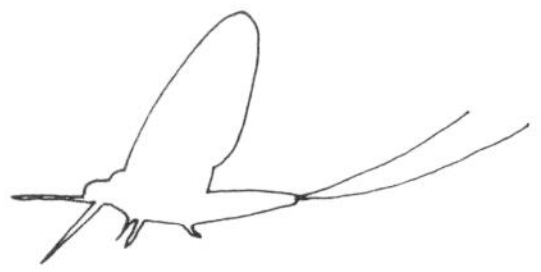

SIZE RANGE: 13 to 16 mm

HOOK SIZES:
SURFACE (dry): #8, #10 4x long
SUBSURFACE (wet): #10, #10 3 × long

IMITATIONS:
NYMPH: Zug Bug, Sadleri Compara-nymph
DUN: Dun Variant, Sadleri Compara-dun, Sadleri Hackled Compara-dun
SPINNER: Sadleri Compara-spinner

Needham, Traver & Hsu list over 25 species of Isonychia in *Biology of Mayflies* (Edmunds now lists 27), all of which are quite similar in size, color and configuration. These Isonychia species are surprisingly tolerant of pollution and are adaptable to various geographic areas; from the lush Eastern mountain ranges to the Midwestern plateaus. Western watersheds, including those of the majestic Rockies, also harbor these fast-water swimmers of Isonychia such as *velma*, but there they seldom reach the angling status typical of the East and Midwest.

In our judgment, the two most important Isonychia species, as far as fly-fishermen are concerned, are *bicolor* and *sadleri*. Another species that may be important to the angler is *harperi*. It emerges in September in the East and Midwest.

Although each of these Isonychia species enjoy a large geographic domain, it has been our experience that *bicolor* is dominant in the East, while *sadleri* represents a major fishing hatch in the Midwest. Unlike *bicolor* (whose emergence is generally sporadic from late May to September), *sadleri's* hatching span is generally three weeks in duration; from June 18 until July 12 in the Midwest, where the best hatches occur. Greatest hatching on the Au Sable system and other neighboring river systems of northern Michigan is during the Hexagenia *limbata* activity; between June 20 and July 12. Wisconsin and Minnesota hatches of *sadleri* also coincide with the H. *limbata* emergence. The best hatches on Wisconsin's Wolf and Peshtigo Rivers usually occur in late June while the northern rivers like the Namekagon and both Brule Rivers should be right during the second week in July.

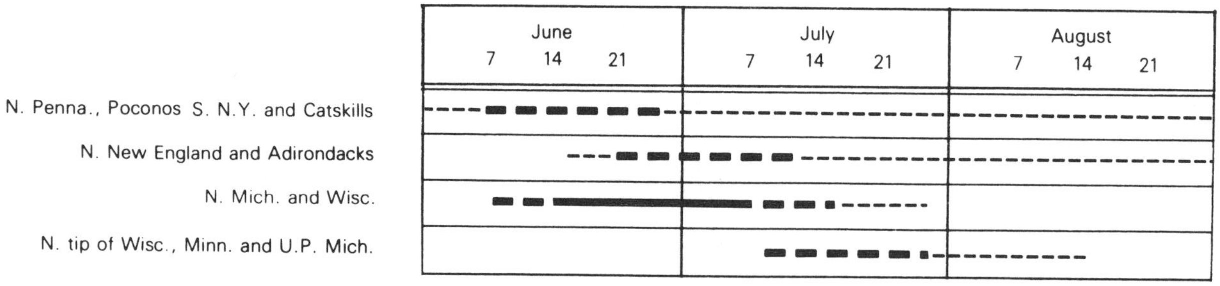

	June 7	June 14	June 21	July 7	July 14	July 21	August 7	August 14	August 21
N. Penna., Poconos S. N.Y. and Catskills									
N. New England and Adirondacks									
N. Mich. and Wisc.									
N. tip of Wisc., Minn. and U.P. Mich.									

NYMPH

sadleri nymphs inhabit the fast-water stretches of both freestone and limestone streams. Their agility and sleek bodies enable them to swim in the fastest torrents where they collect minute organisms like tiny Diptera larva, as well as diatoms and microscopic algae.

Identification characteristics between the *bicolor* and

sadleri nymphs has been somewhat controversial. Needham and Leonard in their respective books, *The Biology of Mayflies* and *Mayflies of Michigan Trout Streams,* claim that the *sadleri* nymph has an uninterrupted pale mid-dorsal abdominal stripe extending from the head to the ninth segment of the abdomen near the tail.

Conversly, Ernie Schwiebert in *Nymphs* states, "The nymphs *[sadleri]* closely resemble those of *Isonychia bicolor,* a related species of our eastern rivers. However, it is somewhat larger and lacks the pale dorsal stripe singularly descriptive of the better known *bicolor* species."

Our stream and lab research agrees with the Needham and Leonard findings in that the stripe on the *sadleri* nymph extends to the ninth body segment while the *bicolor* stripe terminates slightly past the thorax.

As far as the angler is concerned, the most significant difference between *sadleri* and *bicolor* lies in their emergence characteristics. *bicolor* generally crawls out of the water to hatch, while *sadleri* usually hatches on the stream's surface. This factor may be more circumstantial than hereditary, as most Midwestern waters, where *sadleri* predominates, lack convenient boulders for an out-of-the-water emergence. Although *sadleri* emergence usually takes place in the riffles, the nymphs may at times migrate to the quiet eddies or back-waters to emerge out of the water on deadfalls or debris that has washed against the undercut banks.

During emergence, anglers should work the riffles with nymph imitations, jigging them off of the bottom and bringing them to life with imitative twitches that resemble the fast-swimming nymphs. When working the back-waters and shallows, casts should be made a considerable way up-

Left: I. *sadleri,* nymph. *Right:* Ideal stretch of *sadleri* water on Michigan's Au Sable river. Note the absence of boulders.

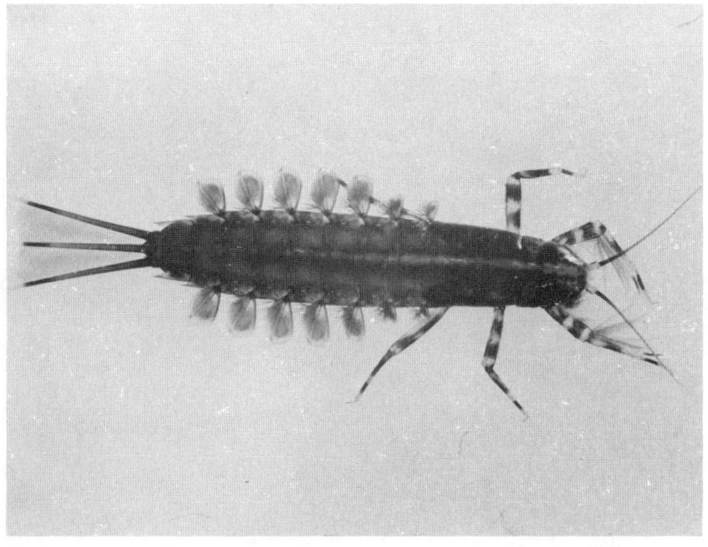

stream, as not to spook the wary fish. The imitation should be allowed to float dead-drift past suspect deadfalls and undercut banks.

The Sadleri Compara-nymph is an excellent imitation and is identical to the *bicolor* pattern. As mentioned in the *bicolor* chapter, the Leadwing Coachman and the Zug Bug are popular and sometimes effective patterns for this hatch.

DUN

The large smoky-winged duns of *sadleri* are commonly known as Maroon Drakes in Michigan fly-fishing circles. Midwesterners may also refer to them as the Mahogany Dun or Mahogany Drake.

These large duns have two tails, having sacrificed their middle tail during emergence as duns. The body averages 15mm and the wings 13mm; about the same size as *bicolor*. At first glance the two-toned legs of the *sadleri* dun seem to be the same as those of *bicolor* (dark forelegs and pale yellow middle and rear legs). The key to separating the species is that the foretarsi of *sadleri* are dark, while *bicolor's* tarsi are whitish.

The importance of *sadleri* hatches in the Midwest is on par with the *bicolor* hatch of the East. Although both species are look-a-likes and exist in the same type of habitat, their individual emergence traits prompt different feeding activity from the trout.

The importance of *sadleri* raises the legitimate question of why this species has been so unpublicized in past angling literature. We believe that the lack of adequate coverage was probably due to the distraction caused by the spectacular and bizarre activity of Hexagenia *limbata*, which takes place during the same time period.

sadleri hatching activity is especially ideal- for the dry-fly

Left: sadleri, female dun. *Right: sadleri,* male spinner. Note dark foretarsi of dun and spinner.

addict, because the duns usually emerge on the stream's surface and in good number. Concentrated hatching activity is caused by the prolific nymph populations which hatch within a relatively short span; about three weeks. This compact emergence prompts exciting surface activity from the trout who feed deliberately and predaciously. *sadleri* hatching action is in sharp contrast to the *bicolor* emergence activity which takes place out of the water, permitting only occasional duns to fall or be blown onto the stream's surface. Even on those uncommon occasions when*bicolor* hatches on the stream's surface, they seldom appear in the quantity of *sadleri*, as their emergence is more sparse due to the long, drawn out hatching period of approximately twelve weeks.

sadleri nymphs usually emerge between 7 and 10 P.M., but the peak activity takes place about an hour or so before dark. On overcast or cloudy days, hatching frequently takes place in the afternoon, after midday. *sadleri* duns usually hatch in riffles and in medium-to-fast runs. They float placidly immediately after hatching, but they twitch and skip momentarily at takeoff. We have occasionally witnessed good hatching in the back-waters and eddies of river-bends where the nymphs had migrated to hatch on deadfalls and debris that accumulated about the banks.

The trout seem to crave these duns and dry-fly action often parallels those theoretical fantasies we all indulge in during the off-season. As previously mentioned, the *sadleri* duns are on Midwestern waters at the same time as *limbata* and although daily hatching activity usually precedes *limbata* by about an hour, they may also hatch simultaneously. On streams that have good populations of both, *sadleri's* impact may lose some punch. Nevertheless, we've enjoyed excellent fishing for trout in the 10 to 14 inch range during this *sadleri* activity just prior to the H. *limbata* hatch. On streams that have little or no H. *limbata* activity, the *sadleri* influence is usually terrific!

Due to the subimago's calm composure on the stream's surface after hatching, we are partial to the Sadleri Compara-dun which has identical dressing to that of *bicolor*. On those windy occasions when it's necessary to impart a fluttering action, or in riffles where it's smart to dance a delicate, high-riding hackled imitation over the diffused and deceiving currents, anglers should switch to hackled patterns. The Hackled Compara-dun and Art Flick's Dun Variant are good patterns for this job.

SPINNER

The spinner flights of *sadleri* are impressive and can present excellent angling opportunities when they are present in good number.

The mating ritual is often first sighted high above the stream. The spinners are large and the dark silhouette of the hovering males are usually quite distinct against the twilighted sky.

Soon after mating takes place, the females flit to the surface and release their dark egg masses.

The first sighting of the males high above the riffles is usually witnessed about an hour before dark. The descent and subsequent nuptial ritual often takes place within about 30 minutes; so, by the time the females are ovipositing, it's usually close to dusk. Anglers should utilize the spinner descent time wisely to select proper imitations and to obtain advantageous casting positions.

The spinner action, though brief, is electrifying and it precipitates fierce feeding activity. Fly-fishermen will be surprised by the size of the trout attracted by these short but highly concentrated spinner-falls. Large trout usually migrate to shallow-water feeding positions during these falls and the hooking and playing of a good trout in these knee-deep riffles is an ideal way to draw the curtain on a day astream.

Our choice for this spinner activity is the Compara-spinner. Sometimes duns may emerge simultaneously with the spinner-falls. When this is the case, we think the Compara-dun is a good compromise. This imitation serves the dual role rather effectively due to its flush-floating characteristics (as in the spinner) and the high wing silhouette (as in the dun).

Art Neuman, the famous Michigan angler, claims that the Madsen's Barber Pole (spent-wing) is an excellent imitation for the imago activity and that it is used quite extensively on the Au Sable and neighboring Michigan river systems. The late Earl Madsen developed this fly in the Wakely Bridge section of the Au Sable River.

Genus Siphlonurus
(Family Siphlonuridae)

GENERAL EMERGENCE:

rapidus . . . . May-June
alternatus . . . . late June-July
quebecensis . . . . . . late May-early June
occidentalis . . . . July-October

The relationship to angling importance between the "large swimmers" of the Isonychia and Siphlonurus genera parallels that of the "clinging" Stenonema and Heptagenia genera; the Stenonema being important in the East and the Midwest, while the status of Heptagenia assumes real importance mostly in the West. So it is with the "large swimmers" of Siphlonurus which are of limited importance to the Eastern trout fisherman and become rather significant in the West.

Unlike their Isonychia relatives, the Siphlonurus nymphs seem to thrive best on rich alkaline streams. We found fair populations, even in the East, when we seined limestone waters like those found in western Pennsylvania. The populations got better when we researched the Midwestern streams; however, the emergence period of these insects in the Midwest conflicts with major activity of the prolific Hexagenia, Stenonema, Isonychia and Ephemera mayflies. Only when they returned en masse, as spinners, did we enjoy excellent fly-fishing to these mayflies in the Midwest.

We found surprisingly good populations of these nymphs in the West to rival the Isonychia populations of the East and Midwest. We had the good fortune to observe and fish a good hatch in the Park waters of the Yellowstone River, where we caught and released large numbers of the illogical population of native cutthroats up to 20" in length. They were feeding on the Siphlonurus duns as well as the smaller Ephemerella mayflies and the ridiculously large Pteronarcys stoneflies (Salmon Fly). We also researched and experienced hatches and spinner-falls of this genus in Montana and Idaho, but our work on these Western species is not near complete.

Siphlonurus, nymph

Needham lists 19 species of Siphlonurus in *Biology of Mayflies*. After much revision due to the addition of new species and the deletion of synonymous species, the latest number of species is now 17, which range in size from 9 to 17mm.

NYMPH

According to entomologists, the nymphs of this swimming genus are quiet-water dwellers and they inhabit lakes and still-water stretches of warmer streams as well as trout streams. We have found their populations in medium-to-fast current as well as in the quiet eddies along the edge of the stream. Their emergence is similar to the out-of-the-water emergence of the Isonychia mayflies, but they will frequently hatch in typical mayfly fashion; on the surface. Angling tactics should parallel those described in the I. *bicolor* and I. *sadleri* chapters. The imitations used, of course, should be lighter in color.

The nymphs of Siphlonurus are similar to those of Isonychia in body form and tails, but the instant recognition factor is that they don't have the telltale mid dorsal stripe found on the Isonychia nymphs. Their darting, minnow-like swimming motions are also typical of the Isonychia nymphs and of Siphloplecton, whose physical characteristics are almost inseparable from Siphlonurus as well as are their emergence traits. Anglers can, therefore, apply the same techniques to both genera.

DUN

The duns of Siphlonurus are called "Grey Drakes" both in the Midwest and the West. They are big (approx. 10-17mm), and usually prompt good feeding by the trout, even though

Siphlonurus, male spinner.

the hatches are sparse in relation to other Western hatches. Typical of Western hatching, emergence temperature is dependent on the erratic and complicated influences acting on each river and stream; hence, the hatching periods shown in the species chapters are general and should be used only as an approximate guide.

Best hatching usually takes place when water temperature is around 60°F. which is generally in late July and August. The weather is usually hot then, so hatching may take place between early evening and dusk or in the morning. Both Compara-duns and hackled patterns are required for this hatch.

SPINNER

The spinners create the best opportunity as they are highly concentrated. We have experienced excellent spinner fishing to S. *quebecensis* on Michigan's Au Sable River, even during "*limbata*" time. The spinner-falls preceded the dusk and after-dark flights of the *limbata* imagoes and decent fish rose selectively to them. Although the spinner-falls occur during the twilight hours in the Midwest, the evenings are generally too cool in the Rockies for the spinners, especially in August and September. Also, the afternoon air temperatures are normally too hot; hence, the spinners generally fall in the morning when the air temperature is between 60° and 70°F. The spent and semispent Compara-spinners are excellent for this activity.

The wing configuration of the dun and spinner is almost identical to the Isonychia mayflies, but they can be easily separated by wing venation, eye configuration, legs, abdomen and tails.

NYMPHS

SPECIES	DIST.	SIZE	GILLS 3-6	VENTRAL MARKS
alternatus	E, M, W	13-16	*double	lateral line
quebecensis	E, M	12-15	single	u-marks
occidentalis	M, W	12-16	single	lateral triangular
columlianus	W	12-13	– – –	– – –

*small recurved flap near base

MALE SPINNER

SPECIES	DIST.	SIZE	BLACK U-MARKS STERNITES	TWO DARK DOTS STERNITES	DUNS
alternatus	E, M, W	13-16	none	present	Purplish-gray insect with gray wings.
rapidus	E, M	9-12	none	none	Similar to *alternatus*, but with darker wings.
quebecensis	E, M	12-15	partial	partial	Almost indistinguishable from *alternatus*.
occidentalis	M, W	12-16	present	present	Similar to *alternatus*.
columbianus	W	12-13	present	present	Body: gray with brown bands. Wings: medium gray.

Genus Ameletus
(Family Siphlonuridae)

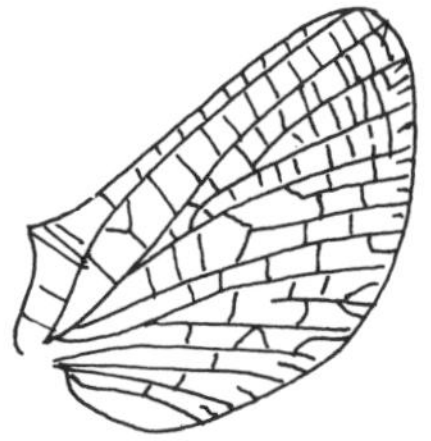

Hind wing of Ameletus adult. Note pointed projection.

Gill of Ameletus nymph with dark "stiffener".

SIZE AND DISTRIBUTION

ludens	E, M	9-12
lineatus	M	11-14
sparsatus	W	10-12
velox	W	12-14
cooki	W	9-11

GENERAL COLORATION:
Brownish or yellowish brown.

Ameletus mayflies are unimportant in at least the east and midwest. Only one remote species is listed for the northeast, that being A. *ludens*. We collected several dozen Ameletus nymphs in the park waters of the Yellowstone River some years ago and photographed them. However, we have not come across them since, in all of our years of subsequent research.

Species are difficult to identify due to the scant entomological information and lack of keys. One gets the opinion when looking through entomological publications, that relatively few of these insects were collected in large enough numbers to determine the variation within the species for accurate keys.

These strong swimming nymphs prefer the runs and riffles of both small and large streams and rivers. Reports of good populations of Ameletus nymphs have been found in streams just inches wide and at elevations as high as 11,000 feet.

The nymph has three heavily fringed tails. They have single, plate-like gills on abdominal segments 1-7. Each gill has a dark "stiffener" located near its dorsal edge. Pale abdominal segments exist on at least segments 1-2.

The adults have two tails. The hind wings have a pointed projection near the base of its leading edge.

Ameletus nymph (Western species)

Genus Siphloplecton
(Family Metretopodidae)

The Siphloplecton mayflies are no longer listed under the Baetidae family. Instead, entomologists have placed them in the Metretopodidae family for taxonomy reasons. For angling purposes fly-fishermen should refer to the imitations and fly-fishing tactics recommended for the more important Siphlonurus mayflies.

There are five species listed in this relatively unimportant genus. They are: *basale, costalense, interlineatum, signatum and speciosum.* Its remote, unimportant sister genus, Metretopus has but one species named *borealis.*

Although the Siphloplecton mayflies are generally insignificant, they may be important locally where decent populations exist, as they are large mayflies. S. *basale* approaches the size of the Eastern *guttulata* (15-20mm) and you can be certain this species will cause interest from the trout where they are present.

We have captured only a few of these nymphs in all our years of seining. Although the nymphs are almost identical to Siphlonurus, both physically and in their swimming traits, upon closer scrutiny, the differences in the nymphs are shown in the drawing below.

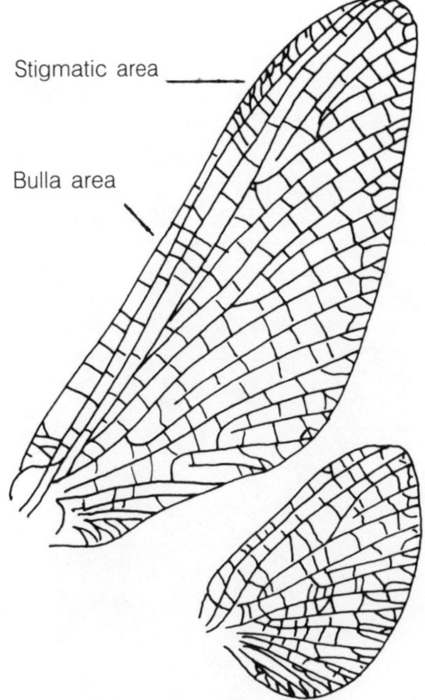

Fore and hind wing of S. *basale.* Leading edge of forewing has two dark brown areas in the stigmatic and bulla region.

DISTRIBUTION

basale . . . . E, M, W
costalense . . . . E
interlineatum . . . . M
signatum . . . . E
speciosum . . . . E

General color: Chiefly a brown insect with pale body markings.

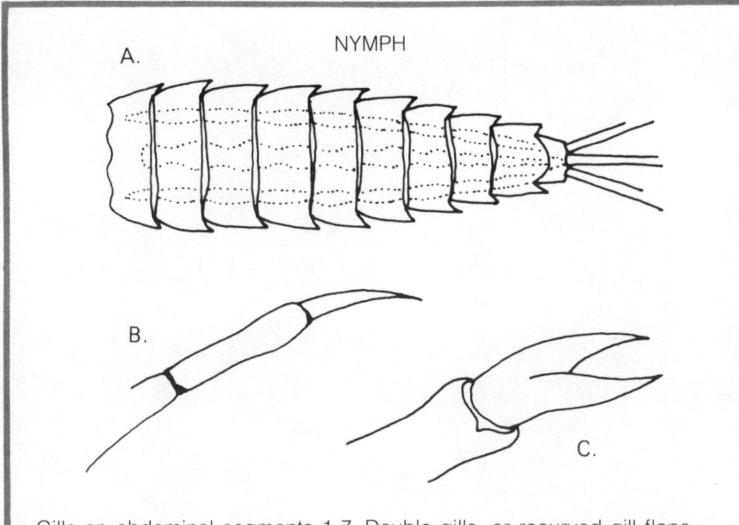

Gills on abdominal segments 1-7. Double gills, or recurved gill flaps that appear double, on segments 1 and 2 or 1, 2 and 3. Single on 3-7 or 4-7. The tarsi of all legs longer than tibia.

The Siphloplecton nymph is visually identical to the Siphlonurus nymph with the following exceptions: A, Detail of three longitudinal stripes on the sternites (underside); B, Long tarsal claws are almost as long as the tarsus; C, cleft in tarsal claw of forelegs.

What Makes a Stream Tick

Stream Research

Any angler can, in a relatively short time, learn how to determine which insect populations exist on a particular stream and even predict when the hatches will occur. This chapter was written to accommodate that curious angler who is not completely satisfied with his current fishing results; the one who is willing to invest the necessary half hour of his fishing day to observe and conduct a few simple operations that will enable him to determine what makes his stream tick.

A seine test quickly tells what makes a stream tick, yielding the secret of those aquatic insect species most abundant and how their populations compare to other streams. During this test, one of us holds the seine while the other kicks up the bottom. After the final kick, the contents of the seine are brought to the bank for examination. At first glance the seine's contents may seem lifeless and filled with only debris and vegetation. If you train your eye on several square inches of the seine for thirty seconds or so, it will usually come alive with subaquatic nymphs and larvae.

When we collect insect specimens for our aquariums or for preservation, we coax the delicate nymphs off of the screen with a thin-bladed flllet knife and place them into a thermal bucket filled with stream water. This keeps the nymphs cool until they are released in our tanks.

On some streams where the vegetation is very thick and the nymphs very small, they are hidden and difficult to detect on the seine. When this is the case, we place a bit of the vegetation into a clear plastic jar or vial full of stream water. The nymphs are then shaken free and closely scrutinized with a magnifying glass through the clear sides of the jar. The body configurations and swimming characteristics of the nymphs soon indicate the species.

At first, the novice may find it difficult to determine the mayfly species, but he should have little problem in recognizing the family or basic nymph type; the flattened clinger, the more rounded feeble-legged crawler, the tusk-bearing burrower or the swift swimmer. After some experience, he should be able to discriminate among the various mayfly genera at streamside and perhaps even determine the species if he has done his homework. Our *Comparahatch* hatch plates are designed for the purpose of streamside identification and they can be very helpful to potential researchers in the East and the Midwest. Immediate streamside identification, however, is not a necessity. Instead, after the angler estimates the contents of the seine, he can put samples of the nymphs in plastic bottles and later identify them at home, comparing the photographs and the entomological keys in this book to his captive nymphs. The jar's cap will

Al and Bob scrutinizing captured nymphs at streamside.

serve as a perfect receptacle for examination of individual nymphs. The nymphs are best examined alive and the lip of the cap serves as a confined reservoir for the nymph when filled with water. Final examination can be made with an ordinary magnifying glass, however an 8x magnifier is usually better for identification purposes.

Indiscriminate use of the seine can disturb both anglers and the streambed. So, unless we are conducting a survey for conservation groups or private clubs, we use our mini-seine. This valuable piece of equipment is a simple spaghetti or fruit strainer, preferably with a strong handle. The versatile strainer can be held behind rocks in the riffles where the clinging nymphs hide as well as some of the fast-water crawlers of Ephemerella. When the rock is lifted and shaken vigorously, the current sweeps the nymphs into the strainer.

Underwater vegetation is a good spot for swimming nymphs such as those of Baetis and Pseudocloeon, as well as the tiny crawlers of Tricorythodes and Caenis. To capture the nymphs, shake the vegetation in the same manner as previously described.

Our invaluable mini-seine.

The strainer performs another very important operation; sifting through the silt for the burrowing nymphs. We dig into three to five inches of silt, swish the strainer around a few times in a circular motion, until all the silt is washed out, then we carefully rummage through the remaining debris for the nymphs.

The strainer will also come in handy during a hatch for capturing emerging nymphs just under the surface film or for scooping floating duns off of the surface during the actual hatch.

Aquarium nets of various sizes are also excellent for this procedure. Hold the net taut against the frame and the duns can be lifted from the surface without wetting or damaging their wings. Spent or semi-spent spinners can also be collected in this manner. An additional use for the aqaurium net is to snare airborne duns and low-flying ovipositing spinners.

An efficient method for collecting duns from the water's surface.

Butterfly nets are the most efficient way to capture airborne duns and spinners. Station yourself in a riffle where most of the mating swarms take place and you'll have a net full in no time. Specimens can be put into the same plastic jars or vials used during nymph research. If the weather's cool they will stay alive for surprisingly long periods. The vials can be tucked into your vest pockets or carried in your creel. We carry the jarred specimens and other equipment in a canvas creel similar to the Articreel. This type of creel has a plastic waterproof liner which, when the outside is soaked with stream water, keeps the nymphs and adults cool and out of the hot sun which can kill them rather quickly.

The best way to contain and transport adult mayflies is with an ordinary coffee-can having a plastic top. We perforate the metal bottom of the can for air circulation. To prevent tiny mayflies from escaping through the holes, we also tape fine screening to the bottom.

Not all potential adult captives are airborne. Discriminate shaking of streamside shrubs and bushes disturbs the resting duns and spinners, making them easy prey for your net. By checking the captured specimens, this practice also gives you a good idea of what species have been active over the past few days. Other methods of determining which species have been hatching are the inspection of spider webs on bridge abutments or around window sills where there is enough light to attract them; i.e., motels and restaurants. Make it a practice to stop at a streamside gas station on your way home or, preferably, the night before you fish. Most mayflies are attracted by the intense light of these service stations and they can be found on the gasoline pumps and brightly lighted signs.

During our stream research we conduct relatively simple yet important analyses such as air temperature, water temperature, ph factor of the water and we sometimes record the carbon dioxide content of the water. It only takes a few minutes to conduct all of these tests as well as to record them.

The stream thermometer is a valuable little instrument that tells a big story. It will indicate when to expect hatching activity in all seasons and helps you seek out coolwater influences during a heat wave. Remember, hatching generally occurs when the water temperature is between 50° and 68°F and the greatest hatching takes place between 55° and

65°F. If you have been fishing without the aid of this wonderful instrument, you've been operating under a terrible handicap. A regular atmospheric thermometer indicates when the best spinner flights will occur (usually between 60°F and 70°F if the weather is right).

Our accumulated recordings of steamside information—air and water temperature, ph, weather, insect activity (hatching and ovipositing), fly pattern evaluation—are one of the key factors in producing this book. We likewise urge all potential stream researchers to record their findings. In a few years, you will amass a surprising amount of important hatch data. However, unrecorded, the information acquired will be functionally lost and unavailable for reference and analysis.

There are various stream diaries and notebooks available for purchase or you can make your own. Due to the volume of our research, we also use tape cassettes for recording information and transcribe it later.

Before we leave the stream we fill our plastic jugs with stream water and collect a bit of habitat from the stream's bottom such as rocks, detritus and a few subaquatic plants. This is only done to stock our aquariums when we are collecting mayfly nymphs or the larval stages of other insect orders such as free-ranging caddis larvae, cased caddis, stonefly nymphs, Diptera larvae and nymphs or larvae from lesser orders.

Our aquarium setups vary from the elaborate to the very simple; the latter being the rule when we're at various stream locations, operating from a cabin, motel or motor home. The nymphs can also be reared naturally through many instars and even from eclosion if fine-meshed wire "live boxes" are used. They are fastened to a raft anchored

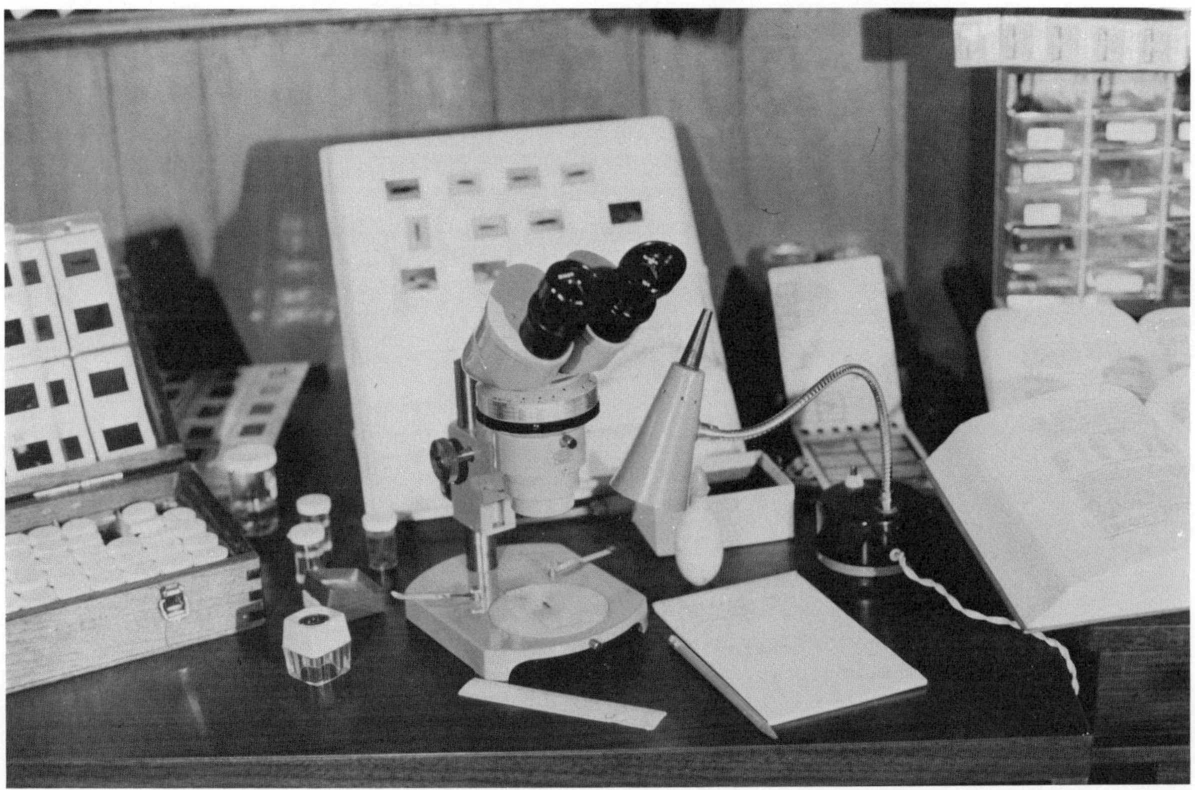

in an eddy of a brook or a side rivulet of a small stream. We have raised most of our immature nymphs to adults by creating the required environment for each nymph type in our lab aquariums, ranging in capacity from three gallons to twenty gallons. The controlled temperature of a small room (55°-65°F) accelerates nymphal growth and produces advanced hatching; we have experienced excellent hatching of the early-season Ephemerella, Baetis and Paraleptophlebia mayflies during mid-winter.

The fast-water clingers are of the most difficult nymphs to raise. Their turbulent habitat can be imitated by the bubble-streams created by portable vibrating aerators such as are used in tropical fish aquarium filtration systems. We run a plastic air line from an aerator to the input nipple of a manifold which has several outlets. The air flow is controlled at these outlets. Therefore, several air stones can be attached to the manifold; each can be adjusted to the desired air flow. When these airstones are covered with the proper rock or stone formations, the correct amount of current and oxygen can be produced for the various species. This setup may sound like an extravagent expense, but the total cost of the aerator, plastic tubing and manifold is less than ten dollars plus the cost of the aquarium.

It is not our intention to advocate the more complicated

aquarium assemblies or lab procedures here. Rather, we believe it will be more helpful to encourage simple but functional setups for the average angler. The most important aspects of aquarium rearing, as far as the angler is concerned, are the observation of the nymphs swimming characteristics, the emergence act and the hatching of the nymph into the subimago. This can be accomplished by collecting mature nymphs from the stream (those with black or dark wing pads) and placing them into tiny aquariums or even quart-sized jars. This is also an excellent way to segregate various species or types for adult identification.

A filtration system will not be necessary if overcrowding is prevented, but an aerator will be needed. A few sprigs of vegetation for food and resting perches and some stones should also be added to create hiding places. The aquariums or jars can be placed in any room in the house, but the best place is a small room with a window that will provide a proper "light cycle". Once your family gets over their initial shock, the antics of the nymphs can be enjoyed by all.

The preservation of mayfly nymphs and adults are important to the angler. The preserved specimens should be labeled and keyed to an index or catalog which describes the date, stream, habitat, initial identification and any other notes that will help him later when he attempts to finalize or confirm the insect's identification. A good practice is to key the specimens to your stream diary.

Unfortunately, one of the biggest problems related to all entomological studies over the years has been the lack of a preservative that retains the original color. We had a terrible time correlating our live or freshly preserved specimens with those described in *The Biology of Mayflies,* most of which were identified from dried or faded preserved specimens from various collections. (Another plus for preservation through photography.)

Over the years, we have tried many solutions for preserving insects, but until recently most have given relatively poor results. The best preservative formula we have found, we have used for almost three years and our specimens have held color almost perfectly—only time will tell if this preservative is the real answer. We have listed it below for the collector's convenience.

FORMULA

Sodium phosphate Monobasic, 8.9 gm.
Sodium phosphate Diabasic, 11.3 gm.
Formaldehyde Solution-40%, 95 CC.

Distilled water, Q.S., add 190 CC.
Divide solution in half—mark solution I and II.
Add sodium hydrosulfite to the extent of 0.5% to solution II only.
As soon as the specimen is captured, place it in I (it will lose most of its color). Allow it to remain in I for 3 to 7 days. Now, transfer the specimen to II where it is kept permanently. II restores the natural color of the specimen.

Various preservative solutions have been recommended in the past by the following authors and they are also listed for the collector's convenience.

Needham, Traver & Hsu, Alcohol of 70 to 80% strength.

The Leonards, 85% solution of ethyl alcohol.

Art Flick, Recommended for adults: 1 part formaldehyde (40% solution), 19 parts distilled water.

Recommended for nymphs: 1 part formaldehyde (40% solution), 10 parts distilled water.

FISHING
TROUT STREAMS

Imitation

Fly Pattern Rationale

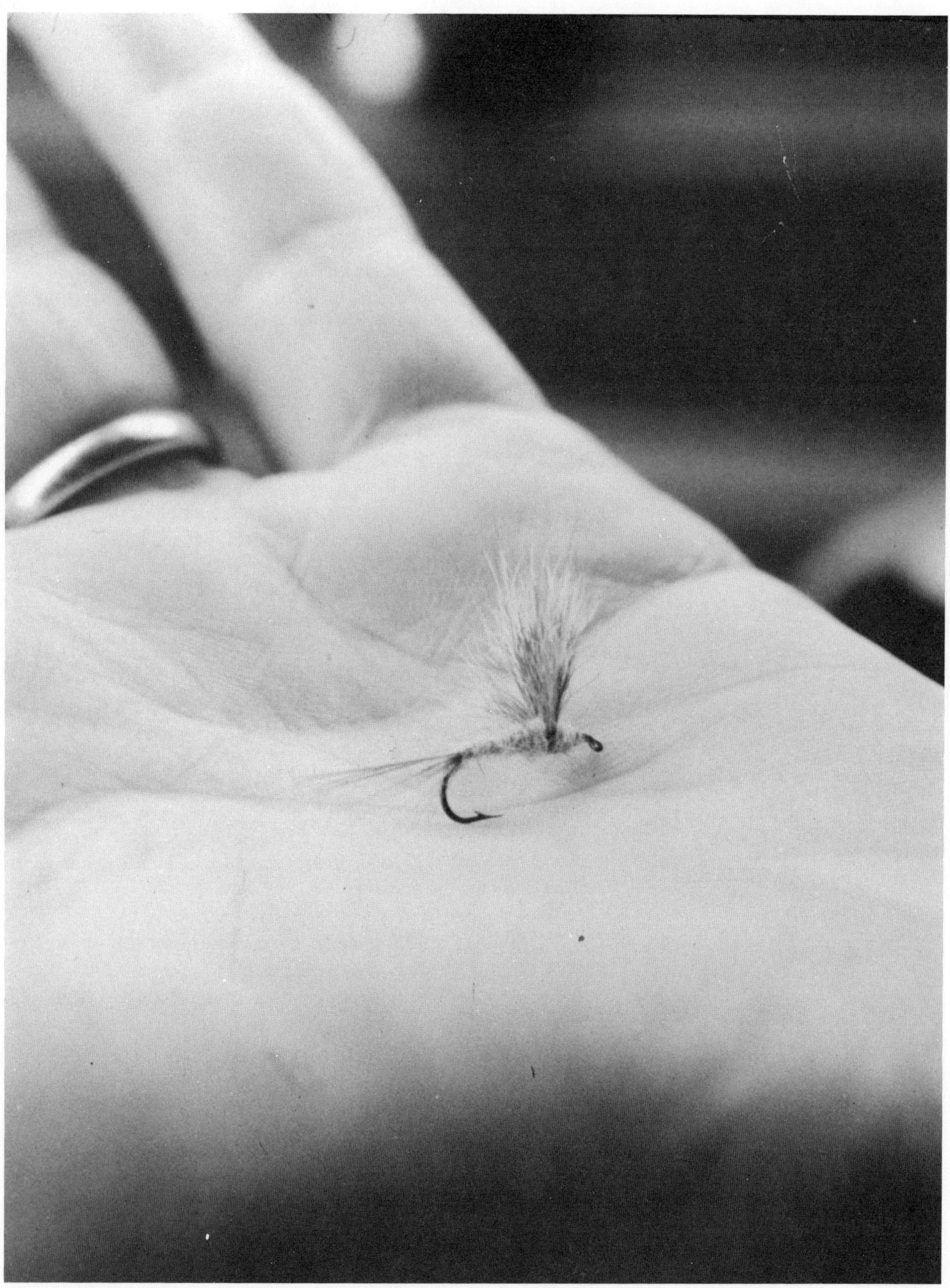

Fly Pattern Rationale

The single-most important question that every fly-fisherman must ask himself every day before he makes his first cast on a trout stream is, "What imitation shall I use?" Whether the angler is a green rookie, a died-in-the-wool veteran or a famous expert, this decision must be made each time the fly-fisherman steps into a trout stream. After the best plans are laid, arrangements made and the most elaborate equipment purchased, the angler will eventually find himself hip-deep in a favorite trout stream where he will ultimately come face to face with a feeding trout. At this point the "moment-of-truth" will have arrived—all his preparation and skill will depend on the single bit of fluff he decides to tie onto the end of his leader.

Over the centuries, in order to cope with this nagging problem of imitation selection, fly-fishermen have developed many methods. A most common method is for the angler to choose one method of fly-fishing over another (such as dry-fly fishing or wet-fly fishing or nymph fishing) and stick with it "come hell or high water". Cracker barrel discourse concerning the pros and cons of each method have gone on eternally; from close, friendly rivalries to famous debate by experts which can later be studied and enjoyed in the hundreds of books on angling.

To further reduce the decision-making problem in pattern selection, many fly-fishermen have reduced not only their methods, but the number of their patterns to a precious few and finally then to a particular size or style. We have probably all witnessed this dogged approach many times. It can be carried to the extent that an angler will fish a weighted nymph through a pool of rising fish without getting even a tap from the trout, seldom questioning why he didn't arouse the interest of a single fish. Conversely, we have witnessed the persistent dry-fly fisher casting his arm off when there wasn't a sign of a rising fish.

This myopic type of approach to fly-fishing may even pay off reasonably well for many fishermen; especially those who have found through long years of trial and error that a certain pattern will produce at a given time even though they may not know why. But, would a Catskill fisherman be equally successful in the Adirondacks or on the rich streams of Pennsylvania? Would this approach work in the Midwest where the alkaline streams are so rich that only a major hatch or ovipositing flight of insects could move the fish?

The problem of imitations is as old as the institution of fly-fishing itself. As with any tradition, change evolves slowly and painfully as its practitioners are reluctant to break with the traditional practices. Although very important inroads have been made recently in the area of pattern innovation, most notably by Vincent Marinaro, Carl Richards and Doug Swisher, the process of change is still in its embryonic stages.

We have elected to by-pass the interesting subject of the *evolution* of fly patterns and leave this analysis for the angling historian; besides, there are already many fine books on this subject. Instead, we believe it to be more constructive to state a case for the resolution of the imitation problem and why we believe it to be the most effective way to take trout.

As we stress throughout this text, the trout is a master of efficiency in his relatively hostile, swift, cool and shallow environment. His survival is directly related to the food and shelter available in such a habitat; principally to the insect populations and particularly to the mayfly, the key link in converting microscopic plankton and algae into trout food.

Normally, the mayfly nymphs, as well as the underwater forms of other important orders (i.e., caddis, stonefly, and Diptera) are well hidden and camouflaged, making them relatively unavailable to the trout until they are ready to hatch into an adult. At that time they become available in great number and are very vulnerable to the trout who feed on them greedily and selectively.

Habitat of the camouflaged nymphs.

The ultimate! A score with the correct imitation.

When trout are feeding on a hatch they become ultra-selective to the species available in the greatest quantity. They usually become oblivious to anything that does not resemble the size, shape, color or antics of the dominant emerging insect. Herein lies the key to the entire problem of imitation. Once the angler accepts this fact, he has taken his first important step in solving every hatch-matching problem he will ever encounter during his days astream. It should by now be evident to the reader that there is no *one* method or *one* miracle fly pattern that will enable the angler to take feeding trout consistently, especially during a hatch. To the contrary, as the various hatches occur, the need for different fly patterns to duplicate the size, shape and color of the available insects is imperative to successful angling. As the trout's attention is shifted from the subsurface nymph to the surfaced, struggling dun or to the ovipositing or spent spinner, so the angler must also switch from nymph or emerger patterns to delicately hackled or flush floating patterns in order to be consistently successful and to increase the challenge and enjoyment of his sport.

We believe the selection of the imitation should be dictated by the stage and behavior of the mayfly that the angler intends to simulate. For example, if a dun is being skittered across the surface by gusts of wind or if it is constantly struggling on a surface that is relatively broken, the choice should be a hackled pattern. On the other hand, if the water is relatively calm and the duns are riding the current peacefully, a hackleless pattern such as a Compara-dun, which features a distinct wing silhouette, would be the correct choice. Hence, the various imitation styles or constructions are almost always dictated by the job they must accomplish. Even when the selection of a pattern becomes obvious to the angler on sight, he should always capture a natural to check the size and color before making his final choice of the imitation.

Over the years, we have evaluated and tested hundreds of fly patterns in various sizes, shapes and construction during countless mayfly hatches throughout most of the country and under almost every conceivable circumstance. We believe our fly pattern recommendations to be based in logic and meet three very important criteria; they are highly imitative, practical and extremely durable. Regretfully we cannot so simplify the problem as to recommend only a handful of patterns, nor can we recommend the use of a particular type of fly exclusively over all others. Nymphs, wets, emergers, variants, spiders, bivisibles, conventional hackled or hackleless flies were all designed and constructed to do a specific job.

* * *

The following chapters on the Compara-dun, Compara-nymph and emerger and Compara-spinner give a comprehensive account of each pattern type in a consolidated format which could not be done in the species and genera chapters without repetition. Although *HATCHES* is not a book on fly tying technique, we thought it would be helpful to include tying instructions for the Compara-dun, a unique dry-fly concept which we first introduced in *Compara-hatch* (1972) and the Compara-deerhair emerger which we developed shortly after the first edition of HATCHES. For the same reason, we have also included a listing of the important advantages of the Compara-dun and a brief synopsis of its origin.

In 1978 we published *FLY TYERS COLOR GUIDE* which focuses on fly tying, fly pattern design and new concepts in materials. The book depicts, in detail, all of our imitation designs, as well as, the dressings for all the important species in *HATCHES*. We also delve into underwater vision, and our "spectrumized" dubbing concept, an amazing process where hundreds of different colored furs can be made from a mixture of the primary colored furs of red, blue and yellow plus white.

The Compara-nymphs and Deerhair Emerger Patterns

As previously stated in the "Life Cycle of the Mayfly", the mayfly spends 99% of its life underwater as a nymph; in the trout's own back yard. Contrary to popular belief however, most mayfly nymphs are not readily available to the trout during this period. If they were, surely the trout would never have to waste his energy and rise to duns and spinners—instead, all he would have to do is to cover a few feet of bottom like a vacuum cleaner and in short order, he would be satiated.

Although mayfly nymphs are rather defenseless, they have an uncanny ability to survive through hiding and camouflage. They hide under rocks, debris and in vegetation and they burrow into gravel and silt. Their colors and shapes blend with their surroundings and they are very difficult to detect. When disturbed, most species are amazingly quick and agile in their underwater habitat.

The point is that the nymphs only become vulnerable or available to the trout in good number during their emergence period. True, some nymphs will be available during high water when they are dislodged or when they moult their skins between instars, but these incidents never approach the impact of an emergence.

Throughout the various genera and species chapters we have tried to convey to the reader the behavioral aspects of the various species of nymphs during the emergence act. If the angler is to score consistently with nymph imitations, he must simulate the emergence process of each species with the proper pattern. This method of taking trout is probably the most difficult to learn because in almost every case the imitation must be fished blind; the angler cannot see his imitation or the trout. However, once the angler knows what species is emerging and understands the emergence traits of the natural, he will usually catch more trout on the proper subsurface patterns than on any other type and his fishing time won't be limited to just the hour or so of hatch time.

For example, if it were late April in the East or Midwest you would know that the early Ephemerella nymphs of *subvaria* were ready to emerge and would probably select a #10 or #12 Subvaria nymph pattern, dressed on a regular wire hook. If it were noon, you'd probably anticipate that the nymphs were seeking advantageous emergence positions, that they would be more accessible to the trout and that the trout would be selective to them. If you were a fly tyer, chances are you would have weighted a few patterns for maximum "sink" while dressing them. It doesn't matter much however, as you can use split shot or wrap-around leaders instead to obtain maximum sink. Using the across and downstream method and fishing the runs and pockets, you score pretty well and take six nice trout.

Around 1 P.M., the nymphs are swimming toward the surface with a peculiar wiggle and gliding back to the stream's bottom; they repeat this over and over. Some float just under the surface while they drift with the current and a few actually pop to the surface as duns. Bright flashes can be seen beneath the surface as the trout turn to intercept the ascending nymphs, but no fish has yet risen to the surface.

By now you realize that the trout are taking the nymphs at mid depth, so you unweight your nymph by removing the split shot. Using the same across and downstream presentation your imitation is now floating at the mid depth and you're getting action on almost every cast. Your success continues even though fish are rising sporadically. Result; eight more trout.

It's 2 P.M. and closer observation shows that the trout are still not taking the duns on the surface which are ever increasing in number. Instead, they are picking off the helpless floating nymphs which are hatching into duns a few inches beneath the film; though some are also evacuating their shucks in or on the surface. You decide to change your fly to a light wire subsurface pattern. Will it be an emerger

The Deerhair Compara-emerger

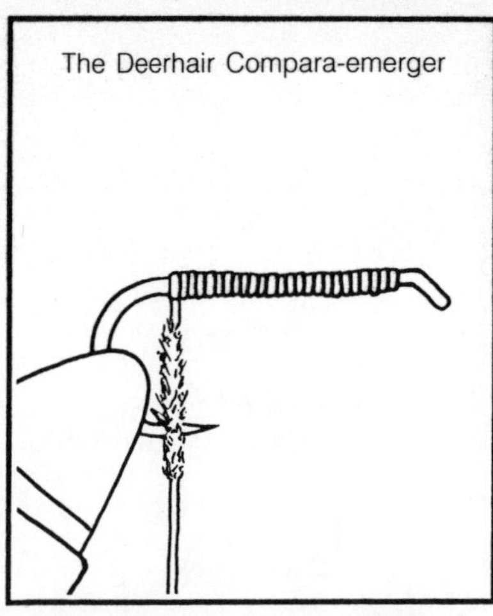

1) Wrap tying thread around shank of hook and add tiniest bit of dubbing.

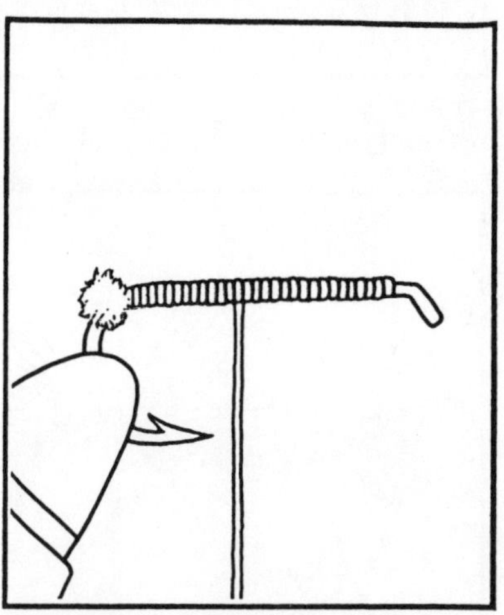

2) Form tiny ball with dubbing at bend, then bring thread to center of hook shank.

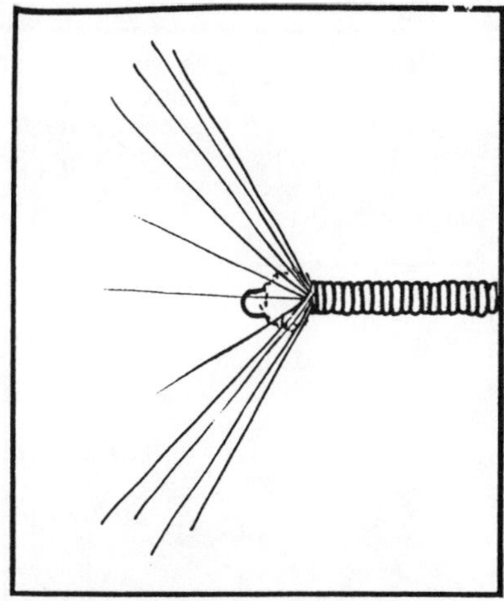

3) Tie in stiff tailing fibers, making sure webbing of hackle barbules are well under wrappings around shank of hook. While still holding clump of fibers with thumb and forefinger, wrap thread to just short of furball, then let go and continue winding thread towards ball. This will force tailing fibers to splay to each side of ball in pontoon fashion.

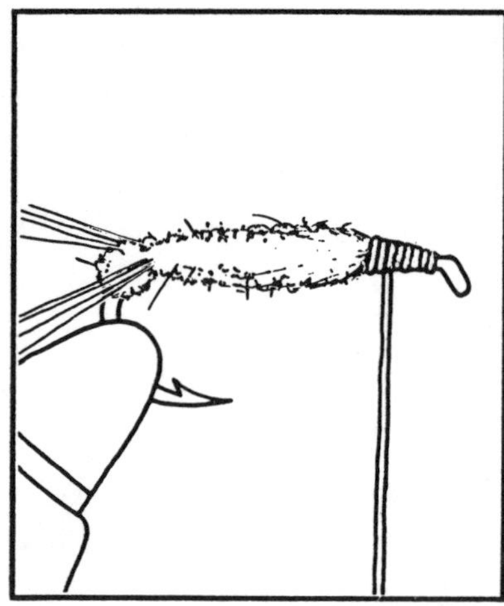

4) Add more dubbing to thread and wind a neatly tapered body as shown.

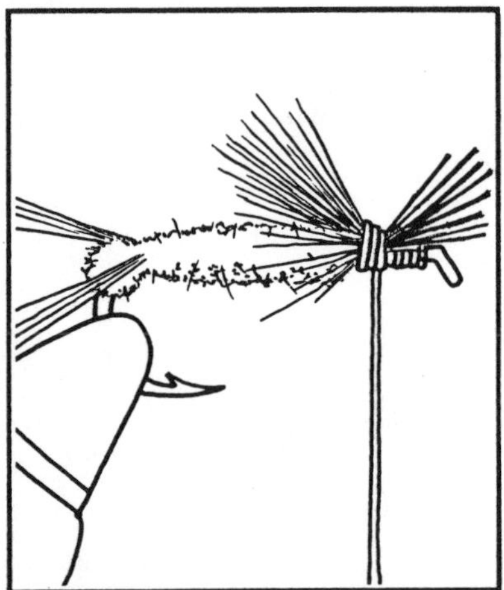

5) Place deerhead fibers (tips pointing towards bend) and wrap two loose turns. At completion of second wrap, tighten pressure for several turns to splay deerhair, securing it to hook shank.

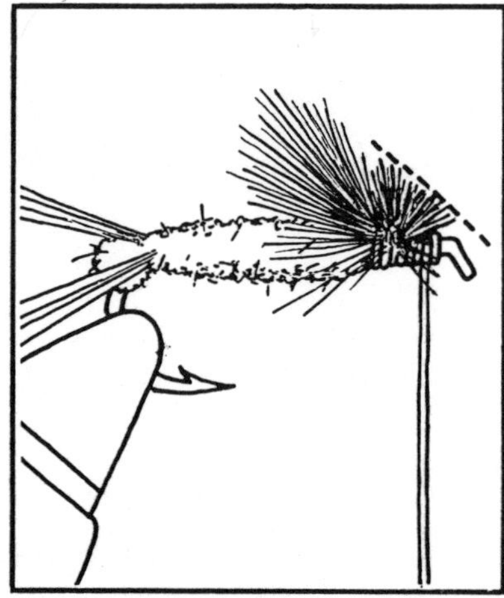

6) With thumb and forefinger, pull back butt ends and wrap tight windings in front of butt ends until they are vertical or leaning toward rear. Trim butt ends as illustrated to form a thoracic hump and finish head with several jam knots.

pattern with a deerhair wing or a "stiff hackled" emerger? You go with a #12 Deerhair Compara-emerger. This time, however, you're casting upstream ala dry-fly method into a medium run studded with boulders. Although your fly sometimes sinks just beneath the surface tension, it's still easy to spot because you're making only 15 to 20 ft. casts and keeping out of sight. I'll be damned!, you're even developing a reflex; a flash beneath your imitation, you tighten the line and the rod bolts forward, throbbing, which can only mean "trout". Chalk up another seven fish.

It's 2:45 P.M.; the trout are rising everywhere and the surface is covered with duns. Now's the time to float a dry-fly over the greedy trout who are completely preoccupied with the *subvaria* naturals. A trout practically shoots between your legs to take a partially emerged dun parting from its shuck. In that instant, you decide to go with the "stiff hackle" emerger instead of a dry fly. It's practically identical to the emerger pattern, like the spent Compara-spinner, except it has stiff pontoon tails and dry-fly hackle in the thorax area, trimmed top and bottom. It's tied on an extra fine wire hook.

After an application of dry-fly solution, you fish it upstream, dead-drift, exactly the same as a dry-fly. By 3:30 P.M., you've hooked, landed and released nine more trout; a total of thirty trout in about three hours. The hatch is over.

You're tired, but never too tired to fool a few more trout, so on your way to the car you stop at the head of a large pool. Experience has taught you that there are many crippled duns during a heavy hatch and that they are flushed through the white water torrents until they land in a flat stretch where they linger helplessly. Trout are never too tired either; especially when it comes to an easy meal such as helpless crippled *subvaria* duns. You spot a few nice fish working leisurely while you tie a #12 Subvaria Compara-dun to your leader. Your cast is true, the trout takes. What a sweet way to end a successful day astream.

IMPORTANT TYING NOTES:

If tailing fibers point upwards after they are splayed, the ball of fur should be moved a little further down bend of hook and vice versa if they point downward. Fibers should splay on the same plane as the hook shank.

If tailing fibers splay in random directions, the fibers are probably too soft. Use only stiffest spade hackles, or for larger flies, the longer and stiffer gaurd hairs of mink tails or similar furs might be necessary.

If secured deerhair (step 5) swivels around shank, tie tighter turns or reduce density of deer hair clump. Also make tighter wraps in front of butt ends (step 6) and weave a few turns of thread through trimmed butt ends before finishing head.

The Indestructable Compara-dun

The emerging squadrons of duns were becoming fewer now; the rises less frequent. A placid, floating Subvaria dun approached the forward edge of a large, slanted boulder and suddenly disappeared, leaving only the telltale ring of a rising trout.

"Take him!" I told Bob. Bob nodded approvingly and edged cautiously closer. In short order he laid a smartly executed curve cast to the left of the boulder and three feet in front of his taking position.

"Right on the money," I yelled.

He fought the urge to strike as a shadowy figure suddenly appeared from a secret underwater cavern. The fly disappeared and he tightened the line deliberately. The light rod nosed into a tight bow and the brown retaliated with a strong leap, clearing the water in a series of catapulting tail walks, its brightly spotted body and golden buttery undersides shimmering in the weak rays of the late April sun. After a few more spectacular leaps he dove doggedly into a heavy, deep run, testing Bob's 5x tippet to the limit.

After several more minutes of cat and mouse tactics, Bob carefully eased the tired brownie, as if he were walking a

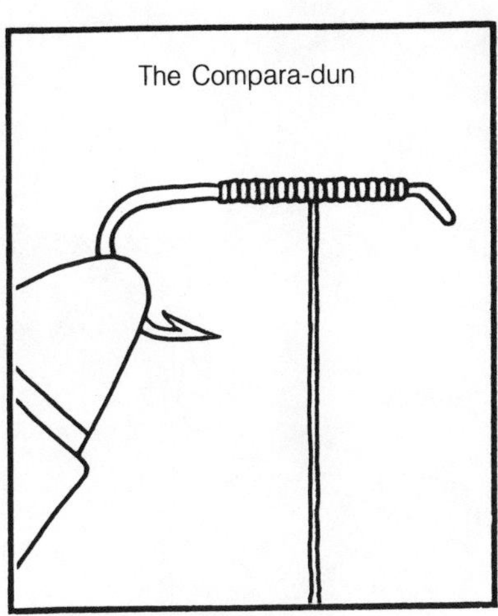

1) Wrap tying thread around shank of hook to a position 3/5ths the distance from hook bend to eye.

2) Pinch a bunch of deerhair fibers and push forward with thumb to separate from rest of patch.

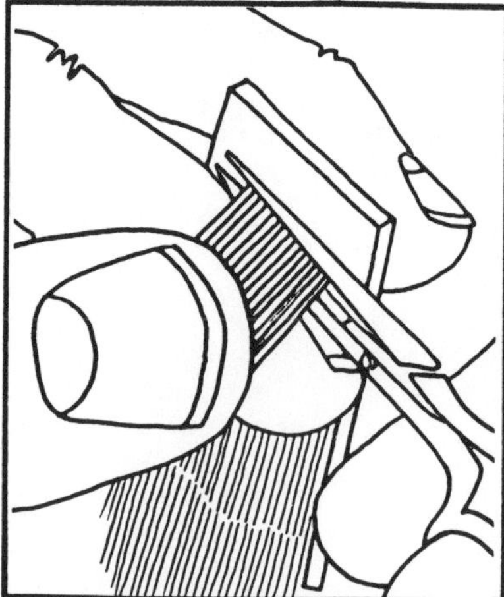

3) Grasp separated clump of hair with thumb and forefinger and cut with scissors.

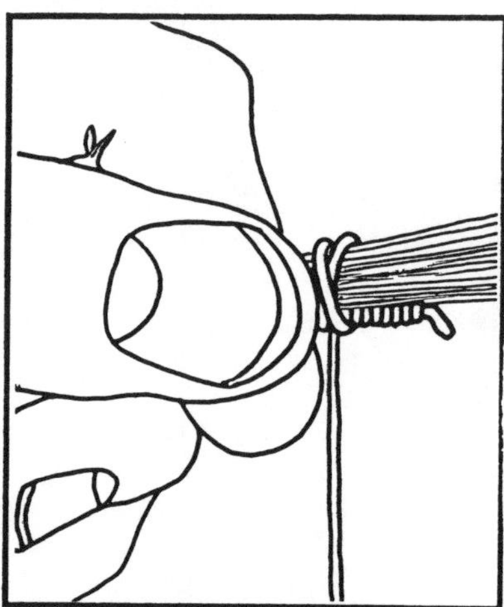

4) Invert cut clump of deerhair 180° in fingers, with both hands, so that deerhair tips extend beyond hook eye. Firmly position clump of deerhair with thumb and forefinger on shank of hook and wrap two loose turns with thread.

dog on a leash, to the pebble beach where I was kneeling. I grasped the eye portion of the Subvaria Compara-dun and eased the barbless hook from his lower jaw. The trout lay in the eddy, exhausted, as we admired its prime condition. I cupped my hand lightly around his girth, faced him gently upstream and methodically stroked him into the current. His pectoral fins started to fan rythmically and with a powerful sweep of his tail, the 14-inch brown disappeared into the Beaverkill as quickly and mysteriously as he first appeared.

Bob smiled tiredly and then grew serious. "You're right Al, this fly pattern is dynamite and as durable as steel! Hell, this is the same pattern I started the hatch with an hour ago," he said, preening the still fresh-looking Compara-dun.

"I landed at least fifteen fish, but lost count," he added. "How about you?"

I let my mind roll back. "About the same," I said proudly. "And all on the same fly too!"

As we climbed the bank I bragged of a 16-incher that I had landed and released.

"Did you measure him," he kidded.

"Of course," I lied.

I designed my first Compara-dun in the mid '60's, adapting the basic concept from an old Adirondack pattern called the "Haystack". It was introduced to me by Francis Betters, who runs the famous Adirondack Sport Shop at Wilmington, New York on the banks of the rugged and legendary West Branch of the Ausable River. Francis is an expert fly tyer and fisher in the valley, and knows the West Branch like the back of his hand; he wades its treacherous currents like most men walk across their own living room.

The first time I saw a "Haystack" I winced. It was like a "bass bug" and tied on a #6 hook—it had a dubbed fox fur body about a 1/4″ in diameter and a large clump of deer hair for a tail. Francis explained that it was used to drum up trout from the depths of the awesome Ausable runs, especially when the river was off color. He added that he had tied the "Haystack" for 20 years and that his father and several of his fathers close friends had tied large versions of the fly for this purpose for as long as he could remember. I've searched exhaustively for its origin in every fly tying book and dictionary imaginable, but have drawn a blank.

In the following years, I modified and refined the large bass-bug-like "Haystack" into a highly imitative and durable series of patterns which duplicated the duns of the various mayfly species I fished to in the Northeast.

From that memorable spring day on the Beaverkill when I first introduced this fly pattern to Bob, we have tested and evaluated the Compara-dun exhaustively during the countless hatches of the various mayfly species studied in preparation for our initial book, *Comparahatch* and, subsequently, for this work.

We fashioned specific patterns for all of the Midwestern, Western and Eastern mayfly species; testing and comparing them to patterns of many styles, including the traditionally accepted patterns for the various hatches. On many occasions we also conducted tests with friends and recorded the results. The recommended uses of the Compara-dun and other fly patterns, including traditional and local patterns, were suggested in the respective species chapters as a result of this testing.

Over the years, the Compara-dun has lived up to every one of our expectations and even beyond. Its acceptance throughout the country since the publication of *Comparahatch* is short of amazing. Thus far, we have not met an angler who has used them during a hatch that wasn't completely impressed, and thereby converted, by its performance. The Compara-dun meets all of the criteria needed for dry-fly perfection; it's highly imitative; practically unsinkable; it's both practical and economical; and it's extremely durable.

The highly imitative characteristics of the Compara-dun are due mainly to the absence of hackle, the prominence of the deer hair wing and the pontoon-like hackle tails. The distinct advantage of the wing silhouette was aptly covered by Vincent Marinaro in his 1950 work, *Modern Dry Fly Code,* and subsequently stressed by Swisher-Richards in *Selective Trout* (1970) where they formally introduced their no-hackle flies. We also cover these points in *Comparahatch.* Recently, the voices from streams as well as the commentary in fishing books and magazine articles on this

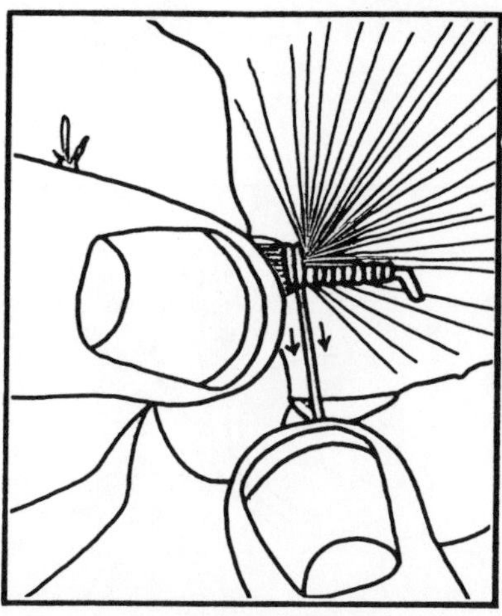

5) At completion of second loose wrap, apply a firm downward pressure, splaying the deerhair 180° at right angles to the shaft. Maintain firm pressure with thread while continuing 5 or 6 tight turns, winding progressively towards rear with each turn.

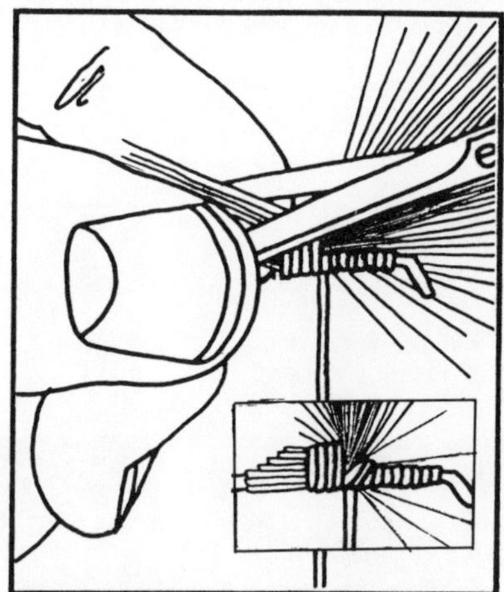

6) Trim excess butt ends of deerhair on bias as shown. Thickness of remaining clump will serve as a bouyant underbody for the thicker thorax area (see inset).

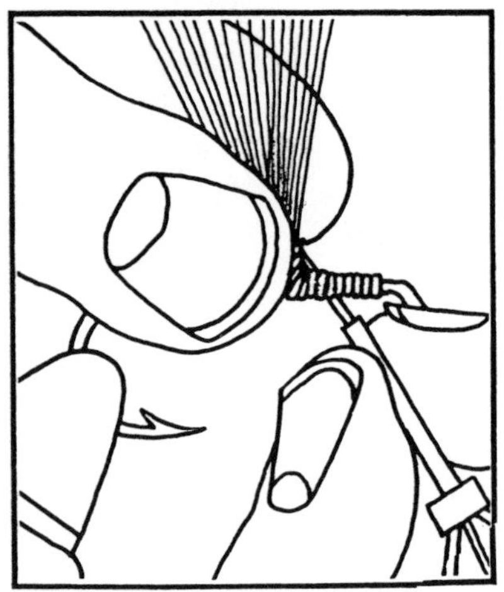

7) Grasp deerhair with thumb and forefinger and pull back, winding 8 to 12 tight turns of thread at its base, forcing the wing into an upright position.

subject have given testimonial to the distinct wing silhouette as a criterion in deception.

The Compara-dun is a very practical fly pattern. It's easy to tie and probably the most economical in terms of materials. The only materials needed are deer hair, spun fur and good tailing fibers. The money saved on hackle alone can pay for the required materals. A single piece of deerskin will serve the tier for years; we average about two dozen flies per square inch. Thus, according to the tying traits of each angler, an 8″ × 10″ piece of deerskin will produce 1,000 to 2,000 Compara-duns. A whole deerskin is ideal because it normally provides every texture and color of hair needed for the various sizes and colors of the species to be imitated. The texture and color of the deerskin will vary; the small deer or the coastal deer, or those with fall coats generally have the most desirable texture of hair. If you can't find the right color for a specific pattern, dye it or bleach it.

Rabbit fur is probably the most economical material on the market. It comes in, or can be dyed to, almost every color. By blending different colors, the hues that can be obtained are limited only by your imagination.

A very important factor in the creation of a good

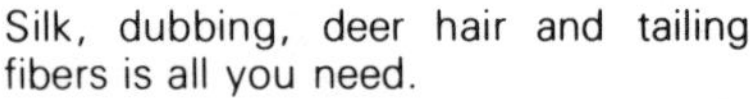

Silk, dubbing, deer hair and tailing fibers is all you need.

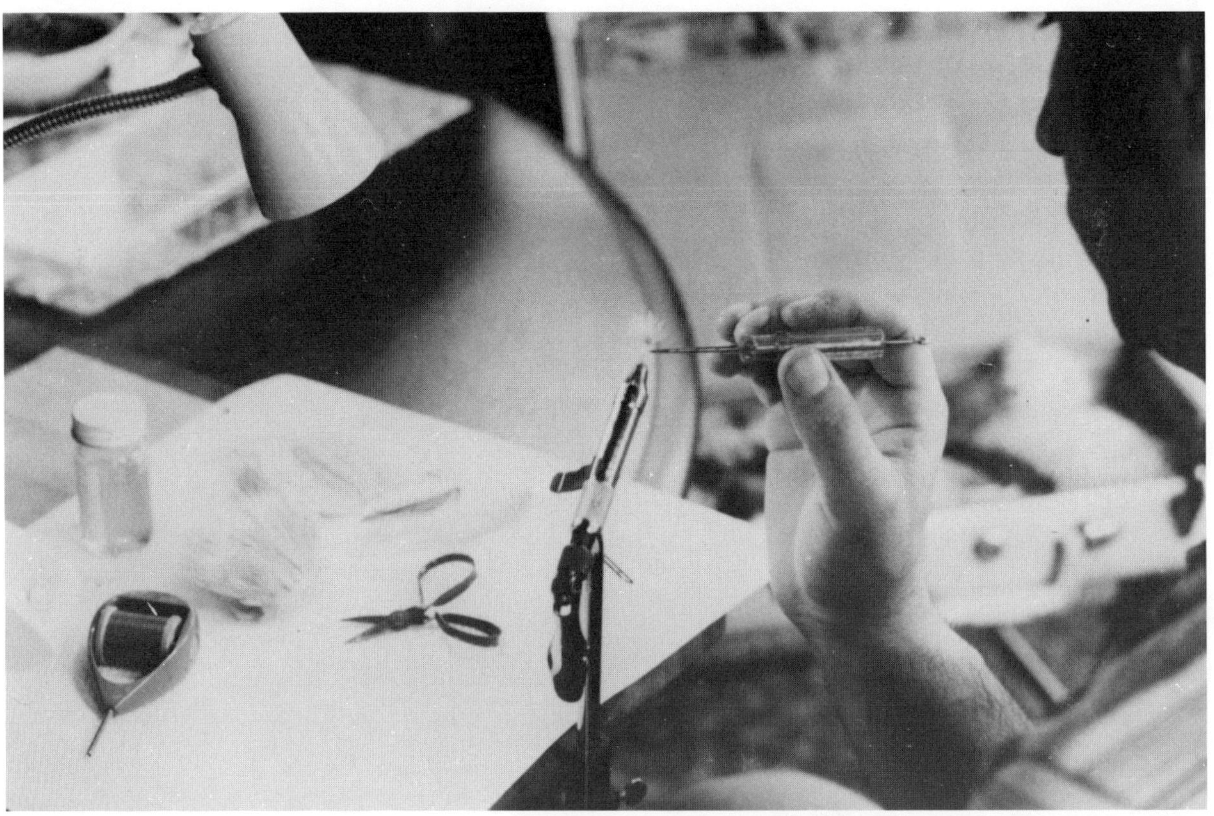

Compara-dun is that the tailing fibers be of excellent quality. We generally use good dry fly necks or saddle hackle for medium and small sized flies. However, the long fiber required for a #10 hook or larger is best acquired from the guard hairs of animal tails. Mink, woodchuck and badger are just a few of the animal tails we use.

The greatest attribute of the Compara-dun is its durability and ability to float; the durability cannot be stressed strongly enough. The more durable fly means fewer fly changes; the fewer fly changes keeps your fly where it should be, on the water where the trout can sock it. When tied properly, this rugged fly will take the abuse of 20 or 30 trout during a single hatch. All that is needed when removed from the jaw of a trout is a few swishes in the stream to rinse off the slime; a few false casts and it rides the current again like a cork. The secret of its bouyancy is in the hollow deer hair wing and the stiff outrigger tails which cover more area on the surface tension and insures a right-side-up landing every time.

To increase fishing time even more during a hatch, an important consideration should be given to the barbless hook. The case for this point has been made in countless books, periodicals and magazine articles and should not be taken lightly. To expand on the virtues and advantages of the barbless hook would be repetitious and I'm sure we could scarcely add to the reams of verbiage that have been so expertly done in the past. The Compara-dun or any pattern tied on a barbless hook is a definite advantage. The time saved in releasing fish from the barbless hook will give you extra action-packed minutes of fishing pleasure. When a pinched down barb is honed needle sharp, you will hook at least twice as many trout; hits that would normally result in misses.

Although the recommendations throughout the various species chapters indicate *when* and *how* to use the Compara-dun during a specific hatch, perhaps it's best to review its general application here.

The Compara-dun is tailor-made for the complacent attitude of the duns as they float flush on the stream's surface in all types of current, but especially on relatively flat water where trout are hyper-selective. Our observations in the lab, and on hundreds of streams, show that the body and tails of practically all mayfly species rest flush on the surface. Hence, if you are to dupe a trout on these flat surfaces, the Compara-dun is the best choice. It should be fished in a dead-drift method directly in the feeding lane of the trout.

Another application for the Compara-dun is when the duns and spinners are on the water simultaneously and the

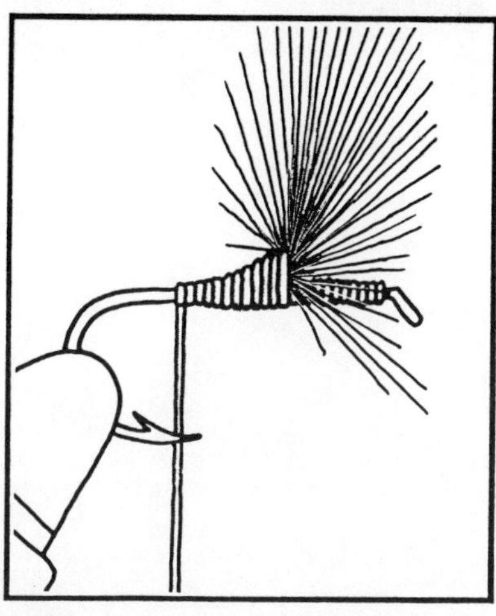

8) Wind thread back underneath to rear of wing and tightly wrap trimmed butt ends. Continue to wind thread to rear of hook and apply tails as per instruction in deerhair "Compara-emerger" on page 305.

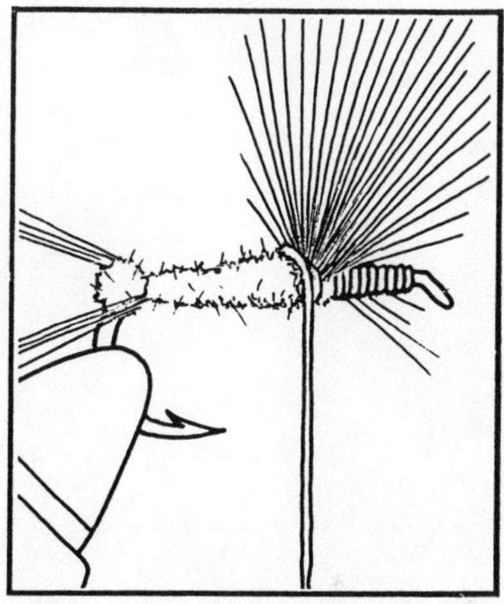

9) Dub thread and wind a neatly tapered body to just short of deerhair wing. This slight space will enable wing to slant backwards during step 10.

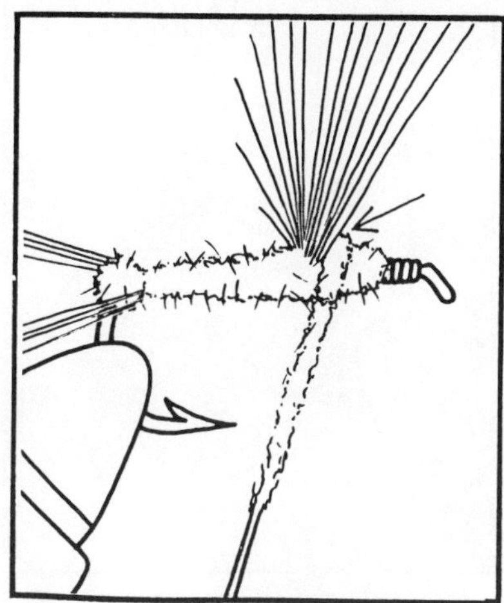

10) Wind dubbed thread underneath wing to its front and tightly wrap dubbing into base of wing at an angle (4 or 5 wraps are ***not*** too much). The wing will slant back into space left in step 9 and insure a permanent upright position.

The versatile and durable Hackled Compara-dun

angler has not been able to determine on which stage they are feeding. The Compara-dun is a good compromise during this mixed activity—it floats flush on the surface like the spinner and, of course, has the wing silhouette of the dun.

The duns of many species have difficulty during takeoff. They flutter and flit in their attempts, creating disturbances in the surface that trigger spectacular rises from the trout. This behavior by the dun is particularly prevalent in the large genera such as Ephemera, Hexagenia and Stenonema. The large Western Ephemerella flies also have this characteristic. In order to closely duplicate the struggling antics of the natural, a generously hackled dry-fly is needed. The hackle cuts down on the friction between the imitation and the stream's surface and enables the angler to closely duplicate the struggles of the dun when he applys a series of timely twitches. This can be accomplished without undue disturbance or unnatural commotion which would not be the case if a flush-floating pattern were used.

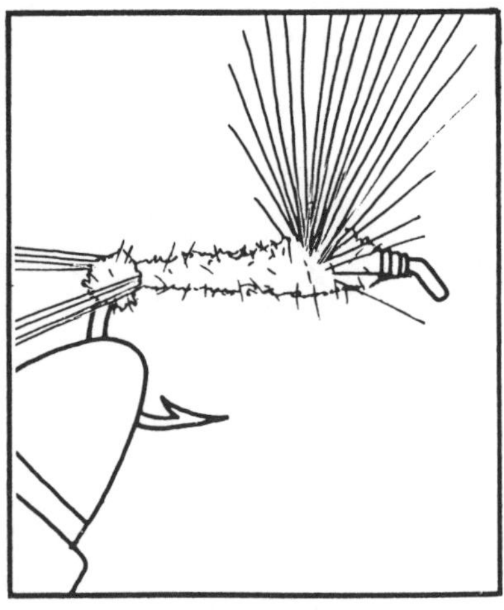

11) Complete dubbing of thorax, tapering towards eye and finish head with 4 or 5 jam knots.

Another application for hackled patterns is when the naturals are being blown and skittered about by the wind. During this period, instead of just twitching the fly, try fluttering or skating the imitation several feet or yards in one sweep to duplicate the wind skittering the naturals. Many times we actually use the wind for this tactic by holding our rods high with a relatively short line; the wind raises and lowers the fly from the surface.

Riffles, pocket water and tricky runs have deceptive mini currents and tiny whirlpools where the naturals are twirled and tossed about. Most of the time, hackled patterns are required during these circumstances. The friction caused by the relatively heavy imitation (as compared to the natural) is amazingly compromised by a generously hackled pattern; the delicate hackle barbule tips respond to the miniature whirlpools and wavelets by automatically skittering the fly across the mini cross currents in a manner similar to the natural.

We have experimented with various styles of conventional hackled patterns, bivisibles and spiders and have listed optional recommendations in the respective species chapters. In recent years, we have abandoned many of these patterns for the Hackled Compara-dun. It has all of the durability of the Compara-dun and the hackle can be snipped off with scissors at streamside if a hackleless fly is required. (See tying instructions for both the Compara-dun and the Hackled Compara-dun).

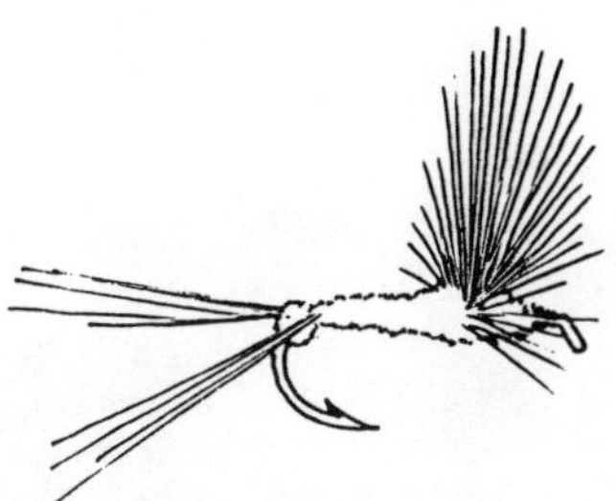

Finished Compara-dun—Side view.

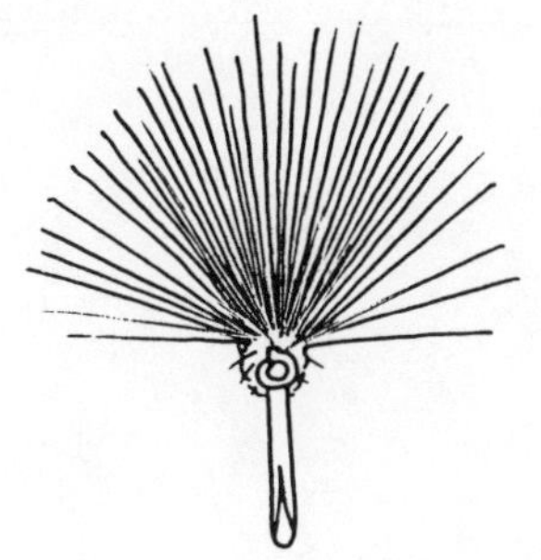

Finished Compara-dun—Front view.

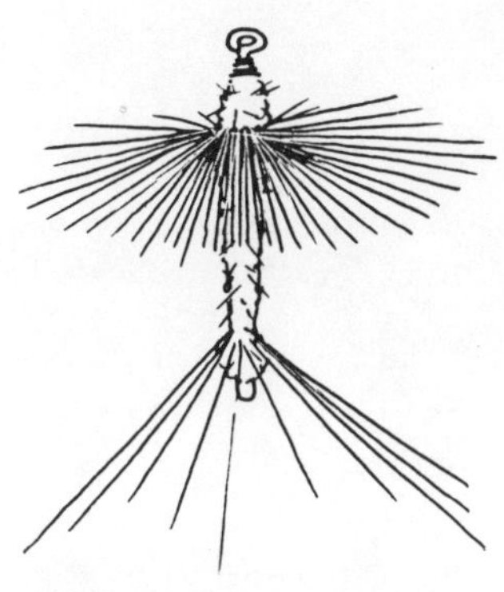

Finished Compara-dun—Top view.

IMPORTANT TYING NOTES:

Do not cement or lacquer head. It is not necessary and quite often the lacquer bleeds back into dubbing affecting the bouyancy of the fly. Four or five tight jam knots will outlast the materials of any fly you can tie.

Steps 9 and 10 are very important as they counteract the memory tendancy of the thick deerhair fibers from leaning forward, into their original position creating an unnatural silhouette of the wing.

Steps 5, 7 and 8 insure a tight adhesion of wing to shank, thus avoiding a loose swivel of wing off its plane.

If you have a problem with step 4, try using a stack-pack. You will still have to transpose deerhair from hand-to-hand, but a least the fibers will remain even during this process.

Compara-spinners and Spinner-falls

The Compara Spinner

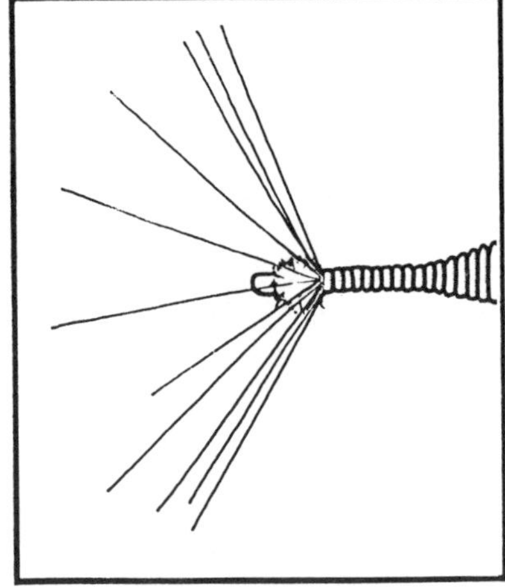

1) Tie in tails as per "Compara Deerhair emerger" instructions on page 305, and/or . . .

Fishing the spinner falls is one of the most exciting and challenging aspects of fly-fishing for trout and also the most underrated. Through the years, we have found that the ovipositing or spent spinners of the various mayfly species usually produce the most reliable rise of trout. This is mainly due to the unbelievable concentration of imagoes that are present on the stream's surface in such a short time span. The magnitude of a spinner-fall can be amazingly dense even during days of sporadic mayfly hatches, as the duns that have hatched intermittently throughout the day arrive en masse for the mating ritual. After mating takes place and the eggs are deposited in the stream, the imagoes fall spent, blanketing the stream for a brief 20 or 30 minutes. Trout relish the egg-laying females as well as the spent spinners and take greedy advantage of this great opportunity when so many mayflies can be eaten with such little effort. The specific mating and ovipositing characteristics of each species is covered thoroughly in the species chapters.

Just as the best hatches occur at ideal water temperature (55°-65°F), the spinners also have a temperature criterion—the temperature of the air. The best spinner flights occur when the air temperature is between 60° and 70°F.

This ideal temperature for spinner flights occurs at various times of the day during different seasons. For example, during the early season, in April and early May, the correct air temperature for spinner flights occurs around midday, when the sun warms the chilly early spring landscape. The midday temperatures during the latter part of May in most localities often approaches the 80's. This is too hot for the imagoes, keeping them in the cool foliage where the heat cannot sap their strength before their eventful and strenuous mating flight. Remember, once the mayfly's remaining strength is gone, it cannot be replenished as their mouth parts are atrophied. They can make their appearance only when the air temperature is favorable, which in the case of late May is later in the afternoon or in the early evening when the thermometer drops toward 70°F.

In late spring and early summer, the spinner flights normally occur in the early evening, at twilight or after dusk; again according to the ideal air temperature. The hot daytime temperature which often approaches the 90's is completely unsuitable.

During the late season months of August and September, the evening air temperature is usually too cool and the afternoon temperature too warm for spinner flights in many areas, especially in the Rockies and the northern mountain sections of the East. At this time the mating flights generally occur in the morning as soon as the ideal air temperature is reached.

As with most rules or generalizations, there are exceptions. For instance, it's very common for spinner flights to occur on the abundant streams of the Midwest during mid morning in April and May. Although ideal water temperature exists for hatching very early in the season, due to the springhead genesis of the rivers, the late afternoon or evening air temperature is still too low for spinner flights. Hence, the spinner activity will generally start in the morning, as soon as the air temperature or angle of the warming sun becomes ideal. The Midwestern flights are only one exception from the norm, dozens can be cited for various localized conditions. The important thing is that anglers must be conscious of weather trends if they are to hit the spinner action squarely.

Rain, mist, high humidity and heavy gusts of wind are a few of the conditions that can spell disaster for the spinner flights, so during these conditions the flights are usually cancelled. Remember, the mayfly's whole life has been in preparation for this mating destiny, which will mean the perpetuation of the species, and their instincts will hold off the flight until the conditions for successful mating and egg-laying prevail. When undesirable conditions continue for

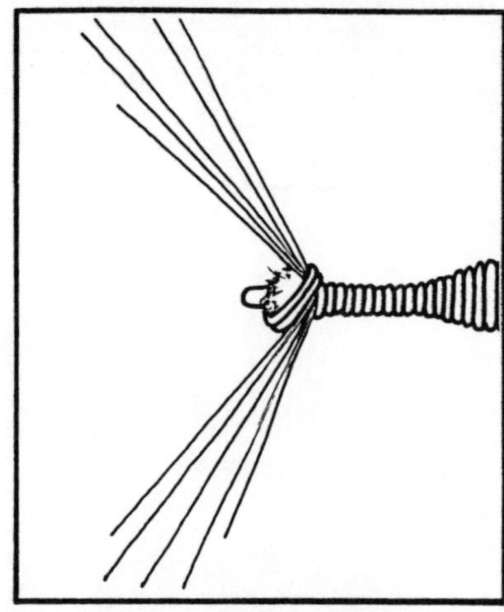

2) . . . accentuate splayed tails into two separate clumps with thread as illustrated (optional). This step can correct, with a little manipulation, an improper splay of fibers that might be a little high or tilted. With a little practice, this slightly tricky maneuver can save considerable tying time.

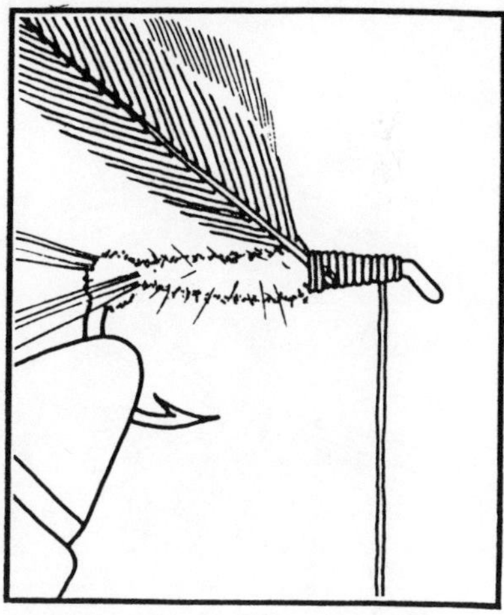

3) Wind a tapered, dubbed body to approximately 3/5ths the distance from hook bend to eye, and tie in one or two (depending on length and quality) dry fly hackles.

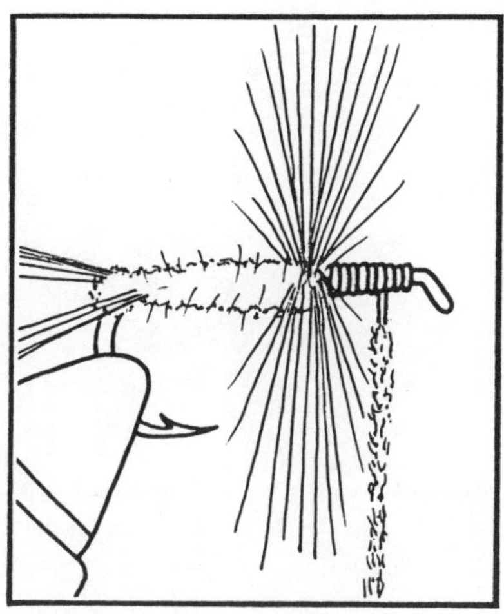

4) Wind hackles in the traditional dry fly fashion and tie off securely, then add more dubbing to thread.

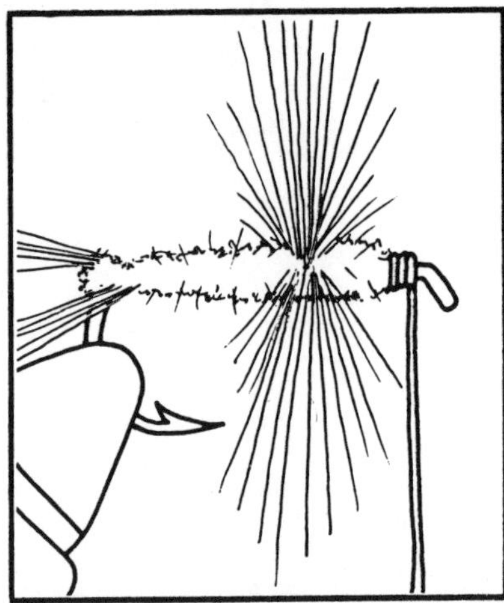
5) Form a tapered thorax and finish head with 4 or 5 jam knots.

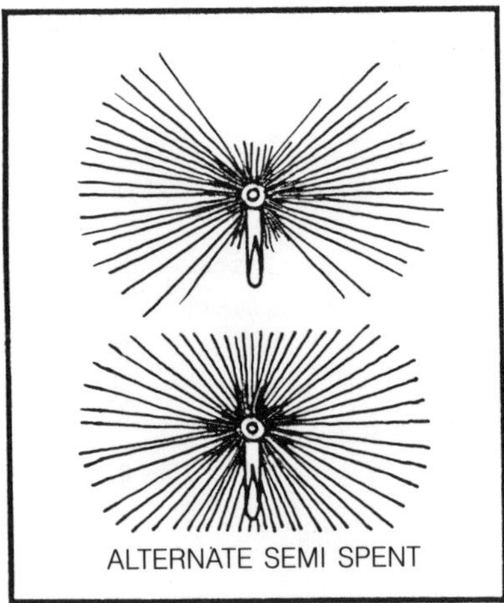

6) With scissors, trim hackles top and bottom to a semi-spent . . .

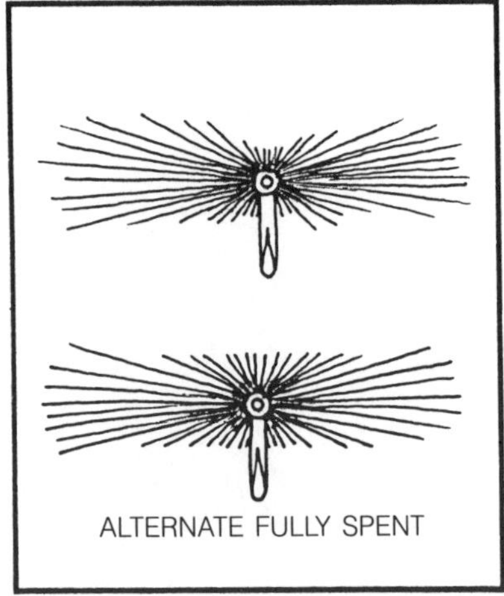

7) . . . or a fully-spent configuration, depending on your pattern needs.

several days, anglers should look for the first break in the weather when the air temperature is ideal. The spinner-fall should be exceptional then.

In the early season, when the spinner flights generally take place at midday or in the afternoon, they are normally less important than those flights of the mid summer and late season, as they must compete with the prolific hatching of the early season Epeorus, Paraleptophlebia, Ephemerella and Baetis mayflies. Yet, they are still surprisingly reliable and produce excellent feeding activity in the faster water. Trout sip these spinners inconspicuously within the white water pockets or heavy runs, so if you're not looking for this activity, chances are you'll pass it by completely unaware. On more gentle streams, the falls are more obvious and produce first rate angling opportunities.

When fishing the faster water, cast semi-spent or spent spinner patterns to eddies and pockets at the base of boulders and obstructions and allow your fly to float drag-free. Full-hackle versions are also required when trout are slashing at dipping spinners; twitching and skittering are necessary to duplicate this activity. Line control is imperative in these tricky sections, so anglers should wade as close as possible to their target and keep casts short.

The late spring and early summer season offer the enormous and legendary spinners of the Ephemera and Hexagenia genera. They create the most spectacular twilight aerial display in all of fly-fishing. These heavy flights are the object of many fishing tales and are of the most difficult to fish, as the trout become amazingly selective, due to the large size and great abundance of the insects. During the same period, the larger spinners of Stenonema, Isonychia and Siphlonurus are almost equally significant in the faster water sections.

Although each species has its own mating flight and egg laying characteristics which are depicted in the specific chapters, they all serve warning of their occurence with impressive treetop appearances at twilight. When the treetop flights are spotted, the angler should use the 20 to 30 minutes grace period it takes for the spinners to fall to obtain an advantageous casting position; if possible he should select and tie on his appropriate fly pattern ahead of time. (This is the only time we recommend the selection of a pattern without properly scrutinizing the naturals). When the falls occur, whether on a quiet pool or in the fast water, the action will be brief and furious.

When fishing the medium or slow currents where the large Ephemera and Hexagenia spinners fall, the angler will do well to select one or two fish during this action and concentrate on them specifically. Some trout will gobble up the spent spinners in side eddies while others will take the big females that are struggling and extruding their eggs in the middle of pool. The selectivity of the trout during these hair-raising moments is painfully acute and anglers must observe individual fish cautiously if they are to dupe them into taking their imitation. Spent, semi-spent or even full-hackled patterns must be considered here, and the ultimate pattern decision will be dictated by the behavior of the individual fish the angler is stalking. On the other hand, the fast-water spinner falls of the Stenonema, Isonychia and Siphlonurus genera call for short line tactics and pattern selection typical of the early season, except that the challenge will be greater, due to the quickly fading light. Hence, you should make the preliminary preparations when the flights are first spotted at treetop level as described for the spinner falls of the Ephemera and Hexegenia flies.

During late July and early August, the evenings may be too hot for twilight spinner activity; thus, morning spinner flights will predominate. Late Ephemerella species like *lata* in the Midwest, *inermis* and *infrequens* in the West and the prolific Pseudocloeon and Tricorythodes mayflies, which are prevalent throughout the country, generally blanket the water in the morning hours, causing extreme feeding selectivity from the trout. During this period, the problems associated with low, clear water and seasoned trout who may prefer dipping spinners to spent spinners, truly represent an opportunity for post graduate fly-fishing techniques and patterns.

Through the years, the Compara-spinner has been a highly imitative and extremely durable imitation which was introduced in our first book, *Comparahatch*. During our *Comparahatch* research and subsequent pattern evaluation for this book, we experimented with many other types of spinner patterns. The results of our findings show that the durability of the Compara-spinner is far superior to every type we tested.

Throughout the chapters of this text we recommend the Compara-spinner in four versions; full hackled, semi-spent, full spent, and in "Figure 8" style.

Like the Compara-dun, the Compara-spinner is easy to tie. It has a body of rabbit fur and pontoon tails; except, the wings are formed by winding two or three grade A hackles (depending on the size) which produces the full-hackled version. The spent and semi-spent versions are created simply by trimming the full-hackle version top and bottom with a sharp scissor as shown. The figure 8 Compara-spinner is of typical construction. Instead of clipping the hackles in "v"

IMPORTANT TYING NOTES:

Make sure the quality of the hackles used are top notch and generously wound—sparsely tied hackles won't cut it, especially after they are trimmed.

We recommend trimming patterns to semi-spent, as they can always be trimmed to flush floating, fully-spent versions on the stream. The semi-spent versions are more easily seen in riffles and pocket water.

fashion on top and bottom, the hackle wings are formed by a "Figure 8" winding of dubbing, which separates the wings and creates a segregated and fatter thorax. Tricorythodes and Pseudocloeon spinners are good examples of imagoes for which the "Figure 8" technique is best suited.

For exceptionally large spinner patterns such as are used during the Ephemera *guttulata* and Hexagenia *limbata* activity, we use modified versions of the Compara-dun, Hackled Compara-dun and Compara-spinner on #6 through #10 hooks, 4x long. These large spinners are extremely difficult to imitate. Although we're not completely satisfied with the results, they work much better than do the extended body type patterns, where the tail curves away from the water unlike the naturals.

Another pattern which shows promise is the relatively new poly-winged spinner. Although they are not as durable as the Compara-spinners, they held up surprisingly well. Their construction is typical of the large thoraxed "Figure 8" Compara-spinner except that it has a single strand of multi-fibered polyurethane for the wings instead of the divided hackle.

We sincerely hope our fellow anglers will try this neglected and exciting facet of fly-fishing. We also hope the talented and innovative fly-tyers of this country will experiment and develop new and appropriate ties, so that the tackle shops will have patterns available for the nontyer. The spinner techniques, photographs of the naturals and patterns pinpointed in the various chapters of this work, should serve as a good base for anglers to develop their skill and technique in solving the spinner activity problem on their favorite streams.

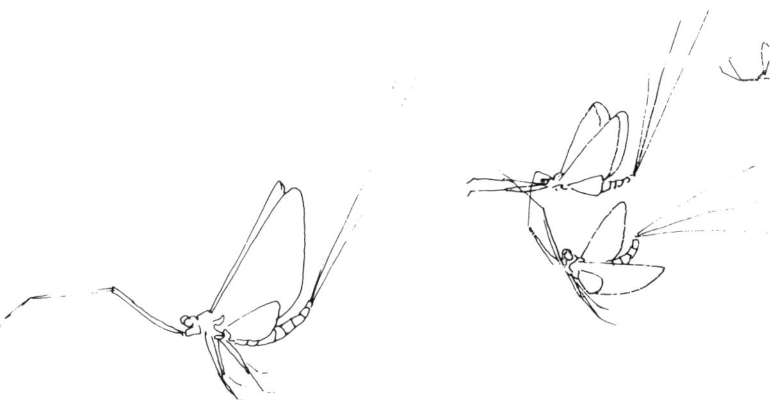

Hook Rationale

We have stated that the single-most important problem that the angler must resolve before he can fool selective trout is the selection of the proper imitation. It is essential that he finally select a fly pattern of the correct size, construction and color; the greatest emphasis being on size.

For example, when selecting imitations to duplicate the tiny Tricorythodes or Pseudocloeon mayflies (which average 3 to 4mm in length), a size mistake of 1 or 2mm (1/32 to 1/16″) represents a size discrepancy of approximately 50% and would surely result in refusals from the trout. The size range of the large mayflies is normally much greater than the smaller mayfly species. Ephemera *guttulata* and Hexagenia *limbata* mayflies range in size from 18-30mm and 16-35mm respectively. Hence, the angler has more latitude in selecting hook sizes for the larger species.

A serious problem confronting the fly-tyer and the angler are the hook size recommendations given in countless angling texts which have, in most cases, evolved from very early works. These early suggestions were usually derived from limited information on the sizes of the actual mayfly species or by well-intentioned compromises arising from the lack of technology to produce efficient hooks of proper specifications in both the small and large hook ranges. In *Comparahatch* we somewhat reluctantly compromised our size recommendations because our work on mayfly sizes was not yet complete. With the conclusion of this work, it became apparent that the blow of proper hook size suggestions could not be lessened further without sacrificing this most important criterion of imitation.

At first glance, our hook size recommendations may seem drastically different to the angler who is accustomed to the traditional hook sizes that have been passed on through the decades, but the facts are plain and simple; the size of the imitation must fall within the size tolerance of the naturals. The hook size recommendations for the various mayfly species throughout this text were determined by the size of the actual insect. We collected and measured thousands of mayfly specimens from streams throughout the country and from our aquariums and correlated the size range for each species with the appropriate hook size (see Hook Chart). This rationale has been extremely successful for us in practically all of our hatch matching situations.

The reader will notice from the Hook Chart that we recommend Mustad 94840 or 94833 hooks of 3x fine or regular wire and 4x long standard hooks (#79580) for dry-fly or surface application to keep the hook's weight to an absolute minimum without sacrificing the proper hook shank length to duplicate the natural's size. This results in a smaller, less

RECOMMENDED SURFACE FILM HOOKS

Hook Style	Hook Size (Actual size is shown)	Body Size of Natural (mm)
Mustad 4x long MP #79580 or equiv.	#4	29–32
	#6	22–25
	#8	18–21
	#10	17–19
	#12	14–16
Mustad 3x fine MP #94833 or #94840	#8	12–14
	#10	11–12½
	#12	9–11
	#14	8–9½
	#16	7–8
	#18	5–6
	#20	4½–5
Mustad t.u.e. #94842	#22	4–4½
	#24	3½–4
	#26	3–3½
	#28	2½–3

The turned-up-eye hooks are recommended in sizes #22–28 to improve the small gap on these tiny hooks, improving hook qualities.

RECOMMENDED SUBSURFACE HOOKS

Hook Style	Hook Size (Actual size is shown)	Body Size of Natural (mm)
Mustad standard wire 3x long MP #9672	#2	31–35
	#4	25–28
	#6	20–23
	#8	17–19
	#10	13–16
Mustad x heavy wire MP #7948A	#10	11–13
	#12	9–11
	#14	7½–8½
	#16	6½–7½
	#18	5–6

Note: for #20 and smaller patterns, nymphs should be dressed as emerger patterns with stiff hackles for fishing in the surface film as it is impractical to fish these small nymphs on the bottom.

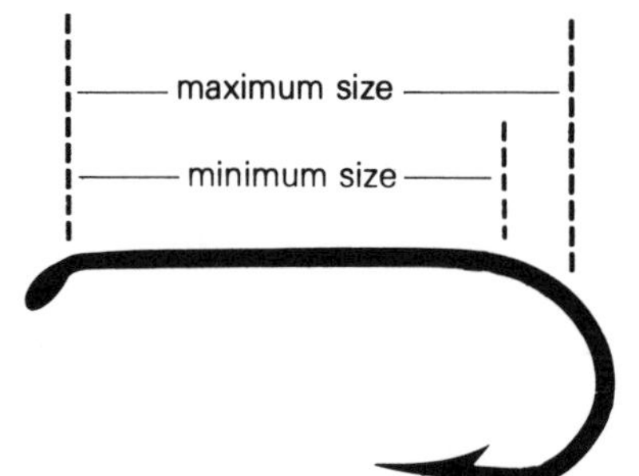

cumbersome hook bend which also improves the imitative qualities of the fly. The angler will also notice that if a hook shank length of over 14mm is required, we recommend a #12, 4x long standard wire hook instead of a #6, 2x long, 3x fine hook. The reason for this switch is that the weight of the standard wire #12, 4x long hook is less than the 3x fine wire #6 hook by 30% or 40% due to the extremely large periphery of the hook bend of the #6 hook. In fact, the #12 4x long hook standard wire hook is even lighter than the #8, 3x fine hook by approximately 25%.

Anglers should not feel that they are restricted to the manufacturer, model or style of the hooks suggested. Any hooks with the proper specifications can be substituted as long as the all-important hook shank length is relative to the size of the insect he intends to imitate and that some consideration is given to the hook weight.

As shown in the chart, we recommend hooks with "turned up eyes" in sizes #22 through #28 because the hook gap is more exposed and accounts for more hooked fish. Also, it's much easier to thread your leader through the "up turned eyes" of such tiny hooks.

Our axiom for leader application and tippet size is to fish as fine a leader as possible under the prevailing circumstances. Remember, the most natural floating imitation is the one without a leader attached. Once a tippet is attached, no matter how fine, it will begin to hamper the natural floating ability of the imitation. Each individual must decide when a leader is too fine to maintain control of his line or too impractical for its application.

Compromise Fly Pattern Charts

The Compromise Pattern Charts are not a panacea for all of the angler's imitation problems. However, they are a practical answer for the imitation dilemma of the non-fly-tyer and the well-traveled angler who fishes to scores of hatches on many rivers across the continent. It would certainly be impractical to expect this angler to carry over 100 specific nymph, emerger, dun and spinner patterns for the 30 or 40 important species he might well encounter during his travels. Although the condensed pattern charts consist of only 8 Compara-duns, 4 Compara-nymph and emergers and 4 Compara-spinner patterns, they correctly imitate over 80% of all the important hatches in the country.

Specific pattern dressings are recommended for fly-tyers and for fly-fishermen who fish only a few streams that have heavy hatching activity of specific species, thereby maximizing their imitating capabilities.

We carry "specific patterns" to match the hatches of our favorite rivers and those we expect to fish fairly regularly during the season and rely on "compromise patterns" for unscheduled trips or for surprise hatches on unfamiliar streams. We believe the choice of both specific and compromise patterns is a practical and efficient approach to the problem of imitation.

NYMPHS

TYPE #, PATTERN	BODY (FUR DUBBING)	LEGS AND TAILS (HACKLE)**	WING PADS (QUILL SEGMENTS)
1) Yellow-brown Compara-nymph	yellowish-brown (amber)	light ginger	brown
2) Red-brown Compara-nymph	reddish-brown	medium ginger	dark brown
3) Olive-brown Compara-nymph	olive-brown	dark ginger	dark brown or dark gray
4) Dark brown Compara-nymph	dark brown	reddish-brown or brown	black

Formula for dubbing: Brown is a medium brown. Pattern 1) 1 part cream, 1 part yellow, 2 parts brown; 2) ¼ part yellow, ¾ part red, 3 parts brown; 3) equal parts olive and brown; 4) equal parts brown and black.

*For the nymph, use soft wet-fly hackle.

**For Stiff-hackled Emerger patterns, the dressings are the same as the nymph, with the following exceptions: they are tied on light wire hooks; stiff dry hackle barbules are used for the tails which are splayed the same as in the Compara-dun; the legs are wound on with two or three turns with a stiff dry hackle before the wing pads are tied down. Tie the wing pads down over the wound hackle and trim the bottom.

GENUS	SPECIES	HOOK SIZE	NYMPH PATTERN TYPE #
Baetis	all	varied	3
Brachycercus	all	varied	4
Caenis	all	varied	1
Callibaetis	all	varied	2
Centroptilum	all	varied	1
Cloeon	all	varied	1
Epeorus	*pleuralis*	#10, #12; std.	3
	vitreus	#12, #14; std.	1
	other light species	varied	1
	other dark species	varied	3
Ephemera	*guttulata*	#4, #6; 3x long	3
	simulans	#10; std. and 3x long	2
	varia	#10; 3x long	1
	other light species	varied	1
	other dark species	varied	3
Ephemerella	*attenuata*	#16; std.	3
	cornuta	#12; std.	1
	doddsi	#10; std. and 3x long	3
	dorothea	#16; std.	1
	flavilinea	#12, #14; std.	4
	glacialis	#10; 3x long	4
	grandis	#10; 3x long	4
	inermis	#16, #18; std.	3
	infrequens	#14, #16; std.	3

GENUS	SPECIES	HOOK SIZE	NYMPH PATTERN TYPE #
	invaria	#14; std.	2
	lata	#16, #18; std.	4
	rotunda	#12; std.	2
	subvaria	#10, #12; std.	3
Ephoron	all	#10; std and 3x long	1
Heptagenia	all	varied	3
Hexagenia	all	#4, #6; 3x long	3
Isonychia	all	#10; 3x long	4
Leptophlebia	all	#10, #12; std.	3
Paralepto-phlebia	*adoptiva*	#14, #16; std.	1
	other light species	varied	1
	other dark species	varied	4

GENUS	SPECIES	HOOK SIZE	NYMPH PATTERN TYPE #
Potomanthus	all	#10; 3x long	2
Pseudocloeon	all	#20-28; t.u.e.	1
Rhithrogena	all	varied	4
Siphlonurus	all	varied	3
Stenacron	*canadense*	#12; std.	1
Stenonema	*fuscum*	#10; std. and 3x long	1
	ithaca	#10, #12; std.	1
	vicarium	#10; 3x long	2
	other light species	varied	1
	other dark species	varied	2
Tricorythodes	all	#24, #26, t.u.e.	2

DUNS

PATTERN, TYPE #	WING	BODY*	TAILS	HACKLE**
1) White-body Compara-dun	creamy white	creamy white	creamy white	creamy white
2) Cream-body Compara-dun	light gray-ish-cream	cream	light ginger, cream or badger	light ginger, cream or badger
3) Yellow-body Compara-dun	creamish-yellow	medium yellow	light ginger	light ginger
4) Yellow-olive-body Compara-dun	light gray	yellow with tinge of olive	light gray	light gray
5) Olive-body Compara-dun	dark gray	medium-dark olive with tinge of brown	medium gray	medium-dark gray
6) Gray body Compara-dun	medium gray	light yellow-ish-gray	medium gray	medium ginger
7) Brown-body Compara-dun	dark gray	dark brown or mahogany	dark gray	dark gray
8) Black-body Compara-dun	pale gray	blackish-brown	pale gray	pale gray

Formula for dubbing: Pattern 1) equal parts, white and cream; 2) cream; 3) equal parts cream and yellow; 4) 2 parts yellow, 1 part cream, 1 part olive; 5) 3½ parts olive, ½ part brown; 6) base gray = 25% gray (3 parts cream, 1 part black) 3½ parts base gray, ½ part yellow; 7) 2 parts medium brown, 1 part red; 1 part black; 8) equal parts medium brown and black.

* Color based on abdominal sternites

**For Hackled Compara-dun only, tie several turns of hackle fore and aft of the deer hair wing.

GENUS	SPECIES	HOOK SIZE	DUN PATTERN TYPE #
Baetis	Olive Species	#16, #18;	5
	Brown species	#16, #18;	7
Brachycercus	all	varied	8
Caenis	all	varied	2
Callibaetis	all	varied	6
Centroptilum	all	varied	4
Cloeon	all	varied	2
Epeorus	*pleuralis*	#10, #12;	6
	vitreus	#12, #14;	4
	other light species	varied	4
	other dark species	varied	6
Ephemera	*guttulata*	#6, #8; 4x long	6
	simulans	#8, #10;	6
	varia	#8, #12, 4x long	2
	other cream species	varied	2
Ephemerella	*attenuata*	#16, #18;	4
	cornuta	#12, #14;	5
	doddsi	#8;	5
	dorothea	#16, #18;	4
	flavilinea	#12, #14;	5
	glacialis	#8, #12, 4x long	5
	grandis	#8, #12, 4x long	5
	inermis	#18;	4
	infrequens	#16;	4
	invaria	#14;	4
	lata	#16, #18;	5

GENUS	SPECIES	HOOK SIZE	DUN PATTERN TYPE #
	rotunda	#12, #14;	4
	subvaria	#10, #12;	6
	other sulphurish species	varied	4
	other gray species	varied	6
	other olive species	varied	5
Ephoron	all	#8,#10;	1
Heptagenia	light species	varied	3
	dark species	varied	7
Hexagenia	*limbata*	#6, #8; 4x long	6
	recurvata	#6, #8; 4x long	7
	other light species	varied	6
	other dark species	varied	7
Isonychia	all	#8, #12, 4x long	7
Leptophlebia	all	#10, #12; 2x long	7
Paralepto-phlebia	all	#16;	7
Potomanthus	*distinctus*	#8, #12, 4x long	3

GENUS	SPECIES	HOOK SIZE	DUN PATTERN TYPE #
	other yellow species	varied	3
	other whitish species	varied	1
Pseudocloeon	light species	#20-28; t.u.e.	4
	dark species	#20-28; t.u.e.	5
Rhithrogena	all	varied	7
Siphlonurus	all	varied	6
Stenacron	*canadense*	#12;	2
Stenonema	*fuscum*	#8, #10;	2
	ithaca	#10, #12;	2
	vicarium	#12; 4x long	6
	other cream species	varied	2
	other yellow species	varied	3
	other whitish species	varied	1
Tricorythodes	all	#24-26; t.u.e.	8

SPINNERS

PATTERN, TYPE	WINGS (HACKLE)	BODY*	TAILS
1) Cream-body Compara-spinner	cream or light ginger and white	cream	cream
2) Yellow-brown-body Compara-spinner	light ginger and pale gray or white	amber	medium gray
3) Olive-body Compara-spinner	light gray	dark olive	dark gray
4) Brown-body Compara-spinner	light gray	dark reddish-brown	medium gray

Formula for dubbing: Pattern 1) cream fur; 2) 1 part cream, 1 part yellow, 2 parts medium brown; 3) 3 parts olive, ½ part brown, ½ part black; 4) 3 parts medium brown, ½ part olive, ½ part black.

* Color based on abdominal sternites.

GENUS	SPECIES	HOOKS SIZE	SPINNER PATTERN TYPE #
Baetis	olive species	#16, #18;	3
	brown species	#16, #18;	4
Brachycercus	all	varied	4
Caenis	all	varied	1
Callibaetis	all	varied	2

GENUS	SPECIES	HOOKS SIZE	SPINNER PATTERN TYPE #
Centroptilum	all	varied	2
Cloeon	all	varied	1
Epeorus	*pleuralis*	#10, #12;	2
	vitreus	#12, #14;	2
	other light species	varied	2
	other dark species	varied	4
Ephemera	*guttulata*	#6, #8; 4x long	**
	simulans	#8, #10;	2
	varia	#8, #12, 4x long	1
	other light species	varied	1
Ephemerella	*attenuata*	#16, #18;	3
	cornuta	#12, #14;	3
	doddsi	#8; 2x long	3
	dorothea	#16, #18;	2
	flavilinea	#12, #14,	3
	glacialis	#8, #12, 4x long	3
	grandis	#8, #12, 4x long	3
	inermis	#18,	2
	infrequens	#16;	2
	invaria	#14;	2
	lata	#16, #18;	3
	rotunda	#12, #14;	2

GENUS	SPECIES	HOOKS SIZE	SPINNER PATTERN TYPE #
	subvaria	#10, #12;	4
	other light species	varied	2
	other dark species	varied	3
Ephoron	all	#8, #10;	1
Heptagenia	light species	varied	1
	dark species	varied	4
Hexagenia	**	---	—
Isonychia	all	#8, #12, 4x long	4
Leptophlebia	all	#10, #12;	4
Paralepto-phlebia	all	#16	4
Potomanthus	all	(*distinctus*—#8, #12, 4x long)	1
Pseudocloeon	all	#20-28; t.u.e.	3

GENUS	SPECIES	HOOKS SIZE	SPINNER PATTERN TYPE #
Rhithrogena	all	varied	4
Siphlonurus	all	varied	1
Stenacron	*canadense*	#12	1
Stenonema	*fuscum*	#8, #10;	2
	ithaca	#10, #12;	2
	vicarium	#12; 4x long	
	other pale species	varied	1
Tricorythodes	all	#24-26; t.u.e.	**

** It is suggested that "specific dressings" be used for Ephemera *guttulata,* Hexagenia *limbata* and *recurvata* and Tricorythodes.

Specific Dressings

Baetis *vagans*

NYMPH:
Silk: olive
Tails: dark ginger wet hackle barbules
Body: Yellowish-brown with tinge of olive dubbing
Wing Pads: brown turkey wing
Leg: amber dyed mallard flank feathers
DUN and EMERGER:
Silk: olive
Wings: Medium-dark gray deer hair (fine texture)
Tails: Dark gray dry hackle barbules
Body: Brown with tinge of yellowish-olive dubbing
SPINNER:
Silk: Olive
Tails: Dark gray dry hackle barbules
Body: Medium-dark brown with tinge of yellowish-olive dubbing
Wings: Light gray dry hackle

Ephemera *guttulata*

NYMPH:
Silk: Olive
Tails: Medium ginger wet hackle
Ribbing: Yellow cotton thread
Body: Olive-brown dubbing
Wing pads: Dark brown turkey wing
Legs: Medium ginger wet hackle
DUN and EMERGER:
Silk: Yellow
Wings: Light brownish-gray deer hair (coarse texture)
Tails: Dark brown (mink tail)
Body: Creamy white dubbing
SPINNER:
Silk: Yellow
Tails: Ginger or brown mink tail
Body: Creamy white dubbing
Wings: Ginger and dark grizzly dry hackle

Ephemera *simulans*

NYMPH:
Silk: Olive
Tails: Dark ginger wet hackle barbules
Ribbing: Olive cotton thread
Body: Olive-brown dubbing
Legs: Dark ginger hackle
DUN and EMERGER:
Silk: Olive
Wings: Brownish deer hair (medium texture)
Tails: Dark brown mink tail
Body: Medium brownish-yellow dubbing
SPINNER:
Silk: Olive
Tails: Dark brown mink tail
Body: Brownish yellow dubbing
Wings: Ginger and dark grizzly dry hackle

Ephemera *varia*

NYMPH:
Silk: Olive
Tails: Medium ginger wet hackle
Body: Brownish-olive dubbing ribbed with yellow cotton thread
Wing pads: Brown mottled turkey wing
Legs: Medium ginger wet hackle
DUN:
Silk: Yellow
Wings: Cream deer hair (medium texture)
Tails: Ginger dry hackle barbules
Body: Cream dubbing
SPINNER:
Silk: Yellow
Tails: Ginger dry hackle barbules
Body: Cream dubbing
Wings: Ginger and light grizzly dry hackle

Ephemerella *attenuata*

NYMPH:
Silk: Black
Tails: Ginger wet hackle barbules
Body: Olive-brown dubbing
Wing pads: Dark brown turkey wing
Legs: Ginger wet hackle
EMERGER:*
Silk: Yellow
Tails: Medium ginger wet hackle barbules
Body: Bright olive-yellow dubbing
Wings: Dark gray mallard primary (wet style, cut short)
Legs: Medium ginger wet hackle
DUN:
Silk: Yellow
Wings: Medium-dark deer hair (fine texture)
Tails: Medium ginger dry hackle barbules
Body: Bright olive yellow dubbing
SPINNER:
Silk: Olive
Tails: Medium ginger dry hackle barbules
Body: Dark brownish-olive dubbing
Wings: Pale gray and ginger hackle dry hackle

Ephemerella *cornuta*

NYMPH:
Silk: Olive
Tails: Ginger wet hackle barbules
Body: Medium-dark yellowish-brown dubbing
Wing pads: Black dyed mallard primary
Legs: Ginger wet hackle
DUN and EMERGER:
Silk: Olive
Wings: Medium-dark gray deer hair (medium texture)
Tails: Dark gray dry hackle barbles
Body: Greenish-yellow (almost chartreuse)
SPINNER:
Silk: Black
Tails: Dark gray dry hackle barbules
Body: Dark greenish-olive dubbing
Wings: Light gray dry hackle

Ephemerella *dorothea*

NYMPH:
Silk: Black
Tails: Medium ginger wet hackle barbules
Body: Yellowish brown dubbing
Wing pads: Brown turkey wing
Legs: Amber dyed mallard flank feathers
DUN and EMERGER:
Silk: Yellow
Wings: Pale gray deer hair (fine texture)
Tails: Pale gray dry hackle barbules
Body: Pale yellow dubbing
SPINNER:
Silk: Yellow
Tails: Pale gray dry hackle barbules
Body: Yellowish-brown dubbing
Wings: Pale gray dry hackle

Ephemerella *flavilinea*

NYMPH:
Silk: Black
Tails: Dark brown wet hackle barbules
Body: Very dark brown dubbing
Wing pads: Black dyed mallard primary
Legs: Dark brown wet hackle
DUN:
Silk: Black
Wings: Dark gray deer hair (medium texture)
Tails: Dark brown dry hackle barbules
Body: Brownish-olive
SPINNER:
Silk: Black
Tails: Dark brown dry hackle barbules
Body: Dark brownish-olive
Wings: Light gray dry hackle

Ephemerella *glacialis, grandis* and *doddsi*

NYMPH:
Silk: Olive
Tails: Dark brown wet hackle barbules
Body: Dark brown dubbing
Wing pads: Black dyed mallard primary
Legs: Dark brown wet hackle
DUN:
Silk: Olive
Wings: Dark gray deer hair (medium to coarse texture)
Tails: Dark brown dry hackle barbules
Body: Brownish-olive
SPINNER:
Silk: Olive
Tails: Dark gray or brown dry hackle barbules
Body: Dark brownish-olive
Wings: Light gray and ginger dry hackle

Ephemerella *infrequens* and *inermis*

NYMPH:
Silk: Black
Tails: Dark ginger wet hackle barbules
Body: Dark brown dubbing
Wing pads: Black dyed mallard primary
Legs: Dark ginger wet hackle
DUN:
Silk: Olive
Wings: Light-to-medium deer hair (fine texture)
Tails: Medium gray dry hackle barbules
Body: yellow olive
SPINNER:
Silk: Olive
Tails: Dark gray or brown dry hackle barbules
Body: Olive with tinge of yellow
Wings: Light gray dry hackle

Ephemerella *invaria* and *rotunda*

NYMPH:
Silk: Olive
Tails: Ginger wet hackle barbules
Body: Yellowish-brown
Wing pads: Dark brown turkey wing
Legs: Ginger wet hackle
DUN and EMERGER:
Silk: Olive
Wings: Light-to-medium gray deer hair medium texture)
Tails: Light gray dry hackle barbules
Body: Light brownish-yellow dubbing with tinge of olive
SPINNER:
Silk: Olive
Tails: Light gray dry hackle barbules
Body: Golden brown dubbing
Wings: Pale gray and pale ginger dry hackle

Ephemerella *lata*

NYMPH:
Silk: Olive
Tails: Dark ginger wet hackle barbules
Body: dark reddish-brown dubbing
Wing pads: Black dyed mallard primary
Legs: Dark ginger wet hackle barbules
DUN:
Silk: Black
Wings: Dark gray deer hair (fine texture)
Tails: Light gray dry hackle barbules
Body: Brownish-olive dubbing
SPINNER:
Silk: Black
Tails: Light gray dry hackle barbules
Body: Dark brownish-olive dubbing
Wings: Light gray dry hackle barbules

Ephemerella *subvaria*

NYMPH:
Silk: Black
Tails: Amber dyed mallard flank feathers
Body: Dark olive-brown dubbing
Wing pads: Black dyed mallard flank feather
Legs: Amber dyed mallard flank feathers
DUN and EMERGER:
Silk: Yellow
Wings: Medium-dark gray deer hair (medium texture)
Tails: Medium gray dray hackle barbules
Body: Light gray with tinge of pink
SPINNER:
Silk: Black
Tails: Medium ginger dry hackle barbules
Wings: Light gray and medium ginger dry hackle

Epeorus *pleuralis*

NYMPH:
Silk: Black
Tails: amber dyed wood-duck
Body: Olive-brown dubbing
Wing pads: Black dyed mallard primary
Legs: amber dyed mallard flank feathers
EMERGER (wet-style):
Silk: Olive
Tails: Amber dyed mallard flank feathers
Ribbing: Brown cotton thread
Body: Tan dubbing
Wings: Medium gray mallard (short)
Legs: Amber dyed mallard flank feathers
DUN:
Silk: Olive
Wings: Medium gray deerhair (medium texture)
Tails: Dark gray dry hackle barbules
Body: Light-gray with tinge of yellowish dubbing
SPINNER:
Silk: Olive
Tails: Dark gray dry hackle barbules
Body: Yellowish-brown dubbing
Wings: Light gray and medium ginger dry hackle

Epeorus *vitreus*

EMERGER:*
Silk: Olive
Tails: Light ginger wet hackle barbules
Body: Olive-yellow dubbing
Wings: Medium, gray mallard primary cut short
Legs: Light ginger wet hackle
DUN:
Silk: Olive
Wings: Light-to-medium gray deer hair (fine texture)
Tails: Light ginger dry hackle barbules
Body: Olive-yellow dubbing
SPINNER:
Silk: Olive
Tails: Light ginger dry hackle barbules
Body: Olive-yellow dubbing (male); tinge of red (female)
Wings: Light gray and ginger dry hackle

Ephoron Genus

EMERGER:
Silk: Yellow
Tails: Medium grey dry hackle barbules.
Body: Creamy white dubbing
Thorax: Gray mallard primary and white maribou
Legs: Pale cream dry hackle
DUN:
Silk: Yellow
Wings: Creamy white deer hair (medium texture)
Tails: Medium gray dry hackle barbules
Body: Creamy white dubbing
SPINNER:
Silk: Yellow
Tails: Medium gray dry hackle barbules
Body: Creamy white dubbing
Wings: Pale cream and light gray dry hackle

Hexagenia *limbata*

NYMPH:
Silk: Yellow
Tails: Dark ginger wet hackle barbules.
Body: Medium gray and amber dubbing
Wing pads: Dark brown turkey
Legs: Dark ginger wet hackle
DUN and EMERGER:
Silk: Olive
Wings: Medium gray deer hair (coarse texture)
Tails: Brown mink
Body: Creamy yellow dubbing
SPINNER:
Silk: Olive
Tails: Ginger mink
Body: Creamy yellow dubbing
Wings: Light gray and ginger dry hackle

Litobrancha *recurvata*

NYMPH:
Silk: Olive
Tails: Dark ginger wet hackle barbules
Body: Dark reddish-brown dubbing with yellow cotton thread ribbing
Wing pads: Black dyed mallard primary
Legs: Reddish-brown wet hackles
DUN and EMERGER:
Silk: Black
Wings: Dark brownish deer hair (coarse texture)
Tails: Dark brown mink tails
Body: Dark brown dubbing with yellow cotton thread ribbing
SPINNER:
Silk: Olive
Tails: Dark brown mink tail
Body: Reddish-brown ribbed with yellow cotton thread
Wings: Dark reddish-brown and grizzly dry hackle

Isonychia *bicolor* and *sadleri*

NYMPH:
Silk: Black
Tails: Ginger wet hackle barbules
Body: peacock herl ribbed fine gold wire
Wing pads: Black dyed mallard primary
Legs: amber dyed mallard flank feathers
DUN:
Silk: Black
Wings: Dark gray deer hair (medium texture)
Tails: Dark ginger dry hackle barbules or mink tails
Body: Dark reddish-brown dubbing
SPINNER:
Silk: Black
Tails: Dark ginger (dry hackle barbules or mink tails)
Body: Dark reddish brown dubbing
Wings: Light gray and medium ginger dry hackle

Leptophlebia Genus

NYMPH:
Silk: Olive
Tails: Light ginger wet barbules
Body: Olive, yellow-brown dubbing
Thorax: Dark brown turkey wing
Legs: Light ginger wet barbules
DUN:
Silk: Brown
Wings: Dark ginger and light grizzly dry hackle
Tails: Dark brown dry hackle barbules
Body: Dark reddish-brown dubbing
SPINNER:
Silk: Brown
Tails: Dark brown dry hackle barbules
Body: Dark reddish-brown dubbing
Wings: Dark ginger and light grizzly dubbing

Paraleptophlebia *adoptiva*

NYMPH:
Silk: Black
Tails: Amber wet hackle
Body: Yellowish-brown dubbing
Wing pads: Black dyed mallard primary
Legs: Amber wet hackle
DUN:
Silk: Black
Wings: Medium gray deer hair (medium texture)
Tails: Brown dry hackle barbules
Body: Reddish-brown dubbing
SPINNER:
Silk: Black
Tails: Medium gray dry hackle barbules
Body: Dark reddish-brown dubbing
Wings: Pale gray and pale ginger dry hackle

Potamanthus *distinctus*

NYMPH:
Silk: Yellow
Tails: Ginger wet hackle barbules
Body: Reddish-brown dubbing
Wing pads: Brown turkey wing
Legs: Amber dyed mallard flank feathers
DUN:
Silk: Yellow
Wings: Pale yellow deer hair (medium texture)
Tails: Light ginger mink tail
Body: Light creamy yellow dubbing
SPINNER:
Silk: Yellow
Tails: Light ginger mink tail
Body: Light creamy yellow dubbing
Wings: Light ginger dry hackle

Pseudocloeon Genus

NYMPH:
Silk: Olive
Tails: Pale ginger dry hackle barbules
Body: Brownish-olive dubbing
Wing pads: Brown turkey feathers
Legs: Pale ginger dry hackle
DUN:
Silk: Olive
Wings: Medium dark deer hair (fine texture)
Tails: Dark gray dry hackle barbules
Body: Olive-brown dubbing
SPINNER:
Silk: Olive
Tails: Dark gray dry hackles
Body: Dark olive-brown dubbing
Wings: Light gray dry hackle

Stenonema *fuscum*

NYMPH:
Silk: Olive
Tails: Medium ginger wet hackle
Ribbing: Brown cotton thread
Body: Yellowish-brown dubbing
Wing pads: Dark brown turkey wing
Legs: Medium ginger wet hackle
DUN:
Silk: Yellow
Wings: Medium-light gray deer hair (medium texture)
Tails: Medium gray dry hackle barbules
Body: Yellow-cream dubbing
SPINNER:
Silk: Yellow
Tails: Medium gray dry hackle barbules
Body: Yellowish-brown dubbing
Wings: Light gray and ginger dry hackle

Stenonema *ithaca* and Stenacron *canadense*

NYMPH:
Silk: Olive
Tails: Light ginger wet hackle barbules
Body: Yellowish-brown dubbing
Wing pads: Dark brown turkey wing
Legs: Light ginger wet hackle
DUN:
Silk: Yellow
Wings: Light gray (medium texture)
Tails: Light gray or light ginger
Body: Yellowish-cream dubbing
SPINNER:
Silk: Yellow
Tails: Light gray dry hackle barbules
Body: Yellowish-cream with tinge of brown dubbing
Wings: Pale gray and ginger dry hackle

Stenonema *vicarium*

NYMPH:
Silk: Olive
Tails: Dark ginger wet hackle
Ribbing: Brown cotton thread
Body: Yellowish-brown dubbing
Wing pads: Dark brown turkey wing
Legs: Amber dyed wood-duck
DUN:
Silk: Yellow
Wings: Brownish deer hair (medium texture)
Tails: Brown (mink tail or dry hackle barbules)
Body: Yellowish-tan dubbing
SPINNER:
Silk: Yellow
Tails: Brown (mink tail or dry hackle barbules)
Body: Yellowish-brown dubbing
Wings: Light gray and medium ginger dry hackle

Tricorythodes Genus

NYMPH:
Silk: Olive
Tails: Ginger dry hackle barbules
Body: Olive-brown dubbing (heavy in thorax area)
Wing pads: none
Legs: Ginger dry hackle
DUN:
Silk: Black
Wings: Light gray deer hair (fine texture) and light gray dry hackle
Tails: Light gray dry hackle barbules
Body: Medium-dark greenish-grey (abdomen) and black (thorax) dubbing
SPINNER:
Silk: Black
Tails: Light gray hackle barbules, extra long
Body: Dark gray, almost black, dubbing
Wings: Oversized light grey hackle and figure 8 to spent position with dubbing

TRADITIONAL WETS & NYMPHS

BLUE-WINGED OLIVE WET
Silk: Olive
Tails: Medium blue dun
Wings: 'Gray', mallard quill
Body: Medium olive rabbit fur
Hackle: Medium blue dun

EMERGING MARCH BROWN
Silk: Orange
Tails: Wood-duck or imitation wood-duck
Ribbing: Dark-brown cotton thread
Body: Medium-brown rabbit fur w/guard hairs
Wings: Wood-duck or imitation wood-duck
Legs: Medium-brown partridge

HARE'S EAR
Silk: Olive
Rails: Wood-duck or imitation wood-duck
Ribbing: Dark-brown cotton thread
Body: Medium-brown rabbit fur w/guard hairs
Wings: Medium-gray mallard primary
Legs: Dark-brown partridge

LIGHT CAHILL WET
Silk: Yellow
Tails: Light-ginger hackle fibers
Wings: Imitation wood-duck
Body: Cream fox fur
Hackle: Soft light-ginger

LITTLE MARRYATT WET
Silk: White
Tails: Pale-ginger hackle fibers
Body: Medium-yellow rabbit fur w/tinge of orange or olive
Wings: Light mallard primary
Legs: Pale ginger hackle

ZUG BUG
Silk: Black
Tails: 3 strands of green peacock sword herl
Body: Heavy peacock her ribbed with silver oval tinsil
Wings: Mallard flank cut short extending over forward ¼ of body
Hackle: Long soft brown

TRADITIONAL DRYS

AMERICAN MARCH BROWN
Silk: Orange
Tails: Dark-brown hackle fibers
Ribbing: Light brown cotton thread
Wings: Darkly barred wood-duck or imitation wood-duck
Body: Grayish tan rabbit fur
Hackle: Dark brown and grizzly mixed

BLACK QUILL
Silk: Black
Tails: Dark blackish-gray hackle fibers
Wings: Black hackle tips
Body: Stripped badger hackle quill
Hackle: Dark blackish-gray

BLUE-WINGED OLIVE
Silk: Olive
Tails: Medium blue dun hackle fibers
Wings: Dark blue dun hackle points or medium blue dun web section (trimmed)
Body: Medium olive rabbit fur
Hackle: Medium blue dun

CREAM VARIANT
Silk: White
Tails: Cream hackle fibers
Body: White hackle quill stripped and soaked
Hackle: Cream and honey dun mixed

DARK BLUE QUILL
Silk: Black
Tails: Dark bluish-gray hackle fibers
Wings: Black hackle tips
Body: Peacock quill unbleached and stripped.
Hackle: Dark bluish-gray

DARK GREEN DRAKE
Silk: Brown
Tails: Brown hackle fibers
Ribbing: Brown cotton thread
Wings: Lemon wood-duck flank
Body: Gray and brown rabbit fur, mixed dubbing
Hackle: Olive gray dun, dark grizzly and brown mixed

DUN VARIANT
Silk: Olive
Tails: Dark blue dun hackle fibers
Body: Reddish hackle quill (stripped)
Hackle: Darkest blue dun

GREY FOX
Silk: Olive
Tails: Light ginger hackle fibers
Wings: Gray mallard flank
Body: Creamish tan rabbit fur
Hackle: Light ginger and grizzly mixed

GREY QUILL
Silk: Black
Tails: Dark grizzly hackle fibers
Wings: Barred teal flank
Body: Badger quill stripped
Hackle: Dark grizzly

HENDRICKSON
Silk: Yellow
Tails: Medium blue dun hackle fibers
Wings: Lemon wood-duck or imitation wood-duck
Body: Medium-gray rabbit fur w/tinge of pink
Hackle: Medium blue dun

LIGHT CAHILL
Silk: Yellow
Tails: Light ginger hackle fibers
Wings: Gray mallard flank feather instead of wood-duck
Body: Cream fox fur
Hackle: Light ginger

LITTLE MARRYATT
Silk: White
Tails: Pale ginger hackle fibers
Wings: Light blue dun hackle points or light blue dun web section (trimmed)
Body: Medium yellow rabbit fur w/tinge of orange or olive
Hackle: Pale ginger

PALE EVENING DUN
Silk: Primrose
Tails: Light ginger hackle fibers
Wings: Palest starling
Body: Yellowish cream spun fur
Hackle: Pale ginger

PAULINSKILL
Silk: White
Tails: Cream hackle fibers
Wings: Barred mallard flank
Body: Cream red fox belly fur dubbing
Hackle: Cream

QUILL GORDON
Silk: Olive
Tails: Medium blue dun hackle fibers
Wings: Lemon wood-duck or imitation wood-duck
Body: Bleached peacock
Hackle: Medium blue dun

RED QUILL
Silk: Olive
Tails: Medium blue dun hackle fibers
Body: Reddish hackle quill (stripped)
Wings: Wood-duck or imitation wood-duck
Hackle: Medium blue dun

WHIRLING DUN
Silk: Brown
Tails: Brown hackle fibers
Wings: Dark bluish gray hackle tips
Body: Gray and brown rabbit fur mixed
Hackle: Medium bluish gray dun and brown,. mixed

TRADITIONAL SPINNERS

NELMS CADDIS
Silk: Yellow
Tails: White porcupine guard hairs
Body: Creamish yellow deer hair lashed to hook shank or extended body
Wings: Cream and light gray hackle feathers (2 each side)
Hackle: Bronze blue dun (parachute style wrapped above wings)

WHITE GLOVED HOWDY
Silk: White
Tails: Brown hackle fibers
Ribbing: Dark reddish brown, cotton thread
Body: Beaver and brown dyed seal, mixed
Wings: White hackle tips, tied spent
Hackle: Honey dun faced with two turns of brown

POSTSCRIPT
Gary LaFontaine

It is fun to sit on the bank of a beautiful trout stream and watch Al Caucci and Bob Nastasi fish a rise. It is a routine they have obviously developed through their years as friends, through their seasons as fishing partners. They work as a team, calling back and forth, not duplicating each other's efforts but instead testing separate elements of that puzzle that means success, until they have found the right combination of tippet size, fly pattern, and presentation to fool the fussiest trout.

They worked in tandem like this, spaced no more than 50 yards apart, during a mayfly spinner fall on the Big Hole River. They had to hurry, both because of the short duration of the spinner fall and the coming twilight, but they found the solution to those devilish rainbows sipping on the flat; and quickly enough they both started catching those fish—as they stood out there waist deep in my favorite Montana trout river they seemed like personifications of the major message of their book: *Don't fish harder, fish smarter.*

It is possible to ignore imitationist theories, or, for that matter, even the actual insect hatches, and still catch trout. But that is not my way—nor is it Al and Bob's. The process of learning about aquatic insects is fascinating in itself, and needs no angling justification; but such knowledge pays off many fold on the water. The real message of *Hatches* might be, "Fish simpler."

That is the force behind the entomological wave that has swept fly fishing in the last few decades. It takes so much more effort to blunder around a trout stream, flailing with nondescript patterns, in effect, guessing, than it does to observe the natural clues. There is no fun in inefficiency and ignorance; even a basic understanding of the trout's food reduces the probable angling choices to a workable number.

Since its original publication in 1975, *Hatches* has been a popular and important part of entomological angling literature. It started with a sales bang, a commercial success almost before the first copy was offered in a store, because it was a main selection of the Field & Stream Book Club. One of the leading executives of that organization, Eric Peper, estimated that the club sold over 25,000 copies.

"By far the best selling fly fishing book that we ever handled," he told me.

Hatches outlived that initial boom—it was simply too good of a book to fade into publishing oblivion. It settled into a steady sales pattern, indicating that new fly fishermen, fresh and eager for information, were getting word-of-mouth recommendations from more experienced anglers. It was making it onto "must-read" lists in magazines and other books.

The major contribution of *Hatches* was the incredibly complete survey of trout stream mayflies. Certainly, no angling entomology had ever covered so many species from across the country; and no other book had ever provided so many important details about specific hatches. It represented a clear jump, not just an evolutionary shuffle, in mayfly knowledge for fly fishermen.

But no fly fishing book can hold an audience with just scientific facts. There has to be a solid connection to fly fishing techniques for it to be interesting—and this book provided that link: the Comparadun flies. This series of dry flies, a refinement of the old Haystack pattern, appeared (or, at least, made its public debut) after the innovative no-hackle theories and patterns of *Selective Trout*, but the Comparadun concept, with durable and buoyant wings of deer hair, proved so much more practical than the delicate, feather or quill winged flies that they quickly captured the loyalty of many flat-water anglers. These new patterns, with their sturdy construction and intelligent color concepts, became a rallying point for followers who might have otherwise avoided an entomologically oriented book like *Hatches*.

It became difficult, and economically unfeasible, for the authors' company, Comparahatch Publishing, to keep *Hatches* continually in print in later years. As the sales hit that respectable, but lower, plateau that even the most revered fishing books reach, it became harder to justify the work of maintaining a distribution network for a single title. So, in spite of a demand, there would be periods of time when *Hatches* was simply not available to the buying public.

This new edition, under the Winchester Press imprint, insures that the book will be distributed through book stores and fly shops. *Hatches* will now be at hand for both experienced and novice anglers; and for those of us who have virtually worn out our originals, the paper edition offers the chance to purchase a "work copy" for the fly tying bench.

There are additions and changes in this new printing, also. The authors heeded the suggestions of mayfly expert Dr. George Edmunds—they corrected the minor inconsistencies that he found in the book originally. They updated facts about the distribution and habits of some species; it was inevitable that their continuing research since the first appearance of *Hatches* would uncover more information.

They included a new, bonus hatching guide, full of valuable data about important hatches on waters across the country.

This edition of *Hatches* confirms the lasting place of the book in fly fishing literature. It is always a source for a complete education about trout stream mayflies; it joins, rather than competes, with other fine works (most notably, *Selective Trout* by Doug Swisher and Carl Richards and *Mayflies, the Angler and the Trout* by Fred Arbona, Jr.) to lead anyone serious about their fly fishing to a better understanding of the aquatic world. By making people smarter anglers it not only makes them bettter ones—just as importantly, it helps them enjoy their days on the water more.

SELECTED BIBLIOGRAPHY

Entomological References

Burks, B.D. "The Mayflies or Ephemeroptera of Illinois"; Ill. Natur. Hist. Surv. Bull. 26(1) (1953)

Edmunds, G.F., Jr., S.L. Jensen and L. Berner "The Mayflies of North and Central America"; Univ. of Minn. Press, Minn. (1976)

Flowers, R.W. and W.L. Hilsenhoff "Heptagenidae (Ephemeroptera) of Wisconsin; "Great Lakes Entomol. 8:201-18 (1975)

Hubbard, M.D. and W.L. Peters "Environmental requirements and pollution tolerance of Ephmeroptera"; Environ. Monit. Sup. Lab. Off Res. Dev. U.S.E.P.A. Cincinnati (1978)

Leonard, J.W. and F.A. Leonard "Mayflies of Michigan trout streams"; Cranbrook Inst. Sci. Bull. No. 43 (1962)

Lewis, P.A. Taxonomy and ecology of Stenonema mayflies (Heptagenidae: Ephemeroptera)"; U.S. Environ. Prot. Agency, Environ. Monitoring Series, Report No. EPA-670/4-74-006 (1974)

McCafferty, W.P. "Aquatic entomology"; Science Books International, Boston, Mass. (1981)

Meritt, R.D. and Cummins, K.W., "An Introduction to the Aquatic Insects of North America"; Kendal/Hunt Publishing Co., Dubuque, Iowa (1978)

Morihara, D.K. and W.P. McCafferty "The Baetis larvae of North America (Ephemeroptera: Baetidae)"; Trans. Amer. Entomol. Soc. 105:139-221 (1979)

Needham, J.G., J.R. Traver and Y.C. Hsu "The Biology of Mayflies with a systematic account of North American species". Comstock, Ithaca, N.Y. (1935)

Angling/entomological references

Arbona, F.L. Jr. "Mayflies, The Angler and the Trout". Winchester Press, Piscataway, N.J.

Caucci, A. and R. Nastasi "Comparahatch" (1973); "Flytyers Color Guide" (1978); "Instant Mayfly Identification Guide" (1984). Comparahatch Ltd., Tannersville, Pa.

Flick, A. "Art Flick's new streamside guide to naturals and their imitations." Crown, New York (1966)

Hafele, R. and Hughes, D. "The Complete Book of Western Hatches". Frank Amato Publications, Portland, Oregon (1981)

McClane, A.J. "McClane's standard fishing encyclopedia". Holt, Rinehart and Winston, New York (1965)

Schwiebert, E. "Matching the Hatch" (1955) and "Nymphs" (1973). Winchester Press, New York

Swisher, D. and C. Richards "Selective Trout". Crown, New York (1971)

Index